Remaking Liberalism

Remaking Liberalism

*The Intellectual Legacy
of Adam Shortt, O.D. Skelton,
W.C. Clark, and W.A. Mackintosh,
1890–1925*

BARRY FERGUSON

McGill-Queen's University Press
Montreal & Kingston • London • Buffalo

For Natalie Johnson

© McGill-Queen's University Press 1993
ISBN 0-7735-1113-X

Legal deposit fourth quarter 1993
Bibliothèque nationale du Québec

Printed in Canada on acid-free paper

This book has been published with the help of a
grant from the Social Science Federation of Canada,
using funds provided by the Social Sciences and
Humanities Research Council of Canada.
Further financial assistance has been received from
the Department of History, the Dean of Arts, and the
Office of Research Administration at the University of
Manitoba.

Canadian Cataloguing in Publication Data

Ferguson, Barry Glen, 1952–
    Remaking liberalism: the intellectual legacy of
    Adam Shortt, O.D. Skelton, W.C. Clark, and
    W.A. Mackintosh, 1890–1925
    Includes bibliographical references and index.
    ISBN 0-7735-1113-X
    1. Liberalism – Canada. 2. Economics – Canada.
    I. Title.
    HB121.A2F47 1993   320.5'13   C93-090262-9

Typeset in Baskerville 10/12 by
Caractéra production graphique inc., Quebec City.

Contents

Acknowledgments

During the all too many years this project has taken me, I have received a great deal of help from many people.

My interest in political ideas was awakened and given direction by my first undergraduate teachers at the University of British Columbia, Daniel Klang, Robert Rowan, and especially Adrian Marriage, who devoted themselves to that marvellous and successful experiment, arts one and arts two. The fact that I am thanking an historian, a philosopher, and a sociologist indicates the rare intellectual vision the program offered. The possibility that Canadian history could constitute a subject in which to pursue the questions raised in arts one and arts two was nurtured by all my teachers in the history honours program at UBC, but especially Margaret Prang, who first taught me Canadian history, Murray Tolmie, who helped me and all his students to discern the insights and the illusions that history and historians offered, and Allan Smith, who inspired my first explorations into Canadian political ideas. Later, at Carleton University, I was fortunate enough to study in the prep school for Canadian intellectual history that S.F. Wise made of his seminar on colonial Canada.

At York University, where this book began as a dissertation, I benefited from Jack Saywell's tough preparation in modern Canadian history, Albert Tucker's splendid seminar on nineteenth-century Britain, and the late Virginia Macdonald's patient and careful teaching of political theory to a novice. Later, reading of my dissertation by Albert Tucker and by Carl Berger of the University of

Toronto encouraged and helped in equal measure. Jack Granatstein at York and Doug Owram of the University of Alberta exchanged ideas and information while we were engaged by similar questions and their enthusiasm for my subject and their help and encouragement from thesis to book always sustained my energies.

Above all, however, the support of Ramsay Cook has been crucial. In his enthusiasm for (perhaps I should say defence of) intellectual history, in his supervision of my dissertation, and in his gentle reminders that there was a manuscript to rework, he ensured that I kept at the project and in the university without succumbing to delusions or doubts. I know that the result only partially reflects his help and his criticism.

Many other people took the trouble to read all or part of the manuscript and were kind enough to discuss it with me. Without of course implicating any of them in the result, I wish to thank Paul Voisey, David Mills, Doug Francis, Leslie Pal, Martin and Joy Cohn-staedt, Francis Carroll, Mark Gabbert, Ed Moulton, Doug Sprague, and particularly Tom Vadney. Over many years, conversations with these people and others, especially Nancy Adamson, Paul Axelrod, Curtis Fahey, Natalie Johnson, Ed McKenna, Don McMahon, Car-mela Patrias, Dave Roberts, and Ray Thompson, have helped in more ways than they may think. If I have forgotten anyone, I apologize. Students in Canadian intellectual history seminars at the University of Manitoba have tolerated my ideas and enriched my perspective with their own work in so many ways. St John's College provides a most congenial place to work.

My research was made immeasurably easier by assistance from archivists and librarians in many places, starting with the Queen's University Archives and its archivist, Mrs Anne MacDermaid, and including the National Archives of Canada, the Robarts Library at the University of Toronto, the Institute of Historical Research in London, England and the university libraries at the University of Alberta and the University of Manitoba. At the dissertation stage, Mrs MacDermaid, the late Professor F.W. Gibson, and Professor M.C. Urquhart, all at Queen's University, secured permission for me to read university records.

Transferring a typescript to the word-processor, and my first use of the computer, were greatly assisted by Joyce Laird, Betty Jennings, and Lynn Kopeschny at St John's College. My thanks to them for their careful work.

At McGill-Queen's University Press, I have been encouraged by Philip Cercone, guided through the assessment period by Peter Blaney, and helped through the publication process by Joan

McGilvray. Curtis Fahey, a good friend for many years, did a wonderful job as manuscript editor, and René Fossett Jones helped immeasurably by preparing the index. I also wish to thank the Aid to Scholarly Publications Program for assisting with publication costs and the two readers who took the trouble to provide reports.

Despite the efforts of all the above, any errors or weaknesses that remain are my responsibility.

Preface

The following work examines the ideas of four political economists at Queen's University – Adam Shortt, Oscar Douglas Skelton, Clifford Clark, and William Mackintosh – and the place of these scholars in the history of twentieth-century Canadian political thought. At this stage, I will explain the thematic and interpretative framework in which I place the work of Shortt, Skelton, Clark, and Mackintosh and suggest why their ideas are important to modern Canadian history.

In the books and essays of the past three decades that have charted the outlines of Canadian intellectual history, Queen's political economists have a notable enough presence. Their place is found in the discussion of such key topics as the changing role of the university and especially the emergence of professional social science, the definition of an autonomist or liberal-nationalist interpretation of Canadian history, and the related issues of social reform and the rise of the positive or – as it is commonly known – interventionist state.

The scholarly work of Shortt, Skelton, Clark, and Mackintosh was central to the emergence of the social sciences and the modern university, particularly the way in which the methods of political economy were applied to the problems of agricultural and industrial expansion and depression between the 1890s and the 1930s. Their participation in the debate about Canadian nationalism was based on highly visible commentaries about national status and politics from the crisis of the Boer War to the transformation of Canadian nationhood in the 1920s. Finally, their discussions of the role of the state were stimulated by their consideration of major social reform movements and then punctuated by their eventual participation in a public service that supported the shift in the 1930s and 1940s to a positive welfare state.

My examination of Queen's political economists tests assertions about their priority in the emergence of the social sciences in Canadian universities, about their strategies and goals as nationalists during major Canadian debates, and about the factors behind their remarkable migration from the university to the public service. In addition, and more importantly, I argue that there was a relationship between the social science of these scholars, on the one hand, and their nationalism and their statism on the other. I think that recognizing the interplay between social science, nationalism, and public-policy proposals leads to new perspectives about the role of the academic in Canadian society and the characteristics of Canadian reform in the first half of the twentieth century.

IN THE PAST TWO DECADES, histories of ideas, including social science, in Canada have emphasized the impact on social and political reform movements of Christian and neo-Christian philosophy, particularly the idealist creed and the social gospel.[1] Yet these studies of the cultural environment in the period from Macdonald and Laurier to Borden and Mackenzie King, important and convincing as they are, over-extend the Christian and idealist continuities into broad social, political, and economic thought. The unwary reader would doubt whether there was much important discussion among the middle class that was rooted in a secular rather than a Christian cast-of-mind. At the same time, historians writing about political reform creeds, among both the middle class and the working class, have concentrated on the background to indigenous social democracy. They have stressed this socialism's Christian/utopian, or, even admitting its extreme minority status, Marxist origins. Their work leads to the conclusion that the liberal or liberal-labour position – a position they dismiss as weak-kneed labourism – lacked theoretical rigour and had no significant impact on any aspect of Canadian society, including the evolution of social democracy.[2]

In contrast to this view, I maintain that earlier studies of Canadian social reform and social science, however prone to examine ideas chiefly as they contributed to present-day scholarly thinking, were not totally wrong to emphasize the "great tradition" of political economy as part of the Canadian debate about public issues in the period of industrialization. Further, I believe that more attention should be paid to claims that popular debate – which included working-class as well as middle-class participants – referred as much or more to Mill and the historical economists than to Marx and the scientific socialists.[3] Their outlook shaped by political economy, Adam Shortt, Oscar Skelton, William Clark, and William Mackintosh presented a revisionist account of political economy, one that reflected American and British scholarly debate about the workings of capitalism and the nature of politics and government. This "new political economy" seems to me to have been, at the very least, equally as important to twentieth-century political and economic debate in Canada as the application of idealist philosophy, social gospel theology, and social democracy. In one direction, then, to focus on Queen's political economists is to recover an important line of intellectual influence over early twentieth-century Canada. Here the influence of John Stuart Mill, Thorstein Veblen, L.T. Hobhouse, John Hobson, and R.H. Tawney is more germane than that of Hegel and Marx and Rauschenbusch or their Canadian devotees.

Historians of nationalist thought have explained the shift from a colonialist to a nationalist mentality by examining the intense debate between imperialist nationalists, who identified Canada's national evolution as a political equal and economic partner of Britain, and liberal nationalists, who favoured constitutional autonomy and/or continental economic alignment. There is little doubt that, in trying to understand the questions of Canadian trade relations and constitutional status, Adam Shortt, Oscar Skelton, and William Mackintosh rejected the imperialist position. Their own ideas have long been classified according to historiographical categories in which Shortt and Skelton are subsumed under a dreary formalist theory of constitutional nationhood and Mackintosh, with distant links to Shortt and Skelton, is seen as a minor contributor to Innis's staples/environmentalist account of economic nationhood.[4]

I see things differently. It is my contention that the ideas of the "Queensians" show the development of a distinct economic and environmentalist interpretation of Canadian nationhood. Their new interpretation of Canadian nationality reflected the fresh insights of the reformed political economy of the early twentieth century. Far from being narrowly constitutional and simplistically continentalist, their nationalism was rooted in economic as well as political debate and was designed to elude both the imperialist and the continentalist visions. Finally, rather than showing isolationist or continentalist proclivities, their nationalism reflected an intellectual style and orientation that was thoroughly based in the North Atlantic community.

As for their emergence in the public service, a couple of flattering arguments may be found. Among historians of Queen's, an impression is often left that Queen's social scientists captured Ottawa and reduced it to their agenda.[5] Recent work on the emergence of the mandarinate of the 1930s and 1940s has suggested a more subtle alternative account of the rise of the bureaucracy in the social circumstances of the period. For all its insights into the details of programs arrived at during the Depression and the Second World War, this work nonetheless relies on a remarkably smooth amalgamation between politicians pressed to adopt reform measures and social scientists eager to implement programs that were similar to, if not the same as, the politicians' vague goals. The specific role of Queen's political economists in the introduction of the welfare state has usually been illustrated by Mackenzie King's testimony in confessions to his diary. In 1938 he complained about the organized, centralist, and Keynesian influence of Skelton, Clark, Mackintosh, and sometime-political scientist Norman Rogers in supporting measures to extend the government's role in managing economic demand.[6]

In fact, for Shortt, Skelton, Clark, and Mackintosh, involvement in the public service came about only after a long and frustrating period of trying to remake the university. Over the course of thirty years they strongly promoted new scholarly approaches to political and economic questions and a pivotal teaching and research role for the university as an autonomous institution in society. Most tellingly, only after Queen's had consistently declared its reservations about and then objections to their research and curriculum agenda within the university did they begin to migrate to Ottawa. The particular influence of Keynesian theory on Canadian fiscal policy occurred some years after Queen's scholars had devised their central arguments about political and economic life, the public service, and public policy. Long before the technical triumphs of economic theory, their arguments favoured major reforms designed to change the nation by opening government and politics to influence from all members of society and by demanding equal economic and social benefits for all citizens from the market economy.

THIS BOOK BEGINS WITH an examination of the origins and development of political economy and an account of the careers of Shortt, Skelton, Clark, and Mackintosh at Queen's. I then study the evolution of their ideas about the leading issues of their times – industrialism, agrarian expansion, the imperial question, wartime economic and political crises and reconstruction, Canada's constitutional status, and political and administrative reform. Within each discussion of these issues I also consider their statements about and understanding of basic political/economic problems. These problems were twofold: the underlying tendencies of capitalism and the capacities of parliamentary government. Finally, I explore their views on the possibilities of human control over and the role of the individual within the political economic order, particularly the place of the social scientist in modern society.

As I have suggested already, I will argue that the ideas of Queen's political economists reveal an intellectual position in early-twentieth-century Canada that has not been taken very seriously by historians. This position, contrary to recent histories of both philosophy and social reform in Canada, was based upon debates and concerns different from those shaped by Christian philosophical idealism and by social democracy or Marxism. It was also distinctive from the programs generated by the demands of government on compliant social science, demands that have been identified by the recent studies of the emergent welfare state and Keynesianism.

In suggesting an alternate approach to the discussions of reform and indeed political and economic debate in early-twentieth-century Canada, I am adapting arguments from historians of British and American social science, who have examined the remarkable reinterpretation of liberal-democratic thought that occurred between the 1890s and 1920s. This work has identified a vigorous, distinctive, and coherent new liberalism which arrived at arguments in favour of equal individual political and economic rights and a more active role for the state. Widely accepted in Great Britain and ·the United States, the views of these scholars have not much been credited by interest-group and class-based studies of political and economic reform in Canada.[7]

I hope that my examination can make substantial room in historical understanding of twentieth-century Canada for a liberal-democratic position distinct from the paternalistic reform program of social gospelers and sociologists, from the limited welfare-state-capitalism of post-social gospelers, and from the doctrines of social and political inevitability that each was based upon. Reconsidering the liberal-democratic frame of mind should at last force us to understand how powerful and pervasive was its vision.

Remaking Liberalism

1 The New Political Economy and the New University: The Case of Queen's

From a single course in political economy offered in 1886, Adam Shortt built up a department of political and economic science and attracted a band of adepts who followed him in two major undertakings from 1890 to the Second World War. The first was to study, teach, and write about Canadian economic and political questions using the tenets of the new political economy. The second was to move from commentary on to participation in national affairs by becoming senior federal civil servants. These two goals emerged from the intellectual and institutional environments of Canada and Queen's University in the period from 1890 to 1925.

WHILE ADAM SHORTT WAS LEARNING his political economy, nurturing his academic discipline, and encouraging his protégés at Queen's, Canada itself was undergoing formidable changes. Transcontinental expansion, industrialization, sustained introspection about national status – all suggest the swirling complexities that the small nation experienced after 1880 and that, according to the standard history of the Laurier and Borden governments, resulted in a "nation transformed."[1]

The roots of this transformation dated to the 1880s at least. In its economic form, the transformation can be seen in the industrial development attending the National Policy and its tariff and railway building programs. During the 1880s and 1890s, despite a cycle of boom and depression, the four original Canadian provinces,

particularly Ontario, were evolving into industrial and urban societies.[2] The resulting signs of class, ethnic, and even gender conflict,
as well as a great deal of intellectual confusion, were to become after
1900 basic concerns in public debate. In its political form, Canada's
reshaping can be seen in the swift escalation of French-English confrontation following Louis Riel's execution in 1885 and the subsequent reorientation of party politics and loyalties during the 1890s.[3]
Later, new provinces, new ethnic groups, and a new awareness of
economic conflicts and political frustrations were to accelerate the
nation's movement toward its characteristic twentieth-century problems and form.

In the post-1900 period of a transformed nation, the exacerbated
economic and political strains resulted in considerable discontent,
particularly among hard-pressed farmers and workers. Stress was
further intensified by the fixation on Canada's national status by
public commentators and politicians. For both ideological and strategic reasons, these public-policy debaters sought a common denominator to interpret or organize politics. In a world of imperial
struggles, a fragile national consensus based on the nation-building
goals of John A. Macdonald's Conservative alliance was subject to
almost constant debate over material questions such as tariff and
defence policy and more ethereal if equally contentious ones of
national purpose and status. Stimulated by the Great War in 1914,
the English-speaking majority's loyalty to Great Britain prompted
near-disastrous confrontations by the end of the decade. One battle
was between French and English, and the other pitted economically
discontented farmers, workers, and, to a lesser extent, women against
a comfortable and confident business middle class.[4] In this environment of accumulating unease and disruption, the political and economic systems were severely strained and the reconstruction of both
was demanded.

Among the groups engaged with these national problems and
solutions were the political economists at Queen's. They themselves
helped to identify the critical importance of the changes remaking
the country and the difficulties its institutions and peoples were
experiencing. They also suggested that a new approach to the problems confronting the nation was needed. This new approach was
based on two broad claims. First, the political economists asserted
that they could identify the outlines of the emerging political and
economic order and the forces making it. Secondly, they argued that
political economy could also suggest the only effective means to shape
and control the forces so rapidly changing the nation. To make these

claims, they drew on new currents of thought in social science in the English-speaking world and emphasized their relevance to Canada.

The Darwinian revolution in science and the emergence of Marxism in social science were only two of the many fundamental challenges to the intellectual foundations of Western society in the last half of the nineteenth century. Furthermore, the intellectual shifts of that period suggest a vital part of the context in which the Canadian academics were working. The decades from the 1860s to 1920s witnessed what has been characterized by European and North American intellectual historians as a "reorientation," a "revolution," or, more modestly, an "emergence" of distinctive goals and methods to guide mankind in the study of the social order.[5]

The revolution in social-scientific theory involved a complex and remarkable set of changes in the way people thought about the world and their response to it, particularly the characterization of the political and economic systems and human nature. The model of scientific study was revolutionized as the Darwinian synthesis, based on an inductive and empirical method, displaced the previously dominant Baconian approach, which rested on a deductive and metaphysical approach. The revolution in the physical sciences soon influenced the social sciences. The very organization of knowledge was broken down as holistic natural philosophy was fragmented into distinctive and often new disciplines such as economics, political science, sociology, and history. The methods of inquiry changed too: the formalistic or deductive, positivistic, and determinist forms of inquiry were discredited and replaced by the inductive and empirical, historicist, and voluntaristic approaches of the new disciplines. Through the new scientific method applied to social questions, understanding material forces as well as the social traits and individual characteristics of human beings was now to be fully achievable. This was to be based on observation and measurement of reality rather than on speculative deduction. The present world rather than the next became the only one that could be understood and the only one that mattered. All this was to result in cumulative and correct knowledge of humans in the social order.

The emphasis on new methods of inquiry and a new focus on this world led to fierce debate with and then rejection of the older deterministic and pessimistic accounts of humankind's possibilities found among pre-1870 social scientists and philosophers alike. The novelty of the emerging cast of mind also became apparent as the new men and women made a claim to exclusive understanding of the social order, again dismissing the authority of moral philosophers and theologians with considerable vehemence. Stressing their peculiar competence to understand the world and the human race, the emerging corps of social scientists aspired to both comment on and guide society's political and economic affairs.[6]

When in 1932 Oscar Skelton reflected on the ways the new social sciences had become so central to modern public debate, he too emphasized the considerable intellectual ferment in the last three decades of the nineteenth century. Instead of examining the fundamental debates about knowledge and its organization, however, Skelton pointed to the direct stimulus of social conditions in changing the basis of social science. He identified the political and economic dimensions of this ferment in radical criticism of society by revolutionaries, especially Marxists, and by utopian reformers such as Georgeites and Fabians. The result was a challenge to both the social order and to orthodox intellectual systems. This challenge, Skelton thought, led to a major re-evaluation of political and economic sciences after 1870.

In economics, the dismal science as a deductive chain of pessimistic conclusions about the human struggle to produce goods and compete for them was rejected under the influence of two important schools of thought. The historical economists, German and English, turned to the study of particular industries and social groups through time to explain how capitalism and industrialism emerged. This led to a new account of the development and operation of industries and markets under capitalism that found precedents and continuing strategies for challenging the torpor of *laissez-faire* policy. From another direction, chiefly among highly skilled mathematical thinkers within the ranks of Austrian and English economists, there was an outpouring of "theoretical restatements" in economic science. Here Skelton identified what was later known as the "marginalist revolution," a new paradigm shifting the theoretical basis of economics from the classical and Marxist "labour" account to the neo-classical "utility" explanation. The result was a reinterpretation of capitalist economics as a system in which the demand for a good stimulated productive capacity, created its value, and therefore met individual needs efficaciously and efficiently.[7]

Examining political science, Skelton was briefer, warning that nothing like the satisfactory construction of a convincing account of politics had emerged to compare with the new economic theory. But he claimed that a new realism had reformed political science. Reflecting the new sociological and psychological dimensions that so obviously impinged on humankind's public behaviour and institutions, political science was escaping from formalist anatomies of institutions and from rhetorical recitations of political doctrines. It had begun to examine actual institutions in their social circumstances and was starting to explain the factors that shaped political behaviour and prescribed political choices."[8]

With his usual optimism, Skelton claimed that the new disciplines had made possible the salvation of Canadian thought from an ignorance that had long constrained national understanding and response to political and economic problems. In this way his survey argued that the new modes of thought helped to remake Canadians' views of their world, and, more obliquely, it indicated the new importance of the university in society. In sum, Skelton suggested that the possibilities for rational and effective resolution of economic and political questions had emerged with the new social sciences.

Skelton hinted that economic thought in the late nineteenth century, as reflected in the work of the historical economists, was notable for an active and even interventionist mood. It was characterized by a shift to a positive assessment of capitalism's productive capacities and by a recognition of the critical place of the rational individual in this economic order. Such optimism was also an important consequence of the neo-classical restatement of economic principles. If considerable disagreement lay between the historical and the neo-classical economics – the "war of the schools" between German historical and Austrian marginalist economists is a cliché among historians of economic thought – they were united in raising the possibility of improvement in humankind's material condition. It would be an exaggeration to suggest that the new formulations were wholly optimistic, but they certainly argued for great material potential within capitalism and greater human agency in shaping that potential. Economists were still aware of the scarcity of resources and the elusiveness of economic efficiency. But their most distinguished practitioners, including their leading textbook writers, Alfred Marshall at Cambridge and Frank Taussig at Harvard, accepted the need for interventions in the markets, both by the state and also by other collective agencies, to fulfil John Stuart Mill's goal of the improvement of all people.[9]

In contrast, political science in Skelton's era undoubtedly tended to find more constraints upon than possibilities for political rationality and collective fulfilment. Distaste for the practices of mass democracy particularly disturbed the new American and British political scientists. Their fellow students of mankind, psychologists and sociologists, especially in Europe, were overwhelmed by their discovery of powerful unconscious, irrational, and destructive impulses in each individual and society at large. Both groups also admitted that theirs was the age of irresistible democracy. They acknowledged, or warned, that all men's claims, and perhaps women's, must be reflected in political participation and public policy. From their insights into human nature and political behaviour, the new political scientists were cautious in their predictions about democracy's future. They struggled to find the means to remake political institutions in the wake of expanding democracy. Undoubtedly, the dominant stream of political science wanted to shield political institutions from the influence of the masses by strengthening autonomous administrative agencies. But this group did not carry the day, as Skelton noted, and another group was equally vehement that the chief political problem was to expand humankind's capacities for effective political thinking and participation. Uniting them was a warning that existing practices and behaviour were not acceptable.[10]

The ferment of economic and political theory had important results. Economists and political scientists shared the conviction that the wants of all people in society must be met or the social order would face severe pressure if not outright revolution – no longer would men and women be satisfied by limited and inequitable economic opportunities or political influence. There was a notable divergence, however, between the economists' and the political scientists' assessments of the possibilities of human beings within the political and economic order. For the economists, opening possibilities and greater potential was discernible in capitalism; for political scientists, dangerous tendencies and narrow choices were observed. This difference indicates the boundaries of choice that Queen's political economists would draw upon in their work. Their own choices help us to locate the distinctiveness of the conclusions they reached.

Queen's political economists agreed that their analyses comprised the most significant accounts of reality, indeed the only useful responses to the fundamental reorientation of the political and economic orders. For each discipline, their insights were the result of a lengthy and assiduous learning of the many factors that explained social reality. This contributed to a sense of exclusive knowledge as well as a special ability to instruct society. The tendency to exclusivity is suggested by the conception of "professionalization," the chief means by which the new social-scientific groups tried to make themselves equivalents to physicians and lawyers, preachers and philosophers, in their competence and influence. The development of professional social science has been seen by American and British historians as a key step by which social scientists promoted themselves as commentators and defended their special insights into public policy.

Finally, the adherents of professional social science argued that their new status should be realized within the university. Although this was more the case in the United States than Great Britain, in both nations the new social-scientist reformers insisted that scholarly research and teaching were essential to the maturation of the new disciplines and the success of the new public-policy agenda.[11]

In a nation where the traditions of intellectual inquiry and public debate were highly limited, such conclusions were both exotic and exhilarating. The intellectual community in late-nineteenth-century Canada, as the recent outpouring of scholarly work has revealed, was highly sensitive to the broader currents of thought in Great Britain and the United States, if not to those in continental Europe. This new group of intellectuals was extremely uneasy about its own role as a participant in the larger cultural environment, particularly Canada's.[12] Concern about rapid secular changes and eroding spiritual underpinnings was perhaps all too congenial in a colonial culture long dominated by evangelical fervour and economic and political insecurity. But, as Ramsay Cook argues in his recent study of late Victorian Canada, the traumatic impact of Darwin and Marx reinvigorated intellectual debate among the orthodox and the critic alike after 1860.[13] Within the universities, debate between the neo-orthodoxy of Christian idealism and the secular optimism of social-scientific empiricism was central to the scholarly debate in what S.E.D. Shortt has aptly termed an "age of transition."[14]

The Queen's where Shortt, Skelton, Mackintosh, and Clark studied had embraced the doctrines of philosophical idealism under the powerful influence and compulsory curriculum shaped by philosopher John Watson. Whatever its impact on the broad intellectual community, and that remains open to interpretation despite A.B. McKillop's persuasive suggestions, idealist philosophy was important in reorienting Canadian universities such as Queen's towards critical intellectual issues and important public questions in the late Victorian era. Idealism did so by offering a doctrine unafraid of the new Darwinian or Marxian materialism and downright hostile to the older positivism of the utilitarians, above all John Watson's enemies – Comte, Mill, and Spencer.[15] In both directions, its opposition to evolutionary naturalism and to deductive positivism, idealist philosophy asserted that the human sciences and human reason could triumph over the natural sciences and the mechanistic model. This intellectual aggression suggests how the idealist position was central to the new social science in the late Victorian world in both America and Britain, as do the careers of leading social-scientific theorists who emerged from the bosom of idealism and influenced Canadians

– figures such as Thorstein Veblen, John Dewey, Leonard Hobhouse, and John A. Hobson.

A sense of human direction as well as intellectual mastery over the social order emerged from the lecture halls of the idealists at universities such as Queen's by the end of the nineteenth century. Schooled to oppose the errors of Darwin and Marx as well as those of Mill and Spencer, students of the idealist philosophers – at tiny Queen's as much as at major universities such as Oxford and Johns Hopkins – were introduced to the dominant modes of scientific and social-scientific inquiry in the English-speaking world. It was in this environment that the investigations into economic and political issues were undertaken. Queen's, like only a few other Canadian schools, incorporated the new political and economic sciences into its curriculum. Its decision to do so was the result of the efforts of Adam Shortt, a philosophy major, and Oscar Skelton, a classics graduate.

Political economy had long been taught in Canada but only as a branch of philosophy. Courses were characterized by the formalist and ethical preoccupations of the clergymen who usually offered them. The refusal to identify a separate political economy was exemplified by Queen's refusal in the 1840s to appoint John Rae to its faculty. Although Rae was a capable philosopher and an outstanding economic thinker, indeed the only outstanding theorist Canada produced until modern times, his work was not appealing to colonial universities. Of course, serious discussion in Canada of economic issues such as colonization and settlement, tariffs and taxation, banking and public finance was central to public life. But participation by the university in these debates was extremely rare and often considered unacceptable, while theoretical rigour seemed almost as rare and unwanted.[16]

Beginning in the late 1880s, however, Canadian universities felt new intellectual currents from Britain and the United States as well as spray from the nation's own economic and political storms. The University of Toronto appointed William Ashley, a distinguished British economic historian, in 1889 and replaced him with the Scottish economist-sociologist James Mavor when Ashley went to Harvard in 1892. Mavor was assisted at different times by a number of Canadians who received advanced training in the new methods, men such as Morley Wickett with his Vienna PhD in political science and Simon J. Maclean with his Stanford PhD in economics. Mavor discouraged the social-scientific studies of another Toronto graduate, but William Lyon Mackenzie King was confident and clever enough to ignore Mavor's judgment and take graduate training at Chicago and Harvard, where he ultimately received a doctorate in political economy.

McGill, the other major Canadian university, appointed a notable economic theorist and student of Alfred Marshall, A.W. Flux, in 1892 and later, in 1901, hired one of Thorstein Veblen's protégés from Chicago, Stephen Leacock. Even tiny New Brunswick found room for a bright Scottish political economist when it hired John Davidson in 1892. Davidson unwillingly taught philosophy for the most part and left, exhausted and frustrated, in 1905. He was eventually replaced by his former student, W.C. Keirstead, a clergyman who, like other Canadian Baptists, took doctoral training in political economy at the University of Chicago. Queen's appointment of Adam Shortt in 1886, then, was not unique. Like Toronto and McGill, the Presbyterian school was making the new discipline part of its arts curriculum, separate from philosophy and history. The three universities anticipated developments elsewhere by twenty years or more, although it cannot be said that they made much of their lead.[17]

For their part, the economists at these schools were to extend their work beyond the confines of the university, not only as teachers, writers, and commentators on political and economic questions but also as public servants. Again, activities at Toronto and McGill, if not as vigorous in their concentration on Canadian issues, were similar to those at Queen's. Toronto economists such as Wickett, Maclean, and Mavor were intensely interested in public policy, Wickett and Maclean devising careful studies of municipal government and railway freight rates respectively and Mavor contributing highly critical views on the prospects of Prairie settlement and the wisdom of public ownership. Similarly, Toronto economists were active in moving to the public service or politics. Wickett was a long-time Toronto alderman and Maclean was the first social-scientific expert in the federal civil service, joining the new Board of Railway Commissioners in 1903. Maclean beat a path followed by other Toronto professors such as S.A. Cudmore and R.H. Coats. The post-second World War generation of Harold Innis, A.F.W. Plumptre, and Joseph F. Parkinson was distinguished by both scholarly analysis of Canadian questions and government service. Plumptre and Parkinson led an exodus of economists to Ottawa just prior to the war and Innis, contrary to reputation, shamelessly recruited and culled for the civil service. While McGill's political and economic scientists were somewhat less visible than their Toronto counterparts, they were nonetheless led by a fierce policy debator, Stephen Leacock, whose partisan writings on trade and foreign policy from the imperialist position undoubtedly made him the most widely known social scientist prior to the Second World War. McGill also sponsored more sober work. Its monograph series on Canadian industries during the 1920s and its social-research series of the 1930s were much more substantial scholarly work on public policy than Toronto's publication in the 1930s of annual volumes on political economic issues, let alone Queen's occasional reprints of papers from the *Queen's Quarterly*. Finally, led by F.C. James, Leonard Marsh, and Benjamin Higgins, McGill political economists also sought government employment during the war and for a time shaped the reconstruction agenda.[18]

Far from being unique, Queen's political economists were to some extent laggards in seeking and getting extracurricular employment. At a time when their American and British counterparts were almost obsessed by the effort to implement theoretical studies by public service, the Queensians were following the examples set by professors at the two dominant universities in Canada. This emulation was significant since Queen's was smaller and much poorer than Toronto and McGill, and, unlike them, was officially a denominational college until 1912. Despite these differences, or perhaps because of them, Queen's invested itself with considerable secular purposes; more specifically, it justified its existence by emphasizing its service and value to society. These goals will be looked at later, but for now it can be noted that the arrival of political economy at Queen's was one indication of the broader reorientation of the school towards a role like that of the two dominant universities.

The significance of developments at Queen's is best shown by comparing it with another religious foundation, the Baptist-supported McMaster University. Both schools worked in the shadow of the resented University of Toronto. For McMaster, this was literally true since its campus was beside Toronto's until McMaster moved to Hamilton in 1930. At both Queen's and McMaster there were similar histories of expanding secular concerns, intense and divisive internal debates about the church's role, and painful transformations of the denominational college into a secular university. Moreover, the social sciences were nearly as well developed at McMaster as at Queen's after 1900. Despite its college status and evangelical links, McMaster introduced a political economy curriculum under A.L. McCrimmon after 1903 and produced several capable political economists. The most notable of these, W.J.A. Donald, D.A. MacGibbon, and Harold Innis, were inspired by McCrimmon to follow his example and take postgraduate training at Chicago, noted for its residual Baptist legacy as well as its eminent social science.[19]

Differences in the evolutions of the two colleges help to identify the uniqueness of Queen's and its political economists. The first was that Queen's broke from official church control some forty years before McMaster. The second was that, by the Second World War, Queen's had managed to remake itself as a multifaculty university similar in form if not size to Toronto and McGill, again four decades before McMaster was to do so. The third – and most important – point in gauging the uniqueness of Queen's political economists to the history of Canadian social science was that at Kingston political economy meant teaching and writing about Canadian issues and not just the methodology of political economy.

SEVERAL FACTORS EXPLAIN why Queen's political economists applied the tenets of political economy to Canadian topics – and why they did so with such powerful ambitions and with such distinction. But the animator of it all was Adam Shortt.

The son of a miller, born in 1859 near the town of Walkerton in Bruce County, pioneer fringe of Upper Canada's agricultural lands. Shortt experienced in childhood and youth the vicissitudes of the miller's trade in a marginal agricultural area during the pioneer phase. Disqualified by place of residence from free elementary schooling, he went to school only because free tuition was provided by the local Mechanics' Institute. His first teacher was a Presbyterian clergyman, the Reverend George Bell, who was Queen's first graduate and a long-time member of its governing board. Shortt benefitted from Bell's encouragement and from improved family fortunes when his family moved to Walkerton but he entered the town's high school at the foot of the class, a victim of Ontario's notorious departmental examinations. Shortt's hoped-for passage to university was delayed by his father's economic reverses; however, at the age of twenty and with a very careful budget, he began the arts course at Queen's.

Adam Shortt's interests soon shifted from preparation for theology to more secular fields, especially philosophy, which he was taught by the renowned John Watson. Considerable academic success and continued family prosperity meant that Shortt, the medalist in philosophy as a BA graduate, travelled to Scotland in 1883 for further study. He spent two years taking courses at Edinburgh and Glasgow universities, where he followed tradition in taking up the sciences, under the rubric of natural philosophy, as well as continuing his liberal-arts reading in moral philosophy. (His earlier plan to study philosophy at Oxford with T.H. Green had been stymied by the latter's premature death.) Shortt returned to Canada in 1885 without another degree but, on the basis of his Scottish work and undergraduate record, Queen's awarded him the MA in 1885. At this point, his formal education ceased.[20]

After his return to Canada, Shortt applied for but failed to receive university appointments in philosophy at Dalhousie and in chemistry at the Ontario Agricultural College. His prospects and spirits low, he retreated to Walkerton and gloomily prepared to take up school teaching. Then his old mentors, Principal George Grant and Professor John Watson, intervened to find him odd jobs at his alma mater. In 1886 Shortt was assigned the single course offered in political economy with Grant's polite hope that he would give the course a decent burial.

Queen's was not quite as cynical about political economy as Grant suggested, and indeed Grant himself was hardly hostile to economic speculation. He had written two books, *Ocean to Ocean* in 1873 and *Picturesque Canada* in 1882, that contained detailed appraisals of Canada's material resources and prospects. At Queen's, political economy had been taught since 1878 but it was treated as a minor offshoot of philosophy with a single course offered first by Watson himself and later by a local clergyman, the Reverend James Campbell. Rather than bury the course, Shortt revived the dismal science and made an academic position for himself. His success led to an appointment as lecturer in 1889 and to his subject's new status as a field for major and honours specialization in 1890. Shortt was made professor in 1891 and promoted to an endowed chair in political and economic science in 1899, a position aptly named after the maker of Canada's industrial strategy, John A. Macdonald. Adam Shortt was the first Canadian-born practitioner of the subject.[21]

During the 1890s and 1900s, Shortt taught a number of students who became his protégés, including several future social scientists. Among them were Andrew Haydon, the lawyer and Liberal Party chieftain and senator, and Edward Peacock, the schoolmaster and financier, who became a governor of the Bank of England, as well as political scientists William Bennett Munro, professor at Harvard University, Walter McLaren, professor at Williams College, and William Swanson, professor at the University of Saskatchewan. Shortt also became acquainted with Oscar Douglas Skelton, a classics undergraduate whose research and succession to Shortt's teaching post were to extend his work in many ways.

In the 1890s Shortt began the research into Canadian economic policies and history that would result in the major studies of his relatively brief scholarly career and lead later economists to see him as the founder of their discipline in Canada. While still a professor, Shortt also became one of the rare scholars who was simultaneously a prominent commentator on current affairs and virtually the only academic who conducted research on Canadian political and economic issues. He engaged in considerable scholarly and popular writing on such contentious matters as tariffs, western settlement, and imperial relations. He also began to serve as an expert consultant to governments. In 1904 he was co-chairman of an Ontario report on railway property taxation. In 1907 and 1908 he chaired a dozen conciliation boards set up under the federal government's experimental Industrial Disputes Investigation Act. Finally, in 1908 he became one of two members of the new Civil Service Commission. As was true of Simon Maclean at the Railway Commission, Shortt's appointment was an experiment: he was one of the first social scientists hired by the federal government to solve economic and political problems using technical knowledge.[22]

Long before this move, Shortt had been deeply involved in Queen's gradual transformation into a secular and multifaculty institution. His experience in the debates surrounding this development was important to the university and to his own outlook on the social scientist's role as a professor.

Queen's had been founded in 1841 as a Presbyterian college for arts and theology students. During the thirty years after 1880, it emerged from the shadow of bankruptcy and the threat of takeover by the University of Toronto as well as from its own religious orientation to aspire to the status of a "national institution," as its historian Hilda Neatby has put it. Careful recent work has shown that this role was an aspiration rather than a reality during the period before the First World War. In Shortt's time, Queen's was the college for Ontario's older and poorer eastern district, particularly for its Presbyterians. Moreover, it managed only after considerable internal and external debate to establish itself as more than a liberal arts and theology school. The result was a careful expansion into applied science and medicine and some difficulty in maintaining the new schools, particularly medicine and mining engineering.[23]

The hopes and frustrations Queen's experienced in finding a national role can be seen in the career of its Nova Scotia-born and Glasgow-educated principal from 1877 to 1902, George Monro Grant. Under Grant, Queen's pursued an active and distinctive role in Canada's intellectual and academic life. In the 1880s he defended his school against centralizing pressures from the Ontario government and the University of Toronto. He strengthened its financial status by several endowment campaigns. He pressed for the addition of new faculties. By 1900 he was determined to lead Queen's away from Presbyterian control to the status of a public institution. This secularization campaign became a decade-long dispute that pitted Grant as well as Adam Shortt and his social-scientist colleagues against traditional-minded faculty and churchmen.[24]

In contrast to its later growth, the Queen's Adam Shortt encountered in the fall of 1879 appalled him by its physical shabbiness. Yet he was won over by its intellectual vitality and so did not carry out his threat to transfer to Toronto at the first opportunity. The school's expansion suggests something of Queen's health after 1880. Enrolments grew from 249 students in 1881 to 774 by 1901 and to 2,247 in 1921. Women were first admitted to selected lectures in 1869 and allowed to register for degrees in 1878. To the faculties of arts and theology were added science, applied science, and medicine as well as an affiliated school of mining. Medicine had been part of the college from 1854 to 1865 but then was loosely connected until reaffiliation in 1893; it too was notable for admitting women to degree programs after 1879. Much of this expansion was made possible by George Grant's skill in persuading a reluctant provincial government and the Presbyterian synod to support the college and in raising alumni, faculty, and student enthusiasm for changes and their costs. In all this, the university's historian has shown, the Presbyterian Church was committed only to the theology faculty and was never enthusiastic about supporting the kind of university Grant wanted to create.[25]

The growth of Queen's and indeed other Canadian universities after 1880 suggests that Canadian society was turning to the schools to produce the men and women schooled in the liberal arts, the traditional professions, and the new applied sciences that an urbanizing, industrializing, and growing nation needed. The reinvigoration at Queen's resulted from its corporate efforts in redirecting itself into new areas and reflected its sensitivity to new opportunities. Prodded by Grant and others, Queen's remade itself in the image of the secular universities, Toronto and McGill, rather than remain a denominational college such as Bishop's, Mount Allison, or even McMaster. The universities grew surprisingly quickly and provided the trained men and women to manage business and government for the transforming nation.[26]

Queen's expansion had its academic side. In addition to the proliferation of faculties, this was found in the scholarly work, noteworthy in the somnolent air of academic Canada, of professors such as the Kantian philosopher John Watson and the Arnoldian literary critic James Cappon. Expansion also meant curriculum reforms that by 1890 included a formal honours course as well as some of the earliest graduate and social-science teaching in Canada. It was reflected too in the publication after 1893 of the first university-based intellectual periodical in the country, *Queen's Quarterly*.

The *Quarterly*, its editors announced, was written for two audiences. It was aimed at Queen's own alumni who maintained their interest in public affairs and cultural questions and comprised a foundation of readers and contributors for a national intellectual journal. It was also written for a larger community that shared the concerns of Queen's graduates. Shortt was one of its editors and, like them, he doubted whether Canada had the range of writers and readers to ensure the journal's financial or aesthetic success. As an editor he was often annoyed by Principal Grant's enthusiastic domination of the *Quarterly*, a domination that countered its stated policy of balanced and informed judgments.[27]

The number of subscribers was minuscule, remaining at less than 750 between the late 1890s and the mid-1920s. In comparison, other periodicals appealing to the privileged, such as the church journals with their serious topics, had thousands of subscribers. In 1898 the *Presbyterian News* claimed 6,750 subscribers while the *Christian Guardian* had more than 22,000; by 1924, the successor *Presbyterian Witness* had 22,500 subscribers and the *Christian Guardian* more than 30,000. The academic competitors to the *Queen's Quarterly* did a little better. McGill's *University Magazine* claimed 2,000 subscribers in 1917 while the *Canadian Forum* had less than 1,750 in 1924, but the former died in 1920 and the latter stagnated despite its magazine format.[28]

The *Quarterly's* editors and the university as a whole took comfort from the importance of their enterprise rather than its growth. Nonetheless, it was the only scholarly forum during the 1890s and one of the few for twenty more years in Canada to publish informed general essays on science, literature, and public affairs. In its "Current Events" columns, the very title redolent of a nervous appeal to civic duty, it provided a place for discussing a surprisingly wide range of topics and perspectives on political and economic questions.

Principal George Grant expressed both the peculiar goals of Queen's and the importance of the university to Canada in the course of his twenty-five year defence of his idea of a university against Presbyterian clergymen, Ontario politicians, and Toronto academics. One important facet of his vision can be gleaned from his account of student and faculty life at Queen's. He argued that students were treated as "men" rather than "boys" (he persisted in thinking of college education as chiefly for males) and were responsible for their own behaviour and education. As a consequence, their responsibilities as scholars and later as members of society were all the greater. In this environment, the faculty were not reduced to the status of "haughty dons" shepherding children. According to Grant, they were not constrained in their teaching but were "independent thinkers" whose very intellectual autonomy was the basis for their authority and their contribution to their students' educational advancement and social responsibilities. Given these standards, a small school such as Queen's could aspire to comparisons with the major universities of Britain and Canada. That was indeed a brave aspiration in the 1890s.[29]

Whatever his reservations about the principal, Adam Shortt habitually pointed to Grant's work in "vitalizing" the intellectual environment at Queen's and in defining a new role for the university in a democratic society. "A university in a democratic country must keep itself in touch with the living needs of the people," Shortt wrote in his eulogy of the principal. He continued:

While it is necessary that [the university] should not lower its high ideals, yet it must be certain that these ideals are truly high, and above all, that they are real and living. The university cannot, on the one hand, seek a superficial popularity by pandering merely to low and short-sighted standards of the useful or expedient, nor, on the other, can it afford to maintain an intellectual aloofness, which will not deign to recognize in a free and liberal spirit the great practical interests of the nation. The university must actively and with enthusiasm assist in raising the spiritual tone of the country, and in promoting an enlightened and tolerant public spirit, which will regard the great issues of life, personal and national, from a wide and self-responsible [*sic*] point of view.[30]

Shortt's emphasis on service as the key to the university's new status also reveals his adoption of the social role of the intellectual and his estimate of the extent to which scholars could influence society.

Probing that role and its impact was often on Shortt's mind as he reflected on his discipline and its function in Canadian society. Practical public questions, Shortt argued, required theoretical, abstract study. But he also warned that theoretical inquiry could be correct only if it were anchored by practical tests (a tenet of Skelton's and Mackintosh's social scientific faith too). Similarly, the material conditions of the world, determining the general environment in which human beings lived and thought, could be transformed by the people who correctly understood those conditions. Conducted in and by the university, intellectual inquiry was crucial to society in forming that reasoned understanding (what O.D. Skelton was later to call the "ordered experience of mankind") that was prior to effective action. The university was the institution dedicated to identifying those malleable parts of the social environment that Shortt the social scientist particularly aimed to analyze. Just as political economists delineated material limitations and possibilities, so academics as a group defined social potentials and limits. The social scientists, like all academics, eschewed mere technical expertise or mindless publication of research. Freedom from the need to provide "practical" answers and independence from special interests, Shortt asserted, comprised the sources for the superior insights that groups such as the Canadian Political Science Association could provide. The university and its academic analysts served a mediatory role in examining public questions, a mediation based on the intellectual's capacity to distinguish between the objective and determined and the subjective and mutable factors shaping the social order.[31]

Queen's ambitions, fostered by Grant, Shortt, and other faculty members, were revealed most clearly by the campaign to break with the Presbyterian Church. This campaign was begun in 1900 but only after a protracted and bitter twelve-year effort did it result in independence from the Presbyterian synod, guaranteed Ontario government financial assistance, and access to non-denominational support from organizations such as the Carnegie Foundation. The length and complexity of the arguments used in the course of the struggle show the novelty of the secular view of the university. It also sustains the point that the "national university" Grant, Watson, Cappon, Shortt, and the other senior professors thought they were shaping was not yet popular among the majority of Queen's own alumni, Ontario politicians, and other colleges.[32]

Grant and Shortt were the chief public spokesmen for the faculty in the earliest secularization drive. They did not, it appears, foresee any of the strong opposition that emerged. Their confidence rings through arguments aimed at the Presbyterian Church and Queen's alumni as well as the Ontario government and the University of Toronto. Like Canadian university heads before and since, Principal Grant insisted that provincial government financing was imperative for Queen's new work and that it would not lead to government control. On the contrary, he explained, government assistance would mark the "co-operation of the Province with our work ... to meet the expansion of the country, the promise of the new century and the restless demands of human intellect." For his part, Shortt insisted that the university had undertaken new and larger responsibilities for higher education in all of Canada, moving from "a denominational college to a national university."[33]

Despite the call on provincial money, if not because of it, Grant and Shortt made a point of distinguishing Queen's national role from Toronto's provincial one. They were careful to refer to Toronto by that ambiguous phrase, "the provincial university," and eager to avoid its connotations for Queen's. Strategically, the claim to a national constituency drew on the national Presbyterian community, which was already somewhat oriented to Queen's, and looked beyond the southwestern Ontario metropolis and hinterland served by Toronto, McMaster, and Western. Shortt cleverly suggested that the proposed constitutional changes were, like the evolution of the British constitution, a natural and organic adjustment.[34]

Perhaps these arguments were a bit too clever because no "evolution" occurred. Grant's successor as principal, the Reverend Daniel M. Gordon – like Grant a Nova Scotia Presbyterian trained in Scotland – rather feebly and unsuccessfully pressed for change. By 1910 an influential group of alumni, led by Edward Peacock and Andrew Haydon, bypassed a conciliatory Principal Gordon and actively fought entrenched Presbyterian opposition to secularization. They reiterated Grant's and Shortt's points about the natural evolution sustaining proposals that reflected the diversity of students, the multifaculty duties, and the financial pressures faced by the institution. Queen's was in effect a public university and reform was simply a "clinical" change reflecting this fact. Stiffened by these wealthy and influential alumni, Principal Gordon successfully led the changes through the Presbyterian synod and the parliament of Canada, the latter revising the Queen's College Act in 1912 so as to turn Queen's into a secular university. By this time Shortt had turned away from a Queen's he had come to see as stultified and frustrating.[35]

The key argument in Shortt's agitation for changes at Queen's was the broad relationship between the university and society. To Shortt, the university must be beyond government interference. At a time when government assistance meant that universities nervously considered politicians' reaction to academic appointments (at least Toronto had a long history of this), Shortt did not find any direct danger to Queen's. He was more worried about the University of Toronto's imperialistic ambitions. Any move towards "university monopoly," he warned, would threaten intellectual and educational innovation as well as Queen's distinctive national ambitions. Shortt certainly hinted that innovation and national status were beyond Toronto's ken.

He made further room for the distinctiveness of the university by contrasting the broad social goal of efficiency with the particular academic project of variety and experiment:

In all the efforts of men to provide for themselves the means and instruments of life, the utmost economy and efficiency in organization, with concentration of knowledge and skill, resulting in the maximum of product for the minimum of human effort, is altogether admissible ... But when it comes to a question of the aims and ideals which inspire life, and for whose realization alone the vast economic resources placed at our command have meaning, we are at once on different ground, We are no longer dealing with means to an end, but with the end itself. This is not to be cramped, abbreviated, robbed of its individuality, and reduced to a characterless series of indistinguishable unity.[36]

The university was exempt from the standard tests to which secular institutions were put. It was also somewhat immune to the materialistic forces that shaped most parts of society. It was, in Shortt's reckoning, a partner of those non-economic and non-political forces that formed the innovative edge of society. In this fashion, it was a source for the discovery of those transcendent ends to which all human activity was directed, at least on one level of existence. All this invested the university with precisely those responsibilities for the reshaping of Canada which he continually argued was crucial if the nation were to avoid the worst effects of its material transformation by industrialization and expansion. The intellectual and cultural weaknesses of Canada only underlined the problems and the opportunities open to the universities. Queen 's at least was prepared to acknowledge these problems and grasp at the opportunities they presented.

The secularization campaign, like Adam Shortt's earlier move from theology to political economy, was very much a professorial bid to launch the university as a directing institution in society. Ironically, the university was to become responsible for adjudicating questions of social ends and human behaviour in a fashion previously appropriate to clerical expectations about the churches. In relation to Shortt's own career, however, it is most significant that Queen's did not adopt his position. To pursue the role he sought, he had little choice but to move towards the public service.

AS FAR AS SHORTT HAD BEEN concerned, a secular Queen's was justified because such a university would have a chance to attend to the critical problems Canada faced. This emphasis might not be surprising from a social scientist, but it should occasion more interest from historians of Canadian reform, who have tended to insist on the latter's essentially "Christian" or else its wholly pragmatic basis. Shortt's emphasis also indicates the need for more attention from historians of the Canadian university who have not examined the interventionism the universities aspired to in early-twentieth-century Canada.[37]

Reflecting his ambitions, Shortt strongly encouraged his students to continue their social-scientific studies, particularly in American graduate schools. From a small college in a country where academic prospects were even smaller, especially for native-born Canadians, Shortt inspired an impressive group of students. William Bennett Munro and Walter McLaren moved to Harvard, Cecil Lavell went to Cornell, and William Swanson, Hector MacPherson, and Oscar Skelton went to Chicago along with J.A. Donnell and A. Calhoun. All kept in touch with their mentor through the vicissitudes of graduate study.[38]

While most of his students turned to the civil service, schoolteaching, or business, Munro, McLaren, Lavell, Swanson, and Skelton all became university professors, the latter three returning to Queen's. Shortt's putative first choice as his successor at Queen's in 1908 was his former student, Edward Peacock, who had gone from teaching at Upper Canada College to selling bonds for a Toronto merchant bank. Shortt apparently thought that merchant banking was sufficient preparation for a political economy appointment. He expressed this support in terms of the general value of social-scientific study and the unique influence the trained social scientist might exert in Canada. In 1905 he pointed out to the deputy minister of labour, Mackenzie King, himself a social scientist by training if not temperament, that these young men would certainly "lend their aid in keeping our intellectual standards abreast of our rapidly expanding material prosperity." King undoubtedly agreed with his older collaborator.[39]

Above all, Shortt made his arguments to another convert to political economy, Oscar Douglas Skelton. Skelton was born in 1878 and spent much of his youth in the farming village of Orangeville. He completed high school at Cornwall, where his father had become a public school principal. Cornwall was within the traditional hinterland of Queen's but it was a unique town for all that. By the late nineteenth century, Cornwall had become a meeting-ground of British and French Canadians, the latter migrating from the exhausted farmlands of Quebec to the rocky soil of eastern Ontario. Cornwall was also a witness to the two major economic underpinnings of old Canada, the timber trade and the St Lawrence-Great Lakes transportation network. Although a small town, Cornwall was not isolated from important currents in Canada.

Oscar Skelton spent his undergraduate days at Queen's mastering a field far removed from such material subjects. He was an enthusiastic and capable classics student, winning the award as outstanding Latin scholar and receiving an MA with first class honours in 1899. After another year at Queen's polishing his Greek, he went on to graduate study in classics at the University of Chicago. The tiny

Baptist college in Chicago had been revitalized after 1893 by huge Rockefeller endowments and raids on other universities to recruit distinguished scholars such as the classicist Paul Shorey and the economist J. Laurence Laughlin, each of whom Skelton studied with. Skelton did not continue with classics after his first year. Instead, he headed off in 1901 to England, where he sought his fortune. In addition to selling "stereopticon" equipment to make his living, Skelton wrote the civil service examinations. He did well, for he was the "first known Canadian," as the *Times* once phrased it, to have passed the exams for the Indian Civil Service. But his eyesight was too weak for Indian Civil Service standards and he did not receive an appointment. In 1902 Skelton surfaced in Philadelphia where he served as an editor with the *Booklovers' Magazine*, an undistinguished popular digest. At the magazine, Skelton worked with another Canadian exile and future social scientist-public servant, F.A. Acland from Toronto. After surveying programs and possibilities for fellowship support at several institutions, including Pennsylvania, Harvard, and Columbia, Skelton accepted Chicago's offer and re-entered the doctoral program in 1905. This time he was a student in political economy.[40]

While considering his prospects during his Philadelphia years, Skelton struck up a friendship with Adam Shortt who, oddly enough, had not been one of his professors at Queen's but who became a strong supporter. His English adventure suggests that Skelton had strong contemporary interests but it seems that his Philadelphia interlude and his correspondence with Shortt sharpened those interests into a feasible course of action. Skelton worked through his graduate courses in 1905 and 1906 and lectured at Queen's in 1907. At Chicago he had been struck by the iconoclastic economic thought of Thorstein Veblen, who was pressured to leave the university in 1906 owing to his equally idiosyncratic private life. Skelton also studied with the ultra-orthodox economist, Laurence Laughlin, champion of the Federal Reserve System, and the somewhat more radical political scientist, Robert Hoxie, a student of the American labour movement.

By 1908, when Shortt left Queen's for the Civil Service Commission, Skelton had lectured for a year and was wrapping up his dissertation. He then accepted an appointment as the Macdonald professor of political and economic science at Queen's, turning down American offers and consideration for the deputy ministerial post in labour vacated by Mackenzie King. He taught the political science side of the department for the most part, offering courses in government and political theory as well as more experimental ones from time to time in areas such as sociology, public finance, labour problems, and constitutional history.[41]

Between 1908 and 1924 Skelton wrote five books and dozens of essays, all the while taking on consultative work with government. His status in the university led to his appointment as dean of arts from 1919 to 1924. In 1923, however, he had served as adviser to Prime Minister King at the Imperial Conference and during 1924–25 he was special counsellor at the Department of External Affairs. He then decided to remain in Ottawa. From 1925 to his death in 1941 he was Canada's undersecretary for external affairs. He became a valued adviser to both Liberal and Conservative prime ministers (each of whom took up the external affairs post), a remarkable commentary on his capacity to provide crucial advice given the different styles and mutual suspicion of Mackenzie King, Arthur Meighen, and R.B. Bennett. Skelton was the architect of a foreign service that, at his death, was distinguished by its talented recruits, sense of purpose, and influence on the gamut of national policy.

In his early correspondence with Skelton, Shortt had emphasized forcefully the ways graduate studies could be important to the younger man, noting, for example, the peculiar impact the political economist in particular could achieve in Canada. For this reason, Shortt never doubted that Skelton would refuse American academic offers and return to Canada. He claimed to have had "impressed on [Skelton] the greater opportunities for men in our line to exercise a strong influence on the future of a country like Canada just expanding into national existence with great possibilities before it. Whereas in the U.S. they are past the formative stage and personal influence counts for less." These "opportunities," of course, were based as much on the country's lack of intellectual and material development as on the political economists' training or insight. The very weakness the *Queen's Quarterly* editors had worried about was the basis for the social scientists' potential impact. Canada was unique in offering individuals the chance to "exercise" personal influence.[42]

Through a curious set of calculations, Skelton satisfied himself that his opportunities to contribute to national life were indeed greater in Canada than the United States. Before the professorial chair came open, he reconciled himself to a Queen's lectureship at two-fifths the salary of a professorship at Washington and Lee University, just as he had refused a teaching job at the University of Chicago the year before, by adding "prospects," "patriotism," and "opportunity" to his income in order to make up the spread. This was clearly a case where only the trained economist could measure the utilities of motivation and hope. Later in 1908, Shortt ensured that these calculations would work out by promoting Skelton as his replacement.[43]

Prior to his intellectual adoption by Shortt and his successful work at Chicago, Skelton had morosely surveyed the "opportunity" for work in Canada. To his life-long friend, William Lawson Grant, the son of the late principal, Skelton noted that Canada provided rather more for farmers and shopkeepers than for teachers and writers, even though the nation also required informed social commentary from the educated man and woman. Like Skelton, Grant thought that an active and critical voice was both a peculiar need of Canadian society and a particular talent of the academic. The two men were forced to spend some years in limbo, Grant teaching at St Andrew's College in Scotland and then lecturing in colonial history at Oxford, Skelton seeking niches in England and the United States. Only after they had completed substantial academic work as mature graduate students did Queen's create positions for them. Not for them the youthful appointment in colonial universities then reserved for Englishmen and Scotsmen. Grant and Skelton had all the more reason to invest their work with considerable significance and to reshape the university.[44]

When O.D. Skelton was appointed, he immediately cast about for an assistant. One legacy of the Shortt years was a strong place for political economy and the possibility of expanding the teaching. When Shortt and Skelton set about to find a political economist whose areas complemented the new Macdonald professor, they decided to hire William Swanson, a classmate of Skelton's at Chicago. This was not easy for Swanson was *en route* to Seattle where he had been hired as an assistant professor at the University of Washington.[45]

Little is known of William Swanson's early or his private life, an appropriate veil given the formal and conservative economist he became. Born in 1879, he had emigrated from Scotland and completed his high school education at Oshawa before entering Queen's. Swanson took the political economy program, gaining his first class MA in 1904. Graduation at age twenty-four suggests that he had worked for a few years in order to finance his education. Once at university, however, he did not pause and immediately went on to Chicago. Like Skelton, he was a faithful correspondent of Shortt and was strongly supported by him during his graduate years. Swanson studied economic theory and finance with that doughty defender of classical economics and the gold standard, J. Laurence Laughlin. Swanson was deeply impressed by Laughlin and contrasted the eccentric and irreverent Veblen most unfavourably with the conservative and conventional Laughlin. For his part, in addition to fighting his losing battle against the new marginalist economists, Laughlin was an eager and influential government adviser, especially on federal banking policy for President William Howard Taft's Republican administration. Laughlin's penchant for such work provided Skelton with much amusement in his reports to Shortt, but had little impact on the staid Swanson, whose only outside activity mentioned to Adam Shortt was his tennis game. Swanson completed his dissertation in 1908, later published as *The Establishment of the National Banking System in the United States*, a study that, like his supervisor's work, challenged the decentralist and populist tradition of hostility to "national" banks in the Great Republic.[46]

When William Swanson accepted the post of lecturer he too was gambling that a poorer salary and term appointment would lead to the opportunities Shortt promised him in Canada. Swanson remained at Queen's until 1917. During this time he taught the economics courses in the department of political and economic science and, with Skelton, supervised the correspondence courses in banking that Queen's undertook for the Canadian Bankers' Association after 1912. If not as vivid a writer, brave a controversialist, or incisive a thinker as Skelton, Swanson did not shrink from scholarly or extracurricular work. During the 1910s this meant writing for the Montreal financial weekly, the *Monetary Times*. After 1917 when he moved to the University of Saskatchewan as professor of economics – he had previously applied for a position at Toronto with the full support of Skelton – he wrote steadily and consulted with provincial and federal governments. During the late 1920s he was appointed to two commissions by the Saskatchewan government, one on colonization and settlement, the other on livestock exports. This employment with Premier James Gardiner's Liberals did him no apparent harm for in 1930 he was an adviser to the new Conservative federal government of Prime Minister R.B. Bennett both before and during the Imperial Conference. Swanson remained at Saskatchewan, writing and teaching but somewhat detached from his duties in later years, until his retirement in 1947. He died at Saskatoon in 1950.[47]

Swanson had returned to Canada because he shared the aim of influencing and reshaping society. In 1911 he bravely criticized the president of Dalhousie University and sometime moderator of the Presbyterian Church of Canada, the Reverend John Forrest, who had dared to call for the disengagement of the churches from political and economic issues. Forrest's line of thought irritated the young economist, who explained that it was precisely this disdain for secular issues that had left many otherwise committed men "repelled" by the churches. "They want a man's work," he asserted, "and a man's work does not consist in avoiding the moral issues of the day. And the moral issues of the day are bound up with the economic and political problems of the day. Indeed, what the Presbyterian Church most needs is a ministry trained to deal with these issues; and to deal with them in a frank and fearless way, regardless of wealth, prestige or power."[48]

Swanson demanded an activist clergy but one benefitting from the political economist's educational influence. He even hinted that the social scientist might well be better equipped to fulfil the mission of Christianity than the disengaged, inactive, uncomprehending clergy that Forrest venerated. Swanson was not calling for an engaged Christianity so much as for a secular form of Christian mission on the part of those with a correct understanding of economics and politics. The role for the political economist that Swanson embraced was an extension of the sort of activities Shortt had engaged in with the Queen's theological alumni conferences a decade earlier. His agenda reflected Shortt's influences and coincided with the secularized mission current at the University of Chicago of the 1900s. Perhaps Swanson did more than study and play tennis after all. (At least one student of Swanson, Bryce Stewart, dropped theology and an intention to become a clergyman in favour of political economy and labour relations.)

More anti-clerical than Swanson was O.D. Skelton. He was totally impatient with the "backwoods preachers" who continued to control Queen's despite, he implied, the wishes of the professors and students. When still at Chicago, Skelton had written to Shortt that "strikes, trusts, taxes, socialism, tariffs, banking, bulk a great deal larger in the public mind than the authenticity of St. John's gospel or the wherefore of the whyness of Hegel. Possibly they shouldn't, but here for once Providence and the stream is with the righteous, otherwise the political scientists."[49] Like his colleague, Skelton contrasted the traditional disciplines and the new ones by asserting that the social sciences dealt with immediate issues in both their practical and ethical dimensions. Whatever else this comparison suggests about Skelton's cast of mind, it indicates a belief that his discipline was central to the significant questions of his time and the university must reflect that fact in its own structure.

This practical role for the social scientist remained Adam Shortt's guiding principle throughout his career. He explained to the inaugural meeting of the Canadian Political Science Association in 1913 that its members were going to be extremely influential in Canada because the nation had now entered fully into an era in which political and economic questions were central and because they were part of that "select, active minority" who shaped society. The political scientists' work was to study all political and economic matters but above all government policy, and provide "an accurate and full knowledge" of them. What distinguished their examination was not any "exclusive or transcendental knowledge" but rather their independence from special interests and capacity for reflection. Freed from the constraints of special interests or incomplete information, the political scientists' "free discussion" and "full knowledge" meant that their work was essential in determining policy alternatives and public choices.[50]

Shortt looked to the example of one of the traditional professions. The surgeon's work best exemplified the role of the social scientist. Just as "the surgeon's injecting needle [introduced] into the proper tissues" of the body the means for recovery, so too would the advice of social scientists enter the body politic and "diffuse itself by way of the proper channels throughout the whole system." To be effective, social scientists must recognize the complex interrelationship of the factors shaping the social world. This recognition would allow them to intervene at those crucial points that could influence future development. Shortt made no serious distinction between theoretical inquiry and practical application. Social-scientific studies were not "objective" but "disinterested" and social scientists were not constrained in the application of their knowledge to practical questions. There was a broad avenue connecting academic inquiry and its application in society.[51]

Shortt pursued this line of thought during the 1900s by working on the Ontario railway taxation commission and by acting as a mediator on industrial disputes boards of the federal government. He undertook these tasks while continuing to teach at Queen's, emphasizing that this outside work was the means for studying political and economic problems and for contributing to rational public policy. Just as practical and theoretical questions could not be separated, neither could the professor be isolated from policy making and public service. Shortt's argument and example found ready support from O.D. Skelton, who lavishly praised his work and cheerfully took up his absent colleague's teaching duties.[52]

Skelton's position on these matters points to the double-edged quality of his and Shortt's position. If their society required their services, they needed society's re-evaluation of their worth. Arguing as they did, they were consciously shaping a role for themselves that was larger than the one they or any professors actually had in Canada. Perhaps more important, this role was to be somewhat broader in its sense of social responsibility and areas of knowledge

than the concept of "professionalism" or "expertise" that characterized the work of their American social-scientific contemporaries. A
comparison of the university cultures of late-nineteenth-century
Canada and the United States indicates the uniqueness of the Queen's
political economists' position and task.

American economists and other social scientists devised elaborate
methodologies and adopted the guise of expert precisely in order to
insulate themselves from the fires of public controversy and disputes
about the quality of their advice. As a result of this insulation, they
extended their influence within the universities and over government
and business during the so-called progressive era.[53] In Canada, the
situation was different Despite an extended campaign to claim an
important role, notably by the teachers of the liberal arts in the last
half of the nineteenth century, Canadian universities and colleges
simply did not matter very much to the larger society, as the more
honest academics of the time ruefully admitted. Recent historical
scholarship focusing on the triumph of idealism or social Christianity
does not make clear that Canada's philosophers and theologians,
however much they may have been intellectually intoxicated with a
sense of mastery, were a beleaguered lot. The proliferation of faculties
and the emphasis on research in science, engineering, and medicine
meant that the main thrust of the university was towards usefulness.
The humanists were left asserting a doctrinal triumph that was a
logical rather than a practical success. According to both politicians
and university presidents, influence and authority came from the
useful faculties not the cultural ones.[54]

The problem for the arts faculty as the Queen's social scientists saw
it was to get the attention of government and the public as well as to
maintain a key place in the university. To extend their authority
within the university meant taking ground from the older disciplines
as well as the useful sciences while simultaneously beseeching society
to pay some attention to the university. Anxiety about the influence
of the *Queen's Quarterly* suggested how marginal the scholars thought
they were in Canada. That was why secularization was important,
for both autonomy and recognition could ensure that society took
seriously the work and findings of the new social sciences.

In pressing for these goals, Queen's social scientists owed as much
or more to the concept of the autonomy of the intellectual than to a
strategy of an alliance with the governing classes. In this way, as
Shortt's careful arguments indicated, they identified with a British
model of the intellectual engaged by the broad concerns of society
rather than an American model of the expert insulated from the
rest of society.

The position they took was epitomized by a minor incident involving one intellectual, Mackenzie King, who readily parlayed his expertise into considerable influence. King was a political economy and law graduate of the University of Toronto and proceeded to take graduate training at Chicago and Harvard. He was later awarded a PHD degree for his collected labour relations reports at the Department of Labour. In 1908 he decided that a permanent lectureship at Queen's would be a perfect billet should his transition from the public service to politics fail. Accordingly, he called upon his fellow Presbyterian, Principal Gordon, and other board members, who warmly supported King's fuzzily conceived proposal to join Skelton and Swanson in the political economy department and specialize in international law.

Skelton and Shortt heard about King's project and strenuously rejected it. Skelton explained that the department had mapped out a coherent curriculum and bluntly questioned King's competence to lecture in any aspect of the theoretical political science and economics that a university department properly concerned itself with, including "international law." Shortt allowed only that King would be an excellent choice to deliver a talk or two on his experiences as a civil servant, while Skelton thought that King's "breezy personality" would ensure the "popularity" of a set of lectures on labour relations.[55] Given this cool response, King backed away from Queen's.

If the new social scientists thought that they should influence all of society, they did not propose to do so by surrendering their intellectual autonomy and authority to presidents and politicians. This position alone indicated their resistance to the older, cosy basis for winning influence and power in Canada. At Kingston, the disturbing question remained that the university corporation would not go along with the social scientists' plans. Could they then pursue their attack on social questions? Shortt left Queen's having failed to convince the college that secularization was necessary. But even when in 1912 the school became a public and secular institution, would it reorientate its arts faculty in the way Shortt and his protégés thought correct? The answer to that question was made during and after the First World War when Skelton and his colleagues refined their arguments about university reform.

THE GREAT WAR PRESENTED many problems to Canada and they tended to defy Adam Shortt's complaisant view about the impact of men of good education. Shortt's successors faced these limits using their formal training in a discipline that was evolving more complex methods and making more precise and even more extravagant claims than Shortt was comfortable with. In the war and post-war periods, Skelton became more convinced than ever that his discipline and the university could resolve society's pressing difficulties. He gave substance to these convictions by building up the teaching staff and leading them in pursuit of the secular service Queen's had tentatively ratified in 1912. After 1918 the political economists tried to present new proposals to remake the arts faculty and the university in order to sustain that goal. The university's reception once again indicated a coyness toward the political economists' plans that altered their later work.

The teaching staff in political economy was reshaped to Skelton's plans during these years. An Englishman, Humfrey Michell, arrived in 1914. Michell was a public-school product of Dulwich who had studied at Oxford and Heidelburg prior to immigrating to Manitoba. There, he taught school and college courses at the University of Manitoba's affiliate St John's College. Michell also completed an MA under another Chicago-trained economist, Archibald B. Clark, who was, like Swanson, one of the ordinary and orthodox products of Laughlin's program. Employed as a tutor and lecturer at Queen's for several years, Michell moved to McMaster in 1919 as professor of political economy. This promotion was a recognition of his own solid work as an economist and McMaster's slowly changing outlook, for Michell was a serious Anglican and not the Baptist the college's officials would have preferred.[56]

If Michell had polished his craft while at Queen's by conducting his first research and undertaking a heavy teaching load, two other appointments in the 1910s arrived with ready-made qualifications. William Clifford Clark returned to his alma mater in 1916 after doctoral studies at Harvard. His younger classmate, William A. Mackintosh, came in 1919 after two years at Harvard and two more teaching at McMaster's western Baptist stepchild, Brandon College. Previously, of course, Swanson had moved to Saskatchewan. His departure, along with Michell's, cleared the path for Skelton's most prized students. The two young Queen's graduates were Skelton's true heirs in the post-war era.

W.C. Clark was born in 1889 near Martintown, Glengarry County, where his father farmed the barren soil of eastern Ontario. A prodigious undergraduate, he completed honours work in literature, languages, history, and political economy before moving on to Cambridge, Massachusetts. He received his MA degree from Harvard in 1915 but he did not finish his dissertation on prairie-grain marketing. Despite steady promotion at Queen's – he was professor by

1923 and returned as director of the school of commerce in 1930 – Clark displayed a restless academic career. For many years he sought a variety of outlets for his apparently considerable ambitions. In 1918–19 he went on leave to the federal Department of Labour, assisting his old Queen's classmate Bryce Stewart in planning the national labour-exchange system. Early in 1923 Clark resigned to take up a position with a firm of real-estate developers, S.W. Strauss, first in Chicago and later in New York. While in Chicago Clark managed to find time to teach economics part-time at the University of Chicago. After his brief return to Kingston following a breakdown in his own health and finances subsequent to that of the United States economy in 1929, Clark was appointed deputy minister of finance by R.B. Bennett in 1932. He settled into that post, retaining it through two decades of major changes until his death. Clark died in Chicago while attending the 1952 meetings of the American Economics Association, meetings over which a desperately ill Harold Innis was to have presided.[57]

W.A. Mackintosh followed a slightly more conventional academic career. He was born in 1895 in the eastern Ontario town of Madoc, where his father was a school inspector. After graduating from St Andrew's College, a private school for privileged Ontario schoolboys, he went to Queen's, where he earned his BA in political economy in 1916. His graduating essay for the department was on "The Social Teachings of Count Leo Tolstoy," a speculative as well as analytical piece praising Tolstoy's Christian mission while doubting its direct relevance to more advanced societies than Russia's. Mackintosh followed Clark's trail to Harvard. There he completed his PHD in 1921 under the direction of the eminent F.W. Taussig, free-trade enthusiast and major synthesist, with Alfred Marshall, of the first statements of modern neo-classical economics. In the interim Mackintosh taught for several summers in Saskatchewan public schools as well as for two sessions at Brandon College. While at Brandon he collected research material for his dissertation, "Agricultural Cooperation in Western Canada," and built excellent contacts with leading Prairie grain farmers and merchants, particularly cooperative and pool officials. Like Clark, Mackintosh was promoted quickly, emerging as professor in 1928. He wrote three major works in Canadian economics between 1925 and 1938, each volume concentrating on the development and problems of the Prairie economy. Mackintosh also succumbed to the lure of government. From 1936 to 1946 he was involved in various ways as economic adviser to federal government commissions and to the ministries of finance and reconstruction. He returned to Queen's as dean of arts in 1946 and was made principal in 1951, a position he held for a decade. He thereby achieved the hopes once vested in Shortt and Skelton that a political economist might be made principal and lead the university in the direction which, according to such alumni as W.L. Grant, Edward Peacock, and Duncan McArthur, was the true legacy of George M. Grant as well as a vital prescription for the university's and country's health. Mackintosh began the remarkable duopoly in which political and economic scientists have held the principal's chair for forty years. (His successors have been J.A. Corry, John Deutsch, Ronald Watts, and currently David C. Smith.[58])

Both Clifford Clark and William Mackintosh shared Skelton's concern with the economic dislocation Canada was experiencing. This was most strikingly seen in their post-war concentration on the economic and political problems of Canadian agriculture. It was not just a coincidence of mercenary zeal that Skelton became an occasional adviser to such farm leaders as W.C. Good and Norman Lambert, that Clark began a dissertation and published essays on the grain storage and marketing system, and that Mackintosh produced a thesis and wrote or edited nearly a dozen volumes on the economic problems of Prairie agriculture. Not only agriculture, but all Canadian economic policy comprised an area where their interests and analyses converged.

A major part of their strategy to enhance their influence continued to focus on the university itself. Skelton argued that the Great War's problems and failures presented the university with a great opportunity. In both arts and sciences at Queen's, senior professors such as Skelton and A.L. Clark, head of physics, devised research- and service-oriented reforms that would have greatly extend the work of the faculties. Like Skelton, the American-born and educated Clark had strong research interests and a lengthy publications record and he was brought to Queen's to lead scientific work to a greater emphasis on research. However, calls for new directions were rejected by an administration headed by yet another Presbyterian cleric, Bruce Taylor, a Scot who was not only obsessed with the old issue of relations with the Presbyterian Church but also weak and unpopular with students and faculty. Under Taylor, the university floundered as he re-examined relations between theology and the liberal arts, clung to the Victorian goals of cultural leavening, and found faculty and student alienation exploding until he left in 1928.[59]

The political economists made a proposal in 1918 to Principal Taylor explaining how Queen's could accept new responsibilities. The first way was to make research as central to the arts faculty as it was to other faculties and thus as important as teaching was. The particular skills of the social scientists, they went on, could become important to both the university and Canadian society. This proposal was partly a plea that the university encourage and reward the political economists for doing what they had fit into their summers for twenty years. A second change was to reorient the curriculum itself. For political economy, this meant developing a senior undergraduate program including courses in business management, public policy, and social welfare. This program would result in the "professional" preparation of students in such areas as the public service, social services, secretarial work (presumed to be an exclusive field for women students), and commercial education, as well as business and accounting.[60]

These proposals reflected Skelton's position that business and "social" administrative studies were means to strengthen the traditions of a liberal education and the inquiries of political economy. A liberal education would remain the core of undergraduate studies. The new areas aimed only at major economic and social issues and a narrow technical focus was not the goal. The parallel he drew was the same as Shortt's, between medical or legal studies and social-scientific work. The new areas would not fall into the trap of mere vocationalism any more than the traditional professions such as medicine or law did. Finally, Skelton noted, Queen's and Kingston must realize that this innovative role would further help the university carve out a niche distinctive from that of Toronto and McGill. Both city and university could benefit from the pure and applied research that political economy and other strong departments offered.[61]

The political economists' aims reflected the department's long-standing concerns about Canada's problems and their reading of Canada's circumstances. Such factors as the evidence of administrative failure in business and government during the war and afterwards and the vast expansion of professional and managerial occupations over thirty years heavily influenced their reconsideration. Skelton and Clark had conducted studies during and after the war on changing labour markets, were keen observers of administrative problems, and, in the person of Shortt, had a direct pipeline to Ottawa. Queen's itself only partly addressed either national labour-market needs or the aspirations and analysis of its political economists. A commerce degree program was established in 1919 with Clifford Clark as its first director. The banking correspondence course begun in 1912 was substantially expanded by an accountancy program created in 1921 and the addition of C.E. Walker and R.G.H. Smails to teach in it.[62]

But these changes did not lead to a broad research-oriented and problem-solving attack on the nation's difficulties or to a wholesale reform of the arts curriculum. The new courses in commerce and accountancy were only loosely related to the general arts curriculum and the wider areas of public policy and social services were ignored. In fact, the new programs comprised exactly the narrow and technical courses the political economists disdained and the university's limited adoption of reform represented a rejection of the essence of Skelton's aims. Penny-pinching and rejection by the administration explains Skelton's and Clark's abandonment of their university in the 1920s just as it does Mackintosh's continuous unhappiness in these years. While the political economists welcomed the addition of commerce and accountancy teachers, they were angered by the limited scope of the programs and concerned that the liberal-arts base, the critical perspective, and the social-service goals of the new courses were not maintained.

Broad goals for curriculum reform were made clear in a debate in the *Queen's Quarterly* between Clifford Clark and a long-time friend of the social scientists, J.M. Macdonnell. A Queen's graduate, Rhodes scholar, wartime army officer, and businessman, Macdonnell put the case for the traditional liberal arts. He warned that in the contemporary university the arts faculty was in decline, its position eroded by the increasing popularity of vocationally related studies. This was dangerous because the intellectual discipline of the liberal arts was the best background for later professional work. In contrast, mere vocational training was not particularly useful for such occupations as business. Macdonnell stated that university programs in business were unacceptable if they were not a continuation of the critical tradition of a liberal education.[63]

Clark accepted Macdonnell's position as an important signal to the university in a period of change. He agreed that the university should avoid vocational courses. But new programs such as commerce showed that the university was potentially strengthening itself. Commerce, he admitted, could be narrow technical training but it could also be part of the "broad mental training" sustaining the liberal arts. A commerce program built on a solid arts curriculum would benefit society by leading to critical research into business problems and practices. It could also assist the transformation of business. As Skelton later put it, businessmen would be infused with the "humanistic ideals of the true university" if they went through a rigorous arts preparation for commerce. Like Macdonnell, Clark referred to the powerful advocacy of curriculum reform by the American political scientist and sometime president of Amherst College, Alexander Meiklejohn. Clark thought Meiklejohn's aim of a renewed, critical liberal-arts schooling that blended the new disciplines with the old was a worthy one for Queen's.[64]

Skelton and Clark defended business studies only as a senior undergraduate specialization. They held to the goal of injecting into the business world the critical modes of thought that best expressed the liberal-arts tradition. In this they agreed with Adam Shortt, who had argued twenty years earlier that a university education was the best means to assess public issues and thus the best preparation for a practical life. While Shortt saw any vocational preparation at the undergraduate level as inappropriate, his successors believed that some adjustment was necessary.[65]

In 1930 William Mackintosh further revised the Skelton-Clark version of the relation between liberal and business educations. He used a more thoroughly utilitarian justification, actually writing of the "vocational" preparation that the commerce degree provided. He was unwilling to sacrifice the older goals of education, however, for he asked whether business studies should not be part of a separate graduate program. This innovation would leave the undergraduate courses open to the critical disciplines and, of course, allow commerce to develop even more technically. Mackintosh agreed with an earlier suggestion of Skelton that the Harvard case-study approach was likely to result in a critical approach to business.[66]

Both Frank Underhill and Charles Norris Cochrane from Toronto, notable figures indeed in academic Canada, contributed to the assessment of commerce in the 1920s. Historian Underhill worried about the further diminution of the liberal education that the universities had a duty to provide. The importance of that sort of education was too great to be sacrificed. Like Underhill, classicist Cochrane was offended by the smug practicality of commerce. He agreed with Underhill that commerce probably should not be part of the arts faculty but confined to the postgraduate area. If commerce became an undergraduate program, Cochrane argued, three "self-denying ordinances" must be kept. Commerce must not aim simply to be a means for business success. It must, therefore, concentrate on specific business problems rather than study techniques such as sales psychology or accounting. And it must, finally, adopt a critical approach to these problems, an approach coordinated with the traditions and curriculum of a liberal education. Although perhaps closer to older humanists such as the Queen's English professor James Cappon, who was resolutely hostile to practical studies but eager enough to instruct good citizens, Underhill and Cochrane found one point of agreement with Mackintosh, Skelton, and Clark. Like them, the Toronto humanists hoped that business studies would nurture a critical outlook from a new generation of businessmen.[67]

To Queen's political economists, a commerce program based on the liberal arts and social sciences was to be critical and reformist as well as relevant. Today, when commerce and management faculties have become virtually self-contained programs as little concerned with broad education and reform as engineering, such aims might seem like a quaint plea for tradition. But such was not the position of the political economists in the 1920s. William Mackintosh, in his assessments of contemporary applied psychology and industrial relations, made clear his view that the liberal arts and social sciences were to be central to the new programs. Dismissing both the false science of the behaviourists' claims to understand human nature and the erroneous concept of human motivation displayed by the scientific-management practitioners, Mackintosh asserted that centuries of philosophical and political economic study showed there was far greater human potential and creativity available to all people under capitalism than the shallow technicians contemplated. More was to be learned from R.H. Tawney's social-democratic vision for social improvement than from the narrow world of the management scientists, a point Adam Shortt, for one, agreed with. Rooted as it was in philosophy and political economy, the English economic historian's work was exactly the sort of critical inquiry into capitalism that Mackintosh hoped commerce schools would produce. If academic study of business were based on the old and new liberal arts, it was even possible that business activity would be taught to shift from the limited and perhaps even stultifying profit-making motive to those transformative mechanisms and creative impulses modern economic research saw as central to human nature and capitalism.[68]

Despite an increasing sense of their own relevance, the political economists were unable to lead Queen's administration to understand or support their work and goals. A mundane but telling aspect of their frustration was the issue of salaries. If interpreting salary levels is difficult given limitations on annual data and the inevitable subjective aspects of people's sense of financial entitlement and need, it is not hard to interpret the continual frustration about low salary levels and lack of support for research at Queen's during the 1920s and 1930s. Between Queen's and Toronto, a notable salary differential had been observed for many years. In 1910 Principal Gordon found that professorial level salaries at Queen's – the average was $2,135 – were about $1,500 less than at Toronto. When Adam Shortt moved to the Civil Service Commission in 1908 at more than $4,000 per year, he was vastly increasing his earnings. Though some attention was paid to increasing salary levels in the 1910s O.D. Skelton indicated in 1916 an $1,000 disparity still existed between Queen's and Toronto.[69]

In the early 1920s Queen's political economists remained underpaid if somewhat closer to their Toronto colleagues. Mackintosh received $2,300 as assistant professor in 1920; his Toronto counterparts were paid nearly $500 more. Clark received $2,700 as associate professor while those of his rank at Toronto drew $3,500. The professors in political economy at Toronto drew $5,000 per year, a salary W.C. Clark received only in 1931 and that included a $500 bonus for directing the commerce faculty. As late as 1937, Mackintosh was receiving a raise to $4,750 as a professor while Vincent Bladen was paid $5,400 for the same rank at Toronto. Skelton earned a hefty salary increase to $8,000 a year when he left Queen's for Ottawa in 1925. When Clark moved to Ottawa as deputy minister, his new salary was a lofty $12,000 a year. Queen's professors continued to receive a lower salary than their colleagues at the University of Toronto and the federal public service. This lower salary was, they thought, an economic burden and a snub. Given their ambitions for Queen's and for their own work, their conclusion could not have been otherwise.[70]

In any event, they deduced that economic constraints limited their capacity to conduct their work in the inter-war decades. This limitation was shown by Mackintosh's continuous scramble to gain government contracts and seek out American foundation support as the means to support his scholarly writing. His perambulations also show that the university had utterly rejected Skelton's 1918 proposal to finance independent scholarly research and that it was not displeased if faculty were at least partly employed by others.

Skelton, Clark, and Mackintosh were remarkably active in both taking up research and publishing. But Clark left in 1923 and abandoned his doctoral dissertation. Despite the best efforts of Skelton and Mackintosh, the coherent program of regular study and research into all aspects of Canadian public policy did not emerge under institutional auspices. Skelton regularly undertook consultative work. From 1916 through 1920, with the assistance of friends such as Charles Dunning, Norman Lambert, and William C. Good, he was actively engaged in studies for the Saskatchewan "farmers' government" of Liberal Premier W.M. Martin and for the Canadian Council of Agriculture and the United Farmers of Ontario. Remarkably, he completed major biographies of Alexander Galt and Sir Wilfrid Laurier as well as numerous other writings in this period. Between 1923 and 1925 he took on temporary advisory posts with External Affairs. Then in 1925 Skelton left Queen's to become permanent undersecretary at External Affairs. In this way Skelton pursued on his own initiative a course that would at least partly realize the goal of detailed study of and influence over government policy which he had urged his negligent university to develop. In other words, he undertook his outside work because the university failed to provide institutional sponsorship. While the public record on this, as on other aspects of Principal Taylor's regime, is spotty, it can be suggested that Skelton was not so consumed by ambition that he was chasing about the nation and indeed the world simply to grasp at power. To realize his agenda of research and analysis, government work was essential. This conclusion is warranted by his very proposals of 1916 and 1918 and by his astonishing outpouring of academic work up to 1923.[71]

The futility of plans to change Queen's was shown by continuous squabbles over the principalship. In 1916 people such as Clifford Sifton, W.L. Grant, and Skelton had hoped and worked for Adam Shortt's succession to Daniel Gordon. In their view, Queen's would thereby gain the principal it desperately needed and Shortt, who had earlier vied for presidencies at Saskatchewan and British Columbia, would get the university headship he deserved. But the position went to the Presbyterian clergyman Bruce Taylor.[72]

The political economists never got on well with Taylor and Mackintosh was utterly enraged when Taylor personally selected a distinguished economic historian, Herbert Heaton, an Australian, to replace Skelton. Skelton agreed with Mackintosh that the hiring was yet another example of the principal's incompetence. Having "destroyed" the English department, Skelton raged, the cleric had trained his sights on political economy. Mackintosh actually threatened to resign, though appeased by a promise of promotion to professor. He continued to assert that the political science side of the department, which Skelton had filled, was vacant and that departmental coherence was wrecked. Along with all the other frustrations of the 1920s, Mackintosh inherited a weak department when he became its head in 1928 and Heaton left for Minnesota.[73]

In 1928, the alumni coterie of Andrew Haydon, J.M. Macdonnell, Edward Peacock, W.L. Grant, Duncan McArthur, and Skelton surveyed the disaster when Taylor left. They despaired over Queen's lost chances. William Grant himself had not returned to teach at Queen's after the war, one of the main blows to the university in Skelton's view. The resignations of Clark and Skelton and the dissatisfaction of Mackintosh were other signs of dashed hopes. In 1928 Skelton was strongly supported for the principalship by now-powerful alumni such as Haydon, Macdonnell, and Peacock as well as the faculty. But Skelton did not let his name stand to replace Taylor, demurring because of his indifferent health and governmental commitments.

Such ingenuous excuses suggest that Skelton saw greater stress and fewer possibilities of success in running Queen's than struggling with the federal civil service during a time of minority government and limited public consensus on foreign policy.[74]

Conflict and frustration over university direction continued among the political economists until after the Second World War, when research and teaching were united as scholarly activities in the arts faculty. Mackintosh distanced himself from Queen's for virtually twenty years after his quarrel with Taylor. He spent his summers conducting research for federal agencies, including the Royal Grain Commission in 1925, the Proprietary Medicines Commission in 1926, and the Tariff Board from 1927 to 1929. When the American Geographical Society provided money for a major study of the problems of Prairie agriculture, Mackintosh immediately began to coordinate research and write his own books on Prairie settlement, farming, and grain marketing. He found this project most congenial under the lead of the geologist and University of Alberta president, R.C. Wallace. (Happily for Mackintosh, Wallace moved in 1936 to Queen's as its principal and for fifteen years was highly sympathetic to its political and economic scientists, tolerating their absences and trying to reorient the university to support their goals.) American Geographical Society assistance was a rare example prior to the Second World War in Canada, where opportunities to conduct scholarly research were limited indeed. From 1936 to 1938 Mackintosh was back in government employ, working with the Purvis commission on unemployment insurance. This commission had been struck at the insistence of the minister of labour, Norman Rogers. In 1938 Mackintosh moved to the Royal Commission on Dominion-Provincial Relations and in 1940 to the ministries of finance and reconstruction. During the last year of the war he substituted for an exhausted Clifford Clark as deputy minister of finance. Only at the end of the war did Mackintosh return to the university, a remarkable act of commitment to scholarship because many other political economists, particularly those from Toronto, did not go back to scholarly work.[75]

In the late 1920s and in the 1930s, after Hamilton Fyfe took over as principal and made peace with the faculty, some new appointments were made at Queen's. Economists Clifford A. Curtis, Frank A. Knox, J. Lorne McDougall, and R.O. Merriman and political scientists Norman McLeod Rogers and J. Alexander Corry were hired. They were all diligent researches and teachers who all found time for public activity, all too much time in Frank Knox's view. Rogers and Curtis, for instance, were committed Liberal Party men but equally active scholars. Curtis, with a PhD from Chicago, made banking and credit his specialty and in the 1930s was a key expert favouring the creation of a central bank for Canada, a policy supported by his friend Clifford Clark. Rogers, trained in history and law, had been secretary to the Privy Council between 1927 and 1929. He then spent several years at Queen's, two of them as a sessional instructor, a curiously insecure post for a forty-year-old scholar of his attainments. At Queen's, he framed a singular if incomplete centralist analysis of the historical evolution of the Canadian federation. Following his election as Kingston's MP in the 1935 federal election, Rogers became labour minister. Alexander Corry moved to Queen's in 1936 from Saskatchewan where he had taught law since 1927. Though a lawyer, Corry was chiefly interested in the evolution of administrative agencies and government intervention since 1900. While teaching full-time, Corry wrote studies of administrative law and jurisdiction for the Royal Commission on Dominion-Provincial Relations and he also drafted "Book One" of the commission's report. Through such moonlighting was social-scientific research completed in the 1930s. Only Knox, Curtis, and Corry actually remained full-time at Queen's in the 1930s and during the war and they too undertook government work.[76]

THE SIGNIFICANCE OF THIS PATTERN was not just, as Harold Innis saw it, that these men fell prey to the flattery of governments desperate enough to listen to experts.[77] They had long felt that the university was barely tolerant of their skills. The university was unable and unwilling to support their research and their salaries were too low to subsidize it. They therefore justified consultative work as a mutually beneficial enterprise. The academics were sponsored to study critical economic and political problems. The government received the information and analysis necessary to address the problems, if only to elude them.

From Shortt to Mackintosh, Queen's political economists argued that research into policy areas was their mission and the prelude to the economic, political, and social reorganization they thought was imperative if Canada were to achieve its promise as a liberal-democratic society. They turned to government only after encountering unending obstacles at the university. Similarly, Rogers's intense concern for the reform of the constitution and Corry's unease about the growth of administrative authority reflected their preoccupation with the practical impact of their studies, and in their cases as well cumulative annoyance with the university led to their later occupations. They then brought to government work the same mission they had derived from social-scientific inquiry. It was, then, the productive scholarly work of Queen's political economists that comprised the sources for their analysis of Canada's economic and political needs and prospects. To that work this study will now proceed.

2 Industrialism, Democracy, and the Promise of Political Economy

Our one great aim must be human, and only material and cultural insofar as these are human.

Adam Shortt

In the three decades Adam Shortt was at Queen's as student and professor, the university was transformed. Enrolment doubled each decade and included women as well as men. New faculties such as science and medicine appeared and new subjects such as political economy were added to the arts curriculum. There were intense debates about the role of the university in society and the intellectual and social role of Christian thought in the university.[1] Students and faculty alike were caught up in this atmosphere. The Alma Mater Society, the student government, contributed to the ferment by co-sponsoring with the principal weekly "Sunday Afternoon Addresses" on contemporary ethical questions. These "Afternoons" gave those students still eager after six days of lectures and compulsory church attendance the chance to hear talks. The lectures were given by their teachers and distinguished guests and assessed the momentous changes – historical criticism, revivalism, social gospelism – affecting Christianity.[2]

One talk given during the winter of 1893 struck a slightly discordant note. Queen's University's newly appointed professor of political and economic science, Adam Shortt, warned the students about ominous problems in the economic and social environment of the age and staked out broad claims for the resolution of these problems. His argument, repeated throughout the 1890s, was that the impact of an industrial economy and political democracy created new conditions and stark alternatives for Canada. He concluded that social science offered the most satisfactory means to understand and deal with the two great forces of industrialism and democracy.

SHORTT BEGAN HIS 1893 TALK by noting the widening gap between the "immediate interests" or material concerns of the majority of men and women and the transformative social possibilities raised by contemporary scholarship. He accounted for this gap by surveying the past century of economic development, which he identified as the critical determinant of social change. He also emphasized the increasing extent to which Canada was drawn into the maelstrom of social and economic change. Material progress and material conditions of life, he continued, had become the primary forces shaping society.[3] This had happened because industry and commerce during the preceding century had created an entirely new kind of society in the Western world, one where production was based on machines and human relations rested on the "cash nexus." The resulting division between producer and consumer snapped two characteristics of traditional society. Mechanization and specialization of work broke people's identification with the products of their own labour, while commercialization and a money economy transformed personal relations into contractual ones. The outcome was the degradation of the physical conditions of life and the loss of traditional personal and spiritual ties.[4]

Shortt's exposition was a bleak description of men's and women's alienation from society and from their own work. Yet Shortt did not proceed to yet another jeremiad about the fracturing of "organic" and communitarian social structures and of the "rational" and integrated personality, a message that would have been characteristic of the late-nineteenth-century intellectual. Neither did Shortt proceed to deliver a radical denunciation of the existing material order and a utopian vision for the revolutionary future – an approach that would have been somewhat uncommon, if not unknown, for an academic in North America in the 1890s. While Shortt was no iconoclast, at least this once he did not follow any predictable course in evaluating the historic changes of society.[5]

Shortt's critical account of material conditions and their social impact was slightly peculiar. He first led his audience to imagine the physical and social effects of Canada's integration into the age of advanced industry. "The skies of our towns and cities," he suggested, "would be obscured with smoke, while soot and cinders would begrime our streets and dwellings. Goodly numbers of us, with all our latent spiritual capacities, would be sent to find realization by burrowing in the earth, there to disembowel the hills and strew the surface of the land with their entrails. Others of us with all speed and reckless waste, would strip the otherwise barren hills of their beautiful garment of forests, and hurry it away to other countries in return for their coal." As if material conditions would not be grim enough, Shortt went on to offer a perspective on the end of this social evolution that contrasted markedly with the hopeful conclusions of the social gospel ministers who predominated at the "Sunday Afternoon Addresses." He concluded: "Then, when the fire had followed with its work; instead of permanently wooded beauty, from which we could have taken timber gradually and in all reasonable quantity for our wants for all time we should have blackened, barren waste whose hideousness and desolation no one can realize who has not seen the like. Need we ask what would be the effect on our higher natures while engaged in such work?"[6]

For all its vigour and condemnatory tone, Shortt's account of Canada's condition was characterized by a restrained hopefulness. In his view, Canada would not face the results of the part century's economic revolution until some undetermined time in the future. He actually drew attention away from the vast despoliation already caused by lumbering and settlement in the St Lawrence and Ottawa valleys and ignored the effects of industrialization and mining in Nova Scotia, Quebec, and Ontario; indeed, he even turned a blind eye to the results of industrialization in his own city, which already was a manufacturing centre typical for its harsh conditions.[7] Perhaps it was merely prudent for an academic critic to couch his remarks in such a fashion. To attack the aim of rapid economic development that was itself a staple in late-nineteenth-century Canada may well have been dangerous as well as impudent for an academic. Perhaps, too, Shortt did not wish to be misunderstood in his view that men and women indeed wrestled livelihoods from nature and that exploitation was necessary. The sum of his writings show that Shortt was neither a bucolic sentimentalist nor an opponent of industrial development.[8] (He did not share any of that fear or dread of nature that literary critics think of as forming the Canadian imagination.) Despite his rhetorical flourishes, Shortt was not about to issue a denunciation of industrialism, let alone capitalism.

For Shortt, the nation remained fortunate because it retained options on how it was to be integrated into the dominant material order. But each of these options had the same conditions attached. First, Canadians must admit that the direction the country was currently taking could lead to the very wasteland Shortt described. He condemned that direction as a "perverted" one based on the subsidization of manufacturing and immigration alike, an approach that burdened the nation financially and degraded its real potential. Secondly, society must realize that the connection between economic structures and "social" conditions was fundamental to the formation of Canadian society. The sort of economic environment Canadians shaped would redound upon the social and cultural environment they lived in and an impoverished physical environment would limit human potential.[9]

In language as rhapsodic as his warning had been chilling, Shortt concluded that Canadian economic progress might be redirected and controlled without sidestepping the broad characteristics of contemporary industrial society. He insisted that a careful comprehension of society and its evolution showed that the emerging economic order contained elements allowing for greater human fulfilment within and human direction over that new order than had yet been achieved in Canada or elsewhere. For instance, the nation could strengthen an agricultural economy that was no longer "the lowest kind of occupation," at least not in comparison with the "degrading" work of the industrial nations. Moreover, Canada could conserve its natural resources by planning for long-term and efficient use. Finally, policies could encourage only those industries that did not "degrade" its workers or "pollute" the environment.

Shortt also argued that economic development must be redirected because humanity's well-being demanded it: "Our one great aim must be human and only material and commercial so far as these are human. We must perfect ourselves, and this involves the perfection of all those around us, so that the more perfect we become the more we are bound in a common interest in our fellows. Our destiny must be eternal progress with perfection as its goal. This I take it to be the end at once of true national life and true religion."[10] To Shortt, then, industrial-capitalist development contained seeds for a flowering of human opportunity, including community life and individual fulfilment. But the germination depended on both rethinking and redirecting humankind's purposes and politics. Consequently, understanding the traits of the new material order and establishing human control over it were crucial tasks. Such understanding, in turn, was to be found in the intellectual enterprise that focused on the material world, the discipline of political economy. The "nature and sphere" of political economy, Adam Shortt explained, was crucial to the control of human fate. His adopted discipline contributed to humanity's understanding of social reality and prepared men and women to control their fate.

Curiously enough, Shortt began his explorations into political economy by sharp criticism of the two disciplines of political science and economics that had emerged since the Renaissance. Classical political science, he explained, had been a unified mode of analysis but it had devolved into two distinct and limited fields of study. The separation resulted from the initial influence of seventeenth-century political theorists such as Bodin, Spinoza, Hobbes, and Locke, who concentrated on legal and political relations in society, particularly the authority of the state and the rule of law. A second disruptive influence was from eighteenth-century economic analysts such as Adam Smith and his generation, whose concerns with public finance and commercial policy had led them to examine the economic policies of government and then the sources of commercial dynamism and wealth.[11] This split in political science had occurred during the emergence of the modern state and the modern market economy, two critical developments indeed. By the early nineteenth century, the era in which Shortt had located the fateful fracturing of traditional society, market relations and statist political doctrines had come to dictate the dimensions of social science as well as society.

There were two major consequences to this analytical revolution. The practical study of the conditions by which wealth was accumulated had led economists to raise economic activity into the primary social enterprise, while the study of the basis of authority and law had led political scientists to invest government with fundamental influence on society. In both cases, scholarly activity had acquired an importance that led to a distorted conception of human society and human wants.[12]

Fortunately, according to Shortt, scholars of the last few decades had begun to react against what he termed the "fetishes" of state authority and economic accumulation both as social factors and as modes of analysis. Academic study now recognized a distinct "social" dimension beyond the economic and the political orders and beyond the vision of the economic and political scientists. Legal and political institutions were not the only public agencies affecting humankind; economic accumulation was not an end in itself or independent of other human wants. By examining a vast "social" area, modern social scientists had realized that such elements as religious, cultural, and educational beliefs and institutions as well as individual variation were equal to if not more important than political and economic factors in shaping individual and social development.[13]

Like so many new political economists in Britain and the United States, Shortt was sensitive to the myriad influences that shaped the social order. This realization of the interdependence of political, economic, and cultural factors left him, like many younger British and American thinkers, determined to plot the ways in which political and economic factors influenced, and the ways they did not shape, the social order. Shortt was not encumbered by the common late-twentieth-century view that nineteenth-century political economists were either ignorant of or uninterested in the social impact of economic factors and vice versa. Far from being a technician lulled into fatuous generalizations by a narrow method, he was convinced that the social scientist had to consider the social context in which both political economic factors occurred and the social scientists' analytical generalizations were rooted.[14]

In explaining the correct approach to economic and political analysis, he first made it clear that economics and political science were part of a more general analysis of society. This general study he called, using the language of the very positivists and Spencerians he had been taught by John Watson to abhor, the "science of society." But this social science, unlike its positivist eponym, was directed to analyze the "aims and objectives" of society. For Shortt, unlike Spencer, social science was admittedly both a descriptive and an evaluative examination of the operations and ends of human society. He further interpreted these ends as society's efforts to secure "a continually developing civilization," one enhancing simultaneously individual capacities and those of society. Here Shortt deviated from both the older social scientific and positivist tradition and from Queen's own idealist environment by asserting that interdependence rather than conflict between the individual and the social good constituted the ends of social science and social existence.[15]

The social science Shortt advocated provided mankind with knowledge of the "means and instruments" by which a general understanding of society was to be gained and with the knowledge of the particular purposes and patterns of social development. These "means" and "instruments" included both a "spiritual" element ("mental, moral and religious or aesthetic conditions") and a "material" element (the "physical properties and forces" shaping the human condition). Shortt then defined the "material" element as the wealth and material means valued by human beings. The inquiry into this material side of those "means and instruments" which men used to understanding society and shape its development, finally, was political science as Adam Shortt conceived it.[16]

Political science was remade in the image of its pre-Renaissance precursor, no longer separated into the sciences of wealth and government. But its intellectual importance was far greater than it had been in the past. Part of the "sphere" of intellectual inquiry, political economy encompassed nothing less than the analysis of "the material means for the development of civilization." In this way, political economy could set about to devise a new understanding of the industrial-capitalist order that was now dominant in Europe and the United States and that was about to reshape Canada. Here was a happy coincidence between the the task for political economy and the major forces affecting Canadian society.[17]

IN MAKING MAJOR CLAIMS for political economy and its particular relevance to Canada, Shortt was led to consider further the extent to which political-scientific analysis was comprehensive and correct. Surprisingly, given his assured conclusions about the goal of a holistic social science, Shortt rejected the "scientific accuracy" and much of the validity of existing sociological and political economic writings as well as the direction they were taking. He did so because he found a fatal flaw in much contemporary social science.

Shortt wrote at a time when anthropology and sociology were suffused by doctrines based on the attribution of cultural differences, especially undesirable ones, to permanent, immutable individual or racial flaws. He argued that this point of view not only denied the primacy of freedom of choice in the social order but it concluded that human reason and action were incapable of influencing the broad forces and tendencies of society. One manifestation of this deterministic social science, social Darwinian laws governing society and history, Shortt rejected in numerous arguments. His now-lost "complete critical statement" condemning Herbert Spencer's positivism, as John Watson described Shortt's 1883 honours essay, was an example of his position. Similarly, his rejection of nineteenth-century social-science systems, Benthamite, Marxian, and Comtean, became central to all of his writings about the basis of his discipline.[18]

In particular, he strenuously dismissed the writing of the Englishman Benjamin Kidd, then extremely influential for his theory of social evolution. Kidd had based his theory on the view that individual will and reason were being submerged to the biological and political forces expressed by nations and empires. This approach, Shortt pointed out, severely limited individual well-being and individual existence to the advancement of nations and the species. Shortt scorned that form of reductionism and its support for the new imperialism. He argued that Kidd simply lost sight of the complex variety of the real world – and the place of the individual in it – because of his fixation on simplistic symbols and metaphors about the subordination of the individual to society. Reason and individuality, Shortt objected, simply could not be so dismissed. Kidd and his kind, including philosophers such as Arthur J. Balfour, ultimately accepted the futility of men's and women's efforts to shape their world and even seemed to suggest that human existence was irrational and meaningless.[19] Shortt utterly opposed such conclusions.

Social evolution was much less predictable than the social Darwinists and traditional social scientists assumed. For instance, the relation between the individual and society was much more complex and important than they admitted. Shortt held that any "scientific and accurate" explanation of society must always be regarded as highly contingent. Subjecting the notion of scientific accuracy to severe testing, and reflecting his own training in the natural sciences, he emphasized the incompatibility of social science with the tenets of validity derived from the natural sciences. The accuracy of the social sciences was not limited simply by incomplete information, although this was often a problem. More important, social change was continuous and social "facts" therefore changed with society. The result, of course, was that old data was no longer relevant to changed conditions.

The study of political economy illustrated the difference between natural and social science. "Where the facts of a science remain unchanged," he wrote, as was the case in natural science, "the only requisite is a systematic classification of them, and an explanation of their relations to each other. The facts remain constant, our knowledge of them develops." The study of human society was different. "In Political Science," he explained, "not only our knowledge of the facts, but the facts themselves, are constantly developing." Here were definite limits to predictability.[20]

As his discussion of the relevance of social science shows, however, Shortt did not abandon the goal of predicting the outlines of social change. "Since the development [of society] is not arbitrary," he asserted,

but constitutes, in the main, a progress, we are able to determine certain definite principles in it. In the variable element incident to progress, temporary questions must receive special treatment in accordance with the circumstances and conditions of their time. But, though the results may become obsolete with a change in conditions, they may be none the less scientific and accurate while the conditions continue. The object of Political Science as a subject of study is not to supply definitive and final solutions for all social questions. The great variety in social relations and the constant changes to which they are subject, render this method obsolete.[21]

The positive accumulation of knowledge about contemporary society was confined, true only for a limited period or to a limited extent. Insofar as a "scientific" body of knowledge was attainable, it was available only for a certain period. Even then only a few "definite principles" might be isolated. But for all that, the practicality of the "solutions" found were perhaps even more arresting than the grand generalizations of the nineteenth-century system-builders. Shortt refused to accept that current perceptions about "social evolution" were self-evident. He denied that social change was independent of human intervention.

Formal economic theory was no more attractive than Spencerian sociology to Shortt. He saw too many economists sharing the social Darwinian deterministic approach to human development. Consequently they denied the possibilities of social change and individual influence. Shortt took great pains to reject the claims of objectivity and prediction found in both the classical and neo-classical economists. He countered the classical economists' ready assertion of "objectivity" for their "laws" of political economy by drawing on subsequent scholarly work. For example, the validity of the labour theory of value and the iron law of wages had been central to classical theory. In simple terms, the capacity of the economic system to provide for the increasing wants of both capital and labour had been denied by Ricardo and Malthus. Yet, Shortt said, a rising standard of living in which both labour and capital shared had been shown by subsequent statistical and other historical economic studies. Moreover, the iron law of wages and the labour theory, with all their limits on mass improvement, were utterly disproven by recent history.[22]

Shortt also rejected the predictive capacity which, after the 1870s, the utility school of economists had maintained by the application of the differential calculus to economic activity and behaviour. Shortt scorned the mainstream theory of his fellow economists who, like their classical predecessors, made what he called "the vain attempt to give their study the exactness of the physical sciences." These scholars ignored both the individual and the social variability of economic aims, wants, and attainments that comprised the reality of economic experience. Humanity simply did not behave in the predictable manner the economists so blithely assumed.[23]

In a small paper written in 1894, Shortt glibly refuted the particular claims of Alfred Marshall, the great synthesist of the late-nineteenth-century revolution in economic theory (his *Principles of Economics*, first published in 1890, was the standard text for six decades). Marshall had sought the prediction and measurement of all consumer demand and therefore the measurement of prices by correlating price with a quantifiable and predictable "utility" of commodities. This enterprise, Shortt claimed, was impossible since it was based on a wholly rational calculation by which no men or women actually lived. Shortt sketched his alternate account:

Marshall is mistaken in saying quite generally that every increase in the quantity of a thing which man gets produces diminishing pleasure. His law of diminishing utility or pleasure, which is so very important in his theory of value is, therefore, only true of the barest necessities of life and is no general economic principle. The fact is, that while no man purchases anything without some purpose in view, the purpose has no definite relation to the price he pays for it, neither has the pleasure which he derives from it any definite relation to the price. Purpose and pleasure or satisfaction, while indispensable to economic value, can be no standard for it. The standard is still relative difficulty of attainment, and must be sought not through physiological psychology or the hedonistic calculus, but through the actual experiments of the world's commercial life. Alter the world's fashions, pursuits, or ideals and you have altered many economic values, but still the standard is difficulty of attainment.[24]

Somewhat inaccurately Shortt attributed to Marshall the views of the "ethical" or "historical" school of economists, though it can be granted that both the historical economists and Marshall and his followers argued that the price system potentially ensured the most efficient and satisfactory distribution of goods. Certainly Marshall claimed that the price system meant a distribution that was efficient economically and satisfying to individuals. Though he was equivocal about the justice of that distribution at any particular time, Marshall held that people's hedonistic wants, which determined the supply of goods through the mediation of the price system, were met as efficiently and as justly as possible. To Shortt, however, the rough experiments of the commercial world simply were not open to such a mechanistic explanation. Human behaviour was not as measurable and predictable as Marshall claimed. The price system as the automatic regulatory of supply to meet demand was neither necessarily efficient nor satisfying to individuals. In sum, the scientific theory and the economic practices the neo-classical economist described were unacceptable to Adam Shortt.[25]

In reality, Shortt explained, not the hedonistic calculus and automatically responsive productivity but highly variable perceptions and the physical limitations based on "difficulty of attainment" shaped economic value and therefore regulated the price system. These two determinants had a number of consequences. Shortt agreed that demand and not expropriated labour (as the old classical and the Marxist theorists claimed) determined the value of goods. But he suggested that the way in which demand was translated into prices was more complicated and indeed crueler than Marshall appreciated. Shortt emphasized the factor of "difficulty," echoing John Stuart Mill. He did not see anything automatic or efficacious about how people's material wants were met. If difficulty of attainment and limits in meeting needs determined price, then all men and women did not have their demands met in a satisfactory fashion. Furthermore, the distribution of goods was neither efficient nor just. The very fact that human beings did not act in a perfectly rational manner was also important. This meant that they sought many different satisfactions. Such variability did not necessarily justify deprivations, or if it did, Shortt did not say so. What it did suggest was that men and women should aim at a richer social existence and scale of satisfactions than economists taught or expected. In sum, purely economic satisfactions did not fulfil humankind and economic conditions and social discontent both proved this.[26]

Shortt did not accept the outlines of mainstream economic theory because he scorned the limited form of human satisfactions it promised. He remained hopeful about humanity's larger potential for fulfilment. His discussions of the social effects of the modern economic order and his rejection of the determinism of social science both pointed to the limitations of economic satisfactions as such and the limited effects of economic forces on human beings. This meant that men and women could and should expect better satisfactions and the freedom to choose these for themselves. It also meant that economics was part of the larger and complex array of factors making up the "social" life of mankind.

TO SUSTAIN HIS CONVICTIONS about the malleability of society, the trends of social change, and the role of the individuals, Adam Shortt turned to history. Very soon after his promotion to the post of professor of political economy, Shortt used explicitly historical research to extend his social studies. This work would occupy most of his scholarly research and writing for the rest of his life.

Shortt's shift to historical research has sometimes been seen as a retreat into a narrow, empiricist approach that made him a dry expositor of historical issues, or, to use Principal Grant's description, a "Mr. Gradgrind". This point has led historian S.E.D. Shortt to suggest that the focus on history was the result of Shortt's aim of finding meaning and moral certitude in social studies. By both accounts, Shortt emerged as a cautious empiricist trapped by his belief that all knowledge and patterns of social development were highly contingent.[27]

But such views tend to mistake Shortt for two different types of mid-Victorians, the utilitarian social scientists and the men-of-letters historians. Far from thinking that he was being reduced to timid and contingent observations about historical tendencies, Shortt was convinced that he had found in the empirical method of measurement and the historical approach to social development the means of sustaining an interpretation of the main tendencies of contemporary civilization and of intervening to reshape it. In this fashion, he was in the mainstream of British and American social science as its younger practitioners at the end of the century turned to historical study. Surveying progressive and social-democratic thought on both sides of the Atlantic in Shortt's time, historian James Kloppenberg has explained that the historical approach emerged as central to scholars in social science, who "[located] the foundations of knowledge in experience and [held] that history provides a source of judgement more reliable, despite its uncertainties, than metaphysical or ideological doctrine."[28]

For Shortt too, historical perspective and historical knowledge became the means of validating the reasoned understanding of society in all its aspects. The very breadth of historical study showed its importance. History was the reconstruction not of the "exceptional factors" but of the general traits of society. Shortt claimed that economic, political, and socio-cultural factors together shaped society and must be the basis of historical inquiry. He tried to write social history not just as history with the politics left out, the agenda of a later generation, but as a broad socio-economic inquiry into social change.[29]

His editorial aims and methods in both the *Canada and Its Provinces* series, published from 1914 to 1917, and the Board of Historical Publications volumes published during the 1920s reflected precisely this vast scope. The scrutizing of economic, political-constitutional, and social factors led to meaningful generalizations and understanding. In Shortt's view, politics alone did not explain or necessarily influence economic or social development. Legal or philosophical validity alone did not explain, or justify, particular constitutional development. Bountiful economic circumstances did not ensure the development or structure of a society. Only the totality of factors explained the evolution of a political or economic system or a nation. As Shortt summarized his goals: "Not only therefore does a properly conceived presentation of historical facts afford an indispensable basis for the satisfactory answer to any intellectual question which arises, but it affords the only satisfactory data for political societies of the present day, and the consequent value of practical economic and political programmes which depend upon the soundness of these analyses."[30]

Not just a nation- or a society-building device, and still less a retrospective court of appeal, historical study was crucial to the reasoned understanding and shaping of society. History was not simply the preparation of citizens or teaching about an emergent national community, goals that too readily have been ascribed to Shortt and his generation. On the contrary, historical study was the bridge between the limitations of contemporary knowledge and the general perspective that the "scientific" study of society required. History was vital to the general perspective and interpretation the social scientist aimed at. It was critical to the validation of all knowledge about society.

Shortt also turned to history to achieve his goal of rational understanding of and effective influence over society. He saw in historical study the means to organize the bewilderingly broad range of factors that scholars had come to see shaping the individual and society. Above all, like others of his generation of historical social scientists, Shortt relished the usefulness of history in debunking conventional wisdom. These new historians refuted the deterministic assertions about social change and social possibilities found in the older formalist studies of society, including economics, politics, and philosophy, and in the crudities of the emerging social sciences such as anthropology and sociology. The historical approach also deflated the older idealist and positivist certainties about ultimate social development, chiefly seen in the subordination of human purpose and individual motivation to the destiny of humankind.

In his own reading, Shortt followed the new economic historians such as Lujo Brentano and Arnold Toynbee as well as legal historians such as Henry Maine. These scholars sustained his own commitment to a rational understanding of society and the individual by their recourse to the historical reconstruction of political, legal, and economic theory. Like other historically orientated social scientists, Shortt allowed for a major portion of human intervention and control – a portion for individuality – within the social order. And like them too, he offered an outline rather than a blueprint of the direction society was taking and the process of social change.[31]

To Shortt, conditions in the current industrial age actually contained quite remarkable possibilities for humanity. As much as the breakup of traditional society with all its satisfying social ties had been traumatic, it was in the current age that the "self-actualization" or "self-fulfillment" of all members of society was a primary goal. Human history, in other words, was the story of emerging individual freedom and increased reason. This meant more than some trivial "progress" measured in material conditions. It meant that there existed the possibility for all men and women to "realize" their wants and thus to be fully rounded human beings. Liberal-capitalist societies had evolved to the point where a complete "realization of [individual] personality" was their goal. In the contemporary period, "personality now implies vitality of ideas, independence of judgement, individual initiative, and the demand for creative opportunity. The highest satisfaction given to man is the creative satisfaction." Sharing John Stuart Mill's repulsion at the utilitarian view of human wants and the positivist quietism in the face of mass degradation, Shortt argued that both highly variable and individual tastes and a common right to a satisfactory life characterized the age.[32]

Shortt pointed to an evolution in the notion of individual fulfilment to argue that "democratic purpose" had emerged with the industrial age. Societies such as Canada's were ones in which the views, aims, and needs of all people were to be satisfied by participation in the political order and by the fostering of their economic and social well-being. Shortt explained this to the 1909 graduating class at an American engineering school, the Clarkson Institute: "Democracy is not a political term merely. It is true that Democracy is commonly referred to in relation to political institutions, but Democracy means the realization by the individual of the liberty to think, to criticize, to act. You cannot have democracy in politics without having democracy in religion, in social life, in educational affairs, in action in everything human." The right of men and women to seek their satisfaction in society had indeed blossomed in the contemporary age. No only political institutions but also economic organizations and social institutions must provide for the possibilities of fulfilling human wants.[33]

Like many turn-of-the-century reformist social scientists, Shortt celebrated the ascendency of democracy and simultaneously warned that it must be guided. Just as industrialism contained the possibility both to degrade peoples' lives and to enrich them, so the larger thrust of democratic society simultaneously held the promise of fulfilment for all men and women and required the reorientation of their aspirations. Shortt himself viewed the reality of democracy and the populace with considerable scepticism. This did not mean that he rejected the democratic purposes he had discerned. Rather, it suggested to him how important it was for the educated élite to act as arbiters of purpose and direction while society acclimatized itself to the new environment of democracy.

Shortt occasionally expressed disdain for the political motivations and judgment of most voters. To his friend Andrew Haydon, himself no stranger to the subtle manipulation of human wants in his role as Liberal Party strategist, Shortt complained privately that Kingstonians had been duped about the prospects for a smelter near the town. He concluded that it was "enough to make me despair of democracy to observe how elementary is the stupidity which the common man exhibits when acting in bulk." Much earlier, as an undergraduate Shortt had given vent to criticism of the social attitudes and practices of the farmers and villagers of his Walkerton home. He was never nostalgic about Bruce County. Years later, in his published work, Shortt was quick to note how important was the "minority of shrewd, well-informed and public-spirited citizens" to the advancement and stability of society. Moreover, these reservations about the qualities of "ordinary individuals" and praise for the "minority" were more than just examples of his social snobbery, which became highly developed as he aged, but also an aspect of his surveys of Canadian social history.[34]

Canadian history confirmed Shortt's assessment of the problems of democracy. Like his philosopher-historian friend, William LeSueur, a combative foe of a simple-minded whiggish interpretation of Canadian history (but a devotee of Comtean positivism), Shortt interpreted Ontario history as a conflict between a prudent élite and a scurrilous reform element. Despite his later identification with a "liberal" interpretation of Canadian history, he defended the tory opponents of responsible government as conservatives whose ideas about the constitutional order reflected the colony's economic, social, and political capacities rather than specious appeals to principle. Shortt also argued, and not especially approvingly, that Ontario had been shaped by the particular traits of its original populace as much as by the material environment and government policies. The "American" roots of Upper Canadians, their narrow class origins and social values, and their crabbed notions of what constituted the purposes of organized society and human life all survived in a still small-minded, materialistic, and rather irrational society. True, the benevolent North American natural environment flattered men's and women's capacities by easing their material life and social relations. But, that said, Canadians, like Americans, were "too thoroughly at ease in Zion" to develop high standards for social, economic, and political life.[35]

Like mid-twentieth-century fragment-culture theorists, Shortt was critical of the lack of self-criticism, the anti-intellectual outlook, and the low cultural standards that had resulted from the intellectual and social origins of the majority of its peoples. This legacy of agrarian and middle-class philistinism sustained his argument about the need to change the received order, particularly by the cultivation of those capacities for reason and judgment that had not been widely dispersed.

Shortt's criticism of cultural life and standards of progress in Canada led him to argue for wholesale changes in the values the society held. He wanted to generate conditions that would allow men and women to develop the capacity to weigh the appropriate means for individual fulfilment and social change alike. His effort to retain the role of the individual in balance with the force of social change, an effort reiterated throughout his work, led him to adopt a position about social change that was extremely cautious. In postulating that the individual's aspirations were primary, he limited state action and the role of economic and social institutions as factors in society's reformation. Yet he also emphasized the primary influence of social organizations, including the state, over social development. To the considerable extent that social order and stability were prerequisites for individual well-being, the state was critical in maintaining stability and order.

But there were important limits to state authority. In a discussion of the relation between legislation and morality, he explained why. Contemporary movements supporting state intervention, such as prohibition, were excessive and undesirable because they threatened individuality. Fortunately, perhaps for the first time in history excessive state interventions were being curtailed by legal and social standards sustaining the individual against authority. Unacquainted with the later comfortable myth that the nineteenth-century was an anomalous era of unbridled individualism, Shortt held that an encompassing and often arbitrary authority – clerical, economic, and political – had been sustained by theory and practice until the later years of the Victorian age. (Curiously, the myth ignores the subordination of individuality found in Victorian social, economic, and political theory and it is being dispelled by recent studies about the ruthless authority exercised in the schools and courts of Shortt's nineteenth-century Ontario.[36])

His strong suspicion of the capacity and judgment exhibited by most men and women showed that Shortt did not rely on natural reason (such as the utilitarians did with their hedonistic calculus or the Scottish common-sense philosophers did with their psychology of the "senses" that made moral choice intuitive) to balance the relations between the individual and society. He was left not with the problem of defining the purposes and rights of men and women in society but rather with the prior problem of cultivating their capacities to reason and choose and therefore to develop social life.[37]

Fundamental social, political, and economic redirection was necessary. Reform could emerge only from a social environment in which people could freely and rationally act to reshape those malleable parts of society and human motivation. Indirect influence rather than government legislation or other forms of compulsion was necessary to preserve the balance – to realize the benefits and avoid the dangers – that would sustain the social potential of the industrial and democratic age. Just as those who studied the material half of society possessed crucial knowledge of how society could realize its economic potentials, they could also guide society in shaping a democracy that worked to the fulfilment of everyone. The political economist's role, much more than that of other rational educated men and women, was pivotal.

There was a model for the reform tasks the political economist should undertake – architecture. Shortt wrote that "architecture, in its various branches of building and planting is at once the most eminently social of all the arts and ... it is in many respects the most fundamental." He continued:

It is at once the earliest and the latest, acting both unconsciously and consciously, and touching most closely the everyday life of the people. It is therefore specially suited to a country in our position and is particularly adapted to redeem the barrenness and cheerlessness of so much of our social life, especially in country places. Its important practical bearing on the future of the agricultural classes in this country I cannot dwell upon here. But once some interest in a broader and fuller life is awakened it will not likely end before it has extended to the rounding out of our social life into a happier and much fuller civilization.[38]

Devised in light of of his other concerns about the social development, the architectural reshaping of Canada was an example of the indirect and voluntaristic reform of the environment that the economist sought more broadly. This reshaping was an analogy for the world of interrelated, complex factors the social scientist was trying to control and influence. Like the political economist's work, the architect's job was a link between the material and the ethical, between the individual and the spiritual and material halves of the social sphere that Shortt had posited.

At the ebb of his career in the 1920s, Shortt wrote on town planning and restated his argument about how reshaping the environment would also change social and cultural conditions and standards.
This result, he thought, would be obtained by blending rural and
urban societies in planned cities. Commuter trains and small garden
plots would revitalize urban men and women. Like the architect, the
town planner had the chance to alter society. Shortt did not worry
about the limits of state authority or individual reason in imagining
such changes.[39]

IN STUDYING THE IMPACT of industrialism and democracy on Canada,
Adam Shortt was struck by the difficult choices the nation faced. On
the one hand there was the potential for degraded and crabbed social
and individual life and, on the other, truly satisfactory and fully
realized individual and social existence. Yet the important point was
that there were choices, and they must be carefully examined. Shortt's
account differed from that offered by most social critics in the 1880s
and 1890s. So much intellectual discussion centred around either
utopian schemes raised by religious and social crusaders or else
narrowly political if equally ethereal proposals for annexation or
imperial union.[40]

Shortt entered the fray and offered an alternative to such debates
by considering the historical evolution of the liberal-capitalist system.
This made political economy virtually the custodial discipline for the
main questions affecting the new age of industrialism and democracy.
Shortt argued strenuously that the renewed political economy and
the historical approach refuted the fatalism and determinism of older
approaches to social development. Neither a Mr Gradgind seeking a
utilitarian utopia nor a Dr Pangloss contented with the existing order,
Shortt emphasized the high stakes for scholarship in guiding Canada
through the perils of the liberal-capitalist age.

Undoubtedly he remained in many ways a transitional figure,
moving as he did between idealist philosophical humanism and
empirical social science, bound rhetorically and theoretically to the
philosophy that nurtured him.[41] But the direction of his thought
makes him more than just a transitional figure. Although the terms
hardly fit his personality, his social ambitions, or his career moves,
Shortt's intellectual position was iconoclastic and brave. He was iconoclastic enough to distance himself from mainstream social science,
including economics, as well as traditional humanism, notably philosophy. He was brave enough to challenge the nation and its scholars
to identify the instruments that would enable Canadians at last to

realize the political and economic possibilities, including individual fulfilment and national well being, that the current age offered them.

Like so many of his generation of social scientists, Adam Shortt at once enlarged the claims of the individual in society and recognized the political, economic, and social origins of the individual. He wanted to redefine the roles of the individual and society, as well as the relation between them. He posited a new place for the academic in mediating that relationship. And finally, he set out a new and very broad agenda for Canada and for its social scientists.

3 Imperialism, Nationalism, and Political Economy

> Worrying about our national destiny seems with most
> Canadians to have taken the place of worrying about our
> individual salvation.
>
> O.D. Skelton

From the 1890s to 1914, explosive growth occurred in both Prairie agriculture and central Canadian industry. The conditions and consequences of this growth raised the problem of Canada's economic relations with Great Britain and the United States and led to heated debate about the nation's political and economic course. Eager to prescribe as well as study Canadian problems, Shortt and Skelton joined the debate about Canada's economic potential and its limits. In so doing they emphasized both the political and the economic lessons of political economy.

A VISIT TO THE PRAIRIES in the summer of 1894 gave Adam Shortt the chance to examine the region where so many of the nation's hopes had been invested – and, until then, with such disappointing results. Shortt's trip was a tour of the frontier and included a reunion with his brother, James, a Presbyterian clergyman then living in the district of Alberta in the North-West Territories. Ever the sceptic, Adam Shortt was forcefully struck by the geographical and economic factors limiting the development that had been promised for so long. He cited three major factors – climatic and soil limitations, distance from markets, and, the burden of the Canadian Pacific Railway, high transportation costs – that left the North-West in a weak position as a grain-growing area.[1]

If these material limitations were not enough to smother growth, Shortt also warned about serious social limits on development. There were the social problems of transferring a new population to unsettled territory, an area that lacked the cultural institutions that normally shaped and disciplined people's lives. As well, there were dangers in recruiting what Shortt called an unselected, alien, and often backward population from the leftovers of Britain and continental Europe.[2] All in all, it seemed possible that the whole enterprise of Prairie settlement might yet prove to be a social, economic, and even political disaster for Canada if measured by the standard tests of economic productivity, social stability, and political rationality.

Shortt's discussion about the North-West was much less a report on Prairie conditions in the summer of 1894 than an argument against the misleading plans and reports of the Canadian government and the CPR. He was reacting to matters that continually disturbed him, overblown hopes for economic development and inadequate preparation for the cultural or economic consequences of development. His hostility to British and continental European immigrants and his reservations about the geographical setting of the Prairies only reinforced a more basic apprehension about the kinds of problems that would (and to a great extent did) result from massive, sudden settlement on the plains. Shortt did not suffer from the economic vertigo that affected so many observers of the Canadian Prairies or the rest of Canada by the mid-1890s. His resistance to boosterism led him to warn continually against all the immigration propaganda, mining promotion, and real-estate investment mania that became so common by the end of the century.

Resisting promoters and politicians became a common enough tactic of the new social scientists during the boom period. Two other notable critics of Canadian extravagance and folly prior to 1914 were also political economists. James Mavor was even more pessimistic than Shortt about the potential of the Prairies. He was certainly more persistent in making his case. He wrote highly negative reports on the region to the British Academy for the Advancement of Science in 1903 and to Canada's own development-minded minister of the interior, Clifford Sifton. Mavor's blunt pessimism impressed few Canadians. Similarly cautious but much more effective, Stephen Leacock was bemused by the speculative binge and warned that only the gullible would believe the prophets of boom. Leacock used the gentler form of the satirical essay to warn Canadians against excessive hopes. Yet as he grew older, Leacock indulged in a speculative binge himself and by the 1930s he had become a hopeless convert to the booster's conclusions.[3]

In contrast, Shortt's commentaries maneuvered between Mavor's characteristic denunciation of all national economic development goals and policies and Leacock's exaggerated accounts, fictional or otherwise. He, after all, wanted to influence politicians, businessmen, and the public, not to entertain them.

Not only did Shortt counsel moderation in expectations about the potential return for pioneer farmers, he warned further that only experts in the new commercial ventures – be they agriculture, mining, or real estate – could make significant returns on their investments. The inexperienced farmer or investor had no fair chance to share in the large opportunities that undoubtedly existed. Thus, on both the agricultural and the mining frontiers, Shortt foretold of a much slower pace of development than he thought Canadians expected. He tried to show that limits would defy either rapid growth or widespread sharing in the spoils. Regardless of economic potential, there would be no great transformation in the condition of the small farmer, particularly the immigrant, or the small investor. Of course, Shortt was not as hostile to or cynical about Canadian economic development or long-term growth as Mavor and Leacock were. He wanted to correct false hopes, not to praise the rural life or condemn the new industries.[4]

During Shortt's time on the *Queen's Quarterly*'s editorial board, the magazine carried many studies of industrial processes that were linked to the economic expansion of the country. Almost all of these essays were restrained expositions rather than breathless paeans. The exception that offset the main themes of the essays was a 1904 contribution by Queen's Chancellor, Sandford Fleming. His essay, "Build Up Canada," emphasized the political and indeed spiritual benefits of massive economic expansion. The former surveyor of the CPR was not particularly interested in the social consequences of settlement and he was a generation older than his fellow essayists.[5]

For the most part, the other writers were part of a new generation of experts in business and industry. They carefully reported on the limits and problems as well as the possibilities of regions such as the North-West and New Ontario and of industries such as forestry and hydro-electricity. They also extolled the relevance of university study of the arts and sciences to the improvement of business, engineering, and journalism, and they called for academic research into the technical problems raised by economic development in the frontier regions of the country.[6]

A common theme in these surveys was the danger of diminished or lost prosperity and prospects if economic activity was not subject to research and planning. A second central theme was the emphasis on new technology as perhaps the key to economic progress. Examples of the link between research and industrial development in

Europe suggested the lessons for Canada. A new role was at hand for university-trained "men," since they would apply theoretical knowledge to practical problems and thereby help shift industry from a primitive to a sophisticated basis.

Forestry research illustrated this new framework for the university and economic development as well as Queen's strategy on the subject of industrialization. Both its own past wastage and the example of squandered American forests showed that contemporary Ontario must turn to scientific forestry to maintain a forest industry. M.J. Patton, a researcher with the federal government's Commission of Conservation, expounded on the benefits of the links between university and industry. He claimed that only "organized conservation," based on research and planning for development on the part of dispassionate experts, would sustain long-term, assured development. The arguments favouring forestry research coincided with a Queen's campaign to gain government support for a forestry faculty to complement the mining school, itself a splendid example of the link between university research and study and economic expansion and evolution. Alas for Queen's, the forestry school was eventually located at Toronto.[7]

The broader theme in the essays was that the nation was moving towards technically complex forms of industry and that this move would create an expanded role for universities. This argument had been used for many years by the promoters of the University of Toronto and McGill University in their own successful campaigns to expand science, medicine, and engineering. As already noted, although Queen's was late in moving towards this position, its political economists were prominent in making the case for research and influence. Their activities on this front began with Shortt and his earliest writings but extended to Swanson, Skelton, and the others because Queen's was so slow in adopting the utilitarian agenda. However, the political economists could no more adopt Patton's view that efficient reform and economic development would be implemented with ease than they could presume that the Toronto or McGill agenda of integrating academic work with business and industry would be followed. They had to think longer and harder about the latter than their confrères in Montreal and Toronto.

Although Shortt was suspicious of the extravagant promises of economic transformation and aghast at the prospect of uncontrolled industrial and population growth, he was almost as concerned about the agrarian economy. He expressed this concern in his earliest work and repeatedly called for the cultivation of a mechanized, efficient agriculture to displace what he saw as a backward, stagnant, and simple farm economy in Canada. In fact, Shortt suspected that a rather simple form of farming was exactly what would result from a predominantly grain-growing Prairie agriculture.

Shortt promoted advanced "industrial" agriculture such as dairying and contrasted it with the rude grain-trade economy and its stagnating economic and social effects. He concluded with a harsh critique of agrarian society:

The agricultural life, to be adequate, requires a varied industrial and commercial accompaniment, as a support for those elements of civilization which only the towns and cities can supply, and in more or less intimate contact with which the best rural life must be developed. The agricultural life is followed by some of the highest and by some of the lowest types of humanity ... Outside of a few distributing centres, therefore, the people who make agriculture their national preoccupation must inevitably stagnate intellectually. Whatever spiritual capacities they may have will be lost to themselves and the world, for though they may vegetate they will neither blossom nor bear fruit."[8]

The common view, that settlement of the Prairies held the key to a golden future as the "granary of the Empire," was simply a retreat into agrarian utopianism. Such a vision also led to the larger failure to foresee the problems settlement and immigration augured and an agricultural economy created. All the criteria of social and individual fulfilment as well as purely economic tests showed that an agricultural society should be avoided.

Rather than accept a limited future, Shortt argued that Canada should devise a coherent understanding of national economic potential and realize the political consequences of economic changes. Towards the clarification of that understanding Shortt and his followers brought considerable energy, particularly by debating the question of Canada's imperial relations.

THE "IMPERIAL QUESTION" WAS, arguably, the political and economic touchstone of turn-of-the-century Canada. The problem of Canada's political and economic future was exhaustively considered by zealous proponents and opponents of the imperial relationship at a time when British investment and trade were crucial to the Dominion. Both Joseph Chamberlain's plan for an "imperial zollverein" and the Boer War were catalysts that polarized Canadian opinion about future relations with Britain.[9]

For Adam Shortt, imperial preferential trade and the prospect of imperial economic unity stimulated his most penetrating and lively studies of Canadian economic and social history. Similarly, for Oscar Douglas Skelton, the imperial debate awakened his slumbering academic ambition and focused his ideas about Canadian prospects. For both men, then, the imperial idea was a point of departure in their work. Their examinations of imperialism in its various guises also led them to more general interpretations of the nation's economic history and prospects, with strong political implications.

It was appropriate that two Queen's scholars appear to have drawn Shortt to comment publicly on the post-Boer War imperial question. The first was O.D. Skelton. Skelton's own anger at Chamberlain's imperial plans had first led the footloose graduate to correspond with Professor Shortt. In their exchanges, Skelton encouraged Shortt to write an extended history of Canadian trade policy. For his part, Skelton originally proposed to write his PhD thesis on Canada and imperial economic policy. Skelton cajoled the older man, much of whose work until that time was characterized by either ponderous social commentary or relentless empirical historical exposition, to analyze and criticize Canadian economic policy.[10]

The ideas of Principal Grant also seem to have anticipated, and in turn been shaped by, Shortt. Grant was a longstanding advocate of closer Anglo-Canadian ties based on a Canadian nationalist's goals. He emphasized the civilizing mission of the English-speaking peoples, including the United States, and called for closer cooperation between Canada and the "Empire" so as to strengthen Canadian contributions to Britain's world mission. The Boer War, however, repelled Grant and he became convinced that imperialism was turning towards capitalistic and militaristic aggression. He saw a permanent gulf between Canadian and British self-interest that precluded formal ties, let alone unconditional alliance. Grant's insight strongly informed Shortt's and indeed Skelton's many discussions of imperialism.[11]

Britain's invasion of the Boer republics emboldened Adam Shortt to state that economic self-interest and political aggression, rather than the higher appeal of imperial leadership in the advancement of civilization, had motivated Cecil Rhodes, Alfred Milner, and Chamberlain, the three principal architects of imperial expansion. Great Britain had turned to an unpalatable policy of aggression, part of which was sold to Canada as "imperialism," because it faced challenges to its industrial and commercial strength and its political and military supremacy. Simultaneously, Shortt scrutinized the American invasion of Cuba and the Philippines as a similar movement, in this case that of a rising nation rather than a threatened leader, towards what he termed "imperialism."[12]

For Shortt and Skelton, if not Grant, the Boer War was more than just the unacceptable face of imperialism, an act of "Kiplingism" as Skelton put it. Rather, the war was a key to the danger to Canada of closer imperial ties, and from it there followed a number of factors important to Canadians. But to understand all of this it was necessary first to undertake a basic study of Canada's economic development from a historical perspective.[13]

Shortt's 1904 essay, "Imperial Preferential Trade," not only examined colonial trade policy but also summarized his ideas about Canadian economic history. The essay also illustrated his use of historical study to explain contemporary problems. Shortt's study focused on the Canadas alone; the development of the Maritimes did not interest him. It began by drawing a distinction, echoed by Grant and Skelton, between two kinds of imperial relations. The first was the link based on sentiment. This relationship was desirable. As Shortt explained, this form of imperial tie was "expressive of a generous policy of mutual sympathy and co-operation in the promotion of noble ideas of civilization throughout the Empire." The other kind was a program for economic and political integration – a program that comprised the most "narrow, mercenary and unspiritual conception of imperial destiny." In this form, imperialism was based on a specious and distasteful appeal to Canadian ambition and a misuse of the ties based on sentiment.[14]

To elaborate on the distinction and explain why Canada must reject the second form of imperialism, Shortt surveyed Canada's economic history. Chamberlainism, Shortt pointed out, was a new wrinkle on mercantilism, a program that set out to maintain economic domination by larger powers. Shortt surveyed the evolution of mercantilist theory and practice, arguing that the difficulties created by mercantilist policies had contributed to Britain's woes by virtually causing the American revolution. In its aftermath, Anglo-American relations had been recast in a free-trade mould that had led to vastly expanded economic intercourse and mutual prosperity.[15]

The aftermath of the first British empire explained Canada's economic history to Adam Shortt. He identified the crucial importance to Canada's commercialization played by the grain and timber trades with Great Britain. He explained that the nineteenth-century Canadian economy had been mainly organized around a commercial system centred on the St Lawrence-Great Lakes basin and directed towards British markets. The colonial trade network prospered, when it did, because of numerous economic, geographical, and political factors. This complexity showed that protectionist imperial policies were either marginal or debilitating to colonial development. The grain trade had risen and fallen through the first half of the nineteenth century in accordance with broad market factors.

In the midst of recession in 1840, for instance, the Upper Canadian legislature had complained of limitations on Canadian agricultural trade created by imperial preference and American protectionism. To their sovereign, the Canadians "pointed out that the United States markets for grain were often better than those of Canada. But as they were protected by a tariff the Canadians could not take full advantage of them (as a matter of fact much Canadian grain was sent to the United States). Again, when there is a demand for Canadian wheat in Britain, American wheat comes in to supply the local market, and thus prevents the Canadian agriculturalist from having an additional advantage of his own market."[16] Even in 1840, then, Canadian farmers and merchants bridled at the limits policy placed on their commercial opportunities.

The timber trade illustrated the other side of the preferential coin, its actual debilitation of colonial commerce. Shortt's conclusion about the trade was harsh: "Looking at the timber trade from beginning to end of its preferential treatment, it must be admitted that it was of very questionable benefit to Canada even at the time, while, with reference to the future of the country, it simply encouraged the most wanton waste and destruction of one of the most valuable resources which Canada possessed."[17] Finding further proof for one of his contentions about uneconomic resource use, Shortt tied massive waste to a commercial policy that subordinated Canada to Britain's market and resource needs.

Not surprisingly, Shortt also criticized the public-works expenditures of the colonial period as almost useless. He concluded his condemnation of British imperial policy by claiming that "much of the lavish expenditure of the British Government in Canada was not of a capitalistic nature, and did little or nothing to develop the country. Only part of what was spent on roads and canals was of a productive character." While granting that the British spent a great deal in the colony, Shortt turned even their alleged generosity into a negative conclusion about imperial development policy.[18]

Like Skelton, Shortt had little good to say about the post-Confederation National Policy. Partly this was because neither he nor Skelton perceived the National Policy as an integrated program of development. For them it was protectionism with a slogan. It was devised in reaction to the old colonial fixation on reciprocity with the United

States and it copied American commercial policy. The National Policy
worked in that it stimulated manufacturing and increased government revenue. But industries were too seldom based on Canadian
resources, capital, or entrepreneurial initiative. The National Policy,
in sum, epitomized the vain search for quick economic salvation from
outside typical of Canada's colonial nineteenth century.[19]

Shortt criticized both the social and economic traits of the economy
that had arisen in the Canadas. He noted that the staples-trade
economy had led to a serious internal division between merchants
and producers. "The few wealthy men conducting their chief businesses in the principal towns were inclined, though not always explicitly, to regard themselves as in the colony rather than of it." In
contrast, "only the common people, labouring in the fields, toiling
in the woods, or discharging the more varied functions of the towns,
looked upon the colony as of necessity their home."[20]

There were several dangerous consequences of the division
between those whose economic interests and lives were rooted in
Canada's long-term prosperity and those whose hearts were elsewhere. Too many promoters and policy makers had a transient outlook. Seldom were economic projects undertaken that aimed at
developing new commercial activities and thus providing expanding
opportunities for large numbers of people. As a result, the bulk of
the populace lived for many decades in virtual isolation from the
commercial economy and thus in considerable backwardness. The
stifling of agriculture caused by grain-trade regulation so shackled
farmers' material advancement that they were led to considerable
social and political unrest and protest. The sheer primitivism of
labourers in the timber trade and their inability to advance into
commercial agriculture or other pursuits showed the permanent economic and social debilitation created by the staples base. The colonial
commercial system also perpetuated a feeble response to whatever
opportunities there were. Thus commercial, material, and psychological failures were notable. This was because Canadians tended to look
"eagerly across the Atlantic for all economic direction, encouragement
and bounty." In sum, self-perpetuating class divisions and entrenched
ignorance of commercial opportunities comprised the unfortunate
legacy of the colonial era.[21]

Adam Shortt's economic history was chiefly a criticism of Canadian
economic development and its major policies. As a historian of the
"empire of the St Lawrence," and he was perhaps the first, he wrote
from a perspective opposite of the region's later champion, Donald
Creighton.[22] Shortt's critical perspective aptly illustrates the uses to
which he put historical study and the validity he saw in it. But he

was critical because he saw alternative and greater possibilities for the nation's economy.

The assumption underlying his interpretation of imperial preference was that Canadian development could have been – and could still be – far more successful than it had been. Shortt criticized the nineteenth-century economy precisely because it relied on British direction. This left the nation lacking in fundamental economic sense and endowment. Similarly, he bristled at Chamberlain's plan because it presumed either that Canada did not have the capacity for industrial development or that it did not want such a diversified and mature economy. In both cases, Shortt postulated that Canada could and should follow a course of economic maturation, moving from dependency and the trading of raw materials to self-directed diversification and industry.

Although he did not elaborate on his vision of this maturation, Shortt asserted that Canada's potential should be judged in the light of the American experience. Canada could develop as a manufacturing nation similar to the United States. This was possible because "Canada, like the United States, has within itself such a rich and varied supply of power and resources that it may normally look forward to being a largely self-contained country, of miscellaneous industries, and, therefore, in the course of its development, as already stated, a field for the import of capital in various forms, rather than for the import of goods for consumption." The material and social environment of North America was the major determinant of the means by which Canada would reach its commercial maturation. In this sense the American case was extremely important. But Shortt did not think that Canadians should either copy American practices or attempt to integrate their economy into that of the United States. He advocated the more strenuous course of acknowledging the common material environment of North Americans and learning from the American experience.[23]

Shortt was one of many late-nineteenth-century critics of Canada who used the American experience as a litmus test. Yet the way in which he did so reveals his distinction as an interpreter of Canadian economic and political history. He had struck a dominant note of failure in examining the nineteenth century. In concluding that this pattern of commercial evolution was detrimental to Canada, he had countered the imperialist argument and its faith in the inherited transatlantic connection with his own thoroughly environmentalist account of Canada's economic base. The American example was the model for Canadian development. Yet the United States was not simply another dominant power to which Canada might attach itself.

The bounty of North America's material environment, Shortt continually pointed out, guaranteed considerable economic well-being. This potential was not confined to the United States any more than it had been destroyed by the imperial connection. All shared in the opportunities of the New World, Canadians as well as Americans, farmers and mechanics as well as merchants and financiers.[24]

It is at this point that Shortt did not follow the typical anti-imperialist critics of Canadian development such as Goldwin Smith and Erastus Wiman. They simply concluded that Canada was an economic absurdity or merely a region of Greater America.[25] Shortt turned the continentalist argument on its head by suggesting that the very affinity of Canada and the United States showed that Canada had a separate yet equal potential as an economic as well as political entity. In this way, Shortt could assess Canada's future and rival the imperialists in shaping a vision of economic expansion. But he could do this only by arguing that a self-interested, self-reliant Canada must define its own commercial aims.

"The trouble with both the American and the imperialist view of the Canadian future," Shortt warned, "is, that it is to be that of the saw log, pulpwood, and wheat growing type, with a great market for manufactured goods; and the only question is, who is to capture that market?" By suggesting a third option, Shortt broke out of the moldy and stifling lines of economic reasoning found in the 1890s and 1900s. He anticipated an autonomous economic future and demanded economic policies that would free Canada from the incubi of dependence and backwardness. In a sense Shortt had devised a mediatory position between the dominant views of his time. This mediatory position also led him to escape from the limits that were so often posited for either the nation's economic evolution or its economic self-direction.[26] Shortt did not think that Canada would become integrated with the United States, socially or economically, any more than he thought that Canada would reintegrate itself commercially with Great Britain. Canada shared many social and economic traits with its neighbour. It might well borrow capital from and trade voluminously with the republic. But the American example showed how Canada could break from its current psychological and material dependency on other economies and emerge as an autonomous, effective nation.

It is not coincidental that Shortt drew a parallel between the colonial economy and colonial society. In a manner similar to its social and political evolution, he suggested, Canada must work toward that economic "self-sufficiency" or self-direction that meant the autonomous development of the economy. Only by this means could

Canadians control their economic fate and benefit most from the capitalist system, both as a nation as as individuals.

FROM THE ENVIRONMENTALIST perspective, Shortt and his successors devised two major explanations about national policies. The first involved Canada's political status and orientation, especially towards the British empire and the United States. The second comprised the ways in which Canada's economic maturity would come about. Since both Shortt and Skelton tended to explain political and diplomatic questions as the consequences of economic conditions, it is appropriate to examine the latter topic first.

By 1904 Shortt had found the goals that should guide Canadian development, demanding an economic order leading away from economic backwardness and class division. This order should be based on the environmental determinants and economic experience of the New World. Behind these factors were tenets of economic self-interest and self-direction that Shortt thought were crucial to the positive evolution of both society and the economy.

He had thus noted that, in spite of increased investment, expanded transportation, and industrial development, mid-nineteenth century Canada had remained "absolutely dependent upon the mother country." It had been incapable of moving beyond a dependent economic status. "Industries," he wrote in a later *Canada and its Provinces* survey, "were not sufficiently developed to support a population so well balanced in the production, exchange and consumption of its own products as to be essentially independent of foreign countries or strong enough to hold its own in regulating the trade with them." A powerful version of the need for economic self-direction lay behind Shortt's framework for Canadian economic development. This accompanied his argument that the Canadian economy would be a parallel and distinctive one to that of the United States.[27]

Shortt also revealed an abiding concern that Canada build the economic institutions essential to this self-direction. To examine these institutions, he worked on a series of monotonous documentary studies in the history of banking and currency. Shortt wrote no less than thirty-three papers for the *Journal of the Canadian Bankers' Association* between 1896 and 1906.[28] He went on to chronicle banking developments in one series of essays and currency regulations and growth in three series encompassing the French regime, the immediate post-conquest era, and the period from the Constitutional Act of 1791 to the Union of 1840. This work was his major research into Canadian economic history, supporting the broader statements about imperial preference he later published.[28] Behind the dullness, then, were major ambitions – to pinpoint the indigenous factors in Canadian economic development, and to explain the origin of Canadian specie.

The kernel of the essays lies in his environmentalist explanation of Canadian economic history, but it remained somewhat ungerminated in all of his writing. In the series for the bankers, he seldom probed this environmentalism, though he began his work by explaining that the history of Canadian banks was "one phase of the general economic history of the people." He continued by explaining that "banking operations are so wholly dependent upon the commercial habits and ideas of the people, the character of their business and the nature of their occupations, that they cannot be studied with much certainty or profit apart from the general economic atmosphere in which they are carried on." This dictum conformed to the synthetic approach that Shortt had earlier argued was the aim of social-scientific study. The essays on banking were intended to contribute to an understanding of not only the larger economic factors but also the broad social characteristics of Canada.

Shortt quickly found confirmation of his environmentalist theme in his discovery that Alexander Hamilton's Bank of the United States was the model for the constitution of the proposed Bank of Lower Canada of 1808 and the first Bank of Upper Canada of 1823. This led him to observe that there was a thorough-going North American outlook to the British Canadians, particularly the Loyalists. Here was a pointed lesson for Canadians in shaping economic policies.[29]

He also explained the steps by which the economy emerged from a barter to a commercial one or, in the case of the French regime, failed to do so. The financial networks that extended from the colony to London and, equally as important after the 1820s, to New York and the trade that generated those networks attracted his close scrutiny.[30] Shortt also took great notice of the problems experienced by the colonies in their efforts to establish an adequate system of banking and exchange. This issue had bedevilled colonial business, creating conflicts within the colonies because of the close ties between the political-economic élite and the banks. But he defended the banks as essential to the encouragement of the self-interest and self-generated economic ambitions that were in turn the basis for a commercial economy within the Canadas.[31]

Shortt also noted the important role the banks had in moderating the impact of the recessions that were the inevitable result of periods of excessive speculation, notable in the aftermath of the railway boom of the mid-1850s. He warned that the banks themselves were not immune to speculation. Still, the growth of the branch-banking system so opposed by agrarian reformers in Canada and the United States showed the capacity for adaptation and stabilization that made the banks so important to and distinctive in Canada's commercial development. The adaption to local conditions on the part of the banks was the key to their impact on commerce and development. This process of adaptation was also a major lesson Shortt drew from his essays. The sensible and "natural" adoption of decimal coinage in nineteenth-century Canada, against British fiat he noted, showed the power of the environment on economic institutions even when the latter were controlled by the most loyal of the Loyalists.[32]

In his economic history, Shortt had become convinced that the nation had not overcome the debilitating dependence on primary trade goods and British leadership. Canada's economic history was a story of comparative failure to mature because of the failure to follow the American example. Shortt's early prophecies about Canada's future and his search for an indigenous basis for development in financial institutions were perhaps misdirected. He had first tried to explain Canadian development by a study of the characteristics of economic growth through the circulation of money and development of banking institutions. In this way he was examining the broad characteristics of an emerging capitalist economy rather than the specific traits of the Canadian economy.

Only when his work pointed to the environmental advantages and colonial disabilities peculiar to Canada did Shortt's work become more than simply a collection of facts. At that point he was able to identify specific factors and forces relevant to Canadian development. Shortt established the criteria by which Canadian economic evolution could be explained and tested. This was the breakthrough allowing him to escape from the limitations of both imperialist and continentalist accounts of Canadian development.

Nonetheless, Shortt did not provide his own blueprint for Canadian maturation. He did not list positive policies or exact steps by which his goal of self-direction and balanced development would come about. It is significant here that Shortt did not adopt the then-fashionable "stage" theory of economic development that was so typical of the historical economists of his era and that William Mackintosh later used. Shortt was too suspicious of the underlying historicist or determinist framework of stage theory to accept such an account. He also rejected the staples trade and imperial markets and capital as an economic dead end and dismissed the optimistic plotting of growth curves based on trade data and natural-resource potential. Unfortunately, he had no alternative vision to offer, no real basis from which to guide Canadians about the nation's economic future. By his own standards – the goal of social science, for Shortt, was both to describe and to prescribe – his studies of Canadian economic history remained incomplete.

At this point the work of Shortt and his successor, Oscar Skelton, overlapped. Skelton returned to academe in 1905 just as Shortt became enmeshed in government work. Skelton substituted for his mentor between 1906 and 1908 while Shortt eased himself into the public service. Skelton also took up the subject of Canadian economic history that Shortt had pioneered. But Skelton concentrated on the post-Confederation period Shortt virtually ignored. Working in an era when the national economy exploded with activity, Skelton had to account for the success that Shortt had virtually denied in his work. In so doing, Skelton elaborated on Shortt's critique to devise a positive explanation for an era of positive national growth. In sum, Skelton continued Shortt's inquiries and work by accepting the environmentalist perspective, the concern for economic and political growth, and the responsibility of the academic to offer informed commentary on the issuer of the day.

For Skelton, the chief characteristic of the country founded in 1867 was its vast potential. Its pivotal international location, its immense size and resources, and its healthy populace all contributed to this potential. Like Shortt, he noted that the favourable environment was shared with the United States and in North America generally the abundance of resources and opportunities was remarkable and shown continually by the ease with which men and women could improve their way of life. That capacity for improvement explained the freedom from movements of wholesale revolution that also distinguished North America.[33]

In his survey of post-Confederation economic history, written for Shortt's *Canada and Its Provinces* in 1912, Skelton was enraptured by the environmental blessings of the nation. Though Skelton surveyed the disappointing progress of the second half of the nineteenth century with an accent similar to Shortt's, he interpreted Canada's economic potential in a far more optimistic way. For him, the nation's geography made for great opportunities. Skelton noted that Canada's location made it a link between the Atlantic and Pacific worlds, an echo of imperialist rhetoric that was undoubtedly intended. He emphasized that Canada's major geographical determinants were the two great inland seas, the St Lawrence and Great Lakes and the Hudson Bay-Saskatchewan River systems. Each opened "the heart of the continent" for Canadian exploitation. Skelton pointed to the agricultural, timber, fishing, and mineral wealth that comprised the nation's obvious geographical bounty. But he stressed that their development depended on overcoming barriers of climate and geography, above all the flaws in the two water routes opening the continent. These barriers, however, could be overcome. The potential was there to be tapped.[34]

Given such advantages, the development of a distinctive and diversified Canadian economy was entirely practical. Skelton found that a sensible estimation of these advantages and a coherent program for national development was first and most clearly pursued by the politician and businessman Alexander Tilloch Galt, whom he portrayed in a very long biography. Skelton's Galt, and not John A. Macdonald or any other colonial or imperial figure, was the central political and economic animator shaping the new nation before and after 1867. To Skelton, Galt recognized the possibilities for a united and separate British North America and he created the policies that framed Canada's economy.[35]

Despite's Galt's intentions and policies, however, the history of the first thirty years of the nation was one of sporadic advances. It was only the international economic recovery after 1896 that permitted Canadian intentions to be realized. Skelton thus explained the initial burst of the Laurier-era boom as the result of world changes in settlement patterns and consumption trends. From these changes, of course, Canada was particularly well placed to benefit. This was because of the agricultural potential of the Prairies and the geographical advantages the nation possessed. Thus a "fortunate conjuncture" between international conditions and Canadian geography led to an era of immense national expansion. The country's prospects by 1912 prompted Skelton to offer a hymn of praise to "the world's fairest land of promise."[36]

Indeed, Canada's success prompted Skelton to conclude that the nation had emerged from the colonial status and state of mind that Shortt had seen as its mark of Cain. It also shaped his point of view on the imperial question. Skelton argued that imperialism would fail because prosperity made Canada's economic interests distinct from Britain's. For Skelton, imperialism and continental union were both cancelled by the new national strength derived from the contemporary era of economic expansion. He concluded that Canada was now the strong second transcontinental political economic unit in North America that had been predicted by Adam Shortt a decade earlier.[37]

There were four major elements in Skelton's explanation of Canadian economic history. The prime element was the structure of the international economy. In Skelton's mind, the key to Canada's growth was the "conjuncture" between its economic geography and the world economy, particularly trade. This internationalist explanation improved on Shortt's critique of protectionism by pointing out that tariffs did not necessarily isolate an economy from the rest of the world. The tariff, Skelton made clear, was more a symbol of Canadian aims than a crucial factor in its development. The Canadian economy had become integrated into a world trading system and was developing its own dynamism through expanding settlement and manufacturing. Skelton deftly pointed out how dependent Canada had been on foreign capital for its growth. Protectionists, he noted sharply, seldom complained about this sort of open international market. But, of course, the availability of capital was exactly the sort of benefit from participation in the market economy that Shortt and Skelton well understood.[38]

The second factor – access to and exploitation of the interior of the continent – was also central to Canada's economic success. The St Lawrence-Great Lakes and the Hudson Bay-Saskatchewan River "doorways" between the Atlantic and the continental interior competed with two American transportation corridors, the Hudson-Mohawk and the Mississippi routes. In a misleadingly slender book, *The Railway Builders*, Skelton lauded the railways and railway owners – despite the stock-watering, dependence on government aid, and contributions to pork-barrel politics that he noted – for the great achievement of making full use of the Canadian doorways. Like the railway engineer Thomas Keefer half a century earlier and many nationalists since, Skelton argued that the railways provided the means to overcome both flaws in Canada's geographical ties and competition from the American economy. He concluded that the railways were the "indispensable" device that enabled Canada to realize its geographic unity and its economic potential. But the importance of the railways reinforced his contention about the international sources of Canadian prosperity. The impact of technology and foreign capital brought about the railways that played such an important role in national development. The result was the autonomy of a Canadian economy within the larger worlds of North America and Europe.[39]

In addition to international markets and the improved means of transportation, a third ingredient was important. This was the state. Skelton made this point most clearly in discussing the place of individual initiative in Canada's development. He began with the proposition that the individual was more important than government in developing North America. The toil of individuals had settled and built up the New World. People were freer here than in Europe to pursue the self-interest that so stimulated their efforts. Yet in Canada important limitations on individual initiative and opportunity led to a consistently greater reliance on the state than was the case for the United States. Weaknesses of individual and local initiative, the continued colonial legacy, and the absence of large sources of local wealth – all the burden of a new society – meant that government usually had defined the purposes and coordinated the enactment of major economic projects.

State direction of the major economic goals and activities could be plotted from the French and British colonial eras to the highly centralized federation created in 1867. In the case of railways, for example, in the 1850s and the 1880s major construction projects occurred because of Canadian government promotion, coordination, and financing. Skelton concluded that the success of the Canadian Pacific Railway was the result not just of the talent and labour of its financiers, engineers, and workers but also of substantial government support. It was no casual phrase-making that led him to assert that "the Canadian Pacific is as truly a monument of public as of private faith."[40]

Similarly, Skelton noted that government regulation often served to salvage business from self-inflicted wounds. This was the case for Canadian banking, whose stability had been secured by government regulation. More broadly, the close relationship between government and business was illustrated in Alexander Galt's plans, simultaneously carried out as a politician and businessman, for British North American self-government, union, and expansion into the North-West. These projects defined the economic and social purposes for British North Americans that turned them into Canadians. In all of them, the governments of Canada had played a role of fundamental importance.[41]

Finally, Skelton looked to financial institutions as a sustaining force in Canada's economic maturation. He acknowledged that, like the railways that provided the "physical means of carrying on trade and political activity," the banks were indispensable to economic and political life by providing the "mechanisms of credit necessary to a highly developed and widely scattered community." Skelton tempered his praise by noting that the banks did this in pursuit of their own best interest and that their success was owing as much to prudent state regulation as to their own capacity. Nonetheless, the banks were important indigenous institutions. Although he did not expand the study of financial history or banking to any extent, in 1913 Skelton and Swanson initiated Queen's supervision of all correspondence courses for the Canadian Bankers' Association.[42]

By his four-point account, Skelton shifted attention away from imperial trade policy as the key factor in Canadian economic development. Thus he provided a counterpoint to Shortt's criticism of this fixation in Canadian economic debate. Skelton celebrated Canada's economic potential as a mature, autonomous nation capable of standing apart from British and American domination. He also advanced a positive account of Canadian economic development based on the factors of geographical advantage, international trade patterns, growth of transportation technology, and the role of the state and financial institutions. These factors were seen in the great advance of Prairie settlement, and the harnessing of the west's geographic advantages led to the realization of Canada's promise. Skelton's epigrammatic statement, "Canada's national policy is the outcome of a continuous struggle between her history and her geography," did not imply that the struggle must lead to the triumph of one over the other. Rather his exploration of Canadian economic history showed the "continuous" interplay between the two elements.[43]

CLOSELY RELATED TO THE problems of Canada's economic potential and relations during the 1900s was the question of the nation's political evolution. This was expressed most often in the conflict over Canada's ties with the British empire. It was this debate that prompted Adam Shortt and Oscar Skelton to assess Canada's economic history and to make judgments about economic policy and imperial economic relations. The two men also examined the important political implications of their economic work. Indeed, they both understood the political relations and status of Canada in terms of their prior economic analyses. At the same time, their reviews of politics led them to insights about Canadian nationhood that stood on their own.

For Shortt, Canada's relations with the empire required a careful distinction between what might be termed "natural" ties based on mutual agreement and mutual interest and "unnatural" ones based on Canadian misapprehension about its self-interest and Britain's motives. Consequently, he defended a concept of "spiritual empire" while condemning schemes for imperial economic or political integration. This distinction was probably more clever than analytical. Nevertheless, it allowed Shortt to argue, first, that Canada's international status was evolving from subordination to autonomy and, second, that the voluntary ties of the British nations would continue to define Canada's international status and national character.

The point about political evolution reflected the development of economic autonomy Shortt had come to favour. It was also a result of what he saw as the essence of parliamentary government. The rights of a responsible and democratic national government meant that

Canada must be free to control its own external as well as internal obligations, economic as well as political. Only then would the touchstones of political rights and economic interest be sustained.[44]

These rights and interests supported Shortt's other point, that Canada simply could not follow British dictates about foreign relations. In print and in private, Shortt defended Wilfrid Laurier's foreign policies, and later those of Robert Borden, because they adhered to the touchstones of "the logic of responsible government" and the "free hand" in both "domestic and imperial" matters. This deductive line of thought allowed Shortt to direct his most pointed criticisms against the specious claims of Chamberlainite and imperial federationist doctrines alike.[45]

Shortt sometimes distinguished between the consequences of political and economic autonomy. In the economic sense, the prime effect of autonomy would be greater self-reliance and strength. In the political sense, however, the effect was more subtle. Rather than just supporting freedom of action, political autonomy instructed Canadians in the limitations that went with rights. In this way, autonomy led Canadians to the "larger and more temperate concept of national and social life which is the legitimate accompaniment of modern civilization." While the political lesson did not exactly contradict the economic one, it certainly moderated any excessive Canadian "sense of power." That moderation was certainly desirable. Modern nationhood was internationalist rather than isolationist and nationhood must be based on standards of civilization and culture rather than unbridled ambitions and hopes. Here Shortt's criticism of Canada's political and cultural deficiencies as well as his disdain for its economic boasts supported his emphasis on the need for a "cosmopolitan" and constrained standard of national life.[46]

The ties of British civilization rather than those of empire became Shortt's guide for a reasonable and practical national autonomy. From this perspective, Shortt adhered to a "sane" and "wholesome" spiritual concept of empire which he identified with Adam Smith and John Stuart Mill rather than with Joseph Chamberlain and Cecil Rhodes. This spiritual empire was held together by "bonds of fellowship" and "British civilization" but not governmental institutions. Canada's national status and autonomy, like its economic orientation, was understood by Shortt as a mediation between two positions. In this case, he reconciled the concept of nationhood advocated by imperial federationists such as George Parkin and George Denison and the concept held by independentists and isolationists such as John Ewart and Henri Bourassa. Bourassa for one privately endorsed Shortt's goal.[47]

His mediatory position indicates how appropriate was Shortt's informal association with imperial organizations such as the Round Table movement. In fact it is instructive to note just how frequently Shortt consulted the Round Tablers. By virtue of his attacks on Chamberlain, Shortt was something of a public figure by 1904. In the following decade, he was often in touch with people who shared the concept of an informal empire that was most typical of the Canadian Round Table. Shortt established connections with leading Toronto Round Tablers, notably stockbroker and sometime economics lecturer Arthur J. Glazebrook, and his own former student, the increasingly prominent merchant banker, Edward R. Peacock. Shortt also knew other imperial enthusiasts such as historian George M. Wrong and journalist Arthur Colquhoun. Through these men, Shortt met the major (that is, British) figures in the movement. When Britons such as Lionel Curtis, Philip Kerr, and Lord Milner visited Canada, Shortt usually saw them. He offered a unique perspective, much different from the grand vision of nationalist thinkers in Toronto.[48]

Shortt's response to these discussions was ambivalent. His idea that Canadian society should benefit from British "civilization" and his aspiration to partake of that civilization left him predisposed to associate with prominent men in Canada and Great Britain. Yet he could not accept the military and strategic obsessions, let alone the centralist bias, of the British Round Tablers. He sympathized with Edward Peacock's arguments that British as well as Canadian participants would benefit from mutual association and that the centralists would moderate their views so that voluntary imperial cooperation could occur. In the end, however, Shortt remained a skeptic who did not join the Round Table. Like so many Canadian members, Shortt eventually lost patience and perhaps fell into disfavour with the closet centralists.[49] In the absence of a recorded summation on his part, we might infer that his skeptical fascination left Shortt in the position of another observer, the Winnipeg editor John W. Dafoe. Dafoe had participated in the Round Table for some time, partly to further the "moral" unity of the empire and partly to counter the influence of "Toronto jingoists." But by 1916 Dafoe had seen too many examples of covert imperial federationism and too much arrogance towards the dominions by British participants to sustain his commitment to the Round Table. He then dropped out. Shortt had fallen away some four years earlier.[50]

Shortt continued to praise the cultural and political leavening gained from the voluntary British connection. His unease about the direction of North American society and democracy led him to praise the countervailing influences of the British heritage. He continued to insist on the voluntary and limited basis of any ties or agreements between Canada and Great Britain. In that sense, he was a notable adherent of Canadian autonomy.

Shortt never recoiled from the affinities between Canada and the United States or recanted from his advice about following the American economic example. But he did note the republic's remarkable transformation into an imperial power in the 1890s. Shortt observed that the imperial adventure that the United States had embarked on would lead to practices and policies that were highly ironic given the anti-imperial, republican political faith of Americans. While Shortt did not wholly disapprove of American imperialism, he nonetheless explained its impact in ways highly reminiscent of Canadian imperialists such as George M. Grant. The discipline of imperial responsibility would lead the United States to impose on its subject peoples a deal of inequality and even injustice. Imperialism would force the Americans to abandon the moral smugness of isolationism and probably the folly of protectionism. Imperial administration would draw on the services of the educated and cultivated segment of the populace, ironically the most vociferous defenders of American aloofness and political virtue. Finally, the United States would begin to share the international duties of the Anglo-Saxon peoples and strengthen their influence even as Britain itself flagged.[51]

The main lesson for Canada from American imperialism was to reject continental unity. If the United States was becoming a major world power and more like Great Britain, Shortt explained, then the Great Republic had as little to offer a nation just emerging from the debilitating ties of empire as Great Britain had. Moreover, Canadian reformers would find it impossible to draw on the example of American democracy when that democracy was tarnished by the imperialist venture. In an important way, Shortt's conception of Canadian nationhood was, as S.E.D. Shortt suggests, internationalist and his version of Canadian nationalism bore only faint resemblance to the more powerful nationalist ideologies that were articulated in late-nineteenth-century Canada.[52]

Examining the domestic sources of Canadian nationhood, Shortt held that French and English remained separate nations and that they would continue to be distinctive peoples. He sustained this position by claiming that French-Canadian culture was flawed by a defensive, backwards orientation and he often disparaged the French. He commented to W.P.M. Kennedy that the Quebec Act had "condemned" the French to a separate national life. Assessing a memoir by Hector Langevin, he noted that too many Quebec politicians wanted to preserve their society as a "genuine fossil specimen." Such remarks certainly suggests some regret at the dual basis of Canada and yet he did not seek a means to resolve the misfortune of dualism. But he also saw many benefits from the Laurier equilibrium of French-English relations, benefits chiefly extending to the economic expansion that a government led by a French Quebecer nurtured and that a majority, French and English, enthusiastically supported.[53]

Assessing the external ties of Canada, Shortt had a restrained notion of autonomy. Canadian autonomy must not, he claimed, become a form of nationalism based on isolation from international obligations and influences. Of course, a healthy internationalism should not be twisted into schemes to subsume Canada to British or American domination. In Shortt's formulation, the dangers of both isolation and domination must be avoided if Canada wished to exploit the material opportunities and develop the cultural identity it had.[54]

In sum, Shortt held to three broad tenets about national status. He aimed at the freedom that allowed Canada to act in its own interests. He wished to avoid the dramatic upset of the French-English equilibrium that any radical reorientation of external relations would pose. And he sought to preserve the international interdependence and cosmopolitanism that would measure Canadian society by the most rigorous Anglo-American standards of national achievement.

In his responses to Canada's imperial relations and national status, Oscar Douglas Skelton shared several assumptions and conclusions with his predecessor in the chair of political and economic science. However, Skelton developed sharper conclusions than Shortt did about Canada's international status as well as about the factors that conditioned Canada's place in the world.

Skelton argued that Canadian imperialism was a necessary precursor of healthy nationalism. He noted that imperialism had been the vital antidote to the annexationism rampant in the 1880s and 1890s. From the vantage of 1912, he explained the significance of imperialism:

The Imperial Federation ideal did good service in its day, and its chief service was the development of a spirit which made its own fulfillment impossible. Preached in a time when colonial dependence might easily have merged in continental dependence, it averted that fate and gave time for the development of a nationalism which stands in the way of all proposals for merging our national identity in any larger whole. In those days [the 1890s] Imperial Federation was the only alternative in sight to separation. Twenty years of evolution has developed not merely the theory but the fact of a workable alternative.[55]

This syllogism in which the synthesis of autonomous nationhood emerged from the antitheses of annexationism and imperialism was one that Skelton often framed. His argument was most eloquently expressed in his post-Great War biography of Wilfrid Laurier. There he reiterated his thesis that "Nationalism went to seed in Imperialism" with all the botanical inevitability that was presumed in Canada's new status at the Paris peace conference and at the League of Nations.[56]

Before, during, and after the First World War, periods in which distinctive positions about Canada's status emerged, Skelton held to his basic convictions about national status. These were similar to Shortt's in several ways. He was utterly contemptuous of schemes for economic or political imperial unity, whether proposed by Joseph Chamberlain or David Lloyd George. Skelton saw only folly in the submergence of Canadian interest, potential, and responsibility to plans for rehabilitating Great Britain. He also tirelessly pointed out the many contradictions and conflicts between Canada and Britain. These he found in areas such as immigration, naval and defence policies, and the basic responsibility of parliaments to their electorates. Such basic intergovernmental conflicts, as much as anything, made impossible any programs for centralization. Like Shortt too, Skelton suggested that the voluntary alliance of "an empire which is not an empire" was most beneficial to Canada. This form of the imperial relationship encouraged Canada to acquire responsibilities and obligations in the world. To this end, Skelton criticized suggestions that Canada seek exemption from "most-favoured nation" treaties. Finally, Skelton echoed Shortt in praising Laurier and Borden for devising consistent policies based on Canada's distinctive interests and for avoiding the extremes of imperialism and separation. Each of these arguments neutralized the imperial centralists and imperial sentimentalists.[57]

Skelton eagerly explained the foreign policy that Canada's interests dictated, and in doing so he arrived at a unique position in comparison with Shortt and virtually all other commentators on Canada's status prior to the Second World War. In this respect, terminology alone does little to elucidate Skelton's views. Skelton used words such as "self-government" and "autonomy" and occasionally even "independence" promiscuously. Similarly, he bandied about terms such as "isolationist," "annexationist," and "colonialist" in describing his foes.

The distinction of his position, then, should be seen less in a strict account of the "autonomy" he sought and the "colonialism" he opposed than in the factors which shaped the nation's interests in the world.

Skelton had explained that Canada's economic and political interests as well as the logic of parliamentary government necessitated a voluntary, autonomous response to the imperial connection. The key elements forming the Canadian response were found in the sum of the traits and needs of Canada. This meant calculating its economic interest and its public opinion. Here the sovereignty of the Canadian parliament was central, for it alone expressed the free will of a democratic society. The role of parliament in a democracy, then, was primary and should not and indeed could not be challenged or subverted. Even prior to the First World War, when Canada lacked the institutions for conducting foreign policy, its right to assess its own foreign policy needs was unquestionable to Skelton. Why else had Canada expressed strong differences with Britain about the migration of Sikhs and the building of a navy? Canada had distinct interests that reflected a fundamental capacity for self-government and these interests were everywhere manifest in Canadian resistance to imported plans for the nation's good. Years later, writing after the clash of nationalisms and the carnage that occurred during the Great War, Skelton gave fuller expression to his argument that factors within Canada were primary to all Canadian policies, domestic and foreign.[58]

He honed this reasoning most precisely in a 1922 address to the Canadian Club of Toronto. Assessing "Canada and Foreign Policy" before an audience that included Prime Minister Mackenzie King, Skelton explained how foreign policy was made by nations. He argued that foreign policy was simply the extension of domestic policy and that the evolution towards self-government in both domestic and foreign affairs had been achieved by Canada during the previous century. All that was axiomatic to political economists, if not to politicians and businessmen. What enlivened Skelton's talk was his argument that the peculiarities of Canada's national character and its reflection in public opinion were the basic factors conditioning the making of all Canadian policy. As with most public-policy matters, issues of foreign affairs were rooted in economic interests. Because Canada's economic autonomy was undeniable, the extension of international autonomy was in effect inevitable. The nation's autonomy was thus a further indication that it had generated something like a national identity based on national self-interest and that identity was economic and political. Just as Canada's economic achievements and prospects led Skelton to argue that its economic identity was secure, so did its political and cultural traits enable him to reach the same conclusion about its political identity. Similarly, the determinants of economic identity were crucial to Canada's political character and interests. These factors together showed that there was indeed a distinctive national interest that was economic and political, material and social, upon which Canadian calculations and policy were based.[59]

Following the examples of his most influential mentors, Shortt at Queen's and Veblen at Chicago, Skelton explained that a wide range of factors must be taken into account if political and economic analysis was to be accurate. Foreign policy was thus the result of interrelated facets that made up what Shortt called "social reality." If economic factors were particularly significant in Skelton's assessment of foreign policy, cultural and social factors, including the freight of history, were important in shaping the broad framework and the specific economic environment that explained Canadian foreign policy. This sense of the interrelationship and complexities of the elements conditioning social phenomena explains Skelton's capacity to develop so distinctive a position on Canada's economic and political development, including foreign policy. His peculiar "Canadian" orientation, then, was the result of his approach to the study of the national interest. The national interest, in turn, was the sum of the many factors that shaped domestic and foreign interests and policies.

Skelton's approach to the study of politics and economics points to his divergence not only from foreign policy analysts but from most of his contemporaries, particularly those who interpreted Canadian foreign policy as a result of the broad theme of the "rise of liberty." To the majority of these whiggish-minded thinkers, mostly historians, the rise of liberty was the central theme of Canadian as well as British or American history.[60]

To O.D. Skelton, the rise of liberty was one important consequence of the several factors he emphasized. These factors formed Canada's society and its politics throughout its history and distinguished its national development from that of other nations. Skelton concluded that the domestic characteristics of Canada were unique and that they comprised a sufficient if not a necessary condition for national status. In contrast, Adam Shortt saw only economic questions as the truly "national" ones and interpreted Canadian society as one effectively warped by its dual social traits and history. He therefore concluded that the nation was rather limited in its capacity to calculate and express its distinctive interests in the world. In effect the nation was constrained by a political immaturity that necessitated a highly internationalist culture and foreign policy.

For all his interest in French-English relations, Skelton did not make any general statement about Canadian cultural and political dualism. His cautionary discussions about the rights of Catholic minorities and Quebec public opinion and his strong centralism suggests that he was comfortable with only a degree of dualism and that it was a prelude to or a constituent part of a "common Canadianism." But even so, he sounds more like a prophet of bicultural nationalism in the mould of Henri Bourassa than a a critic of it. He once commented that Canadians should aim at political "unity," not "steam-rollered uniformity." In sum, he was convinced that the cultural life of Canada was not so fragile that it could not support an effective national political life. As shown by the very evolution of nationalist thought and the many examples of unique Canadian interests clashing with Britain's, Canada had acquired a fully mature, distinctive, and therefore autonomous nationhood.[61]

His concept of a self-sufficient national character led Skelton to propose that Canada's international role could end in a neutral but hardly isolationist stance. His "Canadian" outlook meant that he rested content with the nation's identity and capacity to discern on its own the policies, domestic and foreign, that would be in its best interest. That discernment, in turn, was based on the foundations of national self-interest. This was the rational basis of foreign policy. After all, the rest of the world's nations, including Britain when it dealt with Canada, acted in such a manner and Skelton, unlike his contemporaries, seldom if ever expressed utopian hopes for Canada's example to the world. Still, his arguments were based on material factors. These remained independent of any failure to cultivate the administrative machinery or legal declarations that would ensure acceptance by governments, whether Canadian or foreign, of responsibility for Canada's interests. Material arguments sustained his position in the 1900s, 1910s, and 1920s through all the perambulations of Laurier's nay-saying about obligations, Borden's agitation for representation in world councils, and King's resilient suspicion of international commitments.

There was certainly a confluence between Skelton's ambitions (he had long expressed interest in government work, as shown by his application to the British civil service in 1902 and his consideration of an appointment as assistant deputy minister of labour in Canada in 1908) and the serious overhaul of Canada's foreign policy in the early 1920s. In 1925 Skelton was appointed undersecretary in a

Department of External Affairs that was beginning to concentrate on effective policy making and expanded international representation. For Skelton, shaping a foreign policy was another instance of government supervision of Canada's vital national interests, similar to the work of the Department of Labour or the Board of Railway Commissioners. Foreign policy was simply one of the more strategic examples of the kind of government action that Skelton expected a sovereign, responsible government to undertake.[62]

For too long Canadian historians seem to have examined Skelton's thinking about Canadian foreign policy chiefly in terms of his role as undersecretary of state and ignored his substantial academic studies of Canadian international relations. Skelton's renowned prickliness towards British diplomats and politicians has led one historian, Norman Hillmer, in an otherwise insightful essay, to describe Skelton as a case study of the broad Canadian "neurosis" concerning relations with Britain. For his part, C.P. Stacey, the pre-eminent historian of Canadian foreign policy, describes Skelton's scholarly views on Canada's evolving national status as somehow "mendacious." Both of these positions are unsubtle as psychology and history, focused as they are on policy debates in the inter-war years rather than on the logic and purpose of Skelton's own ideas.[63] Yet scholars writing about the inter-war years have usually echoed Stacey and Hillmer and characterized Skelton's approach to foreign policy as isolationist and his attitude to Great Britain as hostile. They have therefore ignored his understanding of imperialism's importance to the growth of Canadian national identity, his acknowledgement of British cultural influences, and his endorsement of the voluntary commonwealth link. Skelton's position as an academic commentator and adviser prior to 1925 was not the result of hidden motives or unresolved attitudes about Canada's autonomy and relations with Britain, let alone a misleading interpretation of Canadian foreign policy. More subtle and more resolute than an anglophobe or an ideologue, Skelton the scholarly student of Canadian foreign policy posited a new way of calculating and a new direction for Canadian foreign policy based on the logic of Canada's material and political self-interest.

LIKE A HANDFUL OF POLITICAL ECONOMISTS and unlike so many scholarly commentators, especially historians, in Britain, the United States, and Canada in the 1890s and 1900s, Shortt and Skelton refused to celebrate the mission and the fusion of the "anglo-saxon" peoples and their imperialist ambitions. If their resistance was not as systematic as that of the Rainbow Circle of economic liberals in

Britain or as well organized as the Anti-Imperialist League of political liberals in the United States, they were nonetheless spirited exponents of a critique of the imperial movement and adherents of a positive analysis of Canadian national development.[64]

This positive analysis had two components. First, Shortt and Skelton were much more than just Cobdenite free traders and it would be highly misleading to dismiss them as such. If nothing else, their arguments constituted a notable alternative both to the ideas of the scholarly and journalistic mainstream, which was faithful to the imperialist dream, and to the small band of visionaries of independence. More important, they identified Canada's autonomy as essentially established, rooted in geography, economics, and political institutions. They therefore defined the grounds of a separate set of Canadian interests, based on the conjuncture of international circumstances and the Canadian material environment, that separated Canada from Britain and the United States economically and politically. Just as they identified Canadian autonomy and its circumstances, they sustained that international orientation which was so characteristic of Canadian national and nationalist thought. Ironically, they preserved at least part of the imperialist vision as well as the imperial connection in spite of their opposition to imperialist movements. Prior to the Great War, they held a concept of spiritual empire similar to the views of Quebec nationalists such as Laurier and Bourassa rather than to those of English-Canadian imperialists.

Second, like the new liberal British critic of imperialism, John Hobson, they saw imperialism not as a stage of capitalism but as a program linking economic interests, which were explicable enough if wrong-headed, with political goals, which were decidedly bizarre and dangerous innovations. If they were not proto-Leninists identifying imperialism as an advanced stage of capitalism, they were Hobsonian in warning that formal economic imperial ties would warp Canadian development. They therefore saw imperialism as both an ill-conceived response to competition and a dangerous threat to parliamentary responsibility.[65] In these ways, Shortt and especially Skelton had defined a new way of thinking about Canadian nationhood and its economic and political bases. If the distinctive interests and the autonomy of Canada were established, then considerable attention would have to be paid to the role of government in reflecting those interests and furthering that autonomy.

4 Capitalism, Socialism, and the State

> The only bulwark against socialism is social justice.
>
> O.D. Skelton

The study of Canadian economic history did not tempt Shortt or Skelton to ignore the new economic order's problems. Simultaneously with their explanation of Canada's economic growth, they explored what they saw as disquieting and ominous aspects of the national boom. They began by questioning the influence of business organization on the economy and politics, continued by assessing the claims of labour for greater rewards, and concluded by explaining the effects of tariff policy on all classes in society. Their concerns with such public issues and the broader impact of economic change led them to face a larger issue still, the stability and justice of the political-economic order. O.D. Skelton in particular was drawn to assess the legitimacy of liberal democracy and to examine the crucial socialist "challenge," a powerful force in pre-war Europe and North America.

WRITING IN *INDUSTRIAL CANADA* in 1910, Adam Shortt once again warned about the major problems that industrialism imposed on the nation. The previous decade's policy of growth at all costs was contributing to economic difficulties and social conflicts. Weakness in the economy was reflected in a dangerous price inflation, for increases in both costs and prices had far outstripped the "real" expansion of productivity or values. This inflation was partly the result of heedless general expansion, but mostly of price increases caused by the "blind duel" between labour and capital. While the duellists each claimed to have profited from this expansionary era and from their conflict, in reality they simply passed on to others their increased profits and wages. This burden was placed on the consumer in general but on the farmers in particular. Significantly, Shortt here relied on and acknowledged the work of the Department of Labour's first statistician, Robert H. Coats, who had identified the sharp inflation since 1899 and its domestic causes principally in increased labour costs. Nevertheless, both capital and labour were to blame for causing casualties among the third group of economic society, the consumers. The unfairness of this situation was matched by the other danger which price instability posed. Shortt predicted that there would be even more casualties during the inevitable slump which soon would conclude the period of rapid expansion.[1]

The economic ills Shortt diagnosed were treated by his successors at Queen's. O.D. Skelton and W.W. Swanson commented at length on the dangers of the decade's inflation and attendant industrial conflicts. Neither shared Shortt's penchant to blame labour for inflation, interpreting it as the result of accelerated industrial production in general and, beyond this, the expansion of gold output and credit facilities. But they did share his concern for the consequences, which included industrial strife and social tensions caused by extensive urbanization and rural depopulation.[2] The general problem, then, was that the process of economic expansion itself resulted in economic dislocation and social conflict. Growth had not automatically provided for the satisfaction of human needs and it had led to heated conflict about the distribution of wealth. While Skelton and Swanson did display some sensitivity to the cultural and psychological dimensions of the dislocation of the era, they were more concerned with the serious economic and political effects to which industrial development was leading and which Ontario was already experiencing.[3]

To Shortt, industrial conflict was partly the result of humankind's tendency toward ill-reasoning and greed. Just as they welcomed eras of excessive growth which led invariably to slumps, men and women also sought more from the economic order than they had produced. Generally, this was a manifestation of the disruptions to the equilibrium of social forces which resulted from flaws in the rational calculations of individuals and in the operations of social institutions. To Skelton and Swanson, the conflict was the result of a subtler process related to the productive capacities and wealth unleashed under the industrial order. The growth of inequality, Skelton observed, was owing more "to the more rapid enrichment of the few than to the impoverishment of the many." Moreover, while "prosperity drove a wedge between the well-to-do and the struggling" in industrial society, the division revolved around the distribution of wealth rather than its production. In discussing this question with such precision, Skelton freed himself from a fixation on limits to the production of wealth that hamstrung Shortt to a pessimistic assessment of the distribution of economic spoils.[4]

The emerging characteristics of capitalism in Canada thus posed two major problems which the Queen's political economists examined further. The first was the so-called consolidation movement and the accelerated growth after 1900 of large business in Canada and the other capitalist nations. The second was the emergence of intense labour-capital conflict and the related phenomenon of the socialist critique of and alternative to capitalism.[5] The responses of Shortt and Skelton indicated their distinctive readings of the economic and political contours of their nation and also marked a parting of the ways in their intellectual progression.

The rise of larger and larger "units" of business, claimed Shortt, was but one result of the drive for economic "efficiency." That thrust was the major characteristic of economic progress. As a result, Shortt "defended" millionaires, explaining that "the whole growth of economic organization, the subsequent development of the millionaire, and the final effort to avoid the ruinous waste of independent competition, are simply stages in the economic triumph of man over nature. This victory secures the supply of an increasing number of wants with a decreasing proportion of human effort." Competition, a fundamental aim of nineteenth-century political economy, declined even though economic efficiency increased. At the same time, however, competition was transmuted into new forms of rivalry under contemporary conditions of industrial and financial organization and development. Business became international, combines appeared, and manufacturers sought barriers to protect themselves from other producers.[6] If there were problems inherent in the organization of capital and business, they might be resolved by distinguishing between those factors which contributed to greater economic efficiency and those which did not.

The simultaneous tendency of business was to internal protection and international operations. To Shortt, this suggested that contradictory economic results might emerge, though all developments which contributed to lower costs of goods were to be welcomed. The drive to efficiency was beneficial, for it encouraged "enterprise, invention, organization and economy." Efficiency also led, on occasion, to monopoly, which was to be feared. Certainly, any reorganization that simply led to increases or manipulations of selling prices were condemnable. For example, "artificial monopoly" made for decreased efficiency and was intolerable. Shortt remarked that tariffs tended to be an artificial means to increase efficiency in operations while combines could be among the natural means to do so. Hence, the former was not acceptable while the latter was.[7]

Shortt found other examples of the ambiguities of the economic order. He criticized the constant lure of "illegitimate" profit-taking by capital, arguing that manufacturers were particularly guilty of this offence. On the other hand, Shortt defended both monopolistic and protectionist practices in Canada. He pointed out that Canadian manufacturers "have learned the value of organization, as at once more economic and efficient than scattered and haphazard competition. Mere competition justifies itself in the eyes of many from the fact that, though it may not produce cheap goods, it does prevent the accumulation of profits." He then claimed that "the wiser process of eliminating over-production and wasteful competition is still going on, enabling Canadian industries not only to hold their own within the country, but to gradually lay a permanent foundation for a sound and profitable, and not merely a sacrificial foreign trade. As a natural consequence of their enterprise and efficiency, the manufacturers of Canada as a class have of late years increased in wealth more rapidly than any other considerable element in the country."[8] This was a rather coy position. Shortt was free to criticize businessmen if their demands outstripped canons of efficiency. He could also praise the dominant course of business organization and practices. Not surprisingly, his plastic outlook was interpreted by the editors of *Industrial Canada* as approbation of all they had been writing for years concerning virtuous business, including price fixing, protection, and monopoly.

His reliance on the test of efficiency and his ambiguous account of how to test it indicate that Shortt was caught between his assurance that economic progress was a hard struggle and his warning that economic growth could be ruined by policy and practice. Between his periodic willingness to abandon doctrinaire free-trade economics and his occasional faith in an invisible hand leading to economic efficiency, there was his mediating concern that economic forces might well regulate economic relations but in the process blot out benefits for individuals and the nation alike. The very ambiguities of modern capitalist enterprise – protected by tariffs and yet international in scope, capable of huge profits both earned and unearned – left him well aware that devotion to theoretical economic doctrines meant blindness to the potential distortions if not monstrosities of the economic order.

Yet Shortt was concerned enough about inefficiency that he reiterated his warning that the force of economic circumstances was not to be trifled with. He thus warned both labour and business to heed the lessons of economic science:

There are but two methods of truly increasing the means for the supply of wants and thus raising the standard of living without increasing the amount of human effort to procure it. One is by discovering how to induce nature to yield more from her storehouse of supplies, in proportion to the unit of persuasive effort; and the other is by discovering how to economize the human element in working up the products of nature into means for the supplying of wants, including the rendering of nature into means for the supplying of wants, including the rendering of services. Under such conditions, incomes may be increased without increasing prices, or prices may be lowered without diminishing incomes.[9]

Increases in productivity must not be tied to any tampering with the distribution of the spoils. Incomes and profits could be increased, but that would cause severe long-term economic dislocation unless based on an advance in efficiency by either harder work or improved techniques of production. His explanation was less an account of how productivity increased than a warning about the results of disregarding the goal of efficiency. He was nearly left in the position of his classical predecessors in arguing that factors of economic distribution could not be divorced from those of production. This was unlike his putative mentor, John Stuart Mill, who had distinguished between production and distribution and argued that the two elements were autonomous, that redistribution could be effected independently of what could be a stable, assured productive capacity. For Shortt there was not an automatic process whereby efficiency increased and more wealth was produced and distributed justly. There was little ground for the redistribution of wealth. The fact that the distribution of wealth could be based only on increased efficiency and increased production was being denied by the world at its peril. The result was inflation and over-burdened consumers. This had made the present an age of ephemeral prosperity – prosperity that would be lost as a result of the unavoidable correcting device of economic depression.

Shortt was uncomfortable with the implicit inevitability of this process. He had been dissatisfied with the operation of market forces in the new era and refused to take a spectator's view of self-adjusting factors. Long unhappy about Canadian economic policy and goals, he expressed his dissatisfaction in two ways: he accepted the monopolizing and protectionist tendencies of capitalism as a means to enhance the stability and efficiency of the economy; and he looked upon the reform of labour relations as a means of both stabilizing and harmonizing the economic order. Behind Shortt's theorizing about economic growth and about labour-capital relations there was a conservative goal. Shortt aimed to sustain the effective operation of existing economic machinery. To prevent inefficiency, distracting and deleterious labour conflicts and similar forms of business competition should be avoided.

Shortt's former student, William Swanson, reflected his mentor's view of the tendencies of capitalism. During his time at Queen's, Swanson often seemed to present the "case" for business. He did this in work for the Montreal *Journal of Commerce* and in regular contributions to the *Monetary Times of Canada* in the 1910s and 1920s. Swanson agreed that trusts and combines were "part of the inevitable evolutionary process of our industrial life" and were commensurate with the necessities of efficient centralized control and large-scale enterprise. He thought that the Canadian government's proposed Combines Investigation Act of 1910 recognized this inevitability. In fact, its aim to subject combines to public (that is, government) scrutiny was designed more to control abuses and to free combines from the crueller punishment of the criminal code than to eradicate the new phenomenon.[10]

Oscar Skelton agreed with the view that trusts and combines were an integral part of the modern age of capitalism. But in contrast to Short and Swanson, he subjected the trust movement to severe scrutiny. While he accepted that trusts were indeed part of a movement toward greater economic efficiency from the capitalists' point of view, he saw another reason for their rise: trusts were the continuing means to inflate the market value of firms. This benefit accrued to promoters and profiteers rather than to honest proprietors. The resulting corporate giants were less than solicitous of the consuming public's economic interests. Worse, their great wealth left them capable of interfering in the political process and they became a threat to the governing power of civil society.

Skelton issued a stern warning about the consequences in his *General Economic History* of Canada. He railed against corporate abuses:

Financial buccaneers who made millions out of merging mills they had never seen; promoters of fraudulent mining companies; members of rings and mergers who held up the public for all the traffic would bear; the owners of bounty-fed or protected industries whose profits did not, contrary to programme, filter through to the common people below; holders of unregulated public service monopolies; speculators growing rich overnight by the increment of land values communally created, did more to bring all wealth, honest and dishonest, into disrepute than the muckraker and the socialist street orator could do in a century without their aid.[11]

Skelton's concern might in part be attributed to the fact that by 1912 he had witnessed the consolidation activities of the efficiency-minded Max Aitken, who earned the loathing of Queen's venerable Chancellor, Sandford Fleming, by absorbing his company.[12] But Skelton's sensitivity to the problem raised by mergers and trusts should also be seen in relation to his consistent analysis of the economic order. Just as he was clearer than Shortt and perhaps more clever in deducing the factors that explained Canada's economic take-off, so too he was more willing to demand that the market economy operate in the interests of all its members, consumers as well as producers. Skelton wanted to ensure that society through its governments could assert legal control over business. His critique of "financial buccaneers" was not a criticism of capitalism but it was a powerful argument against business abuses of the political-economic order, especially by corporations that could distort economic activity and threaten government agencies. This concern was only implicit in Skelton's survey of Canadian economic history; it became more explicit in his arguments favouring reciprocity in 1911.

Like many other issues taken up by Queen's academics, the question of Canadian trade relations was first treated by Principal George M. Grant. A leading imperialist in the late nineteenth century, Grant had experienced a kind of intellectual revolution in his halcyon old age. He bitterly and harshly opposed Rhodes's imperialism in South Africa and suspected similar avaricious motives behind Chamberlain's system of imperial preference. He also served as an active proponent of Canadian-American trade reciprocity. In 1899, for instance, he reported to Prime Minister Laurier on his impressions about the public response to any schemes for reciprocity with the United States, offering to promote the idea in private and public. Grant's position may well have been in part purely tactical, designed to sound out Laurier on the question of trade, and he was never a particularly articulate supporter of reciprocity. Nevertheless, the fact that he offered his services is significant. It demonstrated not only his acceptance of Laurier's liberalism but also his commitment to the strategic role of the academic in public affairs.[13]

When the Liberal government of Canada finally moved to negotiate a natural-products reciprocity agreement with the United States, Grant was long dead. Another Queen's man, Adam Shortt, now a public servant, took a neutral position in private as well as a necessarily mute public stance. He thought that the reciprocity agreement was of minor economic importance and he had never sympathized with the staples dependency of farmers. He also felt that the change of government in the ensuing 1911 election was as good a result as any that might have occurred. In earlier years, Shortt's advice had been solicited by American free-trade devotees such as the prominent Harvard economist F.W. Taussig.[14]

Skelton's attitude towards reciprocity was much different. He spent the summer of 1911 doing research for the Department of Labour on comparative prices in Canada and the United States. These investigations, he admitted, were designed to aid the responsible minister, Mackenzie King, who was busily engaged in persuading the electorate of the merits of freer trade. Skelton also wrote several essays which, as he stated to King, were written "as forcibly as I was able" in defence of reciprocity. The essays were forceful enough, although certainly fair to the anti-reciprocity case. They help to explain Skelton's ideas not only about Canadian trade policy but also about what larger purposes the economic system should be designed to serve.[15]

As Skelton understood it, the reciprocity proposal had several extremely beneficial aspects. Politically, it ended "the unwholesome political stagnation which has marked our public life of late years," provoking a debate that brought principles into party platforms and involved all classes of voters. Economically, the proposed treaty provided an attractive deal which would benefit substantially fishermen and farmers, who had for years paid for tariffs and foregone the American market. The uneven benefits of recent expansion would be partially corrected and the grievances of the rural community redressed.[16]

An additional factor was also important. The Canadian-American initiative showed a new maturity on both their parts, a maturity in accepting the benefits of freer trade to two states long wedded to protection and in realizing the important connections between the two nations. This maturity was more significant for Canada than the United States. Canada had at last attained that economic and political security which inspired confidence in independent efforts for economic improvement and rational dealings with a foreign country. In turn, Canada's confidence was the result of the previous two decades of prosperity and growth. It was therefore one major consequence of the transformative wizardry of economic progress. Skelton also suggested that the inequities which had been a result of these changes would be dealt with by freer trade in natural products. He expected that the mature political economy of Canada would no longer accept its internal economic inequities and political domination by powerful interest groups.[17]

The result of the 1911 election shook most of Skelton's assumptions. To Mackenzie King, one of the many Liberal losers, Skelton suggested that Ontario had shown once more its penchant for jingoistic appeals over evaluations of economic advantage or justice. To the readers of the University of Chicago's *Journal of Political Economy*, Skelton expressed even graver concerns about the consequences of the election. He thought that a greater question than Ontario's particular response had emerged from the defeat of reciprocity. One was not, he wrote, "reassured for the future of democracy by the ease with which interests with unlimited funds for organization, advertising, and newspaper campaigning can pervert national sentiment to serve their own ends. However, this is a stage through which every young nation apparently must pass, and the gentle art of twisting the lion's tail has formed the model for the practice of plucking the eagle's feathers."[18] Aside from his suggestion about the increasing importance of the United States to Canada (and the decreasing influence of Great Britain), Skelton pointed to the dangerous power of large capitalists in subverting what he saw as a clear national consensus. He also expressed continued dissatisfaction with the makers of public opinion and a gullible public. The lesson of the election was that narrow class interests and a protectionist mentality could dominate society against its best interests. This domination was as deplorable to Skelton as it was to his colleague, William Lawson Grant, then professor of history at Queen's. As with so many other questions, Grant and Skelton shared the same sensitivity to the implications of the reciprocity issue, particularly about democratic decision making and public opinion in the face of business interests.[19]

Class and sectional grievances remained. They might yet be accommodated if pressure was kept up and the issues made clearer. These points were crucial to Skelton's generalizations about the trade policies of Canada. The now mature nation, he claimed, must rearrange its policies so as to yield benefits which satisfied certain standards of justice *and* material interest – standards that sustained the demands of the rural population especially. Skelton's support for these demands was predicated on the proposition that the wealth of society could in fact be redistributed to a class of producers unfairly excluded in the distributive process. It was excluded, moreover, precisely because of a preoccupation with increases only in production by tariff-sponsored industrialization. His studies had led Skelton to admit, albeit rather obscurely, that the "costs" of natural-products reciprocity would indeed land on the consumers, but he was quicker to point out that this burden would be manageable if not insignificant. In any case, it was more important to him that positive discrimination in favour of agricultural and fisheries producers was granted. Such discrimination did not mean that the wealth or prosperity of business or labour would be threatened. He foresaw that the increased prosperity of the farmers would then lead to greater economic activity for all within the nation.[20]

Skelton was concerned by the social and economic dangers posed by the unfair distribution of wealth. In contrast, Shortt was not willing to tamper with the given factors of production and distribution, possibly excepting the tariff. Skelton warned that it was precisely the problem of the distribution of wealth which posed the greatest threat to social peace and indeed economic progress. Perhaps mindful of the reciprocity experience, he wrote in his *Canada and Its Provinces* account of 1912 that "Montreal alone claimed seventy new millionaires in a decade." Skelton was not totally impressed, remarking that "where the millions corresponded to social service, where they were the fruit of daring pioneering in the opening up of new resources or the improvement of industrial processes, few grudged enterprise and energy their reward. But most men viewed with growing uneasiness the concentration of wealth in the hands that had done little toward its making, and the domination of industrial and political life by small groups of allied financial and railway and industrial interests in the three or four large cities."[21] The inequitable distribution of wealth was serious enough to comprise a threat to both the political order, as witnessed by the manipulation of the 1911 election, and to the economic order, as shown by popular resentment against the financial buccaneers and speculators. In sum, Skelton raised a number of problems about the contemporary political economy. The division of wealth, the very nature of material development and, significantly enough, the stability of the political and economic system under current conditions were all questioned as Skelton subjected his society to critical attention.

LIKE MANY SOCIAL SCIENTISTS before and since, Adam Shortt dismissed socialism. To him, socialism demanded consideration sufficient only to show its analytical errors and political irrelevance. Shortt had refuted Marx's Riccardian labour theory of economic value in his survey of economic doctrines and he had quickly abandoned the reading of *Capital* by his political economy students. He later found it worthwhile to challenge a Presbyterian clergyman, John Hay, who suggested to the Queen's Theological Alumni Conference in 1896 that "socialism" was now reconstituted on the notion of "sharing" goods and that the extension of state supervision to address the problems of industrial, urban society was the result of "socialism" modified by Christian principles.[22] In an acerbic lecture to the Theological Alumni Conference in 1897, Shortt rebutted Hay's position by emphasizing that the mere extension of state power was not "socialistic." There always had been a great deal of room for "positive functions" by the state – indeed, no one could deny the legitimacy or necessity of that positive role. This positive state could and did provide many social services, for instance, in the operation of the postal system, public school system, or public utilities. But state-owned enterprises contained no socialistic or socialist elements. That was because those enterprises, like all state services, were run on the basis of their economic costs, covered in one way or another by charges such as taxation or fees. There was, as well, no expropriation of property and no exemption from market calculations. By contrast, socialistic schemes would abolish private property, the support of services by taxation, and the economic limitations on their operations. These differences allowed Shortt to ridicule the notion that positive state action was related to socialism of any sort, including its benign new evolutionary version.[23]

He also took the opportunity to point out the practical and theoretical failings of socialism in its own right. Theoretically, socialism appealed to individual self-interest while criticizing the unequal distribution of goods. The doctrine therefore involved itself in an inner contradiction of its own. Practically, socialism was based wholly on a critique of the existing economic order, especially the way production was generated. Yet it failed to devise an alternative account of production. It is clear that Shortt did not entertain the idea that such a flawed analysis, borrowing psychological and economic theory from the very system it sought to replace, should be taken too seriously. He suggested that the whole appeal of socialism could be dissipated by the provision of the kind of "accurate information on economic subjects" which the economist could give, although he was willing to concede that a "wider extension of personal ownership to property rights" would also help. After a tour with Skelton of the American Congress of Socialists held at Chicago in 1908, Shortt wondered to himself whether the adherents of socialism were not simply physically and mentally "abnormal."[24]

Shortt's argument was interesting because it indicated strenuous effort to distinguish between socialist motives or principles and more orthodox ones. He was hostile to the barest imputation of socialist origins or inspiration to state intervention. Unlike the English liberal A.V. Dicey, who had announced that socialism had arrived already, Shortt was uncompromising in his use of ideological terms and determined to preserve the legitimacy of various kinds of positive state activity. He argued in favour of positive state action on a wide scale, using the language of liberal reformers such as T.H. Green and L.T. Hobhouse in his support for that action. He also tried to put considerable distance between himself and both soft-hearted "reformers" and simple-minded reactionaries, the latter of whom held forth in such great numbers in Canadian periodicals, especially business periodicals, of the era. The positive statism which did exist in the 1890s in Canada could hardly be construed as a distinctive break from the tradition of state intervention in Canada, a fact that Shortt's examples well illustrated. His refusal to concede legitimacy to socialism also placed a significant limitation on the inexorable laws of political economy. For example, the commitment of North American society was towards a permanent equality of opportunity. This goal, while not limiting unequal divisions of wealth, did impose state supervision over people's lives in a number of ways. The goal of "self-realization" to which Shortt often referred – a basic freedom in English-speaking North America, he thought – involved consideration of the positive relation between the individual's "self-realization" and that of the whole of society. Shortt therefore argued that the millionaire's wealth was partly a "stewardship" of wealth (the result of the particular economic conditions and opportunities provided in the society) and the outcome of his own efforts at self-advancement. Both individual and society benefited. If, in practice, Shortt did not specify the areas of state activity or supervision necessary for the preservation of the balance between claims of individual fulfilment and social equity, in theory he made room for that activity.[25] The very imprecision of his arguments indicated Shortt's general approach. Here, as elsewhere, his position war that of the conciliator. That is, he responded to the social forces and competing claimants by a mediatory effort to preserve harmony and yet reach the preferred goal of broader fulfilment for all people.

Oscar Skelton's original impulse to begin graduate studies was based on his fascination with the critical problems Canada faced and the opportunities these presented to a trained social scientist. His work at the University of Chicago, however, soon led him towards more general and theoretical issues in political economy. He was especially attracted by the ideas and personality of his teacher, Thorstein Veblen, an impression he revealed in numerous letters to an impassive Adam Shortt. Veblen's teaching and approach he found stimulating, particularly for its "philosophical" and "sociological" perspectives. These, he thought, comprised a vast improvement upon the narrower orthodoxies of the dismal science as represented by a professor such as Laurence Laughlin. When Veblen left Chicago in 1906, Skelton thought it a "blow" to the university. (William Swanson, in contrast, barely noted it amidst his enthusiasm for the conservative economics of Laughlin and the lighter pleasures of tennis.) While both Laughlin, an inveterate anti-socialist, anti-imperialist, anti-marginalist, and anti-bimetallist, and Robert Hoxie, a pioneer student of trade unionism, also taught Skelton, Veblen was the teacher he wrote about and, as we shall see, the writer he referred to most often. Studying with Veblen, Hoxie, and even Laughlin (Laughlin brought Veblen to Chicago) drew Skelton into the ambit of men who were critically examining the significant contemporary political and economic ideas and movements, including protest movements.[26]

In this environment Skelton's academic work turned to the subject of socialism, which he saw as the greatest intellectual and political challenge to the present social order. His focus was clear in occasional writings published in the first decade of the century and was underlined by his choice of a doctoral dissertation topic. As he argued in an essay of 1907, European "leaders of the red host" demanded attention and study partly because they might soon attain prominence in socialist-free North America. His studies reassured Skelton himself at least that socialists were divided into revolutionary Marxists and reformist social-democrats and distinguished by significant national differences. The same studies suggested to him that socialism was more a symptom of social ills than a fatal social disease.[27]

Skelton, therefore, granted a certain validity in the challenge posed by socialist thought and politics. He also recognized that socialism was a condition of the development of industrial society. For Skelton – and in this respect he was almost alone among Canadians at the time – socialist thought and socialist movements demanded the twin responses of intellectual refutation and social reform. These were responses that Adam Shortt, for example, did not seem willing to make. Detailed consideration of Skelton's assessment of socialism is helpful, not only because it reveals his perceptions about the contemporary age and the competing claims of socialism and capitalism, but also because his arguments drew him toward major conclusions about the human prospect under industrial civilization and the relations between the individual and the state.

Skelton based his PhD thesis on the connection between socialism and industrialism. The topic certainly showed that Skelton tried even as a professionally minded doctoral student to satisfy himself about the general characteristics of the political economy he was all too eager to help direct. His later book *Socialism* was a revision of his dissertation and it was submitted to a competition sponsored by a Chicago clothing manufacturer, Hart, Schaffner and Marx, "to draw the attention of American youth to the study of economic and commercial subjects." Skelton won the $1000 award for 1908, his study being judged by a panel of economists including J.B. Clark of Columbia, Henry C. Adams of Michigan, and J.L. Laughlin, Skelton's thesis supervisor at Chicago. The published study of socialism was a broader work than its provenance or its rhetorical flourish as "the case against socialism" suggested. It examined the operations of the capitalist system and its major problems and also analyzed socialist economics, ethics, and programs.[28]

Socialism, explained Skelton, was the alternative to the market-based, private-property holding, economic system. It had emerged as a result of the "excesses of unregulated capitalism" and testified to the failures of the market system in its industrial phase. Socialism was, then, rooted in the industrial system which had come to be characterized by huge enterprises and large wage-earning groups. In reaction, an intellectual and political movement had sought, over the course of a century, to overthrow the capitalist system. Socialism was a movement involving an analysis, an indictment, and a campaign for the victory of a radically different substitute system. As Skelton perceived them, there were two key factors in the socialist analysis and indictment. Socialist critics condemned capitalism for its economic inefficiency and its social injustice. His study proceeded to consider both points.[29]

For socialists, the economic inefficiency of capitalism, which resulted from its distorted productive capacity, was seen in its misuse of human beings, its sacrifice of social to individual acquisition, its waste of natural resources, its tendency to financial fraud or graft, and its general – and chilling – incapacity to supply the goods humankind needed when it needed them. Famines in the midst of plenty showed that even the market's operation in regulating demand and supply was usually in disarray. A couple of examples illustrated this situation. Under capitalism, "utilities of undeniable importance are not provided because incapable of private appropriation and sale. The importance of forest preservation for conserving moisture is undeniable. But climate and rainfall cannot be packaged and trafficked in, and so our forests are swept down by axe and fire." In addition to this wastefulness, there was the disequilibrium between supply and demand. "Haphazardly scattered producers prepare to meet the guessed-at demands of world-wide consumers," Skelton explained. But "the adjustment is never exact. At times it fails utterly, in the periodical crises which throw the industrial mechanism hopelessly out of gear."[30] Hence, people's basic needs were not supplied efficiently or assuredly.

According to socialist doctrine, the ethical failure of capitalism was found in the social conditions it created. People's lives were broken or degraded by conditions in which they laboured and lived. In examining the effects of capitalism on human beings, Skelton elaborated upon the descriptions of a system in which "competition and capitalism spell misery and failure, a precarious lifelong battle with hunger, stunted and narrowed development, premature death or cheerless old age." By the "loss and gain computed in terms of human life" which Skelton thought comprised the socialists' ethical mode, capitalism did not provide the goods which people needed. Or if it did so, it did not distribute them so that they received what they needed or else produced conditions which made the production of goods destructive of the very people who made and needed them. The picture of human misery, then, was a reflection of the befouled mechanisms of the market economy. Business failed miserably, and human beings were even more miserable.[31]

Having established these charges, Skelton responded to each in turn. To the economic indictment, Skelton provided a systematic counter-argument. "The socialist indictment," he wrote, "gives but grudging recognition or none to the proved and tried efficiency of the existing order." He resorted to a psychological explanation of society in order to argue that private property and competition "harnessed in society's service" individual self-interest, which was "the most powerful and abiding force in human nature." In fact, the potential atomizing individualism of humankind was controlled as best it could be. The effectiveness of this harnessing was apparent in the numerous ties that drew people together into cooperative ventures, in business and commerce no less than in philanthropic and social organizations. Under capitalism men and women were actually bound to one another in a system of mutual help through the pursuit of self-interest. In so creating regulated human intercourse and interdependence, the market economy satisfied the material and emotional needs of all people. Through the "barometer" of the price system, demand and supply were usually in equilibrium, as price signalled the required demand to producers and production was thus brought forth. Despite complaints about the justice of the allocation of goods, the sheer capacity to produce and produce in sufficient quantities to satisfy humankind could hardly be doubted. In drawing attention to this productive capacity, Skelton pointed out that the development of industrial production was characterized by the constant expansion of wealth, and that this process, by stimulating the further production of goods, thus tended to the amelioration of everyone's conditions. Even so skeptical an observer as Veblen, Skelton noted, commented on the productive capacities of the capitalist system under conditions of industrial production.[32]

In response to the ethical objections, Skelton referred to the recent history of capitalism. That history, he said, was one of constant improvement in humanity's standard of living and in its prospects. Again the very increases in production brought about expanded wealth and potential wealth for all who came under the ambit of capitalism. In fact, Skelton quickly shifted his ground, arguing that the objection of the socialists was really based on comparative wealth. What they objected to was the relatively greater wealth of a tiny minority of people and the concentration of considerable riches in the hands of this minority. But this objection was beside the point. Inequality based on "differences in enterprise, in industry, in thrift can be levelled only at the cost of paralyzing production and plugging the whole of society into an equality of misery." Because modern society was one in which industry, enterprise, and thrift were encouraged, then "the possibilities of decent living are increasingly brought within the reach of the vast majority.[33] Humanity's wants, in brief, were met only under market conditions that provided rewards commensurate with efforts. This was both ethical and efficient, for people literally got what they deserved from the market dispensation. Any interference in the spread of wealth could destroy the considerable productivity of the system; that productivity was predicated on some degree of deprivation or at least a perception of want.

Another important factor was the new role for the state that had emerged with the more equitable and productive capitalism of recent decades. The state was in fact coming into the service of society in dealing with those problems of human welfare which undeniably existed. *Laissez-faire* was not essential to capitalism. State action to deal with abuses, to regulate the operation of the economy where necessary, was generally admissible and practicable. In cases of conflict between the interests of society and those of one section, group, or individual, state action was proper. Skelton's argument that the market economy harnessed individual interest for social cooperation showed that he escaped from an atomistic view of human beings in society. It also showed that he thought capitalism itself was changing, becoming more responsive to all peoples' claims and less to some peoples' demands. In this way Skelton spoke of "moralizing" the laws of economics. Significantly enough, he therefore called for state action in supporting this greater sensitivity to the basic conditions of human welfare as well as such cooperative activity as trade unionism in order to provide for the redress of social problems. He did, however, hedge his theory of collectivism by claiming that it was only men's and women's individual perception and initiative that led them to take cooperative action. Hence, corporate business enterprises, producers' and consumers' cooperatives, and the apparatus of positive government all reflected the individual's rational perception that the best means to further his or her interests lay in some forms of collectivist action and organization. In this way too, a subtle change was coming over men and women. As they perceived the need to surrender part of their autonomy they were cultivating their own selfless traits and thereby becoming more amenable to cooperation. The individual, then, might be said to exist independent of the state, but the state existed for purposes more important than the interests of any single individual.[34]

Skelton's concentration on the economic efficiency and ethical defensibility of capitalism was similar to the approach that Shortt had taken in his writings. However, Shortt had been far less clear than Skelton in distinguishing the question of economic efficiency from that of social ethics. For Shortt it seemed that the efficient was the ethical, whereas for Skelton each factor was weighed in turn even though his conclusion was similar. Skelton's method of response to the two parts of the socialist charge was also different from Shortt's in that he used the same arguments against each. He supported both the economic efficiency and social justice of capitalism by reference, first, to certain tenets about human nature, second, to economic progress, and third, to the expanding positive state. His conglomerate of psychological, material, and political factors provided a remarkably economical means to refute objections to contemporary capitalism. Each factor was simultaneously a palpable fact in the real world and an impalpable standard by which societies must test their institutions.[35]

Skelton had essentially completed his arguments in defence of capitalism in the two chapters in which he considered the socialist indictment. The balance of his book examined the manifestations of socialism – utopian, Marxist, and social democratic – and forecast its contemporary appeal in Europe and North America.[36] In this survey, while Skelton amplified his chief contentions about the relative merits of socialism and capitalism and indeed left his readers as much inoculated against socialism as Shortt had his, he added the warning that fundamental reforms to the capitalist order were necessary for its survival. This reservation – reiterated throughout the book – allowed Skelton to make the important point that individual fulfilment, economic growth, and the new positive state were as essential to capitalism as supply and demand, profit and loss, and private-property holding.

Skelton granted Marxist thought and politics pre-eminence as a challenge to liberal capitalism, and he devoted the bulk of his detailed critique to the ideas and goals of Karl Marx. In refuting Marx's system, he elaborated on points he had made earlier in his own analysis and built towards a more systematic exposition of market society. But, he began, Marx's ideas were remarkably powerful. "To him," Skelton wrote, "the world in general owes a relentless exposure of the seamy side of our boasted civilization, a helpful if exaggerated – perhaps helpful because exaggerated – recognition of the importance of the economic factor in history, a protest against the shallow optimism and barren traditional deductive reasoning that marked much of the current economic theory, and an attempt to get a close grip on reality and seize the import of the main forces and the broader currents of industrial development."[37] Marx, in sum, was a transformative thinker who devised an authoritative analysis of the kind which modern political economy sought to emulate. In all his writings, Skelton did not utter such praise to any other economic thinker; he omitted the usual banal paeans to John Stuart Mill or Adam Smith that can be found in most Canadian political economic writing by the likes of Shortt, Leacock, or Mackintosh.

Praise registered, Skelton then spent three chapters arguing that the main points in Marx's analysis were incorrect. This curious blend of deep admiration and complete dismissal suggests either that Skelton was engaged in a rhetorical bid for fairness or that he was trying to make clear that Marx's thought demanded an alternate explanation which was just as complete (and more correct). That Skelton was taking the former course seems unlikely given his confidence in the relevance of political economic thought to resolve economic and ethical questions as well as to explain the historical process. He would not trivialize his aims or commitments by specious praise. That he was aiming at something like an alternate explanation must for the moment remain a matter of conjecture, though the sweep of his total refutation of Marx suggests that logically, he must have thought that a similarly complete alternative explanation did exist. The respect in which he held Marx is made clear by comparing Skelton's choice of socialist enemies with that of his fellow economists. Adam Shortt had directed his ire at the Presbyterian clergyman John Hay. Stephen Leacock attacked and refuted socialism with reference to its expostulation by the Bellamyites, of all people.[38] The difference of difficulty in both cases requires no comment.

To Skelton, Marx's intellectual system was based on the materialist conception of historical development, the labour theory of value, and the "law" of capitalist development with its theory of revolution.[39] In response, Skelton argued that an explanation of historical change based upon the tenets of "historical materialism" was an inadequate account of history. This was because economic interests were not the sole, protean fact of human life which Marx claimed; on the contrary, the divisions of interest and affinity that characterized human beings in society led them to be motivated by geographical, religious, and racial ties as well as class interests. The very "range of human interests and motives" included many variables of the uneconomic sort, for instance, sexual impulses, religious values, and social pressures. In shaping human history, ideas were as important as economic interest, just as unconscious motives and habits were as crucial to human behaviour as material calculations.[40] Not incidentally, then, Skelton broke with a simple utilitarian psychology in his assessment of how humans behaved as individuals and social beings.

As for Marx's value theory, Skelton, like Shortt, readily refuted it for a reliance on the notion that physical labour was the only factor that produced the value of goods. For Skelton, Marx's ideas here were based on the disproven Ricardian theory. This "attempt to derive value entirely from cost, with only an indirect and limited recognition of utility, is as futile as the reverse endeavour in many current versions of the marginal utility doctrine." Skelton elaborated on the problems of the Marxian theory, noting that economic value was determined by factors of supply *and* demand. Supply factors determined cost of production, but cost of production did not alone determine value. Anticipation of demand and demand itself were equally as important in creating economic value. Thus the consumer's perceptions and entrepreneur's skills were as important as production of goods and their pricing. No one group – producers, entrepreneurs, consumers – could be justified in taking a dominant share from the economic system in which all were integral parts. If Marx's value theory was discredited (and Skelton observed that Engels and Kautsky has sought to escape from the erroneous doctrine), then his ideas that "surplus value" was expropriated by the capitalist class and that this expropriation caused the impoverishment of the working class were also erroneous. As the method of determining economic value showed, the great strength of the market system was its mediation between the capacity to produce goods and the desire to consume them, the desire to consume being signalled through the price system to producers who then provided the goods consumers wanted.

The satisfaction of both sides in the negotiations was provided for. Thus collapsed the entire edifice of Marx's explanation about a system of capitalistic exploitation which resulted in monopoly and inefficiency, poverty and injustice, or failures of production and distribution leading to the final downfall of the system.[41] (Similarly Skelton attacked the "difficulty of attainment" theory on which Shortt had based his theoretical speculation concerning economic value.)

Above all, Marx's law of capitalist development, and his theory of revolution, was proven wrong both by economic logic elaborated since Marx's time and by the very experience of the previous forty years. Since Marx's day, capitalism was notable for the continuous growth of productive power and the effective distribution of increasing incomes for the benefit of all classes. Made possible by the evolution of the industrial system of production, the real world of industrialism under market conditions was one in which its productive capacity allowed wage earners to gain a larger and larger share of income. This larger share then fuelled the economic engine to allow for still higher productivity and even greater efficiency. The economic process set into motion was one of self-sustaining material expansion and effective distribution which was continuously improving through time. Skelton concluded that "the very essence of modern industrial progress rests in the ability to satisfy specific wants with an ever smaller proportion of society's force of labor and capital, thus setting the rest free for the provision of new services and commodities."[42]

For Shortt, the point of economic activity was to satisfy human wants by more efficient use of effort and resources. But satisfaction was limited by finite resources and productive capacity as well as competing claims on that capacity. For Skelton, in contrast, that aim was met by the industrial system with ever-increasing efficiency; further, the industrial system was constantly expanding to provide for ever-expanding wants as well. The operation of the capitalist market was a kind of refutation of Newtonian laws. Ever-greater efficiency and ever-expanding capacity showed that there was a remarkable dynamism in the capitalist economy's productive capacities to respond to demand through industrial processes. Just as the Ricardian laws of economics no longer held, Newtonian laws of the physical world were defied by the ever-expanding industrial market economy. (Perhaps here we can see that Shortt's anchorage in studies of the physical sciences did not hold Skelton who was trained solely in the new social sciences. Skelton used the verification of biological-historical theory, but even that posited an open-ended process of growth and expansion rather than a closed system in equilibrium.)

Both the historical development of capitalism and the historical model of Darwinism, then, disproved Marx's theory about the inevitability of a socialist revolution and suggested a far different alternative to the human prospect.[43] Skelton had been mindful that Marx's ideas included both an historical theory and an economic one, the results of which converged in Marx's predictions about the demise of capitalism. Skelton's critique, however, did not lead him to object to Marx's grand historical and economical theorizing. Quite the opposite, in fact, for Skelton was able to provide alternative explanations of both history and economics. His crucial point concerned the efficiency of industrial production and market economics, which Marx had misunderstood. As a consequence, the just demands of men and women were (usually) met. The way in which the industrial capitalist order met the tests of efficiency and justice was by escaping the bonds that hitherto existed in the production of wealth. The ever-expanding productive capacity found an economic rationale in Skelton's explanation of consumer demand and industrial efficiency.

Darwinian theory showed that human history was not deterministic or finite in moving to a particular end, such as a socialist world order or the victory of the proletariat class. On the contrary, human history was the process of open-ended and uneschatological change. The powerful verification of Darwinian science, accepted by Skelton and Marx as the basic test of theory, made Marx's theory outmoded, ironically in light of Marx's admiration for Darwin. For his part, Skelton accepted the Darwinian conception of history as a continuous evolution which existed apart from man's direct control and which had no final purpose. This did not lead him to abandon his notion of the purpose of humankind's temporal experience. Rather, the impossibility of human mastery over the social order or control over the precise direction of history was the essence of the psychological and spiritual fulfilment men and women experienced. Indeed, the interaction between human will and wants and the abstract forces of nature provided the only meaning people could find. As Skelton argued, "In the future as in the past progress must be rooted in divine discontent. The goal ever fades into the distance; every step upward opens new horizons; achievement always lags behind conception. If ever the voice of the critic is hushed, it will mean that society has attained not perfection but stagnation. That finality is impossible is not reason for folding the hands and acquiescing in the present ills, but it is a reason for disregarding the factious criticism which would have us scrapheap civilization because with all our progress there yet remain many a blot to be removed and many a manful fight to be waged."[44] Human beings found their fulfilment not in some final stage of history, their mastery over the world, or their post-human state, but in their efforts to master the world and in the history of the struggle to do so. This blunted version of history-as-struggle accepted the pointlessness of theological questions but affirmed that the historical process was the only way in which people's lives gained purpose. Even while criticizing the "utopian" who sought the end of history in perfection, Skelton reaffirmed the importance of the "critic" who goaded and challenged society to renewed effort. But his main point was that just as people were fulfilled in a material sense by an economy providing ever-expanding production, psychologically they achieved meaningful lives through the constant striving towards an ever-receding goal.

So the convergence between Skelton's economic and his historical-psychological theories led to a final summary concerning man in society. The concept of progress as an unending evolution and the idea that human fulfilment was a function of that evolution informed both parts of Skelton's vision about the market economy. His psychological and his economic accounts of "progress" relied on a perception of history as unending growth, change, and improvement. This historical perspective, hardly a systematic theory yet a backdrop to his work, was at once the testing-ground for his economic and ethical evaluation about the benefits of the market economy and an explanation about the purposes which lay beyond that economic order. For it was important that this perspective rested upon a concept of wholly secular fulfilment for human beings. The point of history was not the rise of liberty or the establishment of a heavenly city on earth (let alone a heavenly kingdom in the world to come) but the perpetuation of human history with the aim of an open-ended "progress."

As for the practical prospect of the overthrow of capitalism, Skelton examined contemporary socialist movements in Europe and North America with considerable reassurance. The wisest and most influential modern European socialists, epitomized by Karl Kautsky, had so apprehended the weaknesses of Marxian economic and political thought as to become social democrats whose ideas were based on constitutional-political action and market-economic analysis. As for North America, the conditions of Canadian and American economic and political life were so favourable to an equitable distribution of rewards and to the full representation of all interests that socialism would continue to find few converts. Again, of course, the strengths of the industrial-capitalist system came to the fore. These supported Skelton's assured prediction of the future. There was, he argued, "every indication that private property will remain the dominant industrial feature of our western civilization. In the future, as in the past, it will survive because of its proved social utility, changing its scope and its attributes as new demands are made upon it, regulated by state insistence on the rules of the game, socialized by the extension of joint-stock ownership, democratized by trade-union sharing in determining the conditions of employment, moralized by the growing sense of the trusteeship of wealth."[45] In other words, the susceptibility of industrial economies to revolution was slight because they had been so amenable to the economic, social, and, pointedly, political resolution of problems.

Social change was thus also a result of another trait of market societies. As recognized by social as well as liberal democrats, this was the capacity to provide the political as well as the economic means to translate demands into reform, usually of a state-supervised variety. Hence Skelton's assurances about evolving capitalism included an emphasis on the political capacity of societies to respond to and reshape aspects of the capitalist order. As Skelton had stated in his summation about the capitalist system, factors of "social utility," "regulation," and "democratization" brought about a new role of the state. It then confuted the ethical objections once so central to the socialist indictment by "moralizing" the way of political economy. But elaboration of this political aspect of industrial capitalism and the role of the state takes us from Skelton's *Socialism* to the larger body of his writings.

In the nineteenth century, the state had come to take an active and positive role in ensuring the efficient and just distribution of goods as well as their effective production. For Skelton, this role was found in the analogy to a "referee." He had claimed that the modern state did not interfere with competitive market forces or private-property relations, but rather raised "the ethical level of competition, maintaining the struggle while insisting that it shall not be carried on at the expense of the weak and the helpless. While it declines to follow the advice of the socialist and play the whole game itself, the state gives inestimable service by acting as referee."[46] Despite his tentative language, which was reminiscent of Mackenzie King, this role was not just an umpire's one nor was it as vague as that of raising the ethical level of competition alone. In his writing, Skelton identified the following areas where state intervention in economic activity was necessary: services (education, social insurance), regulation (conditions of work, housing and health, supervision of financial transactions), direct management (public utilities, post offices), and sponsorship or coordination of economic development (Canadian government aid to capitalist enterprises such as the CPR). These were broad areas of state activity; only a few regulatory activities were simply the refereeing of economic relations. Most involved state action in areas with broad political and economic ramifications. Skelton enthusiastically supported both social insurance projects and public-economic enterprise because they provided for "national development and social betterment," as he explained in supporting the British Liberal budget of 1909.[47]

Skelton insisted that state interventions, though providing social services and public works, were not socialistic. He ridiculed the "bogey" of socialism raised against them. Some state activities, such as the operation of public utilities, were sometimes justifiable because these "natural monopolies" were exempt from normal market conditions. Others, such as social insurance programs, were necessary because they raised the level of competition by exempting certain basic needs from the merest whims of the market. Contributory welfare schemes avoided the danger of sacrificing individual self-reliance to social reform because both individual and state participation in their financing and operation was necessary. One reason why Skelton favoured the introduction of a progressive income tax to support government spending was precisely because the income tax signalled that the individual paid for government, but fairly in this case. Skelton followed Shortt in emphasizing that economic calculations of cost, financing, and taxation were used to provide services and to run government businesses in any event. State intervention could be subsumed under the imperative of economic calculations. Justice or other ethical considerations should not be raised above this "primary consideration" even if it could not remain the "sole" basis for decisions. All this indicates the effort Skelton, like Shortt, made to separate his positive, statist reforms from socialist ones.[48]

In a review of Skelton's book for *Queen's Quarterly*, James Bonar criticized Skelton for refusing to admit the similarities between contemporary socialist and more orthodox reform positions. A distinguished British economist, long-time deputy master of the Canadian Mint, and friend of Canadian economists, Bonar was hardly hostile to Skelton. He was making an important suggestion about possible convergence of liberals and socialists. Skelton, however, denied this convergence, arguing that any similarities were owing to modifications not by marketeers but by socialists. He was concerned to preserve reform from any tincture of radicalism, let alone socialism, even as he defended major social reform through the positive state. British social-democrat or liberal reformers did not have to worry about this, but Canadians did. It is a comment on Skelton's intellectual and political environment that he, like Shortt, preserved the distinction.[49]

For all his caution, Skelton's actual formulation of priorities showed his awareness that the market did not naturally and simultaneously provide for efficiency and justice. Efficiency and justice were not concomitant factors either; they were distinct ones by which to judge the operations of the economic system. In reaching this conclusion – and Skelton rather talked around it than stated it so baldly – he placed considerable distance between himself and liberal-minded Canadian reformers of his era. Unlike political economists such as Morely Wicket at Toronto or even Mackenzie King during his Rockefeller Foundation phase, Skelton had no illusions about automatic and just regulation of people's wants and interests.[50] As we have seen in his discussion of trade policies, conflict, through competing claims by class groupings, was essential to the market economy in ways which required mediatory state action. Similarly, his call for state action – in such areas as trade policy, social services, or even direct management – was predicated on the state's action in imposing harmony upon areas of conflict. The emphasis on the "referee's" role in his studies of the positive state was also based upon the essential role of state action as a bulwark against the socialist challenge. The imposition of harmony was an effective means to redistribute income by favouring the claims of farmers above that which they would naturally have received. (By "naturally" he did not mean free market conditions but rather the conditions that emerged from economic competition and the relative power of the various interests in imposing their claims, as with the influence of the manufacturing class in nineteenth-century Canada.) Skelton's plea to "moralize the laws of supply and demand," much like R.H. Tawney's goal to break with the "acquisitive society", was a moralist's call to force recalculations about those laws. This plea was basic to the growth of the "positive" state to which he referred so often.

SKELTON'S ARGUMENTS WERE a substantial advance upon those of most reformers of his time. Their appeal, it might be stated, took different forms. Some Laurier-Borden "progressives" sought more efficient production of goods and greater output. Others, such as the Progressives, looked for a larger share for their particular group. Finally, some, the social gospelers, clamoured for more "moral" behaviour by all humanity.[51] Skelton broke away from these formulae by holding that the state existed partly to redistribute goods and services but also to determine the most effective conditions for their production and/or to redress particular grievances. This was Skelton's basic deduction from his assessment of the characteristics of industrial capitalism and the ameliorative factor of state authority which went with it. Consideration will be given later to the tax reforms and the social welfare proposals that Skelton made during the second decade of the twentieth century. These can be seen as elaborations of arguments about the role of the state which Skelton presented in his theoretical work. Capitalism, he maintained, could only be justified and only survived precisely because of the transformative functions that it had acquired. And it would never had acquired such functions had it not been for the conditions that political democracy and the positive state created.

Skelton's theory of capitalist justice and efficiency indicated a fear that the capitalist system would indeed reflect Marx's forebodings. Reform, he warned Canadian businessmen in 1913 when economic expansion had turned to recession, was not optional but imperative:

Private property today is on the defensive. It has no heaven-born sanction. It will endure only so long as it proves socially beneficial. The hour of social as well as political democracy has come. The ideal which will prevail, the ideal shared by socialists and individual reformers alike, is the organization of industry in the interest of the masses of the people. Our existing order will endure if it can be made, and can be shown to be true, that private property is a better means of attaining this end [of social justice] than collectivist property. It must be shown that within the existing framework of society we can combine private initiative and private energy with social control and social justice. Every tax-dodging millionaire, every city slum, every instance of shady high finance or of overworked and underpaid employees, is a potent argument for socialism.[52]

This rather alarmist message to the readers of a business periodical needs to be considered carefully if Skelton's arguments about the remaking of capitalism are to be interpreted correctly. Reform was an admission of the complexity of the relations between individuals, classes, and sections. The state must indeed take up a coordinating role in economic relations which had been left previously to competing interests or divine hands, just as the political world was the forum for the representation of the multitudinous interests in society. The call Skelton made for "social as well as political democracy" suggested too that he saw the adaptation of the economic system under state guidance as an extension of human rights from the political plane to the economic one. Mere political freedom no longer comprised the great end and tendency of development. The political forum would remain important as the place where "social control" would be exerted and those "social utilities" to which he elsewhere referred would be calculated.

Skelton's suggested reforms were offered in a conservative spirit: they would preserve private property and market relations as much as these were preservable. This conservative bias is significant since it was rooted in Skelton's sensitivity to the fragility of the progressive era of industrial capitalism. Unless men's and women's psychological energies and society's material capacities were wedded to the system of industrial capitalism, the momentum that he had claimed as its special feature might be lost. Similarly, unless the reformism of positive state action was sustained, the economic order would no longer fulfil its purposes. Still, even if social and economic justice could be aimed at, no standard of justice could be devised which was acceptable to all groups.[53] Skelton's theory of historical relativism and historical change helped to prove the contingency of all standards of justice. That same relativism had also shown limitations to the sheer efficiency of industrial capitalism. Skelton thought that it was necessary to mediate between the two poles of efficiency and justice. Neither was wholly attainable or acceptable without the other, for each had its important claim. It was necessary to balance between these two demands. The role of the state finally provided the means of resolution. For the state might be invested with the great purpose of reconciling the two great demands men and women made upon their society and the divergent ways by which the industrial system could claim to satisfy their wants. To put the matter simply, the state was at the convergence of the capacities of industrial capitalism for economic progress and individual fulfilment.

5 The Reform of Government

The chief factor of success in the Canadian system of
parliamentary government is the concentration of power
and responsibility.

Adam Shortt

The practice of politics and government in post-Confederation
Canada was a spectacle of corruption. Voters were often bribed or
impersonated, party politicians rolled out "pork barrels" filled with
jobs, and the public purse was looted. The result was that a ménage
of politicians, businessmen, and party faithful lived off the avails.
The venality of electors and legislators, the effectiveness of the party
machines, and the irregular origins and administration of government policies were much commented on, with distaste and a certain
bemusement, by contemporaries. Foreign political scientists such as
James Bryce and André Siegfried thought that corruption, which
discredited democracy and distorted policies, was perhaps the most
disturbing problem in Canadian politics.[1] Whether or not they were
correct about the effects of corruption, these observers spotted the
peculiarity of Canadian politics.

Not surprisingly, politics in the Laurier and Borden years drew
rapt attention from Adam Shortt and Oscar Skelton. Like the European observers, they were highly critical of many aspects of political
life, including electoral behaviour, the party system, policy making
and administration, and the role of parliament. Acting as the trail-
blazer for his colleagues, Shortt tried during the Laurier period to
reshape politics through administrative reform.

SHORTT CRITICIZED THE machine politics of his age and the sense
and sensibilities of the common voter. Like many others, including

his colleagues James Cappon and George M. Grant, he railed against excessive partyism. But unlike several critics, he tempered his attacks with qualifications: the party system was national and therefore served a crucial role in integrating all parts of the country into a common political order, and the party system was a necessary accompaniment to the operation of responsible government and parliamentary democracy. Shortt thought that the further "education" of the voters was possible and that issues and standards of public affairs could be raised to a more serious and reflective level than the division of spoils.[2]

Shortt's argument, in fact, was not with party politics as such but with the political "character" of the nation, or, to use a modern term, its political culture. This argument led him to criticize the selfish expectations people had of public administration and of public policy. Shortt concluded that reforms should focus on strengthening parliamentary government and the party system in the following ways: the advancement of people of "character" and judgment into the political system as politicians and administrators, the provision of proper information and ideas concerning public affairs, and the improvement of the machinery of government so that the party system and public business could be conducted more efficiently. Hostile not to parliamentary democracy or the party system but to its current manifestations, Shortt sought reform through individual influence and incremental changes in the existing system rather than by a retreat into anti-party coalitions or a bureaucratic government.[3]

If criticism of the political system and conditions for its reform were in order, so too were specific means to bring about that reform. The main point, already alluded to, is that the Queen's academics approached the renewal of Canadian politics from a position firmly within a British tradition of parliamentary government and politics. The party and the role of parliament were, to them, the foundations of politics. Adam Shortt wished to strengthen these institutions and build upon them. In other words, he predicated his criticisms on the intention to rebuild, not demolish. Shortt had emphasized, and Skelton would as well, the crucial role of parties as forums in which all sections and classes of Canada would meet. Moreover, parties provided the means by which the various segments of society would find truly effective representation in the parliament and legislatures of the nation. Finally, only properly constructed parties could make parliamentary government effective.

Prior to the First World War, Shortt argued that the link of the party system to parliamentary government must not be tampered with if the interests of all groups were to have an effective voice in government and if parliament was actually to govern. He then warned that "any scheme for getting rid of the party system simply means another party" and stated that parties alone would concentrate "responsibility" in the cabinet. Only the party system within legislatures would provide for that "concentration of power and responsibility" which he thought was the "chief factor of success in the Canadian system of Parliamentary government." He specifically warned against such anti-party agitation as that indulged in by Herbert B. Ames, Montreal businessman and social reformer, and his fellow spokesmen at the 1914 convention of the Social Services Congress. To Shortt, strengthening political responsibility in the executive by renewing political parties was the key to an efficient and responsible political system.[4]

During the war, at the high-tide of coalition sentiment, Skelton repeated this argument. He noted that the party system was "the essential factor in the working of democratic government, the only means yet devised of securing a stable and responsible majority and organized and responsible criticism." To Skelton, however, the responsibility of government rested on its capacity to represent all interests effectively rather than the paternalistic concentration of power and efficient executive action that Shortt aimed at. Still, for both men, it was important to refute that peculiar and tenacious "tory" suspicion about partyism which had emerged again in the Borden years.[5]

If both Shortt and Skelton were committed to the ascendency of parliament and the strengthening of political parties, they diverged in the ways in which they tried to pursue the renewal. Skelton devoted considerable attention to party platforms and policies and to the fiscal powers of government. He did so chiefly in a number of essays on these problems written for *Queen's Quarterly* and other "serious" periodicals – that is, he wrote for publications which were read by Dicey's "legislative public opinion." Shortt concentrated, at least from 1907 to 1918, on the problem of the administrative machinery of the national government. This work was conducted first through active membership on Industrial Disputes Act conciliation boards and then through his role as civil service commissioner.

Adam Shortt leaped at the chance to assist the federal government when it created a program for mediating between labour and management. This program began with the 1900 Conciliation Act and culminated in the 1907 show-piece of voluntary mediation, the Industrial Disputes Investigation Act. The Lemieux Act, as the 1907 measure was known, was the brain-child of the deputy-minister of labour, Mackenzie King, but named after the minister of labour, Rodolphe Lemieux. It was one of several measures that typified the response of Laurier-King liberalism to the extreme stresses of labour-capital relations after 1900. For King, the importance of easing the strains of industrialism led to a dual strategy: defining the state as society's referee to preserve peaceful economic relations, and obtaining a voluntary agreement between labour and capital to accept this referee state.[6]

For Shortt, the Lemieux Act was a chance to show that the academic political economist could shape public policy and, in this case, redirect it away from King's moralistic purposes. Carefully marketing himself, Shortt became a major participant in the conciliation process, serving on twelve boards while continuing to teach at Queen's. He apparently enjoyed equal favour from management, labour, and Department of Labour officials, and his boards were said by contemporaries from all three groups to have been models of successful negotiation. Shortt's skill drew the praise of labour representatives such as Toronto lawyer John O'Donoghue, the Trades and Labour Congress solicitor and the son of an activist in the printers' union, business appointees such as the Toronto corporation lawyer and Supreme Court of Canada justice, Wallace Nesbitt, and key Department of Labour officials such as F.A. Acland.[7]

Both during his time as a conciliator and in his subsequent reflections, Shortt put some distance between himself and Mackenzie King. He claimed that the Industrial Disputes Investigation Act was misconceived and misapplied by the government because of King's inclinations. He warned that the act was vaguely drafted and probably beyond federal jurisdiction. Yet the vagueness of the act enabled Shortt to develop his own views of how the conciliation boards should work. Shortt regarded himself as a conciliator rather than an arbitrator. Disputes were to be evaluated on the basis of the complexity and ambiguity of issues rather than on legal or moral grounds. Labour relations and labour-management negotiations were not so much ethical or legal questions as economic and social problems to which economic tests tempered by sensitivity to human foibles must be applied. Shortt implied that King was too much concerned with the moral value of conciliation and too enamored of legal machinery. Like King in one way, Shortt was not convinced of the need for, let alone the legitimacy of, trade unions. He went so far as to suggest cautiously that they should be legally liable.[8]

During his time as a negotiator and later, Shortt emphasized that the act provided for conciliation between the sides of a dispute rather than arbitration of the issues. Further, it could be effective only if conciliation was the aim of the negotiators. This meant that decisions must be based on agreements acceptable to all parties and that they were neither arbitrarily imposed nor abstractedly "just" settlements. Consequently, voluntarism on the part of all participants to negotiations was basic to Shortt's approach. Voluntary agreement must be preserved and not replaced by recourse to court-imposed negotiation or agreements. As early as 1910 he noted that the use of legal compulsion – to force the parties to continue negotiation and to provide for adjudication by arbitrators – was beginning to undermine the effectiveness and prestige of the act. His opposition to legalistic procedures and machinery was not based on simple hostility to lawyers or even to compulsory state intervention. Shortt was willing to enforce the meeting of the parties to a dispute via subpoena. As well, he saw the act as a useful means for the mediatory state to "educate" by guiding both the disputants and the public affected in accepting the (state-sponsored) principle of mediation. On the other hand, Shortt was not in favour of the legal practice of "full publication" of negotiations since that easily destroyed the disputants' propensity to frankness and flexibility. It also harmed the negotiator's ability to isolate each side. In sum, the adversarial and public aspects of a court-like setting were anathemas to Shortt. Confirming his attitude in this respect were his suspicions about the legal validity of the act (which referred to the "public utilities" affected in terms that encroached on provincial jurisdictions), suspicions that were reinforced by the private warnings of some labour representatives. In these circumstances, he would have been anxious not to flaunt the provisions of the act and thereby challenge labour or management.[9]

Shortt developed an approach to labour negotiation that reflected his peculiar understanding of the Lemieux Act's purposes. First he developed his anti-legalist *modus operandi*, and then he advocated adherence to principles of "practical justice" as the aim of negotiations. As a negotiator Shortt stressed the need for complete privacy of negotiations once they were begun. The issues were to be presented and settled one by one until the key problems were isolated. Afterwards, private negotiation with each side was conducted in turn, with the chairman acting as the "common medium" between employers and their appointee and employees and their representative. While the act itself provided for public and "open" negotiations, Shortt claimed that this was never followed on boards he chaired, particularly in his work with the two Toronto lawyers, Wallace Nesbitt and John G. O'Donoghue.[10]

An amusing and revealing account of Shortt's "shuttle diplomacy" can be followed from his letters to his wife while negotiating a dispute between Nova Scotia Coal and miners at Sydney, Nova Scotia, in July 1908. The discussions began with judicious visits to the miners, including meetings at their union lodges and place of work, where Shortt noted the effects on his stamina of two day's tramping about in coal mines. Then he concentrated on discussions with the mine owners, including a less demanding day sailing on the president's yacht. Negotiations followed for two weeks and a settlement was finally reached. It was one about which Shortt felt quite triumphant given the original "obstinacy" of Nova Scotia Coal. Working independently with each party to a dispute had allowed the negotiator as "medium" to reach a settlement despite the considerable opposition from the disputants.[11]

Throughout such negotiations as these, Shortt claimed that adherence to a set of general principles would lead to the "practical justice" he sought. The owners must recognize the rights of labour to negotiate collectively over the terms and conditions of work. Shortt actually stated that this meant "recognizing the labour unions," but whether his words were to be taken literally is not clear. The workers must recognize the right of employers to determine decisions about how operations were run and grant "open shop" privileges. Finally, the board must be granted the right to deal with pay rates, hours of labour, conditions of promotion, and "reasonable protection for life, limb and general health."[12]

In these ways, Shortt thought that negotiation would ensure that "the employer was essentially entitled to manage his own business, while the employees should be free to manage theirs." This concept of division of power and responsibility, when tied to Shortt's neutralist precepts about getting a settlement regardless of abstract claims of right or wrong, meant that he was not troubled over the justice or indeed even the specific results of decisions. Agreement was what mattered. Perhaps it could be concluded that agreement was justice in Shortt's estimation. When an agreement was reached, the submission of both parties to it (at least until the next contract talks) was the best protection either side could have. Shortt once commented that strikes were far less often the result of economic grievances than of social conditions and even the perceptions of strikers and the struck. Labour must be made aware of its responsibility in striking and forced to accept the freedom of all workers to strike or not. Capital, however, must be made to abide by the agreements reached during negotiations and to admit that labour's demands were moderate in essence. Shortt found no reason to accept labour's claims to principles of universality of treatment or the seniority basis for promotion. Similarly, he held little regard for management's demand for arbitrary authority or its denial of the right to strike. A division of responsibility and mutuality of obligation served as the best bases for labour peace. These were the only abstract guarantees that labour and capital could point to – and they were the result of practice and not theory. Finally, the provision for such practical justice was also a tribute to the rationality of each side in submitting to necessity by admitting the claims of the other.[13]

To Shortt, the personal skill of the negotiator was essential to winning an agreement that was respected by labour and capital. The skilled negotiator – here a subtle jibe at Mackenzie King can be seen – did not need to have knowledge of economic theory, still less of labour-relations theory. Rather he needed to know about "the concrete economic conditions, historical and contemporary" that could lead to the proper settlement of any particular dispute. Moreover, the negotiator must have insights into human psychology, especially individual foibles, which would enable him to bring disputants into agreement. So equipped, the conciliator would jettison the legalistic and court-room tendencies of the Lemieux Act in favour of the principle of voluntarism and the technique of private negotiation. With his knowledge of the industrial conditions and individual personalities involved, the negotiator could bring about a settlement acceptable to both sides. Clearly, a peculiar kind of person would be best equipped to fill these requirements. Not a lawyer or a moralist, but a scientist of social and economic conditions (and thus a scientist of human nature) was the person to provide for successful labour relations. Yet the negotiator was probably not simply an academically trained professional; actually he was someone remarkably like Adam Shortt. In his apologia for labour conciliation, Shortt stridently warned against "premature" and moralistic appeals to public opinion or the public interest. Shortt himself entertained no recourse to the grand appeals to "public interest" or "public opinion" in his own explanation of successful conciliation. Unlike the Lemieux Act's author, Mackenzie King, Shortt thought little of public opinion as such and he was wary of the grand gesture of publicity.[14]

Both his coolness towards democracy and his distrust of mere moralizing were epitomized in his approach to labour relations. Shortt was adapting to labour relations those principles of successful administration that he so admired in Governor Sydenham, the subject of a biography he was completing at the time of his labour-conciliation work. Shortt's explanation does resemble a version of Sydenham's "harmony principle" of colonial administration with its emphasis on the limited rights of each party, their mutual submission to the other side's rights, and the central role of the chief administrator in making the system work.[15] In any case, he stressed the crucial role of the negotiator as much as any other factor in explaining how labour relations could be effectively managed. The need for conciliation, the principles of voluntarism, and the role of the social scientist-negotiator were crucial for the success of the mediatory efforts of the state.

Two commentators struck notes of praise both for the Lemieux Act and for Adam Shortt's success: Dr Victor S. Clark, of the United States Department of Labour, a classmate of Skelton at Chicago, and Oscar Skelton himself. Both stressed that the act had come about as a result of public opinion exasperated by disruptions to public services in railroads and mines. Both emphasized the non-compulsory nature of conciliation, Skelton also mentioning that the most successful conciliation boards avoided arbitration. Both concluded that the act was supported by broad sections of business and labour. Significantly enough, however, whereas Clark tended to see the Lemieux Act as a model for successful state mediation, Skelton viewed it as a mere "supplement" to more wholesale reforms. He suggested that collective bargaining should be automatically begun by joint committees of labour and capital and not remain an extraordinary measure provided by government in a crisis. He also suggested that the necessity of major social legislation was proven by the current degree of labour-capital conflict. Once that social legislation was implemented, the collective-bargaining process would be much less volatile and much more effective. In his judgment that the Lemieux Act was experimental and contingent, Skelton was one with Shortt. In his expectation that social reform and more elaborate machinery of labour relations were necessary, he left the cautious Shortt behind. In 1919, when Mackenzie King's *Industry and Humanity* was published, with its support for British style "Whitely Councils" comprising joint labour-management committees as the means to promote "industrial democracy," Skelton was quick to see the lesson for Canadian legislators and for labour, management, and the public.[16]

SHORTT'S SUCCESS AS a labour negotiator was established just as the constitutional question at Queen's seemed to be stalled. This combination of personal success and frustration with Queen's appears to have made him amenable to a change. During the first half of 1908 he seems to have been in consultation with the federal government about a couple of positions in the public service. Finally, in September 1908, he accepted the post of commissioner with the newly established Civil Service Commission. His co-commissioner was Michel G. Larochelle, a Quebec barrister and former secretary to Wilfrid Laurier, a person whom Shortt delightedly and erroneously thought he could dominate. Despite his initial hopes and occasional rewards such as his 1911 tour of England, Germany, and Switzerland to study civil-service reform first hand, Shortt quickly became unhappy with administrative drudgery, conflicts with his co-commissioner, and the commission's general lack of impact.[17]

When members of Robert Borden's cabinet defied the philosophy of civil-service reform that the prime minister had proclaimed, Shortt became extremely restive. In 1915 he found himself involved in a fierce and ultimately humiliating conflict with Robert Rogers, Borden's minister of public works, over Shortt's factually incorrect and politically indiscreet charge of patronage in the "outside" service. In 1917 he resigned quietly, tired if undaunted by the disputes over the commission's work, composition, and jurisdiction and fed up with the grinding pressure of hypocritical supporters of "reform" seeking "consideration" for their relative, friend, or constituent.[18]

The details of Shortt's administrative work need not be dealt with here. But his approach to civil-service reform and his understanding of the role of the commission merit attention since they offer further insight into his views of the proper administration and function of government as well as of the social scientist's place as a social reformer. On several occasions prior to the First World War, Shortt drew on his experience with entrenched Ottawa practices and argued for investigations of the public service.

In a 1911 memorandum for Prime Minister Borden, Shortt called for a fundamental re-examination of the apparatus of government administration. His co-author was Governor-General Lord Grey's aide "Dougie" Malcolm, with whom Shortt had had previous correspondence over the Round Table movement. The axiom that supported this appeal was the "remarkable national expansion" and corresponding "complexity and importance" of national issues which had brought about a greatly expanded role for executive decisions and routine administration in the dominion government. Unfortunately, Shortt and Malcolm continued, no corresponding reorganization had been undertaken in the way governments administered their newly complex and momentous responsibilities. This problem was manifest in the lack of coordination and control of government activity. Hence financing of programs was no longer directed by coherent strategies of control and administration and was too seldom managed by people knowledgeable about the purposes of the policies they were executing. A gap between the demand for government services and the supply of services had resulted in the near-independence of each department and the incompetent administration of policies. Government, in sum, was characterized by the kind of "drift" that American

Progressives such as Walter Lippmann so decried. In their case, the Canadian commentators were convinced that coherent organization was essential for effective government, even if they did not commit themselves to the kind of social engineering which the Lippmanns of the Progressive movement sought.[19]

Shortt's and Malcolm's thought about the problems of Canadian public service was inspired, or perhaps captured, by the example of nineteenth-century British reform. The sixty-year-old reformation of the British civil service, launched by the Northcote-Trevelyan report of 1854, had been based on two basic innovations. These were a treasury board to supervise and review public spending and a civil service board to appoint and promote candidates for public service posts. Both measures were enthusiastically promoted by Shortt and Malcolm. A treasury board, which had existed on paper but not in practice since Confederation, must be brought back to life as the agency supervising all spending by each department of government. This resuscitated treasury board would ensure that each department administered its spending on the basis of sound accounting and accountability. During each parliament, the fiscal priorities and strategies of the government would for the first time become the basis of public administration in Canada. The treasury board would begin to guard Canadian public administration against that predator on unreformed government, wasteful and fraudulent expenditure.[20]

While Shortt and Malcolm hoped to revivify the treasury board, they proposed merely to educate the agency that Shortt himself worked for, the Civil Service Commission. They argued that a powerful civil service commission was an essential complement to the Treasury Board because the commission would ensure effective compliance with the new system of financial controls. There were three parts to the commission's broad supervision of personnel: defining the duties of officials, supervising selection and recruitment at all levels of the public service, and assessing the performance and adjudicating promotions of this newly independent public service. A fully operational commission would provide Canadian government with yet another guardian against the patronage evil.[21]

Although Shortt and Malcolm asserted that the two super agencies were basic to the remaking of Canadian government on the model of liberal Britain, they did not pursue in detail either coordination between the two agencies or their relations with parliament. The two reformers simply assumed that once financial control was established by the Treasury Board, the Civil Service Commission would provide management and personnel direction for all departments. They did claim that the changes would free Cabinet to undertake the kind of long-term policy making that it currently could not do. As they noted, cabinet ministers were burdened by the crush of patronage appointments to the vast majority of positions in their departments and by the ignorance about departmental activities that weighed down all ministers. The powerful central agencies, Shortt and Malcolm summarized, would grant to Canada executive and administrative structures that would provide the kinds of benefits that Great Britain had enjoyed over the last half-century.

Admitting the sketchiness of their proposals, Shortt and Malcolm concluded their memorandum with a recommendation that the way to implement reform was by commissioning a thorough study of governmental reorganization from the "ablest and most experienced official of the British treasury who that office can be persuaded to lend." To Shortt at least, such a study would likely lead to major changes in line with the British system of public administration that he placed so much faith in. This thorough study to provide a blueprint for the inevitable reorganization of government was the key to effective reform.[22]

The former permanent secretary of the Treasury in Britain, Sir George Murray, was appointed to conduct such an examination. After a three-month study, his 1912 report set out rather general conditions for reform. These conditions were similar in fact to the Shortt-Malcolm proposals. Murray sought to relieve the bottleneck of administrative burdens which he thought severely constrained the policy-making duty of cabinet ministers. To sustain a distinction between policy and executive action, Murray argued in favour of effective Treasury control. He also suggested that there be developed an elaborate classification and supervision over personnel so as to expedite administrative efficiency and, of course, subvert patronage. While Murray's report apparently had little practical impact on the Borden Tories, it underlined the criticisms Shortt and Malcolm had made.[23]

Murray's work elicited a lengthy commentary to Prime Minister Borden from his civil service commissioner. Again Shortt went over the problems imposed by the new responsibilities of government in the twentieth century. He supported the major recommendations of Murray and of his own previous analysis, and he drew attention to the major problem that the patronage system imposed on civil-service recruitment and government policy makers and policy execution. Then he discussed at length the problems of recruiting able personnel and classifying positions so as to ensure that the civil service might become efficient. The technical questions that so often swamped him, such as superannuation, classification systems, merit promotions, uniformity of salary scales, and the like, occupied much of his commentary. Running through the memorandum, however, were several more important points. First, the abolition of patronage appointments was essential if the service was to attract "thoroughly-qualified" individuals. Only then could the civil service be reconstructed along lines that would ensure the efficient administration which all reformers aimed at. This meant, secondly, that policies could be administered after the best minds in a government had examined priorities under the microscope of Treasury control. Of course, such priorities could be established only if the policy makers were freed of the burdens of patronage considerations. Third, Shortt called for an extension of the Civil Service Commission to empower it to restructure the entire service, in line with both departmental needs and those of a central manpower agency. In this way merit alone would be the criterion for any appointment or promotion. Finally, Shortt vigorously sustained Murray's main conclusions. Murray had written that the "best people in the country" must be drawn to the public service, that the service must be regulated so that merit was the key to advancement, and that the division of policy making and administration must be water tight.[24]

Shortt, clearly, held very high hopes for the reform of the administration of government. He was not simply interested in abolishing patronage and creating efficient government, though he was committed to these, the clichés of the J.S. Willison–G.M. Wrong–W.L. Grant school of civil-service reformers. Rather, Shortt saw the reform of the public service as part of a systematic assault upon old corruption in Canada. The centralization of both financial control and public-service recruitment and administration was the basis for a fundamental reform of government in Canada. Freed of the profligate spending and patronage-management of the existing "independent" departmental system, the government could get down to determining long-term and coherent policies which the nation's contemporary problems warranted. At a stroke the government would be able to deal with the twenty-year backlog of social, economic, and political problems that transcontinental expansion, industrialism, and international obligations demanded. Revitalized, the civil service would at last be able to carry out the intentions of government. Moreover, it would attract the new educated classes – technicians, generalists, and social scientists – that would be committed to the aims of public service and capable of efficient administration. Reform would reinforce demands from informed, concerned citizens for efficient, effective government.

This last point was important in a couple of ways. It was a further elaboration of the complaints Shortt (and Skelton) had made concerning the relation between public standards and the spectacle of government in Canada. Achieving effective government and a civil service based on merit depended on escaping from low standards of political values and political reasoning on the part of politicians, civil servants, and influential community leaders alike. Shortt felt strongly after his 1917 resignation that informed public opinion would considerably strengthen any government's efforts to impose reforms despite the pressures of corrupt politicians and venal citizens. He also observed that the universities had failed to provide enough candidates educated in the new disciplines to fill civil service positions even when reform occurred. He clearly did not see the public service as a haven for superfluous humanistic arts and science graduates.[25]

Shortt was little bothered by threats to the accountability and responsibility of elected politicians either by those civil servants who were to reinvigorate administration or by those ministers who were to coordinate policy. While Shortt's successors at Queen's in the 1930s feared that the executive branch threatened legislative control and even parliamentary government, Shortt did not concern himself with either the relations between the cabinet and parliament or between the legislative and administrative arms of government. The tendency of his arguments was to strengthen the executive branch and administrative capacity of government. In this way, he merely wanted to insinuate a Bagehotian "efficient secret" of strong executive and capable administrative authority into the Canadian parliament. His liberal-democratic understanding of parliamentary government meant that he supported as much centralization of power in the parliament and government caucus as possible. But as long as party lines were firm and "responsibility" rested with the parliamentary leaders, they determined policy and therefore shaped their civil servants' roles. Nonetheless, Shortt did not advocate the American Progressive's goal of a bureaucractic form of government and the subversion of political control. The purpose of civil-service reform was to free the policy makers to make policy, even if the long-term consequences of meritocratic civil-service recruitment may have been to create a group of public servants with formidable knowledge of policy issues and alternatives.[26]

Shortt's concept of the civil service was similar in a number of ways to his view of the industrial-relations negotiator. He devised a theoretically neutral role in describing the purely administrative role of civil servants. Just as the labour negotiator made peace based on the issues involved in the dispute at hand, without reference to abstract claims of right, so too the civil servant was to execute the policy arrived at by the cabinet. The subordination of civil servants to parliament was assured in the manner that personnel management by the Civil Service Commission was dependent on the responsible politicians of the Treasury Board. The very fact that policies were to be made on a long-term basis naturally was assumed to commit governments to courses of action that could not be deviated from. True, the civil servants might well implement policies against the ephemeral pressures of the legislature. But that was not a worry to Shortt. Simple restraint was to be expected from those civil servants who were well informed on how parliamentary democracy worked and who were animated by the British model of relations between administrators and politicians.

Shortt's proposals for civil service and administrative reform can be seen as a kind of architectural restructuring of society. Exactly this kind of restructuring of the superstructure of government would, Marx to the contrary Shortt might have suggested, alter the lines of society to the extent that government affected the economic, political, and social structure. Staffed by men trained in the newly secular curriculum of the university, the civil servants themselves were well prepared to engage in the work of chipping away at the old and rebuilding the new structure of government. To change metaphors, Shortt and Malcolm themselves had used the analogy of the surgeon's work in calling for reform of the civil service – exactly the metaphor Shortt employed in calling for a new social role for the political economist at the inaugural meeting of the Canadian Political Science Association in 1913. That sort of radical activity was to be gained only through the expert advice of the trained student of government. It would, of course, only be implemented politically. Once "surgery" was performed, the rehabilitation of the patient was again the directed task of humble servants such as those in the public service. In each of his metaphors, Shortt was advocating considerable changes to the society with the social scientist both a major consultant to and supervisor of change.[27]

The importance Shortt placed on reform helps to explain the apparently perplexing career change that he made in 1908. The story of his years at the Civil Service Commission is one of considerable tedium and some futility. Unless we are to conclude that Shortt sought a sinecure in which to play at administration while pursuing his historical work (*Canada and Its Provinces* was published during this time) we must wonder just why he took the position in the first place. Despite comments to the contrary from Shortt's biographers, it is clear enough that behind the deputy-ministerial status and salary was a functionary's task of arranging examinations for clerks and fending off old-style cabinet ministers such as Samuel Hughes and Robert Rogers.[28]

Shortt had indeed accepted the position knowing that his role was very limited and that the commission itself was an "experiment." Yet he clearly looked beyond the 1908 Civil Service Commission Act to a time when his position would be at the top of government administration. These hopes were well supported by his exposition and Murray's on the reform of the civil service. If Shortt was stymied by politicians and the strength of "old corruption" in Canada, it was hardly because of any naïvety or idealism (as the chroniclers of the Civil Service Commission put it), at least not if it is remembered how comprehensive was his analysis and prescription for the reform of the public service. Still, his aspirations for the civil service were not fulfilled and his own work ended in something like the failure of the commission itself. Even so, his was a failure only in relative terms. Shortt weathered Rogers's fierce attack of 1915 and did not resign until December 1917, just as the Unionist coalition was supposed to stamp its brand of efficient government on Canadian politics. Shortt had left of his own accord at a point when he was willing to retreat to a sinecure and, perhaps, when he saw a renewed possibility for reform. Before and after his resignation, he acted as the consultant to the British Columbia, Alberta, and Manitoba governments in their own civil-service reforms. Shortt was also active in choreographing new agitation for reform of the federal public service. He called on those whom he described to George Chipman, editor of the *Grain Growers' Guide*, as the "better class" of people to defend the government's plans for the civil service against the attacks of the populace and politicians and to oppose the "trashy American model" of administrative reform. Into the 1920s Shortt encouraged people such as William Grant in his strenuous efforts to secure effective reform.[29]

Both reform and the prestige of the federal public service experienced considerable oscillations during the 1920s and 1930s. Civil service reform reached something of a nadir in the early 1920s and the reorganization that did occur reflected American rather than British influences. An impatient William Mackintosh complained in 1924 about the folly of cutbacks in the size and roles of the civil service. He saw these changes as the unfortunate results of a basic Canadian misapprehension about the public service. He warned that cutbacks impaired the government's capacity to rely on capable permanent officials to carry out its policies. Mackintosh also bluntly observed that only a capable civil service could effectively implement programs during a period of unstable, "shortlived" governments. As if confirming Shortt's warnings and Mackintosh's complaints, the public service in the 1920s endured the ignominy of such scandals as corruption in the customs department and even misappropriation of funds by one deputy minister of finance. But the public service was also notable for attracting people of considerable talent and by the end of the 1930s O.D. Skelton and Clifford Clark, both established as deputy ministers, had helped to transform it. Treasury control over the bureaucracy was established and a new ethic of devotion to the public service, domestic and foreign, resulted from recruiting by Skelton and Clark. For his part, Mackintosh looked to Shortt as the inspiration of what was translated into a "Queen's tradition" of analysis of and participation in policy making and of a spirit of devoted public service.[30]

At one remove from Shortt's elaborate arguments and efforts to schedule a surgical operation to repair the civil service was O.D. Skelton. In the summer of 1912, after Shortt and Malcolm had urged the adoption of Murray's report, Skelton, doubtless privy to the matter, discussed the problems of the public service in the *Queen's Quarterly*. Skelton parroted Shortt's conditions for an effective civil service: patronage must be reduced if not removed from government appointments, staffing policies must be altered so that the "ablest" people were brought into and kept by the public service, and a thorough reorganization of government must be undertaken so that effective planning and administration could be implemented. With his usual terseness, Skelton summarized the arguments flying within the government. To the control and coordination of government policy, Skelton was later to devote considerable attention. Even then, however, he reiterated Shortt's points about the priority of Treasury control over departmental spending and meritocratic civil-service appointments.[31]

ADAM SHORTT STRONGLY CRITICIZED the practice of politics in Canada and looked for reform in the architectural restructuring of government machinery. Only such reform would lead to efficient administration by government and to more rational choices by the populace. His decision about the importance of this restructuring led him to accept first occasional and then full-time employment in the public service. In spite of his rather bitter-sweet experience in the public service, Shortt sustained his commitment to a more effective and more active role for government in contemporary society.

Notwithstanding, his well-earned image as a cautious thinker and his evident skill in cultivating powerful men, Shortt was ultimately proposing novel and innovative changes to Canadian governmental practice. The reformed state machinery, in his mind, would provide new means to implement national policies through an efficient civil service and would contribute a new calculus of the national interest in the notion of "practical justice."

For Shortt, an efficient civil service was above all a key means to reform the basis of political life and public policy in Canada. If he did not go as far as Skelton in condemning the excessive influence of party insiders and businessmen, he nonetheless acknowledged the hyperbolic expectations they encouraged among the general public and the great benefits they derived from the politicians. Shortt well knew the pretense under which political hacks and business dealers had dominated Canadian politics. This political culture was exemplified, he found, in the continuous and distasteful practice of exaggerating the potential value of mineral, forest, and agricultural lands. To insert knowledgeable civil servants into the executive procedures of government was to begin to provide politicians with an alternative source of information, informed about realistic possibilities and disinterested in the outcome. Thus the civil-service expert would assist the politicians in escaping from the tentacles of the "interests" who so often overwhelmed them. Ironically, given his constitutional position calling for autonomy from Great Britain, Shortt appealed to Canadians to adopt the British practice of an efficient, disinterested, and competent civil service. Despite his own reservations about democracy, Shortt's civil-service reforms aimed at encouraging politicians to consider the interests of all men and women in society. He did not worry about the dangers of administrative discretion precisely because he expected the politicians to remain responsible and the influence of the rest of society to become greater.

The other result of reforming the civil service – the emergence of the standard of "practical justice" – was demonstrated in the procedures that accompanied effective state intervention in areas such as labour relations. Shortt had learned from his labour-conciliation work that precepts of practical justice were the only realizable expectations in the contemporary world. These principles, which applied to everyone, were derived from the mutality of individual rights and limitations on individual economic and social rights. In the Canada of the 1900s, Shortt knew, his notion of equal individual rights was a new perception resisted in many quarters. But he had long since outlined his arguments about the claims of practical justice when he had examined the characteristics of contemporary society. He had emphasized the interdependence of all men and women in society as the main source of the rise in labour-capital conflict in the United States and Canada. This sense of interdependence was behind his account to Queen's undergraduates in the 1890s of why Canada faced the full brunt of social conflict. The new approach to political economy that Shortt favoured – an approach that was historical, empirical, and social – was a precise reflection of his interpretation of contemporary society. Here Shortt was adopting the views of those new social scientists who in the United States of the 1890s and 1900s were abandoning the formalist and pessimistic accounts of their predecessors. Shortt used the same insight into the interdependence of individuals under the new industrial social order that so motivated American reformist political economists, historians, and philosophers such as Veblen, Beard, and Dewey after the turn of the century.[32] While Shortt, unlike Skelton, did not actually refer to the works of the American anti-formalists, he did distance himself from the same intellectual antecedents and social theory that the younger social scientists in Canada and the United States did.

6 The War for Democracy

The place of the economist is on the firing line of civilization.
O.D. Skelton

Adam Shortt's attempt to reform the civil service as a means of reorienting government was no more successful than Wilfrid Laurier's policy of commercial reform had been. Both failures were painfully clear to Oscar Skelton. Despite his attempt to maintain an impartial tone in published commentaries, his frustration with obstinate government and public opinion was evident after 1912. He engaged in his own rhetorical rearmament in subsequent years. So equipped, in the years from 1912 to 1919 he unleashed a constant barrage in prose against the existing party system, public opinion, and public policies. His criticisms of Canadian standards in each of these areas led him to suggest numerous ways in which they must be reformed. During the First World War, a period of considerable human suffering, social strain, and abuse of power and democratic opinion, Skelton's concerns and alternatives were most eloquently expressed. He offered an alternative conception of how Canadian political life should be conducted with the abiding aim of creating new standards and goals.

O.D. SKELTON AND ADAM SHORTT shared a fascination with the workings of parliamentary democracy and the party system. As usual, however, Skelton developed his thoughts more systematically and presented a far more devastating critique of Canadian politics than Shortt did. In so doing, Skelton proposed prescriptions more threatening to the existing political culture and more in keeping with the arsenic-cure treatment that was administered to the party system by the rise of Progressivism and the Unionist coalition. Yet, in essence, these prescriptions were still based on the pharmacopoeia of parliamentarianism.

Prior to the reciprocity debate of 1911, Skelton had written that the "lack of substantive debate or real policy alternatives" comprised a major failing of Canada's two-party system, a failing worse in some ways than outright corruption. Related to the lack of debate and corruption was the docility of the majority of members of parliament and provincial legislators. Skelton was concerned throughout the period from 1909 to 1921 with what he characterized as "errand-boy Parliaments." By this he referred to the pliancy of government back-benchers and the lassitude of opposition members in the face of cabinet power. Still more ominous, Skelton thought, was the propensity of the interests who financed the parties to dominate them and the tendency of the state to be used as a funding agency for their business projects. The relationship between governments and business contributed to the waste of public funds and to the typically Canadian disdain for political morality.[1]

Running through Skelton's litany was a social criticism similar to Shortt's. Both were disturbed by the complaisance with which the corrupt and inefficient order was viewed, and they shared the chilling thought that people were indeed satisfied with the contemporary order. To Shortt, this order was perpetuated by the mass of voters that readily accepted the system. But to Skelton, corruption was in fact entrenched by those dominant interests – politicians and businessmen – who were most actively participating in politics and benefitting from it. As he concluded in a 1913 assessment of political reform proposals, "not individual inefficiency; not crude or careless legislation; but sacrifices of public interests to party and to pocket" comprised the core of the problem. He asserted that it was "the brazen insolence of the system by which the money of the people of Canada is spent to maintain the party in power that constitutes the strongest indictment against our political life." Suggesting that "our record and reputation are such as to make us ashamed of what we have made of this, democracy's last fresh chance in the world," Skelton went on to catalogue the manifestations of corruption epitomized by business bribery of politicians and politicians' bribery of voters.[2]

Clearly, Skelton was distraught with Canadian democracy not least because he held considerable hopes for its success and also a distinct moral standard for the conduct of politics. The immoralities of the system – and the subsequent abuse of public funds and public trust – were unacceptable. Behind his criticism were concepts and standards of public good, social responsibility, and equity that must be met if the political system was to be justified. And behind all of this was a conception of Canada's democratic "mission" which fired Skelton's rhetoric. For him, the problem that required immediate attention was not imperfections in the machinery of government, politics, and the civil service (though he certainly took these seriously enough, as we shall see), but basic flaws in the political values of Canadian society.

Skelton was concerned with Canada's failure to perceive, let alone act upon, certain values that were essential to its political well-being. His explanation of the economic order was based on the importance of equity to economic calculations. Similarly, in the political world, this aim of equitable calculation of the rights and wants of all men and women must become the basis for political decisions. That re-evaluation would lead to escape from the existing domination of government by the rather shady forces that so unfairly benefitted from the division of political as well as economic spoils. All things considered, Skelton was more the general social reformer than was the later Shortt.

Shortt shared Skelton's goals of individual fulfilment and social harmony, a similarity that can be found in both men's expectations of the political order. Yet there was an important difference between them. In Skelton's case, individual fulfilment and social harmony were but the foundations for the emphasis he placed upon equity and the public good; in Shortt's, the idea of equity attracted no sympathy. Shortt either did not grasp or did not accept that equality might be the outcome of the fulfilment and harmony that he saw as the purposes of society. Perhaps his attitude may be explained by his scepticism about whether fulfilment and harmony were really attainable in practice. Major limitations on both the material capacities of society and on the rationality of people, in Shortt's view, were enough to prevent any significant fulfilment or to suggest any assurance about such fulfilment. For Skelton, however, the reorientation of the political and economic order must point toward and even assure the equitable fulfilment of all men's and women's aspirations. This difference also suggests a divergence in their reading of the flaws in the political system. While Shortt and Skelton perceived the dangers of the "patronage evil," to use the code phrase each used to describe the larger weaknesses of the party and parliamentary institutions, they differed in their assessments of the long-term threat to democracy in Canada. The contrast in their positions can be seen most arrestingly in their reform proposals, but it was also revealed in their views about the challenge that the First World War presented to Canada.

Prior to the war both Shortt and Skelton had shared in the "great illusion" that the prospects of war were virtually annulled by the dominant interests in Western society. Unlike so many Canadian intellectuals, such as the classicist and imperialist Maurice Hutton of Toronto, they foresaw little need for Canadian military preparedness. Never did they trade in Hutton's typically imperialist-nationalist appeal for greater military "discipline" and state "service" as means to strengthen and fulfil the Anglo-Saxon democracies. This may account for their shock once the war did begin; it may also explain the stiffness they displayed in their backing of the Allied cause. Nonetheless, despite Skelton's reservations about particular policies as the war dragged on, neither he nor Shortt hinted at any uncertainty in their support of the war's purposes.[3]

On the subject of the war, Shortt confined himself to superficial and conformist comments. He described it as a vital conflict between "democracy and militarism" pure and simple. But there were undertones of concern for Canada in his remarks. He argued that the unity of the British empire which emerged in August 1914 was solely a result of this basic confrontation, and he warned that imperial unity would last only as long as the war. Furthermore, if the war was prolonged, he wondered whether the Canadian-American model of peaceful international relations and their unmilitaristic, democratic forms of society and government could survive. This question was one that democratic nations would have to face during the war. It was a question the prudent Shortt did not try to answer.[4]

Shortt's question was addressed by some of his younger Queen's protégés. O.D. Skelton and W.L. Grant were fearful of the dangers posed by the conflict between British democracy and German militarism. They were also willing to face up to the threat that mobilization made to democratic society. In concurrent writings published in October 1914, they looked for the war's causes in the larger structure of international politics. Skelton blamed several factors – the armaments race, the weakness of the "peace movement" throughout Europe, and the ease by which militarist doctrine had come to dominate Germany and Austria-Hungary – and he proclaimed that democratic governments, including that of Canada, would not regain their ascendancy unless the war was prosecuted vigorously. Similarly, Grant saw the roots of the war in the conditions of pre-war Europe. More specifically than Skelton, he condemned the machinery of "secret diplomacy" and excessive nationalism and statism as major causes of the outbreak of hostilities. These, he argued, had been the conditions that had spawned the particular evils of German militarism. And like Skelton too, he urged Canada's complete commitment to the "liberation war of humanity."[5] Both men supported the war wholeheartedly but on the condition that its causes must remain the basis for the democratic nations' war aims. In this way, they were firmly in the vanguard of those who saw the war as demanding the preparation for a "new era" once peace returned and who argued that North America's environment was the likeliest venue for that new era.

If successful prosecution of war demanded post-war reform in the international world, it also meant further attention to reform at home, at least according to O.D. Skelton. This he made clear in a 1915 survey, "Canada in Wartime," prepared for the British journal, the *Political Quarterly*. Here Skelton reiterated his complete, if conditional, support for the struggle for "political freedom and international honour." He then listed the domestic problems – assimilation of immigrants, debate over national autonomy, readjustments to the national economy – that remained potent factors in determining the nation's capacity to respond effectively to the crisis at hand. Within the nation, then, the wartime entente was temporary. After the conflict ended, the internal as much as the international ramifications of "freedom" and "honour" would need to be addressed. "Sordid revelations of political corruption" in wartime Ottawa and especially Winnipeg, both involving the awarding of government contracts, only served to underline the importance of domestic regeneration. In this fashion the war was a kind of catalyst to stimulate, for example, the ending of the "evil of the patronage system." Skelton also argued that both Canada's and other democracies' fate depended upon avoiding the "danger of the war after the war." For Canada, averting this danger meant the "triumph of real democracy." For the world, it meant "the achievement of a sane international organization and of co-operation in trade." To Skelton, therefore, the war did not simply raise hopes about a better post-war world. Rather it demanded attention to the social and economic and political problems of the nation. Like Stephen Leacock with his concern about "the unsolved riddle of social justice," Skelton thought that there simply was no alternative. Unlike Leacock, he reached this conclusion five years before the armistice, the Bolshevik revolution and the Winnipeg strike had so pricked the former's social conscience.[6]

Critical of the existing party system, Skelton assessed the proposals for its reconstruction which were so plentiful during these years of Populist and Progressive unrest in North America. He was mindful, however, of the danger in emasculating parliamentary government though wrong-headed reforms. After 1910, Skelton advanced his own suggestions to strengthen the party system and parliamentary government by rethinking the relations between citizen and state. Although he was not sympathetic to the wholesale importation of American Populist reforms, Skelton praised the western Grain Growers' Association for its attempt to force Canadians to think about political reform. Still, he rejected its proposals for the "initiative" and referendum-legislation, the "recall" procedure, judicial review, and a reformed Senate with veto powers. He also drew on the example of Jacksonian democracy (which he saw as the "defeat of democracy" in the United States) to warn against the subversion of parliamentary democracy. The British political system was superior in a number of ways to republicanism, as no less an authority than President Woodrow Wilson had admitted. Like Adam Shortt, Skelton argued that "concentration of responsibility was the sheet anchor of democracy." The flaw of republican democracy was the absence of a link between legislative and administrative responsibility. Skelton's goals were to strengthen parliamentary responsibility and to rebuild political-party accountability.

In one discussion of so-called direct democracy, Skelton concluded that "whatever accompanying changes in political machinery or in public life are urged, the one essential safeguard must lie in the character and force of our representatives in parliament. Weaken parliament's power to pass laws, which possibly the electorate may exercise as well, and you weaken its capacity to do the many tasks which the general electorate cannot even attempt. Make a parliamentary career less a prize for ambition, and the men who will fill the seats in parliament will be little likely to make a stand against this corroding menace to our national life." The "corroding menace" was patronage; the need to revitalize parliamentary government was overwhelming. Skelton did not reject the referendum or popular initiative as consultative and educational aspects of a new politics. His restrained commitment to Populist reform shows that Skelton was a traditional liberal in his satisfaction with the powers of parliament but a radical democrat in his insistence on the importance of popular consent in democratic politics.[7]

Commission government was the great panacea devised during the Progressive era in the United States. More so than Populist nostrums, this favourite idea of middle-class reformers was coolly received by Skelton and others at Queen's. Skelton saw the 1908 proposal for a tariff commission as a means to screen by economic obfuscation the essentially political calculations about the tariff rates which government alone should face. As he put it, the Canadian Manufacturers' Association aimed to enshrine mathematicians and accountants as lobbyists. An administrative board would only obscure the essentially political considerations of tariff making. Skelton was willing to accept a tariff board by 1911, but he thought that it should have only investigative and not judicial powers. It was true enough that the "new burdens" on government demanded new approaches to government. Moreover, imperfectly effective market forces were being rejected as a sufficient regulator of economic institutions. But the choice of administrative boards – Ontario's boards of railway and municipal commissioners were perfect examples – was only a "confession of the failure of representative institutions." These boards, Skelton continued, became courts rather than administrative bodies because they were independent, unaccountable interpreters of the laws. Because they subverted the British democratic tradition of legislative authority and responsibility, such irresponsible and quasi-judicial agencies, to use J.A. Corry's phrase, were a very dangerous alternative to the renewal of the legislative capacity to govern.[8] Skelton must have appreciated the irony of loyalist-minded Tories applying American schemes to British institutions and thereby threatening their very existence.

The danger of such an overthrow of parliamentary government was also foreseen by William Swanson. He, however, was concerned that the courts were the chief agencies usurping the functions of the legislatures. The possible destruction of anti-combines legislation was a major case in point. Swanson warned that, if court interpretation effectively annulled legislation, it was imperative that the legislators modify the laws so that both the intent of the particular legislation and the supremacy of the legislative branch were sustained. With this position Skelton was in full accord, as he made clear in his assessment of the Lemieux Act and his critique of European social-democratic proposals for governmental commissions. These concerns were not shared by Adam Shortt, whose faith in administration and legislative draftsmanship apparently was unshaken. Moreover, he actively sought a degree of administrative autonomy which at least implied that the quasi-judicial role of commissions did not unduly trouble him. To be fair to him, Shortt's strongest advocacy for the independence of the Civil Service Commission was conceived in line with the commission's subordination to the Treasury Board, a body of responsible politicians. Yet even here Shortt was seeking to strengthen the executive branch of government, conceived as a kind of coalition of cabinet ministers and senior public servants. Skelton and Swanson, on the other hand, did not accept the quiet subversion of parliament by administrators that Shortt leaned towards any more than they

accepted the intrusion by the courts into the intention of the legislatures. The latter was, admittedly, a confrontation Shortt had sought
to avoid in the case of the Industrial Disputes Act. Nevertheless, the
concern of the younger scholars with legislative supremacy was a
significant difference, and not only of emphasis.[9]

While "progressive" reformers in Toronto such as Professor Morley
Wickett and the undergraduate Frank Underhill welcomed Canadian
adoption of commission government in cities, the Kingstonians
resisted. However, it was left to the professor of government at Harvard, Shortt's former student William Bennett Munro, to deliver the
most systematic refutations of the commission idea. In the pages of
the *Queen's Quarterly* and at the inaugural meeting of the Canadian
Political Science Association, Munro supported Skelton's position
against American- or European-style reform. Munro's theme was
argued most succinctly before the political scientists. "Power linked
with responsibility is never dangerous," he concluded, "power
divorced from responsibility is always dangerous." This concern for
the responsibility of governing officials and suspicion of non-account-
able administrators was a theme that Skelton was to use as a spring-
board for further attacks on the reality of party politics in Canada.[10]

In pointing to the dangers of measures inappropriate to the parliamentary system, Skelton also raised some larger issues about the
approach to political reform in Canada. First, the Canadian parliamentary system must be properly understood and its characteristics
preserved if reform was to be effective. The parliamentary system
was potentially superior to a congressional one in its "smoother" link
between public opinion and legislation. In that way, parliamentary
government was indeed democratic. The relations between the legislative and executive branches, the supremacy of the legislature, and
the subordination of legal to legislative authority were the key determinants of this superiority and its democratic capacities. According
to Skelton, even President Wilson was trying to adjust his administration in light of the greater efficiency of responsible parliamentary
government. Skelton's whiggish faith did not lead him to admit to
any intrinsic or actual superiority in the practice of politics in Canada,
let alone Britain – the lurid corruption that oiled the party system
was as condemnable as anything the United States had produced.
Still, drawing the sting of any ultra-imperialists in Canada, Skelton
could reject their ill-informed adoption of European and British
reform ideas partly because they always seemed to do so only by
using American adaptations of such reforms.[11]

This raises another major point. Notwithstanding all the descriptions of Skelton as an anglophobe and republican, he was in truth a
more committed "parliament man" than most of his contemporary

critics of Canadian government. Yet he did not simply trumpet the superior virtues of "British" politics. He as readily examined French, German, Italian, or even Swiss politics for their legislative innovations as he did the American or British systems. His assessments and suggestions were based on the premise that informed understanding was the essential point from which the critic must proceed. In light of a correct understanding of how government worked, it was clear to Skelton that Canadian parliamentary government could work effectively only if it was exactly like the British system. That is, parliament must be supreme indeed. It could not remain vulnerable to the whims of judicial-committee distortions or British parliamentary interference any more than it could accept the interference of Canadian courts or the irresponsibility of the executive. Skelton's many arguments for the autonomy of the Canadian parliament were not deduced from a temperamental anglophobia but rather from the depth of his immersion in the traditions of parliamentarianism. Other factors than this touchstone might be examined in the making of Canadian political machinery, he allowed, but the common denominator of Canadian politics must be the parliamentary system. If the Canadian system was to work as well as it might – and that was very well indeed – then no illusions about its merits or its machinery could be held. Skelton sought reforms that were aligned with that fundamental need to understand the parliamentary system.[12]

Reform of the political system remained to be plotted. This reform, Skelton argued, should take several directions. To begin with, the place of the politicians in legislatures and parliament must be strengthened. As mentioned earlier, he thought that parliamentarians should undertake a far more active scrutiny of governmental business than they had to that point. Unlike someone such as Shortt, for example, Skelton did not rest content with effective government alone. Shortt's Palmerstonian dictum – that as long as there was someone to "hang," concentrations of power were proper – was not Skelton's final assessment, though he liked to repeat it. In his view, parliamentary politics could not be strengthened unless parliament itself became more reflective of groups in society. To this end, proportional representation might well be brought forward. Skelton thought that the kind of over-representation of the majority party, a problem that existed in seven of the nine provincial legislatures by mid-1916, was a condemnation of the first-past-the-post and single-member constituency system. Instead, he suggested that huge constituencies elect eight to ten members according to the percentage of votes for each party. While admitting both the pros and cons of this suggestion with his usual balance, Skelton added a warning:

"A strong, effective, responsible opposition is as essential a part of the machinery of British parliamentary government as a strong, effective responsible cabinet." Accordingly, Skelton suggested a second reform, this one in recognition of the "necessity" of parties. He urged that parties become more broadly based and financed. Publication of all contributions and wide public support of the parties were therefore essential. A parallel with public support of churches was relevant, with the proviso that publication of contributions was necessary given the public interest in parties.[13] So, in both these directions, the salvation of parties, politicians, and parliament was likely. And, if Skelton was sacreligious in comparing political to religious support, it was for the good reason that he thought the reform of democratic politics was essential considering the primary importance of politics to society.

As Skelton often admitted, however, strengthening existing parties and parliament was not enough. Through 1917 and 1918 the disturbances of racial, sectional, and party conflict under the pressure of Canada's war commitments had virtually wrecked traditional party politics. This wreckage, according to Skelton, was both beneficial and dangerous. It was dangerous in the sheer exclusion of many groups – farmers, French Canadians, and labour – from national political life. It was dangerous too in the further excesses of "order-in-council" government and "errand-boy Parliaments." Still, there was some hope in that the problems of the present system were now clear. The most obvious problem demanding attention from politicians and the public was the party system, the key mechanism of political life. Political parties must be reconstituted, but on the basis of the representation of all segments of the society and the emergence of real policy differences between the parties. Skelton, who has tended to be regarded as a Liberal Party apologist on the basis of his biography of Laurier and his employment by Mackenzie King, was disarmingly frank in discussions with Laurier himself about the need for such a revolution in the party system. While defending with vigour Laurier's opposition to conscription in 1917 – for reasons that will be examined below – Skeleton was satisfied with the shake-up of partyism that flowed from the 1917 election. Like the 1911 campaign, it had forced a reconsideration of the basis of political loyalties and political thinking. More specifically, it had made clear the need for reconstituted parties.[14]

At the invitation of Norman Lambert of the Canadian Council of Agriculture, Skelton drafted an electoral platform of thoroughly reformist bent. This platform, he quickly explained to Laurier, was necessary if the farmers were to be heard by the rest of the nation and if democratic parties were to emerge from the present flux. (The so-called Farmers' Platform was, of course, the campaign document of the Progressive Party during the 1921 election.) Skelton could justify his aid to the Progressives in another way too. He often argued that mere mechanical reforms – whether of voting or party finance – were not enough to alter the characteristics and conduct of politics. The populace itself must be prodded into recalculations about why and what it should demand from politics. Here the influence of informed and reasonable citizens was very important.

Skelton's call for the "break up of the old parties," which he published in July 1918, made clear this link between the individual and society.

"Hope for independence lies in the break-up of the old parties and the rise of new groups. The individual member will count again during the process of reshaping of parties; individual Liberal-Unionists, for example, will find themselves in strong strategic positions so long as they are deciding on which side of the hyphen to come down. The organized manufacturers, the organized farmers, the organized veterans, will all be represented, and in addition, it may be hoped, informed and independent study and discussion of public issues throughout the country will create a spirit which should help to check party slavishness and make Parliament a real forum."

In his enthusiasm and idealism, Skelton looked to the representation of all significant interests, key individuals, and the general public in the renewal of the party system. But he also wanted studious and informed activists.[15]

This political catholicism was an essential means to deal with one of the more insidious dangers of the political order in Canada. By the end of the war, Skelton was commenting that either "principles" or else "class" and "section" would be the basis of parties. He saw too many dangers in social confrontation, disunity, and corrupt government to await with eagerness the triumph of class and section. The sorts of economic questions that were now the purview of the state meant that organized economic interests necessarily would be an ominous force indeed. Hence Skelton made an appeal to Canadians to "escape from group selfishness" by a "liberation from individual selfishness." Group domination of party and government was as abhorrent and undemocratic as domination by individuals, and that applied to any group, businessmen, workers, or farmers. Skelton, accordingly, looked to a reorientation of what might be termed the political consciousness and political ethics of Canadians. The same kind of rethinking that was apparent in men's and women's approach to economic calculations in an interdependent society must be applied to the world of politics. Ironically, perhaps, Skelton's analogy between parties and churches was doubly relevant. Given the history of sectarian as well as sectional conflict in Canada, loyalty to class, section, or party had to be tempered by some ecumenicalism if social or political harmony were ever to prevail. The shaping of politics must, therefore, involve a change of spirit and mind. In the political world, of course, the ecumenical council was parliament. The ecumenical spirit, then, was a concept of national interest, precisely the sort of concept that had been so disastrously ignored during the war.[16]

In a tentative return to the paternalistic views of Adam Shortt, Skelton suggested that individual MPs were potentially the best ecumenists. He sought the expanded influence and leadership of key individuals – and, of course, the concentration of responsibility in the legislature. More important, however, was the need to increase parliament's sensitivity to the new conditions and forces which were shaping Canada. That novelty demanded open political parties reflecting the many interests that made up the nation. In his emphasis on the role of individuals and the democratization of party politics Skelton tried to find a way out of the dilemma of parliamentary democracy which Adam Shortt among others had noted. Shortt, somewhat naturally, had concluded in 1907 that parliamentary government could reflect public opinion wisely or act as the agency for special interests and that parliamentarians might be selfish or public spirited. Such a neutral, fatalistic position was not Skelton's. Putting it another way, whereas Shortt's biographical subject was the Benthamite administrator Lord Sydenham, Skelton's was the Gladstonian parliamentarian Wilfrid Laurier.[17]

CANADA'S INVOLVEMENT in the European war imposed heavy and ultimately terrible burdens on the nation and its people. Fulfilling the Canadian government's considerable military and economic commitments in the face of these burdens led, by August 1917, to the adoption of military conscription. This policy was one of the most significant measures of the nation's war effort. It contributed to the fracturing of the post-Confederation party system. It polarized relations between French and English and between rural and urban Canada in a thoroughly ugly and dangerous manner. The conflicts that raged over conscription led Oscar Skelton to further assessment of the nation's political and social life. Conscription raised questions about war policies in general, about Canadian political parties and political attitudes, and about the relations between ethnic groups and between the individual and the state. Each of these questions, Skelton thought, was momentous indeed.

As early as mid-1916, casualties in the Canadian Expeditionary Force had reached high levels. In July 1916 Skelton noted that the strains of simultaneous economic and military commitments were beginning to tell in the declining numbers of recruits. These strains were not easily borne. Skelton argued that a couple of major questions had to be addressed by the policy makers and the nation. Could the economic war effort be kept up if more and more men were diverted to the army? Even if it could, would the citizens of the nation countenance the number of deaths and injuries which the war of attrition caused? Demographic and sociological factors would be very significant in determining the limits of the Canadian people's willingness to follow their government's and the Allies' lead. Disproportionate enlistments from the four major regions of the country were notable already. Problems with the coordination of government policies were apparent in the inefficiency, inconsistency, and scandal that detracted from the general dedication and commitment. Skelton's sensitivity to such social factors as ethnicity, age, and marital status, competing agricultural and industrial priorities, and, of course, flaws in the execution of government policy all indicated how remarkably incisive he was in his approach to the problem. (Indeed, to read Skelton's analysis of 1916 is to see the enucleation of virtually all the issues with which an academic history such as J.L. Granatstein and J.M. Hitsman's *Broken Promises*, written sixty years later, would deal). Once conscription was made law, moreover, Skelton returned to his examination and foresaw even greater danger to the Canadian political community and to the Canadian ability to achieve its economic and political commitments. In reaching his conclusions about these dangers, he was to study and find wanting most aspects of Canadian political values and behaviour.[18]

The most dangerous factor revealed by the government's movement toward conscription was that public opinion was badly divided and confused by the war. To Skelton, this was the fault of parliament in general and especially of the Borden government. Under the pressures of war, the government had not provided coherent policies in managing the war effort, let alone effective leadership and instruction of the populace. Parliament itself, including the opposition, was a mute body in its responses to cabinet initiatives. Canada's ambiguous national status itself was also partly to blame for this unfortunate passivity.

The Borden government was woefully ill-informed about the conduct of the war until the prime minister demanded formal recognition of and consultation with the dominions. At this point, Borden's absence from Canada and penchant for executive action still left the nation and its parliament somewhat unclear as to what was to be done and how Canada would be affected. At length, the tremendous pressure of both Great Britain and English Canada on Borden to sustain Canadian commitments at home and in Flanders propelled the government towards its 1917 reorganization and its adoption of conscription.[19]

Skelton was commenting on precisely these dilemmas in his criticism of the government and in his reflections on Canada's status during the war. He also followed with alarm the shift of English Canada towards an almost unlimited commitment of human and material resources. Finally, he noted distinct and dangerous schisms in the country. The first fault line was between parliament and public opinion. The rising toll of casualties and increasing demands for *matériel* were matched both by considerable public determination and by the people's sense of the politicians' failures to translate determination into action. In other words, Skelton's own increasing criticism of parliament was similar to the sort of criticism of government leadership that precipitated the coalition of 1917. Unlike the advocates of coalition, however, Skelton's aim was a return to strict party government, government under an effective party system.

More obvious than the first political faultline was another national schism. Within the nation by mid-1916 there was a looming gap between the commitment of "English" Canada and the increasing isolationism of French Canada. This national fracture deeply affected public debate and Skelton's own thinking during the last two years of war. But Skelton also believed that a break of sorts between the parliament and the people had preceded the racial conflict.[20]

It was Skelton's contention that the problems of Canada's war effort, which had grown with Canada's commitments, were reflected in a schism between the government and public opinion as well as in a threatening conflict between French and English in Canada. The government acted to reform itself and to rededicate the nation's war efforts after January 1917; the Military Service Act, the War-Time Elections Act, and the Unionist coalition followed. But in the process, the schism between French and English was exacerbated by the government's policies. Skelton also added that the distinctive immigrant population posed a challenge to the legitimacy of democracy and indeed to the unity of the Canadian nation. He reminded Canadians of the need to deal with this group's concerns too. In light of his delineation of the main components of Canadian society, Skelton's concerns about the party system and parliament were closely tied to his anxiety about a potential breakdown in social and political cohesion. The danger was clear that Canada's political parties and government no longer reflected the needs and wants of the social and cultural groups that made up the nation. The war also showed that relations between society's main groups and institutions were very fragile and that social cohesiveness was highly dependent upon the national government's capacity to bring about reconciliation. For Skelton, conscription was a crisis in the nation's existence.

Skelton tolerated the tremendous enthusiasm within English Canada for the war, but he had one major reservation – support for the war was not based on an authentic "Canadian" interest in the matter. Just as Skelton had interpreted the economic success of the nation after 1900 as the result of indigenous factors – material and human – so too he saw the basis for effective political life in the supremacy of the Canadian parliament and its evaluation of Canadian interests and needs. Read in this light, the problem of military recruitment was an entirely Canadian one because only Canada's national needs and capacities (economic, social, and political, he kept reminding his readers) should be the basis for evaluating any policies. The demand of many English Canadians for conscription was unacceptable because it revealed a blindness to these calculations. Skelton argued that the Ontario origin and British birth of most of the vociferous pro-war advocates prevented them from understanding the national interest. He was not opposed to the policy of conscription *per se*. If nothing else, his sympathy with Charles Godfrey's pro-war, pro-conscription *bonne entente* movement should dispell any illusions about Skelton's commitment. When conscription became a mania of English-Canadian public opinion, Skelton's position on the issue was determined not by any ingrained opposition to state compulsion, let alone by any serious opposition to the war, but rather by conviction that the primary calculations of Canadian interest and the sentiments of all elements in the nation must be met before conscription should be implemented.[21]

Following his own prescription, Skelton analyzed the nation's economic and social capacity to provide an unlimited army. Here alone he found grounds to oppose conscription. Since proper analysis also demanded examination of the opinions of all segments of society, Skelton also looked at the French-Canadian opposition with care. He began with the observation that that opposition was very much the counterpart of what he termed (privately to Laurier) "Tory extremists" or (in print) "Ontario imperialism." An ingrained Quebec nationalist extremism, as blind and as detrimental to the national interest and its proper calculations as Ontario's imperialist hysteria, was a potent force that must be faced by the Canadian public and political leaders if the war's conduct was to be successful. Skelton took considerable pains to point out the flaws of Quebec nationalism, just as he had done in the case of Ontario imperialism.[22]

In his 1916 survey of the war effort, Skelton expressed concern over the extremism he saw growing in Quebec. "Quebec, then, is neither British nor French," he acknowledged. "Well and good, if it were Canadian, but unfortunately a large number of its people prefer to be merely 'Canadien'," he warned. He went on to offer one of his most important statements about French-English relations by examining Quebec nationalists.

Claiming to be Nationalists, they are essentially Provincialists. In addition to the factors already considered, the dominance of farming, the small proportion of British-born settlers, the lack of racial sympathy with Britain and of intimate ties with France, weight must be given to the open anti-recruiting campaign of Mr. Bourassa and his lieutenants. There is no question that their influence has been wide-spread. Mr. Bourassa defends his attitude on various grounds ... [but] the real underlying reason [is] the exaggerated sense of provincial and racial separateness, the desire to keep Quebec apart and exclusive. There are elements in Nationalism which deserve sympathy and support – the insistence upon facing frankly our future imperial relations, the emphasis upon Canadian interests, the demands for a recognition of the right of French-Canadians to take a full and equal share in shaping the country's policy. But there are also elements full of danger to national unity and achievement – the failure to recognize our present imperial and international responsibilities, the unjustified suspicion of the aggressive designs of English-speaking Canadians, and the ultramontanism which desires to keep the French-Canadians a race apart to avert the danger of heretical contamination. It is not without significance that Olivar Asselin, a fervent nationalist but liberal Catholic, is raising a battalion, while ultramontane clergy are foremost among Mr. Bourassa's supporters.[23]

The dominant tone of this passage was its firm rejection of the nationalist position. The war was legitimate but a different perspective from the truculent and erroneous opposition to war commitments was necessary. Interestingly enough, Skelton saw the roots of Quebec "ultra" nationalism in Catholicism. Again, a Protestant-born Canadian such as Skelton (his ancestors were from Ulster) would be well versed in the dangers to which sectarian conflict had and still led. His hostility to such religious exclusionism was clear, even if his remark might have been misconstrued. Yet in 1916 and later, Skelton made an argument that relieved the provincialists in Quebec of

extravagant charges concerning their loyalty or of primary responsibility for their extremism. He saw the nationalism of wartime
Quebec as a reaction to the initial aggressive and exclusivist Anglo-
Saxon imperialism that had led in the first place to the erosion of
Quebec support for the war. More, the provincialists in Quebec were
reminding Canadians of their mutual problems, such as the incon-
sistencies of Canada's national status and the anomalies in the status
of French-speaking Canadians. In each of these ways Quebec nationalism was as important and positive as it was for its opposition to
conscription itself.[24]

Supporting Skelton's assessment of the nationalist doctrines – and
all of his discussions of Canada's wartime burdens – was a conception
of a national interest that was to him the primary factor of Canadian
society. This has already been noted in chapter 3, where it was
suggested that Skelton saw the reality of autonomous Canadian needs
and wants as the brute force that defied the impractical, illogical
schemes of Canadian imperialists. Similarly, in the case of Quebec
nationalists, Skelton was concerned about their lack of contact with
what might be termed the reality of the larger world in which they
lived along with other Canadians. So disengaged, the nationalists did
not face up to the war's demands, the legal and moral commitments
that had drawn Canadians to Europe, and the values and goals of
other segments of society. From Quebecers, in short, Skelton
demanded submission to a larger "Canadianism." But he demanded
the same thing from Ontario's imperialists. In both cases, beyond the
narrow visions of exclusivist groups was a unifying means to calculate
national interests and needs. This latter must include all the people
and institutions that shaped Canadian society. Since "Canadianism"
was never fully defined in Skelton's writings, it may be dismissed as
a vague, vapid patriotism. Yet "Canadianism" was a presupposition
in his many assertions about national autonomy and the national
interest. Skelton's concept of Canadianism can perhaps be thought
of as the social embodiment of the holistic, social-scientific understanding that he elsewhere derived from his theoretical studies. To
put it another way, just as there was a holistic approach to understanding social phenomena, so was there a holistic means to conceive
the nation. The "common Canadianism" of Skelton was a kind of
synthesis of the many social groups and economic and political elements that made up the nation.

Skelton's stance regarding the nationalisms of Quebec and Ontario
showed that he regarded a literal synthesis of the two positions as
necessary. The synthesis of imperialist and provincialist nationalism
was dialectical in that it was a progression beyond the two previous

"theses." Only if certain key changes were made in Canadian political and economic life, however, could this synthesis come about. Here Skelton's conception of historical progress was important in leading him to foresee a particular evolution of Canadian history. Skelton's synthesis, therefore, was unlike Shortt's conciliatory and neutralist model of mediation between two equally valid or invalid positions. It was also different from Laurier's political efforts, which were aimed at a similarly neutral racial harmony. Skelton accepted Bourassa's criticisms of Canada's ambiguous national status and the role of French Canadians ("there are elements in Nationalism which deserve sympathy and support") just as he accepted imperialist dissatisfaction with annexationism or isolationism ("a distinct advance over colonialism"). But he was clear in disengaging himself from both these positions because of their equally unacceptable consequences. Each would lead to the isolation of the races from one another and each would lead to the subversion of the legitimate features contained in the other's aspirations. Their mutual exclusivism indicated their basic failing. Finally, each was a limited and flawed account of the forces that shaped Canadian society and determined Canada's national interest. These forces comprised the Canadianism which Skelton saw as the new synthesis of national interest. They were also a "necessity" that Canadians must recognize if they were to gain any control over their fate. In conclusion, and in response to a question raised in chapter 3, Skelton wished to avoid the mere pacification of race relations and the doldrum-like equilibrium of French-English dualism. He sought to submerge them both in the interests of a larger conception of national life and the nation.

Skelton reinforced this point in his discussion of the "language issue" which became so important during the war. That question, linked as it was to the problem of denominational education rights, was, from the 1890s through the 1910s, a momentous one in the politics of the country, involving federal-provincial jurisdictional battles, deep party splits, and racial conflict. Skelton's survey of the issue of language rights indicated his awareness of the subtleties of constitutional rights and concurrent powers as well as racial-linguistic conflict. His plea for the resolution of disputes was based on acceptance of the constitutional factors. He therefore made it clear that he regarded English as the basic language in eight of the nine provinces. Yet, while he accepted the subordination of the French language, he simultaneously called for acceptance of French *and* other languages as subsidiary languages of instruction among the minority groups in the eight English-language provinces. Similarly, although he accepted Ontario's Regulation 17 as legitimate, he considered Quebec's nobler toleration of English-language education as preferable. He also made it clear that French was not simply another foreign language. It had historical, sociological, and commercial as well as limited legal (because of its place in parliament and federal courts of law) claims in provincial educational systems.[25]

Three lessons emerged from this survey: Skelton did not wish to be limited by literal application of education rights; he sought a spirit of toleration in granting French prior claims as a universal second language but also in admitting instruction in other minority languages where ethnic minorities were strong; and, perhaps most important, he wished to submerge the whole issue by an appeal to a new conception of a common Canadian future ("the nation of the future in which all share in common") as the basis for educational language policy. In the last respect, Skelton's position on minority language rights and ethnic groups was a major application of his idea of national life and national interests. These groups' place in Canada could be assured only if the older dualism was in fact overcome. French-English dualism contained monstrous implications of exclusivity and intolerance for the new ethnic population, just as it did for the French and English themselves. If the French in Manitoba or the Ottawa valley could attest to the results of the ambiguities of dualism and constitutional guarantees, so could the "Ruthenians" and Germans of the Prairies and so might the English of Montreal.[26]

Skelton's reliance on a "synthesis" to dislodge provincialism and imperialism and his aspiration for a "Canadianism" to replace the duel of the races led back to his concerns over the problems of Canadian political and social life. These concerns led him to posit an alternative concept of "national interest" and a particular course of national evolution which would together resolve the problems inherent in the present order. A future in which evolved a new conception of Canadian interest and new institutions of national political life was Skelton's own ever-receding goal of human and historical purpose. To that extent, it may be said that he did not elaborate on his concept of "Canadianism" because he did not conceive the need for blueprints of a future whose development he had already denoted in broad outlines. He had already noted a tendency of economic evolution in the "moralization" of the laws of economics through a recalculation of human wants that was both mindful of all men's and women's needs and of the complexities of their valuations. Similarly, he had already noted the democratic forces that would create a truly participatory party system and parliament. He had long since concluded that the logic of Canada's political evolution meant the autonomous sovereignty of parliament. Finally, the impetus of war meant that the people and government agreed to work toward a political future which guaranteed each of these developments.

He concluded his assessment of Canadian public finance with a similar assertion. "The War," he wrote,

has made us realize the immense latent reserves a nation possesses, the unused forces of labour, the added strength that organization and education can yield. The root of the matter is to get more people and more efficient people. If we can put foresight in place of drifting, and teamplay in place of class and race and sectional wrangling, there is no reason why we cannot merely carry the burdens of war, but grapple with the greater tasks of peace, in the effort to enable Canada to take its full share in the work of the world and to make our country in reality a land of freedom and equal opportunity, land where every many and woman among us will have a fair chance to share in the decencies and comforts and the possibilities of development that hitherto been restricted to the few.[27]

Reform of the economic and political order was demanded by the circumstances of war. Indeed, it was essential if one accepted Skelton's analysis of political and economic forces and his reading of Canadian political history. The synthesis of "Canadianism" that Skelton offered was no more or less than a component of his view of the nation's and the world's historical evolution. This view was not simply utopian because it was rooted in the economic, political, sociological, and psychological forces that were paramount in the society. It was, however, a distinctly communitarian vision because of its firm equalitarian, democratic, and cultural orientation.

We can see this communitarianism in the way that Skelton held to the defence of "minority rights" within an enveloping "Canadianism." Skelton opposed both military conscription and a "steam-rollered uniformity" on this basis. As he asserted to correspondents such as W.L. Grant and to readers of the *Queen's Quarterly*, mere majoritarian sentiments (or the aims of a new "common Canadianism") were not a justification for isolating and overwhelming the basic aspirations of minority opinions or groups. This position he defended not on the basis of the primacy of the individual or even of a Laurier-like social and political mediation strategy. For Skelton, like Adam Shortt, John Watson, and most political thinkers in Canada, began with the premise that the state's sovereignty and even existence were primary and the rights and indeed existence of individuals were secondary.

His considered and lengthy discussions of this theme showed how firmly he held to his statism and how he had made room for dissent within the emerging Leviathan. In October 1917 he argued with such conscriptionists as his colleague James Cappon. "While the doctrines of the absolute sovereignty of the state are being sapped by theoretical criticism and practical developments," he wrote, "it may be agreed that no *a priori* limit can be set to the power of the state over the citizen. The state, or the majority, has the right to compel us to pay taxes, or to serve in arms, or to join and attend a certain church." Up to that point the Cappons of Canada would have agreed with Skelton. But he extended his discussion by questioning, "whether, however, any or all of these courses would be expedient is another matter. This only can be assumed in advance, that the state has the power, but that the expediency of using the power must be proved in any specific case if the general presumption in favour of liberty, born of hard and long experience, is to be overcome." The limits of authority were in the first instance practical. But as he had argued in July 1916, these limits were also derived from political theory. He asserted that it "cannot be said that it is beyond the power and right of the state which makes all pay to make all fight, nor that the individual liberty should not be sacrificed if necessary to preserve national liberty. Yet so great is the danger of giving governments power to send millions to battle by compulsion, so great the need of compelling them to have a cause that will appeal to the honor and the zeal of the mass of men, so vital to the working of democracy is the habit of self-determination, so contagious is the Prussian spirit of ruthless oppression of all individual liberties, that this sacrifice of the principle which has been the glory and justification of the British people in this war should be made only as a last resort."[28] In both cases, the state existed, as Adam Shortt claimed in Aristotelian terms, "prior to the individual." It was an embodiment of the people who made up the nation. Skelton himself did not entertain thoughts of rebellion or options of secession. Indeed, he admitted the authority of the state to compel its subjects' obedience. But, equally, there were, to use the phrases of John Watson, "universal principles of reason ... humanity and sympathy" which the state could not disregard without triggering a dangerous if not revolutionary social breakdown.[29]

Skelton made no such direct appeal to natural law, though he certainly apprehended a kind of natural law in the very historical evolution of the political and economic order. That evolution was a progressive unfolding of the potential of all people to derive increasing satisfaction from social relations. In this manner, Skelton could appeal to the rights of the "mass of men," to the vitality of self-determination for all voters in democratic society, and to the state's own agreement to sustain these rights. Skelton's liberal reformism and his aim of a "common Canadianism" were the consequences of his apprehension of general principles of historical evolution towards human freedom and equal opportunity. That is, Skelton's reformist aims were rooted in what he discerned as a potentially ordered and purposeful world system. People's conformity to this world system was guaranteed by the changing power of social forces over individual aspiration or wants. Just as individualistic capitalism or Canadian colonialism were displaced by the evolving economic and political orders, so too the individual was swept along by the currents of history and social evolution. In this regard, Skelton's affinity to Marx's systematic approaches to the science of society and his understanding of historical evolution were reflected in his argument that the state and the individual were subsumed under the larger forces acting on society. Further, the organic/communitarian basis of society was at the core of his subordination of the state and the individual to these larger forces as well as in his perception of their indissoluble, mutual interrelations.

Skelton established a kind of obligatory relation between human beings and state based on their permanent links to each other – links that, in turn, rested on the peculiar social values and political economic relations of people in contemporary society. Skelton drew on these links to set out limitations on the power of the state and the actions of individuals or majorities at any particular time. Given the climate of war and the dominance of the problem of conscription, it is not surprising that Skelton concentrated on the problem of state and majoritarian domination. But, as his assessment of economic questions shows, his arguments equally could be applied to the problem of individuals, especially rich and powerful ones, and their obligations.

One limitation on the state and on majoritarian rule was prudence, or, as Skelton called it, "expediency." Isolating minorities was dangerous. It could lead to social breakdown and ultimately threaten the very existence of the society and state. A second limitation was even more significant. There was at the present time the considerable danger that the state could overwhelm that "general presumption of liberty" which was a principle of parliamentary government. Skelton did not, of course, adhere to a concept of social contract, just as he did not accept that the general will was a final authority. What he did adhere to was the conception of progressive historical evolution in which, in the case of the Canadian people, certain expectations unfolded through time. At the present, "freedom and equal opportunity" were the determining characteristics of that process, as seen in economic goals and political evolution. Furthermore, these traits were the avowed aims of the state.

The implication of Skelton's ideas concerning the role of the state was also important. Since freedom and equal opportunity were the state's priorities, the main *raison d'être* of the State was – in Shortt's terms – to provide for individual personality. To Shortt, first security, later individual fulfilment, and finally freedom were consequences of the state's existence. Skelton certainly appears to have taken up this view in asserting, for instance, that the "hard and long experience" of Canadians now led them to demand freedom and equal opportunity from the contemporary state. It also led them to demand full political and economic autonomy in the international world. Similarly, in both the capitalist order and the parliamentary system, historical evolution had led to precisely this kind of reassessment about expectations and rights. The state's contemporary role at least implied an agreement on the purposes which it served. It also set out certain limits on the demands the state could make on the individual. Again these limits were both prudential (being based on social forces and the currents of history) and, as it were, contractual (being based on human expectations). In both cases, their abrogation led to social upheaval. There was no abstract appeal to right or to revolution here: there was simply the hard experience that certain forces could not be ignored or else society and the state would face the opposition of some of its members and, of course, experience considerable failure in achieving its larger goals (for example, economic progress and political freedom). (Exactly this denial of limits to national action had led Wilhelmian Germany to war, in the estimation of John Watson.) In the end, Skelton could even hint that the evolution of state and society was leading to a practical and theoretical refutation of the nineteenth-century notion of the "absolute sovereignty" of the state. In any event, there was a "necessity" above both individual and state in Skelton's reckoning that was the basis for the only freedom which the individual could ever gain.[30]

To Skelton, the importance of the national community in Canada was the assumption leading him to oppose the polarization which resulted from conscription. Of course, if that national community was not inclusive of all peoples in Canada, one might simply regret the conflict but pursue the larger cause: this was what the conscriptionists did. Skelton did not follow their example because he was not willing to countenance the fracturing of the larger national community in any serious way; consequently, he might be said to have distinguished the community from the state. This distinction was to be seen in the general tendencies of economic and political history as the "necessity" which was beyond society. Skelton's theoretical statism was thus limited indeed. Majorities must recognize minority rights. More important, the state must recognize human rights and aspirations. Skelton could draw on an account of the state that limited its role on the basis of its obligations to all members of the community because, at this point in history, those obligations were to freedom and equal opportunity. To return to his concept of the Canadian nation, we may conclude that Skelton did not simply adopt a concept of a higher "nationalism" above the competing British-Ontario and French-Quebec variations of that faith. The limitations of each limited form of nationalism must be displaced by the inclusive communitarianism which he termed Canadianism. That was the only purpose which the sacrifice of the Great War could itself justify.[31]

THE REFORM AND DEMOCRATIZATION of Canadian politics was necessary and indeed likely for two broad reasons. First, prudence on the part of the state and dominant groups in society dictated accommodation with those groups and individuals who were denied full representation. Skelton's discussion of socialism and its alternatives had also been based on the premise that it was highly dangerous to alienate those not satisfied within the capitalist order. Similarly, his discussion of Canadian politics was suffused with the threat that those who were excluded might grasp at power and in so doing seriously disrupt society. This raises the second point: people had rights which they could demand from their society. In claiming that people properly could make demands based on such rights, Skelton was suggesting that certain abstract rights indeed existed as a result of human beings' participation in a liberal-democratic and capitalist society. Skelton was, for instance, as insistent as Shortt in demanding a recognition of the mutuality of rights. He appealed to the generous sentiments of Canadians by pointing to the "common Canadianism" which might emerge from greater mutual accommodation and respect for rights. (While it has been suggested that no strictly nationalistic basis supported Skelton's communitarian appeal, he certainly did appeal to nationalist sentiments in his broader hopes for reform in the "nation of the future.") Whereas for Shortt, rights were but the result of hard bargaining in the social order, for Skelton such rights were the very fruits of participation in that order. In fact, a number of these abstracts rights could be enumerated. Minority cultural rights, historical language rights, and even rights to dissent were part of the evolving tradition of liberty. They comprised part of the way of life which Canadians were fighting the war to defend. Skelton's reasoning about the potential of the contemporary social order led him to conclude that, in political as in economic terms, certain rights were the essence of men's and women's expectations. In sum, both reasons of prudence and claims of rights constituted a force that would bind Canada to reform itself as a democratic society.

Skelton's democratic faith and his commitment to political means to bring that democracy to maturity contrast with the dominant trend of his contemporaries among American political scientists. As explained by the historian of political science, Bernard Crick, Americans tried to remake politics as administration and to blunt the force of democratic sentiment by emphasizing the "scientific" and deterministic nature of public life. In this regard Skelton's understanding of the potential of humankind and his commitment to the greater democratization of politics fall into what political theorist C.B. Macpherson describes as the "developmental democracy" devised by John Stuart Mill, L.T. Hobhouse, A.D. Lindsay in Britain, and John Dewey and Robert McIver in the United States. To Macpherson, this developmental democracy represents the conception of liberal democracy that provides for the most generous interpretation of human freedom and potential as well as for a sufficient extension of state authority so as to provide for those "positive liberties" that late-nineteenth-century liberals such as T.H. Green sought. Macpherson contrasts this conception with a later version, "equilibrium" democracy, which he sees as far more limiting of human freedom and potentials. Exponents of equilibrium democracy are the self-same scientists of politics against which Crick directs so much criticism.[32]

O.D. Skelton supported Adam Shortt's attempts at political reform through the architectural or surgical reshaping of government. He also devised his own arguments favouring political means to bring about that reform. Aiming at the democratization of Canada, he looked to political means to achieve his goal. He found those means in the expectations of people and in the flexibility of the political system. He identified both moral arguments, or subjective factors, to convince Canadians to reorient their politics, and practical arguments, or material and objective factors, to force that reorientation. As a result, he was willing to use state power to create a democratic economy as well as a democratic politics.

7 Financing a Liberal Democracy

The aim of Canada's Ministers of Finance can be defined as
plucking the most feathers with the least squawking.

O.D. Skelton

During the 1910s Shortt and Skelton continued to deal with the
economic issues confronting the nation. While the Great War was
very important in sharpening their positions, the economic consequences of that conflict related to broader questions. The distinctly
cyclical nature of the Canadian economy, so apparent in the faltering
economy from 1912 to 1915, remained a central problem, disturbing
both the nation's well-being and the economist's explanations. In
addition, the role of government in the economy emerged as a dominant issue by the end of the decade. The attention Shortt and Skelton
gave to these areas led them to refine their understanding of Canada's political and economic possibilities.

ALTHOUGH IMMERSED IN administrative struggles after 1908, Adam
Shortt did not lose his place as a senior Canadian economist. When
the Carnegie Endowment planned a multi-volume series on the economic impact of the Great War, the editor, Professor David Kinley
of the University of Illinois, asked Shortt to write the Canadian
volume. He agreed readily, a sign of both his intellectual resiliency
and his under-employment at the Civil Service Commission. The
resulting study, the last substantial book he actually wrote rather
than compiled, was something of a summation of his economic
thinking in a couple of ways. It was yet another chance for him to
devise the new economic "principles and practical deductions" that
the New World's distinctive "experience and policy" demanded of the

economist. It was also a reiteration of the major themes he had developed concerning Canadian economic and fiscal development, particularly its vulnerability to international factors and its institutional weaknesses in responding to the economic cycle.[1]

To Shortt, the war was a sharp economic blow but hardly a surprising one. Indeed, Canadian economic history revealed a continual pattern of vulnerability to international disruptions such as war and to highly cyclical patterns of development. Shortt had long argued that war had had a major impact on Canadian development during the nineteenth century. In his banking articles he had explained how the indigenous commercial economy had originated in the War of 1812, and he had noted as well that the economic cycles of prosperity and depression had been shaped by variable foreign markets often caused by war.[2]

In the same articles, Shortt had also deprecated the roles of the Canadian and even the British governments in comparison with private financial institutions in the nineteenth century. Governments generally were baffled by humanity's propensity to speculate and by the economic phenomena of over-production and inflation. He claimed that the banks were powerful enough to put "the brakes on the train of general business when the movement or when external financial conditions, upon which the progress of the country depends, are in a state of uncertainty." Nonetheless, both the weaknesses of the state and the dependency of the national economy suggested to him that Canada must live with highly variable economic cycles.[3]

As he pieced together his account of the Canadian economy, Shortt did note a few factors that contributed to measured optimism about its long-term stability and prosperity and about economists' capacity to understand its peculiar operations. The first was the bountiful environment of North America and the example of the United States, each of which showed the potential for economic strength and prosperity. A second factor was found in Canada's experience as a focus for foreign investment. Twice in Canadian history, during the 1850s and 1900s, railroad construction had provided a crucial stimulus to economic development. In both cases the construction boom had occurred because of the "rapid absorption of foreign capital," an absorption that was similar in magnitude on a per capita basis in each era. In both periods, the stimulus of railroad investment led to major industrial development, population growth, urbanization, and finally to speculative hopes and practices. The ultimate result was the seemingly inevitable depression and readjustment through "cheap living and hard times." Foreign investment had the simultaneous benefit of fuelling the period of growth and therefore creating the conditions for economic boom that tended to lead into depression. Canadian control over the larger economic forces, let alone the specific international sources of capital, was very limited.[4]

Shortt discerned a third conditioning factor in the experiences of the Canadian economy in the periods after the railroad booms. The contraction of the late 1850s was corrected by the American Civil War and the economic recession after 1912 was eased by the impact of the Great War. Thus international political crises benefitted Canada. Shortt did not say whether he thought such crises were as inevitable as the business cycle, but he often repeated his remark that the prosperity of the Canadian farmer depended on a good crop and a foreign war. Canada, in sum, was remarkably open to international economic and political influences.[5]

From these reflections, Shortt drew both the obvious lesson about the rather limited degree of control over Canada's economy and the more theoretical one that the Canadian experience was the basis for generating distinctive economic theory and practices. In his 1916 presidential address to the Royal Society of Canada, Shortt struck a theme typical of the historical economist. He argued that, even if the Canadian economy could not move towards autonomy, then the Canadian economist could escape the intellectual dependency on theory and policy based on the vastly different experience of Europe. It might be surmised that he was thinking of the Canadian reliance on tariff policy as the major piece of intellectual borrowing, but a number of other issues were playing on his mind as he considered how to respond to the Great War.[6]

Initially in 1914 Shortt was struck that the war simply perpetuated the ambivalent heritage of the Canadian economy. As he suggested to the Canadian Club in Toronto,

The war has simply ... enforced a condition previously existing and which necessitates financial readjustment. Fortunately, that is easier for this country than for most other countries whose trade was more extended and on higher and more specialized lines. Already the war has increased the value of some of our chief products, such as grain and food supplies generally. Had more of the immigrants who came to Canada gone into farming, as promised, there would have been a better proportion between rural and urban population than at present and manufacturing would have been better supported by a prosperous agricultural class than by stranded city builders and those dependent on them. Borrowed capital built the cities and carried them beyond present needs. Now, agriculture and other natural industries must restore the balance.[7]

Still suspicious of industrialization, uneasy about urban development, and dissatisfied at the speculative basis of the previous decade's growth, Shortt blamed the entire system of immigration, tariffs, and boosterism for Canada's economic jam. At the same time that he posited that the nation should have moved more slowly towards expansion of its population and industries, he drew some solace from the facts that industrialization was relatively incomplete and the national economy was still open to the stimulus of foreign demand – even if that stimulus was a war. Nonetheless, the war placed burdens on the productive and financial capacity of a Canada dependent on foreign capital as well as markets. More ominously, Canadian troop commitment meant that the demand for manpower and *matériel* further increased the pressures on the economy. In short, the European conflict was not quite the tonic for Canada's economic ills that earlier wars had been. While Shortt nowhere ever actually challenged the propriety of Canada's military commitments, he certainly expressed his foreboding about their cumulative economic impact.

This precise problem was addressed in Shortt's Carnegie Foundation study, *The Early Economic Effects of the War upon Canada*, completed in 1917. Reiterating his longstanding views, Shortt examined the broad pattern of Canadian economic growth and the specific cycle that the war intruded upon. In one sense, he explained, the war interrupted the usual necessary contraction that would have corrected the speculative excess. This adjustment should have led to more balance between "natural" and artificial industries, between those based on Canada's environmental advantages and others developed by tariffs and bonuses. But the war quickly led to renewed growth and the same kind of "abnormal and artificial" expansion that had occurred before 1912. There then ensued the familiar pattern of urban and industrial expansion at the expense of more stable rural and agricultural development. In addition, the nation continued to rely on British and American markets for over 90 percent of its trade, with the curious twist, Shortt noted, that American imports grew as British fell and exports to the United States fell as those to Britain grew. Both the enormous debt that resulted from wartime sales and expansion and the narrow dependency on two markets, and one of them chiefly a wartime one, added to Canada's vulnerability.[8]

Although he reached a gloomy diagnosis, Shortt managed to extract a hopeful prescription for the future. He did not modify his premise about the continuing cyclical basis of the economy and at one point he likened these cycles of capitalism to the climate in their uncontrollable if all too predictable course of development. He did

not think that the manufacturing capacity built up from war industries would generate a new base for the nation. But what did strike
him as encouraging was the huge expansion of a domestic capital
market and his estimation that this market would form the basis for
self-stabilization during what was going to be a trying period of
readjustment after the war. The Borden government's policies, therefore, were important and highly praiseworthy in finding new areas
of taxation and in pushing Canadian business to the domestic capital
sources revealed in the Victory Bond campaigns. Unlike Skelton,
Shortt was not a true believer in the transformative power of direct
taxation, but he was certainly intrigued that government fiscal policy
had led to such a remarkable change in the tax base. Canadian policy
had stimulated the redirection of capital flows necessary both for the
war and for the anticipated post-war crisis. In so arguing, Shortt
pointed towards the role of government in at last helping to coordinate and even direct the nation's economy in an effective fashion.[9]

When the war ended, Shortt prescribed a typical nostrum, arguing
in the *Monetary Times* that the nation must continue to save and not
borrow in order to meet its capital needs. Avoiding excess foreign
borrowing emerged as a key lesson of the war. He saw many benefits
from this policy as the basis for both government and private policy.
"If," he wrote,

we can continue to meet the larger part of our domestic requirements, in
the way of industrial capital, from the savings of our people, we shall not
only benefit our international position financially, but save ourselves from
possible embarrassment during the more or less stringent readjustments
following the war. The unpleasantness of being involved in international
financial complications over which we have no control, is a very serious matter.
On every account, therefore, in meeting the requirements of our domestic
reconstruction and essential future expansion, and in avoidng the consequences of being dependent upon the foreign money market at a very critical
period, we must frankly face the necessity of raising from our domestic
resources, the greater part of our capital requirements during at least the
period of reconstruction both at home and abroad.[10]

Beyond this somewhat nationalistic exhortation, Shortt was moving
away from simply warning about Canada's economic openness
towards seeking the means to control the economic storms that were
approaching. As with most areas of human experience, in his view,
control over the economic environment was certainly limited. But
greater self-reliance was a means to assert the amount of control that
could be mustered. He suggested that government policy could

actually be effective in leading the nation towards a more self-sufficient and therefore more stable economic base.

Discretely lobbying on behalf of his proposals, Shortt sent his *Monetary Times* article to the finance minister, Thomas White. In other letters to White and W.G. Gates of the Department of Public Information, he reiterated his call for policies encouraging massive domestic savings and investment. He praised the government for already adopting measures in that direction, hoping that the average citizen would be allowed even greater access to government bond issues. He did not mention to government officials the criticisms he had made to American correspondents about about what he saw as disgraceful tax break granted to institutional investors during the Victory Bond drives.[11]

The circumstances that Canada found itself in and were giving rise to new economic policies – depression, war, and reconstruction – prompted O.D. Skelton to devise elaborate proposals for changing the basis of economic policy. The 1912 depression challenged Skelton's praises of Canada's economic potential. "The world's fairest land of promise" was no Eden after all. But like Shortt, Skelton examined the aftermath of the downturn and the effects of the war not so much as specific problems but rather as the latest manifestations of the disabilities faced by an economy remarkably open to external influences, vulnerable to cyclical disruption, and of course still in the midst of the change from agriculture to industry. In other words, the very factors Skelton had identified as crucial to Canada's economic evolution required further scrutiny. He conducted this new work still concerned about the capacity for social justice and human fulfilment that capitalism in Canada provided. Indeed, his studies after 1912 led him to bold suggestions for fiscal interventions aimed at controlling the Canadian economy and providing major economic redistribution.

In a 1915 survey, "Canada in Wartime," published for the *Political Quarterly*, Skelton showed how dismal were social and economic conditions in depression-prone Canada. Like Shortt, he attributed a series of economic symptoms to the basic problem of a post-boom downturn. The great economic expansion after 1900 imposed a number of strains, the most obvious being immense debt charges against the new transcontinental railroads and the federal government and the rise of protest movements among farmers. Economic difficulties led to tremors within the party political system, and there also remained the social challenge of assimilating the "undigested" mass of immigrants drawn by two decades of expansion.[12]

As if these economic and social burdens were not serious enough, Skelton warned British readers that Canada's participation in the war had created problems. One was to decide how far Canada should commit itself to the military war effort. Already there was disagreement between Quebec and the rest of Canada about the size of the Canadian military force. Another was to face the economic consequences of organizing for war. Economic readjustment following a decade of frenzied growth was made much more difficult by the prospect of major additional commitments to the war effort.[13] Thus, even while he identified the social and political issues seething beneath the surface of Canada in the first year of the war, Skelton suggested an economic origin to most of them. To him, the solution of national problems required fundamental reconsideration of national economic policy.

There was also an underlying assumption to his many essays written between 1909 and 1920: that the chief means to attack the problems the nation faced was through government policy and leadership. The extent to which this assumption reflected Skelton's basic understanding about the impact of government had been revealed in his examination of socialism. But his presupposition about the primacy of government policy emerged forcefully when he made policy proposals concerning the war. Throughout the conflict, he emphasized that the solution of Canadian problems would come about only by concentrating on economic issues and by emphasizing the role of government.

These two points, of course, were fundamental to Skelton's thought. He had scrutinized the workings of the capitalist system and found an economic substructure beneath the social and political edifice. He had also argued at length about the crucial role of the state in supervising all matters affecting the nation, including economic ones. As a corollary, his defences of capitalism and democratic government had plumbed the capacity of democratic political institutions and capitalist economic forces to accommodate calculations of economic and social need based on the wants and aspirations of the whole population and not just dominant interests or classes. Given all of this, he was being perfectly consistent to emphasize public policy as central to the resolution of the economic, social, and political problems Canada faced after 1914. In contrast with Adam Shortt, Skelton was optimistic that the economic order could provide assured and stable prosperity through a rapid orientation towards greater state intervention. Accordingly, he examined fiscal policy in relation to two subjects. The first was the potent impact of taxation on the economy, and the woeful misdirection of tax policy in Canada. The second was the potential impact of government expenditures on economic and social stability.

PRIOR TO THE WAR, SKELTON had pointed out that Canadian tax policies were central to the economic-development strategies of both national and provincial governments. Unfortunately, these policies tended to be inequitable, ineffectual, or contradictory. To illustrate this contention, Skelton considered the case of natural-resource industries, where the goal of more efficient exploitation was a crucial issue. The apparent contradictions between conserving natural resources and efficiently and voluminously processing them within Canada could readily be resolved, he suggested, by more effective provincial-taxation systems.

In his commentaries on resource development, Skelton was quick to condemn both preying speculators and bounty-giving governments. Each of these groups either hindered productive exploitation or shielded the inefficient producer. He noted that the federal government as much or more than the provinces had been prone to encourage such waste and inefficiency. Skelton summarized the typical Canadian practice as "taxing Peter to bonus Paul." The national government, he argued, should retreat from promoting resource development so that the provinces could act alone to devise an equitable development policy. (On this matter, Adam Shortt also favoured provincial taxation of revenues accruing from resource companies and especially the revenues of "public service corporations" or utilities, although he suggested a possible national assessment.[14])

Taxing net revenues, rather than the usual practices of collecting fees from the volume of production or assessing gross revenues, Skelton argued, would ensure the best possible use of resources and the highest degree of processing within the provinces. In the case of forestry, the Ontario provincial practice was already a model for other provinces to follow. In the mining industry, where no such reforms were in place and where the export of semi-processed raw materials was the norm, the identified alternatives seemed to be provincial operation of mines or else federal taxation of exported minerals. But neither constitutional rigidities nor social traditions made these alternatives likely. Hence the provinces should revise mineral taxation along the lines of the forest industry.

The creative approach of taxing net revenues – an approach Ontario followed in the case of pulpwood – promoted efficient use and processing while also enriching the public treasury. The latter advantage of taxing net revenues was important because it meant that development occurred with the maximum return to the people of the province. And Skelton lectured that the people, not only the entrepreneurs, had a claim to the rewards gained from exploiting public resources. Provincial taxation would thus doubly ensure the best development, and by "best" Skelton clearly meant development in accordance with the public interest. Equity, as much as efficiency, was central to his early taxation proposals.[15]

To Skelton, taxing corporate and personal incomes contained remarkable social and economic possibilities. In a number of eloquent analytical studies of public finance written both before and during the war, he made the issue of taxation a fundamental consideration of public policy in a democracy. For instance, in 1912 he linked the current methods of taxation and the provinces' partial fiscal dependency on federal grants to the wholesale corruption that so disfigured the spending of public money in Canada. The dispersal of federal subsidies since Confederation was one more example of the pork-barrel in Canadian politics. Behind the system of grants was the dependency of the national government itself on inequitably raised, irregularly collected, and inconsistently available indirect tax sources, particularly the tariff. Even though the provinces had tried both to balance their own budgets and to reform their politics by imposing taxes on corporate and personal incomes, they were not in a position to generate the necessary root-and-branch reform. Moreover, the imminent expansion of federal fiscal responsibilities – reflected in expanded grants for the newly completed railways and in the commitment of funds for a Canadian navy – was about to overwhelm the existing provincial claims on revenues. This unavoidable expansion of federal spending made it essential to generate more revenues, to collect them more equitably, and to devise more effective controls on spending at both levels of government.

Such considerations led Skelton to warn that fiscal pressures on governments, financial pressures on individuals and businesses, and public opinion about fiscal and taxation policy alike were contributing to a potential crisis over public finance. "There is probably no civilized country to-day in which the rich man pays a smaller proportion of taxation than in Canada," Skelton lectured. He went on more guardedly, stating that "how equality should be secured is a matter for separate consideration; land taxes should be left to provincial and municipal gathering; an income tax levied at the source, a tax on corporations, or possibly a Dominion tax on inheritance, supplementing the provincial taxes, where they exist, in the manner customary in the French system of taxation, must be carefully studied."[16]

Though quietism currently reigned in the area of fiscal policy, Skelton saw dangers ahead. He concluded one discussion with the angry warning that "for the present the mounting customs revenue makes it unnecessary for a Finance minister to hunt for trouble by finding new sources of taxation. But the time will come, and come soon, when the railway king and the land baron and the cement knight will be required to pay their fair share of the cost of the policies they so largely shape."[17] A pointed reminder that public policy as well as public revenue were currently controlled by big business, this remark revealed Skelton's fundamental belief that liberal democracy must change dramatically. It was also a veiled accusation against the financier Sir Max Aitken, who had routed Queen's chancellor Sandford Fleming over control of the cement industry.

The sheer expansion of government and the tenets of individual and governmental efficiency and equity in collecting and disbursing public money sustained Skelton's broad goal of wholesale reform of fiscal policy. He was happy to begin with the issue of the income tax. Skelton favoured the national government as the one to institute tax reform, not because he saw it as more progressive than the provinces, but because of the increasing range of its fiscal obligations and its national jurisdiction over individuals and corporations. The national government was most in need of a reformed fiscal base and its actions would have the greatest impact on the Canadian people. Of course, Skelton's earlier analysis of the 1911 reciprocity proposal had confirmed his dissatisfaction with the dangerous discrimination that was built into national tax policy. It may also have been axiomatic to Skelton that national projects such as the railways and the navy had priority over provincial goals. Whatever the reason, Skelton's intense concern about public policy, including both the actual selection of policy and the ethics of choices made, led to his insistence on a new structure for Canadian public finance. As he wrote in April 1914, "Both to assure responsibility and care in expenditure, and to put the biggest burdens where they belong – on the broadest backs – the income tax must come."[18]

With the coming of war in August 1914 the severity of Canada's public-finance mess and the intensity of Skelton's proposals increased in tandem. Already having explained that the national treasury was vulnerable owing to the conundrum of extensive obligations and fragile revenues in the post-1911 depression, Skelton warned that the extraordinary cost of any significant war effort was going to force a reconsideration of fiscal policy. Since the expense of war would be so great and the cause itself was so compelling, the war made tax reform essential rather than simply important.

The obvious way to address the coming fiscal crisis, Skelton pedantically if foxily explained, was to control Canadians' spending by increasing taxation. In so doing, the national government might at last begin to close what he saw as the longstanding and ever-widening gap between national expenditures and national revenues. But if this was an obvious prescription, Skelton admitted that raising taxes and cutting or controlling spending was a noxious mixture. Canadians already were taxed at a high rate, higher proportionately than the British, although not as highly as the Americans. Similarly, the traditional method of taxation – taxing the consumption of goods via excises and tariffs – was also pitched about as high as the capacity to pay and the need to consume imported goods would allow. As for government expenditure, cutting spending during a period of war and instability would have disastrous consequences for the nation's railroads and war industries. Moreover, both the continuing pressure of patronage politics and the ineffectual administration of government services made difficult any rational scrutiny or effective control over government priorities and policies. Together, these problems and conditions – long since identified by observers such as Adam Shortt as well as his protégé – showed that the obvious cure for the nation's fiscal ills would not likely be adopted.[19]

Yet Skelton concluded that the serious situation would actually lend itself to treatment and to a more rather than a less radical one in the bargain. He argued that new sources of revenue were available and could be used to address the domestic and international fiscal problems Canada faced. Furthermore, he suggested that, if new sources of revenue were likely to be deemed politically and socially acceptable because of the present crisis, they would lead to a number of major and possibly permanent changes to the entire basis of the national government's fiscal and hence social policies. Having extended his ambitions so far, Skelton carefully surveyed the sources of government revenue. In the first place, Canadians should rethink the types of taxation. Rather than choose between "direct" taxes on incomes and "indirect" taxes on expenditures, they should begin by identifying three sorts of taxes. These were taxes on "property," "income," and "expenditure." This was a typology slightly unusual in public-finance theory at that time, but it was not unknown. Skelton borrowed his nomenclature from the British new liberals and from British Prime Minister Asquith's and Chancellor of the Exchequor Lloyd George's tax reforms, implemented as part of the ferocious British debate over the "People's Budget" in 1909. (In Britain, the governing Liberals had proposed to finance major social-insurance and income-maintenance programs as well as land redistribution by extensive land and income taxes. But in Canada, as Skelton and Shortt often noted with mischievous intent, rhetoric about the vital British inheritance seldom led to action based on British practice in economic areas.) Nonetheless, to identify as clearly as possible the broad sources of revenue – land, expenditure, and incomes – was to redirect thinking about how to allocate taxes, and not the least to identify both land and income as major tax sources, favoured panaceas long held by Populists and Progressives trying to defeat the tariff for two generations in North America.[20]

Skelton then considered the effects and the effectiveness of the sorts of taxes available. If they rethought the types of taxes, Canadians should also apply the appropriate tests to each. The effectiveness of taxation, Skelton explained, should be measured by its effects on overall economic output and efficiency, on government revenue, and on the individual's ability to pay. According to this standard, the property and expenditure taxes currently favoured in Canada were flawed. Most obviously, each had limited potential for expansion because Canadians faced such high levels of property and tariff taxation already. Existing taxation was so high that the possible expansion of either form of taxation, moreover, seriously threatened to curb the incentive and even ability to purchase property and manufactured goods on the part of the vast majority of Canadians. Perhaps the greatest immediate flaw in taxes on expenditure was its effect on economic output. Tariffs demonstrated an inverse relationship between revenue gained and economic productivity. Taxing and too often impoverishing consumers in order to nurture inefficient industries, the tariff was a self-imposed economic burden, and no more so than during wartime, when economic output must be most efficient. Finally, taxes on expenditure and on land were unfair in their application and effects on individuals. These taxes were imposed haphazardly, especially in the cases of property taxes, and indiscriminately, in the case of tariffs. They therefore were not fitted to perhaps the chief political test of taxation, its fairness based on the individual's ability to pay.[21]

Having rejected traditional taxation sources, Skelton explained why the income tax was the most appropriate base of public revenue. He argued that income taxation would transform the economic circumstances of government, foster a greater public understanding of economic policy, and subtly alter the essential political and economic relations between the people and their governments.

The income tax would raise revenues for governments without harming economic activity of individuals and businesses. At last public finance would be freed from dependency on duties and tariffs that were notoriously variable given the cycle of international trade. Moreover, simply diversifying the revenue base strengthened the fiscal position of government. The effect of income taxation on business and individuals was also a stabilizing one. Arguing that the income tax would affect business and individual taxpayers only after they had reaped the benefits of their enterprises, Skelton portrayed it as a salutary means to raise revenue and encourage enterprise at the same time. Unlike tariffs, excises, and other expenditure taxes, the income tax reflected rather than interfered with the process of economic expansion or contraction. Consequently, it avoided the unfortunate effect of expenditure taxes to reduce peoples' necessary financial resources and thus to depress their capacity to spend and propensity to earn. Clearly, Skelton envisioned modest rates of taxation.[22]

By encouraging a clearer understanding of the revenue areas and potential open to the levels of government in Canada, income taxation could repair the fiscal imbalances and distortions among provinces and between the dominion and the provinces. Under the existing approach, Skelton explained, there existed both inter-governmental competition for revenues earned nationally, especially by businesses, and significant differences in the potential revenues of the provinces. Property/resource taxes were practically limited to the provinces, of whom several had little or no resource revenue. The major source of income, the tariff, was limited to the national government. This division perpetuated provincial dependency on Ottawa and a wide disparity between the provinces. Moreover, it sustained the waste and corruption of politically biased grants. Only the taxation of incomes could provide effective amounts and a simple division of revenues for both levels of government. Skelton looked forward to a higher degree of equality in the capacity of governments to get money and a greater extent of administrative effectiveness in the actual collection of revenue. Extensive inter-provincial disparities and political favouritism could at last be minimized if not avoided altogether. Finally, the actual administration of the system would be revolutionized. Skelton suggested that an agency such as the Wisconsin Tax Commission, a body composed of dispassionate academic and business experts, was the model for effective adminstration. But national collection and distribution of the income tax would be successful only if key administrative reforms were implemented.[23]

Another merit of the income tax was that it would turn citizens into watchdogs of political and fiscal responsibility and indicate that public finance was conducted on the basis of fair treatment of every individual in society. Skelton explained why this social benefit was important. "In common with all direct taxes," he pointed out, the income tax had "the merit of being felt. So long as we pay our taxes without knowing it, so long will extravagance be at a premium. An income tax would not entirely stop our taxes going up but at least it would impose some drag on the aeroplane – if an aeroplane is a correct simile for taxes, seeing that aeroplanes usually come down some time or other."[24] Rather than countenance what Skelton once termed bribing people with their own money, the income-tax-paying citizen would strongly tend to scrutinize very critically government spending. Skelton even went so far as to propose that not just inefficient but even unnecessary public expenditure would be condemned. Thus, the administrative reform demanded by the shift to the income tax would be supported by a populace newly cognisant of the impact government spending had. In these circumstances, public support and awareness of the benefits of any particular program or project would be widespread. The apathy and cynicism of the public about the roles of government would at last be reversed.

Not just economically sound and politically responsible, the income tax would lead to significant social benefits. Skelton noted that "mere considerations of justice" had seldom been important in Canadian politics. But the war meant that "necessity adds its weight to justice." One benefit of the income tax was, he explained, that "it is on the whole the fairest test of ability to pay." This was both good economics, Skelton explained, and socially desirable:

Under a system of taxation which takes expenditure as the basis [of taxation], the poor man ... is compelled to pay more heavily than the rich. His expenditure swallows up practically all his income, while the millionaire, even with lavish personal and household outlay, usually spends only a minor fraction of his income. Again, given two men with the same income, one with a large family to support and another with no one but himself to spend for, a system of taxation according to expenditure, such as we now have in the dominion, piles up the greater tax on the back of the man who already has the greater burden. A straight income tax of the older type would tax both the same; an improved income tax, as modified by recent developments, notably in the United Kingdom and the United States, would take the size of family into account in determining the amount of exemption allowed, and thus equalize the burdens fairly.[25]

Discounting the tax revenue available among lower- and middle-income groups (most other economists, like successive ministers of finance, would note that there were more poor and modest-income families than millionaires), Skelton pressed the case for shifting taxation to those who could afford to pay more and exempting those who could not. Taxation should not harm the individual's capacity to purchase necessities, let alone his or her ability to live with some comfort. Fairness was also economically sound and politically benefical, since a progressive income tax ensured that a larger pool of tax money was available. Skelton made the claim that there was a relationship between efficiency and justice in the reformed tax system. While he did not assert that the most efficient tax was necessarily the fairest one, he did suggest that the fairness of a tax must be central to evaluating its efficiency. In any case, economic efficiency was sufficiently malleable to include tenets of fairness such as the ability to pay. To Skelton, the exciting prospects of tax reform lay precisely in the melding of economic and political efficiency and social and political justice. Here was policy embodying the central tenets of liberal democracy that he had struggled to elicit from his analysis of socialism.

Despite persistent difficulties in financing the war and in spite of Skelton's hope for the reform that wartime demands would generate, the government moved hesitantly to change the tax system. In the February 1917 budget, Finance Minister Thomas White finally implemented a highly limited individual income tax system at the federal level and revised the year-old tax on the war profits of corporations. In both areas, White worried about this federal intrusion over an area previously left to the provincies, although almost all provinces avoided income taxation, especially of individuals, and he justified the new venture not on economic grounds but solely as a means to share the war's burdens. He said nothing then or in his later book on war finance about the economic benefits of direct taxation of incomes, though he admitted that corporate taxes raised large revenues.[26]

Skelton certainly welcomed these tentative moves towards tax reform. Again he emphasized both the economic and the more ethical reasons for reform. He repeated his warning that the consequences of the unreformed fiscal system were becoming dangerous to both the war effort and the post-war future, and by the latter he meant the economic as well as social environment of the nation. He also noted that cumulative financial burdens were made worse by inefficient administration and war profiteering: excessive government borrowing and continued dependence on indirect taxes were together impoverishing the "poorer classes" in Canada. Moreover, fiscal policy was actually contributing to the price inflation that was so seriously threatening economic productivity and well-being as well as social stability. Skelton pointed out the compelling need to meet present and future national obligations out of the wealth already available in the country. He therefore concluded that Thomas White should immediately expand the income tax and corporate war-profits tax in order to make them the major sources of public revenue. He also warned those most capable of paying taxes, highly profitable businesses and highly paid individuals, that they must pay their full share or the long-term effect of the war would be socially, politically, and economically disastrous.[27]

To support these contentions, Skelton undertook a second careful study of federal fiscal policy in 1917. Here, besides reiterating many of his strictures of 1915 about government finance, he sharply criticized the policy of paying for the war by massive borrowing, as in the acclaimed and successful Victory Loan project. Because of its inflationary effect, such a policy placed the immediate burdens of the war on the mass of the populace, particularly harming poorer people who were least able to absorb price increases. Also, borrowing had the long-term effect of transferring the ultimate financial responsibility for the war to future generations, and as a result seriously risked future economic recovery and future expansion of government activity. Shackling future generations negated a central premise on which the war had been justified, its contribution to a post-war reformed society. Finally, massive borrowing was ineffectual in sustaining war production simply because it was guaranteed by government. The borrowed capital was not carefully scrutinized, as it would have been by project-oriented investors, nor was its pay-back related to the efficiency of the industries created. For these reasons, it was essential to find an alternative fiscal policy to one that only "imperfectly" encouraged immediate production and added so many problems as a consequence.[28]

For Skelton there remained the compelling alternative basis to its wartime fiscal policy, the income tax. By 1918 the government had already acknowledged the inadequacy of traditional revenue sources for the extraordinary expenditures of the war. However, neither the ill-conceived direct-taxation measures implemented in 1917 nor other means to diversify government revenue – savings-stamp programs and savings-bond drives – met the tests of economic efficiency and social and political fairness that Skelton posed. An elaborate progressive income tax program did.

Skelton proposed to tax incomes beginning at $1,500 at an unspecified graduated rate and corporate taxes on a similar basis. But both must be at higher rates than the government had dared to implement. (In contrast, White's first tax was on individual incomes above

$2,000, with rates varying from 1 to 8 percent and he taxed corporate incomes at the rate of 4 percent. Even as late as 1919, White's direct taxes produced only 3 percent of the federal government's revenue.) Skelton illustrated with some rough calculations how the problems of war finance would be resolved by wholesale direct taxation. He reminded his readers that the unfair burdens of the war, such as inflation and profiteering, would be addressed by tax reform. He also claimed that the implementation of an efficient income tax program would demand a new standard of administrative competence and parliamentary responsiblity. Thus, in a more direct fashion than Shortt's administrative reforms, Skelton's tax reforms would ensure that government policy making would be transformed. Treasury control, a competent civil service, and rigorous parliamentary scrutiny of the administrators were each necessary consequences of the new tax system.[29]

In conclusion, the economic, political, and social effects of an income tax would meet the tests that Skelton applied to government tax policy: revenue-gathering would become socially equitable, economically efficient, and politically responsible. In meeting these tests, tax reform was a major application of Skelton's general principles about the purpose and development of government policies. A new tax system addressed the social and political as well as the economic pressures for reform that had been built up in a nation that had experienced both the great economic boom and the immense burden of the war.

IF TAX REFORM WOULD greatly alter the sources of public finance, it would also change the direction of public spending, prompting a reconsideration of what programs and services governments would provide. Skelton, for his part, examined both new areas for government spending and the broad approach to expenditures that tax reform generated. The purposes of stabilizing and enhancing government revenue were not just to make governments richer, to tax the wealthy, or to resolve federal-provincial conflict, although these were important enough. Skelton also wanted to enable the state to meet the burdens of coordinating Canada's economic war effort and adjusting to the post-war, post-expansion economy.

Skelton's purpose in his fiscal-reform proposals was nothing less than to remake the state as a central coordinating agency capable at last of shaping the economy. This was a new departure. It was not simply a negative power of policy interference, such as the market distortion the tariff created, or the extraordinary power of intervention that could be grafted onto the governmental structure of Canada, as in many of the wartime initiatives.

For Skelton, there were important lessons in the positive and interventionist state that tax reform promised. One was that patterns of investment and therefore of the business cycle could be controlled to a considerable extent from within Canada so long as a key role for government was sustained. Skelton's reforms meant the fundamental renovation of state fiscal power to enable it to maintain sufficient revenues and expenditures. Thus government would direct rather than respond to economic circumstances. His entire critique of the role of government in wartime implied that government was already engaging in such direction anyway, but that it might as well do so effectively and equitably. In this regard the proposals were in part a response to Shortt's cautious search for effective government-led stabilization of the economy.

Another lesson of tax reform, Skelton thought, was that remarkable new directions for public expenditure were possible. The new initiatives for state intervention that he proposed – social-insurance and income-redistribution programs – were in accordance with his own earlier strategies for the fundamental reform of the political and economic order. Hence they were fundamentally the result of his broader inquiry into the role of the state and the redistributive and egalitarian potential of capitalism.

It was clear to Skelton that the investment patterns of the nation were changing as a result of the war. This was seen in the shift away from Great Britain as a capital source. With the decline of an overextended Great Britain, the United States had become the major foreign source of Canadian capital and would likely remain so in future. But even more important was the wartime discovery that Canadians could, as Skelton put it, "paddle our own financial canoe." While neutral enough in denoting these new developments, Skelton did so by making a couple of major points.[30]

First, he distinguished between the purposes of foreign and domestic investment. Foreign investment tended to be in industrial ventures and its role was generally to assist economic expansion in "virgin areas." In contrast, Canadian capital supplied the "ordinary needs" of commerce, by far the largest proportion of investment capital. Thus, while British and American capital certainly had facilitated the expansion of the economy, Canada's domestic capital sources and the national financial system sustained the distinctive Canadian economy. Secondly, to the extent that Canadians had been forced to plan and finance new industries, they discovered that they possessed major sources of capital, including investment capital. They also learned that government coordination of financial and industrial development was quite effective. As a result, they realized that Canada was now in a position to act in a self-reliant fashion economically as well as politically. Both greater domestic financial capacity and maturity and the political and administrative ability to coordinate the financial system, then, were legacies of the war.[31]

To a considerable extent, Skelton was merely supporting Adam Shortt's suggestion that Canada could mobilize domestic savings and profits and avoid the old solution of relying on external sources – borrowing and trade – for prosperity. Shortt had railed against the colonial economic outlook and reliance on borrowed capital as detrimental to Canada's economic security and long-term prosperity. Skelton echoed this argument in asserting that a larger amount of domestic savings could support a greater degree of domestic investment. Like Shortt, then, Skelton applied his conception of Canadian political autonomy to the economic sphere. Unlike Shortt, he had a more resonant faith in the capacity of Canadians to shape that autonomy. He looked to the healthy growth of indigenous sources of capital and he expected that economic policy would fully reflect the calculation of interests that in economics as well as politics was now Canadian-centred. To be sure, Skelton does not fit the late-twentieth-century definition of an economic nationalist. He did not seek barriers to capital or ownership, and he rejected the specious nationalist appeal of contemporary tariff-boosters. He was, however, decidedly nationalistic in formulating economic as well as political arguments that made Canada's interests and perspectives the primary factors shaping Canadian institutions and policies. He provided for efficiency as well as justice in the economic order by insisting on the national accounting of Canadian requirements.

Economic autonomy was in fact the only way in which the balance between efficiency and justice could be sustained. This was the case because only then could the concept of the public interest be called on to modify economic policies through the authority of government. Skelton's reformism, based on the key role of government and the recalculation of economic policies by gauging their effect on the entire populace, resulted from his prior concern with the efficiency and the justice of the economic order. In this respect he stood in contrast to contemporary innovators such as Robert Borden and Thomas White, who justified their reforms chiefly because of the war's importance. Skelton was also different from traditional political nationalists, for whom national autonomy was the end in itself of Canadian political-constitutional reform. For Skelton, the ends of efficient economic production and its just distribution came before the reorganization of government institutions and activities. He avoided the fetishisms of statism and nationalism alike, as well as the tendency towards compulsion that seemed to underlie each of these during the war.

In comparison, it is useful to examine the views of two other economists – Skelton's colleague William Swanson, and the McGill economist Stephen Leacock. Swanson revealed his essential conservatism and conventionality during the war by arguing that the British economy would remain Canada's major focus of investment and trade. Writing in 1915, Swanson did not deviate from his faith that the "financial power of the Empire" was unshakable, even if he did admit some concern about the war's disruptions of the open international economy. The subsequent closure of British capital sources must have shocked him, although he was in good company among economists. Perhaps his later appointment to the University of Saskatchewan led him to appreciate economic disruptions at least to agriculture and labour, which he had ignored in his wartime commentary. But even in 1920, he was willing to advocate the need for individual and governmental economy, price deflation, and increased productivity but not new methods or amounts of taxation. In fact, Swanson remained at heart a preacher of restraint. This was still his theme in his writings on the "way out" of the Great Depression, when he called for a general reduction in the standard of living as well as a return to a more rural and self-sufficient way of life and the gold standard as the means to world recovery. Admitting no crises, suggesting no innovations, Swanson offered only submission to the economic cycle.[32]

For his part, Stephen Leacock approached Canada's wartime economic problems by blithely advocating as much foreign borrowing and any other expansion of public debt as were necessary. To Leacock, no doubt about the availability of capital, British, American, or Canadian, was ever entertained. Perhaps his strident optimism in the early years of the war explains his shocked discovery after the armistice that Canada's economic and social structures were threatened by severe strains. He then advocated effective, comprehensive, state-supported social-welfare reform under various social-insurance programs. But he proposed to implement these reforms by the same kind of compulsion – the marshalling of national resources for an emergency – that had been necessitated by the wartime emergency. Leacock did not consider fiscal, administrative, or political reforms, let alone the reshaping of society, as pertinent to the achievement of "social justice."[33]

The second broad area that Skelton thought state economic direction could take was possibly just as innovative. It also showed not simply his capacity for creative and serious public debate but also his belief in the ameliorative powers of Canadian economic self-interest and self-direction. In papers written in 1909 and 1915, Skelton offered the outlines of a theory of "government expenditure in depression" that rejected the orthodox economists' approach to fiscal policy. The earlier of his accounts set out his theory in the clearest terms, although it was really only a note and not an extended discussion. To support a new approach to government spending during Depression, Skelton wrote that

the proper policy of government expenditure ... is exactly the contrary of that currently accepted. Government expenditure should serve as a flywheel to regulate the speed of the industrial mechanism. In times of prosperity, when the calls of private enterprise are draining the labor market, straining credit to the uttermost, and sending prices of materials skyrocketing, governments should as far as possible refrain from accelerating the speed. In times of depression, when private enterprise halts, when men and funds lie idle and prices fall, governments should push permanent work with all haste. The present system accentuates the violence and extent of industrial fluctuations, now retarding the recovery. The contrary policy, if consistently pursued by both national and local governments, would do much to avert crises entirely, or at least to mitigate their severity. The fact that prosperity usually involves abundant revenue and depression falling revenue, is no argument for making capital expenditure follow every fluctuation in revenue.[34]

The mechanical analogy Skelton struck was both a typical specimen of neo-classical economic writing, with its suggestion of the determinism of engineering and its specific allusion to Veblen's emphasis on technology, as well as a remarkable statement on the importance of the state. Using the metaphor of capitalism as an engine, Skelton pointed to the great power of the economic system and also suggested a subordinate yet important role for government. The "flywheel" derived its force from the primary engine but it in turn controlled that engine. Moreover, the very notion of the engine of capitalism reminded readers that the engine was a creation of human ingenuity and susceptible to human tinkering. Unlike Adam Shortt, who used a meteorological metaphor comparing the economy to the climate in its cyclical and ungovernable behaviour, Skelton's mechanical analogy emphasized human control.

The elaborate and novel role for government that Skelton suggested was based on arguments about capital formation, the business cycle, and fiscal policy which themselves were innovative enough in the

economic science of his time. In emphasizing control over the
economy through government and the resiliency of capitalism in the
face of state intervention and higher taxation, these arguments were
consistent with the agenda contained in his other proposals for fiscal
reform and were shared by other progressive-minded economists in
the pre-war period.[35] Skelton credits no writer for his views and,
curiously, he restated his position on counter-cyclical government
fiscal policy only once, in 1915. Given that there is no statement of
the proposal in his major books on Canadian economic history and
socialism, it may be construed either as a theoretical assumption
underpinning his optimistic account of the productive capacity and
governmental regulation of capitalism, or a radical view for Canada
he dare not elaborate on. Or perhaps it was both.

When he did restate his theory about anti-depression state expenditure in 1915, Skelton explained its potential in terms of the broad
reform of the taxation and administration policies of the federal
government. He acknowledged the audacity of his counter-cyclical
fiscal nostrum, but he parried this charge by pointing out that
orthodox and radical alike admitted that current fiscal policies and
powers were already so great that they were often said to worsen
depression. If that were already the case, then his proposal to follow
a counter-cyclical policy was theoretically no great extension of state
activity and probably no more damaging than existing activity.[36]

Skelton elaborated on his proposal by trying to distinguish between
his new principle of fiscal policy and the venerable Canadian tradition of public works and patronage expenditures. Besides explaining that the reform of tax policy had led to a reformation in fiscal
policy, he realized that administrative revolution drove the "post-
reformation" state. As he concluded his account in 1915, "It is one
thing to make government expenditure fall and rise to offset rise
and fall in private undertakings, and another to advocate that it
should always rise and never fall." Neither advocating the traditional
relief measures of the fiscal pork-barrel nor supporting the socialist
panaceas of a bloated public sector, Skelton pressed for a civil service
with the competence necessary to control the business cycle.

If the principles for both collecting public revenue and spending
it must be rethought, what, finally, did Skelton propose that government intervene to do? Clearly, he was content to argue in favour of
a rather broad reorientation of the economic role of government
based on ethical tenets of justice as well as efficiency and on political
tenets of extending national "responsible government" and autonomy
to include economic as well as political areas. Still, Skelton did propose specific social-welfare reforms, particularly social-insurance

measures such as pensions, health insurance, and unemployment insurance.[37] And, while he did not elaborate on the benefits of these measures even to the extent that the post-war Leacock did, he had advocated the new areas of government involvement both before and after the war. Moreover, perhaps Skelton gave short shrift to his own laundry list of social reforms in part because he took seriously the support by both the Liberals and the Progressives for major social-reform legislation. Finally, lest he be charged with excessive naïvety, he actually proposed his tax and fiscal reforms precisely because they were predicated on the removal of excuses for governments, especially the federal government, to avoid implementing social-welfare and broad economic-stabilization measures.

Skelton's reformism bears only faint resemblance to the later Keynesian program of economic management. Unlike any of the Keynesian advocates of a fiscal revolution in the role of government, he did not foresee a heavy-spending and taxing role for government, let alone limitless and unvarying economic growth, and he had nothing to say about the monetary policy so central to Keynesianism. In 1918 and 1919, for instance, he warned about the need for social and economic reform, but he also reminded his readers that productivity and wages must be correlated and that frugality of expectations during periods of economic decline must prevail.[38] Similarly, it has to he remembered that Skelton was addressing only the particular crisis of an economy unique in its stage of development and susceptibility to international influences. His arguments, especially about counter-cyclical spending, were specific ones directed to the Canadian case alone, an example of the empirically derived rethinking of economic theory that Shortt had long prescribed. Skelton's policy was limited to and, perhaps as important, limited by Canadian conditions. This perhaps as much as any other factor explains his refusal, failure, or omission (the reader can make her or his choice) to develop his ideas about fiscal policy. Finally, and more personally, after 1918 Skelton was increasingly preoccupied by his historical work as a biographer and, unfortunately, by administrative work as a dean at Queen's. By the early 1920s, he was drawn towards foreign policy and government consultation yet again. All of these interests led him away from any serious economic analysis.

THE SHORTT-SKELTON EXAMINATION of the economic consequences of the Great War on Canada prompted them to examine the new role of the state, a theme that was only dimly acknowledged at the time and indeed has only barely been admitted by historians in the past decade by their reinterpretion of the Borden government's major interventions to control industrial output and prices. In effect, historical interpretation has shifted from an older view dismissing the Unionist government's measures as temporary intrusions to an explanation which points to that government's significant experiments in fundamental regulation of economic output – experiments that withered after 1921 amidst the triumph of provincial rights and Mackenzie King's form of conciliating interest groups. While this new account is essentially correct, it ignores a key point about the substructure of government.[39]

Between 1916 and 1926 the federal government's revenue base was greatly and permanently expanded with the addition of new taxation areas. Corporate and personal income taxes comprised one-sixth of total federal revenues by 1926 and total budgetary revenues nearly doubled between 1916 and 1926. The result was federal expenditure comprising about one-twelfth of the gross national product of Canada in the mid-1920s, not much less than the 10 percent usually claimed (in the absence of national accounts) for federal spending in the expansionist war years. Clearly something important was going on and Skelton spotted it and explained its significance.[40] He saw the fiscal developments of these years as nothing less than a drastic change in the public conception of the national interests and of the duties of the state itself.

During the war Adam Shortt had encouraged a basic reconsideration of economic policy based on Canadian circumstances and not economic orthodoxy. If he only partly followed his own advice, he nevertheless pointed to a new capacity for economic self-reliance and even economic self-government in Canada. He was also fortunate that his successor at Queen's followed his advice much more completely. Skelton rethought the entire basis of fiscal policy in Canada, taxation and expenditure alike, and in the process was one of the very few commentators to explain how fundamental and not temporary were the actual and potential changes in the economic role of government. Despite his failure to sustain his arguments with extended studies of government finance and policy during the 1920s, his original and creative policy speculations of the 1910s were important. Not only was Skelton virtually alone in the Canada of his time in explaining major changes in the role of government that had already emerged, but he was unique in seeing the links between fiscal policy and broader political change. Skelton was one of a small number of slightly heretical liberal political-economic reformers in his time. These reformers were dismissed by orthodox economists as mere economic populists besmitten by the prospect of vast tax revenues ripe for government plucking. Yet the reformers had more important goals; in the case of Skelton, he aimed at using the fiscal power of the state to assist in the transformation of the political and economic order.

Skelton's speculations are important precisely because they are rooted in his larger examination of liberal democracy. His conception of the state's potential for breaking the impact of recession was a bold claim in itself but it was derived from his observation of the existing impact of state policy and his evaluation of the great potential for reform of its financial base. That evaluation of the potential strength of public revenues was in turn rooted in his belief, first, that government policy could and should be oriented to bring about the efficient and just distribution of goods, and, second, that the interests and needs of all people in the society must be part of policy calculations of efficiency and justice. He showed specific ways by which society's aims of individual fulfilment and freedom for all men and women could be brought about by a revised calculation of the economic duties of the state and by a major interventionist and stabilizing role for the state. Through his studies of fiscal policy, Skelton pursued his most basic arguments about capitalism in a democratic society.

8 The Agrarian Origins of Canadian Democracy

> Canada is a nation created in defiance of geography and yet the geography and economic factors have had a large part in shaping her history.
>
> W.A. Mackintosh

The problems of Canadian farming had interested Queen's political economy professors at least since the last years of George M. Grant's principalship. Long concerned with agricultural settlement in the North-West, Grant supported tariff reform as a means to grant justice to Canada's farmers – a group whose comparatively weak economic and political voice he lamented.[1] Similarly, Adam Shortt, in addition to studying the political economy of the Prairies, explained that the commercialization of Canadian agriculture was central to the country's economic and political development. For many years he had criticized agricultural-settlement and tariff policies as harmful to the farmers' interests. In 1903 Shortt reflected upon the "astonishingly small influence" of farmers in economic and political affairs. He noted that the Canadian Manufacturers' Association and the Trades and Labour Congress acted as representatives for their groups' interests. Yet farmers, equally if not more important to national prosperity, could scarcely be heard. Their comments on such issues as tariff reform virtually were ignored.[2] Oscar Douglas Skelton pursued this line, arguing that the grievances of the farmers were central to the more general problems of Canadian society. The farmers' difficulties had been caused, he said, by the nation's erroneous commercial policies and unrepresentative political system. Skelton supported reciprocity in 1911 partly because it would have addressed the farmers' problems.[3] All three men deemed important the place of the farmers in Canada's social, political, and economic development. Yet each had observed that the nation had not properly apprehended the importance of agriculture to its well-being. Political parties, public policies, and economic strategies were seriously if not critically flawed by their treatment of the farmers and the agricultural economy.

In the years after George Grant's and Adam Shortt's complaints were heard, Canadian farmers had organized to increase their economic and political power. Daunted by the 1911 election results, they spent the decade after Skelton had pleaded their case by casting about for means other than the Liberal Party to exercise greater economic and political influence. By the end of the war, the activism of farmers in various organizations had become a remarkable influence on the nation. In this atmosphere of renewed agrarian vigour, Queen's political economists were active observers of the place the farmers had and should have in Canada.[4] Collectively, their work can be seen as a major facet of the agenda for social-scientific scrutiny of the problems of a democratic society to which their university department committed itself after the Great War.

ADAM SHORTT'S CONCERN with the social role and characteristics of agriculture in society was of long standing. From the start of his career he had not only offered biting comments on the social life of rural Canada but had looked forward to the increasing social integration of rural with urban Canada as well as the advancement of agriculture from simple crop production to mechanized and advanced agricultural processing and production.[5] By the 1910s he was commenting on the depopulation of Ontario and Quebec. Shortt argued that the urbanization of contemporary Canada was part of a major shift of population in the advanced portions of the world. An earlier epoch – the middle ages – had also involved such a population shift with the movement of "anglo-saxon and norse elements" from village communities to individual farm dwellings. While that shift had occurred prior to the capitalist era, the present one was a consequence of the evolution of industrial civilization – and it was not a process that could be avoided. But, of course, accommodation could be reached between city and countryside. Further, while the characteristics of modern cities ("which are not communities") were not totally desirable, the population movement could be a social as well as an economic boon if one of its main causes could be harnessed. Transportation, which had made possible the interdependency of and commercial bonds between city and country, could also be used to create suburban communities in a semi-rural environment. Through construction of street-railway systems in major cities, the urban populace could enjoy both the economic benefits of industrialism and the social benefits of pre-industrial community life. Similarly, the rural populace could now be connected to the dynamic and civilized urban centres. In each of these ways, Shortt suggested, the sense of community and the benefits of economic progress could be maintained.[6]

The rather banal optimism of this assessment may simply have resulted from the effects of administrative drudgery on Shortt's mind. But more seriously, it also indicated his preoccupation with the problems of a declining agrarian population in Canada by the 1910s. By the end of the war, in fact, he was quite concerned with the status of agriculture in the Canadian economy. Like his former student, William Swanson, Shortt thought that the instability of the economy and its post-war readjustments could both be corrected by renewed emphasis on agriculture. In the *Monetary Times* Shortt and Swanson suggested to Canadian business that agricultural improvements were the necessary basis for all economic reconstruction. Neither writer apparently felt moved to explain why this was so. Shortt and Swanson were writing at a time of growing social and economic protest emanating from both industrial workers and increasingly well-organized farmers. For them to demand redress for agriculture was perhaps only sensible advice in a crisis. Still, sympathy with the farmers' grievances as well as a subtle nostalgia for a more rural society and economy were contained in their remarks.[7]

Such nostalgia was not shared by O.D. Skelton. At the demise of the reciprocity proposals in 1911, years before Shortt and Swanson wrote for the financial press, Skelton had expressed his concern for the economic plight of farmers. During the pre-war slump he pointed out that the financial and social problems of the day, and the "over-expansion" which had resulted, were in part the consequence of a neglect of agricultural problems, economic and social. More generally, Skelton placed the successes of agriculture – especially Prairie agriculture – at the centre of Canada's development when the nation's economic "hour had struck." Beneath this appreciation and concern, there was another consideration. In his 1912 survey of national economic history, Skelton had felt compelled to defend Canadian farmers for their achievements in producing and marketing their crops. He had told his readers that, despite critical voices, the farmers' "troubled prosperity" was not their own doing. In fact, he went so far as to focus on the success of agriculture as a major refutation of the socialist indictment of capitalism. That success was owing to the application of scientific skills (rather than merely by mechanization) on the part of Canada's many small-scale producers. It was shaped too by the cooperative movement and by state support. Ultimately, however, it was a result of the "stimulus of self-help." The preservation and reinvigoration of the family farm was a significant example of the capacity for reform and adaptation under the capitalist system.[8]

So, for Skelton, the well-being of agriculture was a major component of Canada's prosperity and stability and an important test of the adaptive capacities of capitalism. Further, though his elaborate discussions of fiscal reforms were mainly generated from his readings of the wartime crisis and his wider perceptions about how a liberal-democratic political economy should work, they were also nourished in part by Skelton's schemes to resolve the economic problems of Canadian farmers burdened by the tariff. Skelton must have felt a fair amount of frustration about society's lack of response to his aims. We can see his frustration in his own gloomy reading of the 1911 election results and in his increasing pessimism about the Borden government's policies. Skelton's considerable concern about the divisive characteristics of the national government by the summer of 1917 explains his later concentration upon political means to deal with agriculture's problems. This link between politics and agriculture was one of Skelton's major public interests from 1918 to 1921.

In 1914 Skelton urged Mackenzie King to examine the problem of rural depopulation as a research topic for the second meeting of the Canadian Political Science Association. Skelton suggested that the ramifications of rural depopulation meant that its political significance was considerable; he did not add how important that might be to an unemployed politician. Later, in 1917, Skelton toured the Prairie west and did research for the Saskatchewan Liberal-Farmer government. He found that "the influence of the farmers' organizations in the West is proving admirable." By late that year, and for the next several, he encouraged Laurier and then King to adopt measures that appealed directly to the farmers and to indicate the Liberal Party's willingness to cooperate with the Progressives.[9]

On the occasion of the armistice, Skelton suggested to Laurier that the Union government would now have to decide whether to "desert the manufacturers or give up the West." He further stated that he was "very hopeful that the organized farmers will provide a sincere and effective democratic force in the next few years: whether within or outside the Liberal party is harder to say. What is your opinion as to that?" Skelton then reported on his authorship of the major revision to the Farmers' Platform, a project he had undertaken for Norman Lambert of the Canadian Council of Agriculture (CCA).[10]

Skelton's draft focused on both international and domestic issues. Internationally, Skelton called for free trade and world peace through an international league of nations as well as full Canadian autonomy within the voluntary British empire. Domestically, he advocated equal suffrage for women and other groups presently barred, freedom of speech and the press, political parties open to full public scrutiny of their finances, proportional representation, parliament's supremacy in all areas, abolition of the Senate and of titles, greater state regulation of conditions of work, greater opportunities for education, major public works, and fiscal – especially taxation – reforms.[11] Although Skelton prepared these points only at the behest of the CCA, his own predilections concerning Canadian trade and foreign policy were clearly evident in the document. At the very least, the document indicated an interesting convergence between Skelton's concerns and those of the CCA leadership.

Laurier, although tartly noting the provincial jurisdiction of some of Skelton's proposals, expressed approval of his letter and enclosures. He too chortled at the divisions within the Unionist caucus over the tariff, but he cautioned Skelton that east-west tension on this matter was a problem even for the organized farmers. This was obviously a reminder that the tariff issue would be a difficult one for any national government.

Skelton's work for and support of the farmers was remarkable. He was sympathetic to both provincial farmers' movements, such as the United Farmers of Ontario and the Saskatchewan farmers, and the Progressives who emerged in 1921. Yet this support was predicated on the notion that agrarian agitation would bring about the reorganization and reform of the two-party system. Skelton thought that the farmers' movement and its reform policies were healthy signs and vital to the recovery of what he termed a "reorganized" Liberal Party, an aim he expressed to Laurier in 1917 and to Mackenzie King in 1919 and 1921. In 1921 he argued that "progressive" forces, low-tariff and "Canada first" in orientation, from all sections of Canada should eventually be drawn into a reform-based Liberal Party. This suggestion was another example of his commitment to parliamentary government as the forum for the redress of grievances and for the maintenance of national unity. The revamped party system was a means to overcome the danger of sectional grievances on the farmers' part. Finally, through his discussion of the farmers' opposition to the tariff, Skelton was continuing his project of making fiscal reform a major point of difference between the parties. Admittedly, he conceded that erroneous views on taxation permeated the farmers' movement too; for example, he corrected William Good's ill-conceived support for the single tax in an otherwise enthusiastic review of Good's *Production and Taxation in Canada*.[12] Nevertheless, Skelton's account of the farmers' movement, like Shortt's views about the social and economic benefits of nourishing a progressive agriculture, placed it at the centre of the political reinvigoration of Canada.

The brilliant success of the sort of political strategy Skelton suggested to Mackenzie King is well known to students of Canadian politics in the 1920s.[13] For his part, Skelton may have emphasized political means to strengthen agriculture's place but he did not neglect other strategies and vehicles. Later, through the examination of rural problems, especially the cooperative movement, Queen's professors followed Skelton in arriving at a broader conception of agriculture's significance to Canada's economic history and development as well as its political and social importance. Humfrey Michell, Clifford Clark, and William Mackintosh studied the cooperative movement and the economic problems of agriculture throughout the 1910s and 1920s. Their concentration on the cooperative movement was a major indication of their sympathy with the agrarian movement and the need to strengthen rural Canada. It was also a sign of their intention to contribute to, if not to direct, an important reform movement. Their studies suggested how significant agrarian and other cooperative reform was. Mackintosh, at least, was able to develop from his studies a brilliant synthesis of Canadian economic history which also encompassed an interpretation of the nation's political life.

It was Adam Shortt, again, who first ventured to consider the question of the cooperative movement. In 1897 Shortt had praised the cooperative movement as a sensible kind of reform. In comparison with the "undisciplined" and "unselfish" theorists of socialism, cooperators "advocate no schemes of total regeneration, they look forward to no utopia where human nature has become inhuman." "They take," he continued, "human nature, economic laws, social and political institutions as they find them." Shortt supported the efforts of both the British "distributive" coops and the European "producers'" coops. Both were important means by which the economic conditions of agricultural and industrial workers were improved by their own efforts. At the same time, however, he suggested that the cooperative movement was not essential in North America, where economic conditions already were more beneficient. Again, the rich material environment, the wider diffusion of wealth and opportunity, and the more powerful and effective commercial and social integration of all men and women into a common market society meant that the problems cooperatives dealt with were already soluble in the New World. Shortt suggested that anyone who wished could become a capitalist. Savings, insurance and investment schemes, the ready availability of credit to any who could prove ability, and the new class of expert and responsible but not proprietorial business managers each provided ample opportunities for the ambitious individual; indeed, Shortt went so far as to conclude that the peculiar North American economic environment was itself "one vast co-operative society." In later years, pershaps because he was not so ready to reach this conclusion, Shortt did not return to the cooperative movement as a basis for reform.[14]

William Swanson adopted Shortt's anatomy and analysis of the principles and basis of cooperative movements. But Swanson went further and condemned as disastrous the producers' cooperatives that developed in Canada. Compared to other tactics, producers' cooperatives were ineffectual in transferring wealth from business to labour or to consumers. Organizing trade unions, adopting protective legislation, and "the extension of public management and control, or even socialism" were more effective and more popular means to provide for equitable economic opportunities. Given Swanson's general hostility to the extension of state ownership and his economic conservatism, it can be suggested that his arguments were tendentious, designed simply to confute the advocates of cooperation rather than to support the alternatives he mentioned. Finally, it is curious that he did not exempt agricultural cooperatives from his charge, especially since he was to spend the bulk of his career in Saskatchewan. The potential of cooperative grain selling and the possibilities of government-supervised grain marketing were not favourably examined by Swanson in his later accounts of the grain industry or in his proposed solutions to the Great Depression. Not from Swanson would an innovative discussion of the agricultural economy or rural Canada emerge; even his criticisms were cast as curt dismissals rather than considered analyses.[15]

This was not the case for Humfrey Michell. For six years at Queen's and occasionally after he moved to McMaster in 1920, Michell wrote on cooperation with considerable sympathy but ultimate scepticism. He studied the cooperative movement first by examining the problems and innovations of the militant farmers. Here Michell was extremely sympathetic to the problems of the agrarians and the social and economic strategies that they adopted. In 1914 he assessed the complaints against the banks made by Saskatchewan farmers, and he did so by considering the larger problems of a pioneering commercial economy facing the need for and consequences of a great amount of borrowed capital. While the farmers' criticisms of the "eastern" banks were in part correct, he suggested, they overlooked the fact that the very novelty of Prairie development contributed to the restrictions on and burdens of credit. In Saskatchewan, a commercialized society only recently evolved was facing what Michell described as "a period of stress, a time of settling and shaking down into place." Both the settlers and their creditors "had freely discounted the future and credit has outrun production."[16]

Michell went on to instruct his readers in the intricacies of farm credit. He noted that options existed to the traditional bank loan and mortgage system. These were found in several parts of the world – in the Germans' "landschaften," in the Quebec cooperative credit unions, and in the Australian state-funded loans. Michell thought that the proposed cooperative credit system to be administered by the provincial government was a clever adaptation of the German schemes. But the revised system was designed as an alternative to, not a replacement of, the banks. Moreover, he warned, the cooperative credit system could work only if several conditions were met. Very important was the effective insulation of the credit cooperative from political control. But equally significant were major reforms in the economic calculations and agricultural practices of the farmers. Farmers could not exempt themselves from blame in the current period of readjustment. Neither could they hope that the cooperative would have a magical economic effect. Although none of these points negated the farmers' aim to reform the credit system, they did modify the extravagant hopes and somewhat one-sided views held by the advocates of cooperative credit. Not only the agricultural credit system but agrarian society required reform.[17]

In a later examination of producers' cooperatives, Michell was more critical still of the experience of North America. A 1918 study of agrarian and industrial producers' cooperatives led him to reflect on their "melancholy story." The economic limitations and problems of these organizations were too seldom understood by their proponents who also seemed to expect too much from their organizations. To Michell, it was axiomatic that the economic benefits of cooperation were extremely limited. Cooperatives were a tool to be used by consumers against producers and especially against monopolists. Again, in Michell's judgment, cooperatives were not institutions that would reshape capitalism; they would only reform it. Nonetheless, the educational and social impact of the cooperatives was significant. Cooperatives had effected an important social and intellectual improvement among their members. They had brought together the farmers of North America so that they escaped from the ignorant isolation which was so lamentably their traditional characteristic. The coops had also taught their members to think about economic and social issues and to strive realistically for reform.[18]

Unlike zealots within the cooperative movement, Michell held no hope for its transformative powers. This moderation was based on his Shortt-like reading of the distinctive economic and social environment of North America. That environment limited the difficulties which farmers, consumers, and producers faced within the capitalist system. Similarly, the economic strengths of the cooperatives themselves were sufficiently limited that they could not bring about any transformation in any case. At the same time, however, Michell did think that the movement had a very valuable educational role as well as a potentially significant social influence. He was eager to point to the success of the Quebec *caisses-populaires* and the Prairie farmers' grain-sales cooperatives as innovations relevant and important to the social and economic climate of North America. These innovations had led rural Quebecers and Prairie farmers to adapt successfully to the conditions and demands of the market economy.[19]

Michell's warnings about the limited power of cooperatives bothered C.B. Sissons, a farmer-professor and enthusiastic agrarian reformer. Sissons refused to accept the material basis of Michell's account of the limitations to cooperatives. Instead, he charged Michell with an imputation of psychological traits to North Americans which somehow warped their cooperative capacities. In response, Michell pointed out how limited was the Canadian adherence to cooperatives and how concentrated it was on the agricultural sector.

In the end, however, Michell had devised a sympathetic yet critical account of cooperation. That account was based on an economic and environmental account of the cooperatives' prospects. It also pointed to the innovation of agricultural cooperation as a response to the important problems of the Canadian economy. Finally, it emphasized the important benefits of self-help and economic rationality in considering reform. On all these points, Michell was in substantial agreement with his Queen's colleagues about the proper basis for economic and social reform and the importance of the cooperative movement, as the work of Clifford Clark and William Mackintosh well illustrated. Michell himself was to refocus his attention toward the Anglican Church as an agency to dispense the prescription of economic rationality. Like the young Queen's scholar Bryce Stewart, he joined the reform wing of Protestantism in order to further the reorientation he sought.[20]

The Prairie farmers' response to the grain marketing system, argued Clifford Clark in 1916, was indeed leading to fundamental changes in Canadian economic and political life. Clark shared Skelton's judgment and Michell's hope that the organized farmers were in the midst of contributing to what Clark described as the democratization of the nation. But he also rejected Michell's argument that the significance of the cooperatives did not lie in their economic impact.

Once again, Clark explained the particular question by reference to the international economic system. In this case, the dynamic change affecting Prairie farmers was the result of their place as international producers. The Canadian farmers' response to the complexities of pricing and marketing in this world system led them to examine both their own practices as well as those of the "middlemen," the people involved in storage, shipment, and sales. In both these areas, and especially the latter, the farmers found considerable room for economic improvement. But this improvement was aimed at increasing market efficiency, not at overturning market structures. As a result of their inquiry, the farmers demanded and obtained state supervision over the inspection, storage, and transportation of grain. Further, they themselves created grain storage and selling cooperatives. The effect of these developments was remarkable and ironic, for the intrusion of the state and cooperation among the farmers unleashed the commercial impulses and self-help ambitions of all involved in the wheat economy. Line elevators as well as milling and selling agencies, private and cooperative alike, worked more efficiently to get grain to market. The availability of capital and profits that resulted testified to the commercial success of the reformed, regulated, and competitive system.

The reformed grain trade, according to Clark, was "the strongest force making for real democracy in present-day Canada" because it contributed to economic well-being and active participation in commerce on the part of all involved in the trade. In addition, the grain trade was an example of the way in which agriculture cooperation plus judicious state regulation could benefit, indeed revitalize, the capitalist system. The important example of the wheat economy in suggesting new roles for the state and for the agricultural sector in Canada emerged as a lesson for all parts of the nation. Clark avoided the intricate and broader proposals for government regulation and intervention, especially state grain selling and central banking, that he would later support in the 1920s and 1930s.[21]

TO TURN FROM THE WORKS so far examined to those of William Mackintosh is to begin a more complex task. This task involves a shift from tentative explorations and somewhat narrow critiques to a remarkably creative and sustained explanation of the agrarian reform movement and of post-Confederation Canadian history in general. It also brings us into contact with the central post-war statement about the characteristics and prospects of liberal democracy in Canada.

Mackintosh's work has been viewed in a peculiar and rather restricted way by historians, economists, and public servants. All three groups have emphasized his important contributions, yet they have interpreted them almost exclusively in terms of the evolution either of Canadian historical writing or of Canadian policy making. On the one hand, Mackintosh's historical-economic studies have been explained in relation to the evolution of the staples approach to Canadian economics and an environmentalist interpretation of Canadian history. In particular, his work has been seen as a prelude to that of H.A. Innis.[22] On the other hand, Mackintosh has been regarded as the fourth of the major Queen's political economists who, in establishing a link with the federal public service, helped to advance the university's national position and the role of its political economy department in public policy making. Mackintosh's staples approach to Canadian regional economic and the "economic background" to federal-provincial relations has encouraged some scholars to interpret him as a sort of cipher for the Rowell-Sirois and Keynesian revitalization of Canadian federalism.[23]

There is no need to claim that either of these characterizations seriously misrepresents Mackintosh. Indeed, this study has relied on each of them. Nonetheless, his work does tend to remain in shadows that should be illuminated. Whatever else they resulted in, Mackintosh's studies of the geographical and economic determinants of Canadian society led him to examine the problem of sectional economic and political conflict. This problem, in turn, drew Mackintosh to consider the democratic potential of Canadian politics and the egalitarian possibilities of its economy. His work continued the broad inquiries of Shortt and Skelton in ways that Clark and Michell did not follow.

In March 1923 the *Canadian Historical Review* published Mackintosh's interpretative essay on "Economic Factors in Canadian History." His preliminary aim in this densely argued study was to correct the constitutional-political bias of previous Canadian historians. He did not identify the sources he had in mind, leaving the impression that he was less concerned with academic historical writing (such as it was at the time) than with a kind of public perception about Canada's history. If he had considered specific writings, he could hardly have accused *Canada and Its Provinces* of this bias; but perhaps he was reflecting upon the constitutional and political interpretation of Canadian history written in light of the Great War. In any event, constitutional-political bias, according to Mackintosh, had led to a misconception about the history and development of the nation. To correct the account, he argued that the geography of the North American continent was "of primary importance" to its historical development. This geographical and continental perspective induced him to consider the "developing life of the people" as a secondary theme. To a degree, therefore, Mackintosh's criticism of the constitutional and political histories focused on their failure to deal with the history of the whole populace as well as to assess the central impact of environmental and material factors.[24]

In studying the impact of the environment, Mackintosh suggested that the history of human settlement was central to Canadian development. This history was one involving the commercial exploitation of what he called, following the work of G.S. Callender, "staple" products. Initially, these were natural resources or agricultural goods, which brought about sufficient material prosperity to sustain settlement and generate other economic endeavours. The most important staple of nineteenth- and twentieth-century Canada, he asserted, was wheat. Ontario's growth in the mid-nineteenth century, for instance, was based on the wheat staple. The sale of wheat then led to the prosperity and expansion that "primed the pump" of industrialism in the new dominion after 1867 and produced plans for Prairie settlement. That settlement in turn was based on the wheat staple and it shaped the economic maturation of Canada after 1900. Against this background, Mackintosh thought, the centrality of commercial agriculture to Canadian nationhood and the material basis of the transcontinental nation were obvious.[25]

Yet the primary place of agriculture in the Canadian economy, Mackintosh continued, rested on the convergence of geographical characteristics with government policy, technology, and, of course, markets. The peculiar growth of Canadian agriculture was determined by the physical architecture of North America. Geography provided Canada with the St Lawrence River, its main transportation link to the Atlantic and hence to vital European markets. Yet the St Lawrence faced the powerful rivalry of the Hudson-Mohawk and the Mississippi River systems as well as the major limitations imposed by the climate and, especially, by the Laurentian "barrier" to the interior. The problem of overcoming the competing transportation corridors and the natural barriers to penetration of the continental interior demanded effective government policies. And, for all its flaws, British colonial trade policy had met Canada's needs. Later, the self-interested trade policies of colonial and independent Canada as well as the adaptation of new transportation technology supported the renewed staples-based economy, railways in particular giving "the

St. Lawrence valley access to a country capable of rapid expansion." The end result was that Canada became a prosperous continental economy and society. Although Mackintosh did not refer to other writers in the course of his analysis, there is no doubt that his discussion of the staples economy and colonial policies drew on the work of Adam Shortt. Similarly, his reliance on Skelton's *The Railway Builders* would have struck anyone who had read that book.[26]

The interaction between geographical and political factors created a staples economy, which itself powerfully influenced the country's evolving political order. In the nineteenth century, the political and cultural distinction of Canada was mainly the result of an environment inimical to settlement. In this regard, Mackintosh drew upon Frederick Jackson Turner's work in explaining a contrast between the Canadian and American economic and political history. The Turnerian account of environmental determinants, Mackintosh claimed, was applicable only as a way of understanding the importance of the environment. For Canada, this account must be turned on its head. Despite a shared continent, Canada's nineteenth-century history was distinct from that of the United States because of Canada's lack of a continuous frontier of agricultural settlement and of assured prosperity. "There was," Mackintosh wrote, "no Jacksonian democracy and no Jackson in Canada" precisely because of the two economic-geographical flaws, those within the St Lawrence–Great Lakes navigation system and that of the Laurentian barrier to agricultural expansion. Each of these so limited staples production and thus settlement and economic diversification that, at least in the past, the nation had not experienced the exhilaration of North American plenty or democracy. A note of regret clearly rang through Mackintosh's account. Yet a defiant tone, emphasizing the differences between the two nations and their histories, could also be perceived. In all this, Mackintosh forcefully emphasized the important impact that geography and economic development had on the nation's evolution.[27]

The Laurentian barrier and the St Lawrence's limitations were overcome. And that fact led Mackintosh to reassert his claim that the transcontinental, staples-based economy was secured with the success of Prairie settlement. In an obvious echo of Skelton's account of the evolution of nationalist thought in Canada, Mackintosh contrasted the present national confidence with what he perceived as the almost forgotten political debates of the previous generation over annexation, commercial union, and imperial federation. He wrote:

It is difficult to realize that Canadians ever believed in them. The difference is not in Canadians. It is in the economic background. When frustration of

Canadian progress was overcome, and a period of expansion resulted, Canadian nationality was assured, and policies which cast doubt upon that nationality fell away. For the first time in Canadian history, powerful and effective western forces made themselves felt. For the first time western problems became capable of solution. The end is not yet; for the West still struggles in time of world-depression with a bulky staple and a long transportation haul. But improvements in transportation have made problems not insoluble. A new factor has arisen in the existence of a manufacturing East. Another is developing in the opening of the Pacific trade; and still another, of unknown significance, will come into play as the forest frontier of the north is attacked in earnest.[28]

A number of remarkable assumptions are embedded in this statement. Mackintosh argued that "Canadian nationality" was determined by material well-being and expansion, thus eluding both the racialist account of nationality that had irritated Skelton and the sentimental account that had offended Shortt. More, he tied Canadian nationality to the success of Prairie settlement, and in so doing he placed the Prairie west at the centre of Canadian political as well as economic life. And finally, he saw the country's present success as doubly beneficial in that Prairie settlement also brought Canada into contact with that Turnerian frontier of settlement – the opening of the Pacific and the northern forests – which had fashioned the democratic character of the United States in the nineteenth century.

In a subtler fashion than Clifford Clark, but for once in substantial agreement with him, Mackintosh asserted that Prairie settlement brought about both true nationality and a proper democracy for Canada. Each of these he celebrated. For he insisted that the nationality and democracy born on the Prairie frontier allowed the nation to escape from the clutches of a dependent, often backward past. This is to say that Mackintosh clearly plotted the roots of contemporary Canadian economic success in the conditions and issues of the past. Yet his main point was that the geographical environmental limitations of the past were now overcome. The distance between the problems of the previous century and the promise of the present signified a major break in Canada's history. The very economic geography of North America had enabled Canadians to devise the kind of liberal-democratic society that Skelton and, in his way, Shortt had sought from their reading of the economic history and potential of the nation. Mackintosh's obvious reliance on Skelton's work can be seen in the fact that he referred to the same dialectic of imperialism-annexation-autonomy that Skelton had. Moreover, like Skelton, he relied on the force of material factors to bring about the transformation of the nation and its character. If this affinity is accepted,

Mackintosh's account may be viewed as the culmination and completion of a thirty-year search by Queen's political economists for the material engines of Canadian national development. His argument showed a satisfaction about Canada's material and social evolution that contrasted with Shortt's concerns and Skelton's exhortations. But he shared with them a fundamental commitment to an autonomous, economically efficient, politically democratic society.

William Mackintosh concluded his 1923 paper, using a phrase that in 1930 would be revised by Harold Innis, by restating the importance of economic and geographical factors to national development. He admitted that this development was ironic in a way: "Canada is a nation created in defiance of geography, and yet the geographic and economic factors have had a large place in shaping her history ... It is not contended that these are the only factors. Others have been often and adequately dealt with. But unless one is to consider Canada merely as a collection of racial types and not as a nation, the basic facts of economic and historical geography can never be ignored." Then he offered the advice that "it behoves present-day historians to perceive the romance of a nation in the story of a people facing the prosaic obstacles of a colonial existence, developing national traits, and winning through to nationhood."[29]

In making this argument, Mackintosh followed his predecessors. Like Shortt, he corrected the continentalist fixation upon Canada's geographical weaknesses. Like Skelton, he rejected the imperialist fixation on race. In refuting such errors, he was forced to admit the successful "defiance" involved in the nation's creation. That defiance, however, was based on the acceptance of certain essential geographical and economic forces, the importance of staple goods and natural transportation routes. The result of this acceptance meant, moreover, the assurance of autonomous nationality. Such an assurance depended too upon a recalculation of the nation's material basis. Just as Mackintosh had proven that a reorientation of the material world might result from the application of proper economic reasoning, so too he demonstrated that a transformation of the nation had resulted from its conformity to geographical and economic reason. Still, there existed the danger of a return to the political and economic vagaries – to Mackintosh, futilities and failures – of the past. But that danger could be overcome by accepting the kind of reasoning about Canada's economic bases which he had provided.

Shaped by its unique agricultural frontier and its export staple, Canada had become an autonomous, distinctive society. Whereas Skelton and Shortt had held this out as a goal, Mackintosh now asserted it as an accomplished fact. Only as a North American society did Canada assure its national well-being. There was a lesson in that shift from defiance of the environment to a state-led and technologically induced resolution of its limitations. This lesson was that only by accepting the characteristics of the environment could Canadians find the basis for national success and a margin for real national prosperity.

There are a couple of parallels between Mackintosh's account of the search for the crucial area of human control and that of Adam Shortt. In Shortt's view, only by coming to grips with the environmental forces that shaped their material life could women and men begin to choose policies and aims which were in their interest. Shortt had also held that, in the hard struggle for wealth, humankind had only a small area in which to assert control over the largely uncontrollable and harsh forces generating and allocating that wealth. While Mackintosh had followed Shortt in recognizing the basic dictates of the environment, he set himself apart from the latter by showing how beneficial were the consequences of human efforts to assert control. In finding the means to ease Shortt's doubts about Canada's prosperity and men's and women's direction of their economic fate, Mackintosh was sustaining the inquiries of O.D. Skelton.

MACKINTOSH'S STUDY OF the Prairie farmers' cooperative movement, *Agricultural Cooperation in Western Canada*, published in 1924, was based on his Harvard dissertation completed three years earlier.[30] The book elaborated and extended his earlier publications on the staples economy and the place of the west in national economic life. As well, it examined the history and prospects of western agricultural cooperatives. The work was written in a clear and occasionally vivid prose that only Skelton among the Queen's academics could equal; it combined a narrative form and economic analysis, perhaps marred by its tendency to anticipate and repeat its arguments. Whereas his *Canadian Historical Review* paper had emphasized the west's impact on political democracy, his book concentrated on the economic transformation the region was both undergoing and inducing in the rest of the nation. In both instances he was echoing Skelton's concern with the economic and political consequences of the capitalist economy's reform.

In introducing his subject, Mackintosh repeated his claim about the larger North American basis and germinal importance of the wheat staple to Canada's economic history. "The most significant phase of the economic history of American," he wrote, was "the endeavour of agricultural regions to obtain access to large and expanding regions." In that endeavour, "wheat brought the expansion of Ontario [Canada West] in the fifties and sixties out of which came the necessity of Confederation, and wheat and the market for wheat produced in the Canadian west gave to it its economic and political importance."[31] As a result of settlement and the staples trade there emerged the struggles of the farmers to devise cooperative-marketing organizations, among other means, to introduce a solid democratic ethic into Canadian life.

Mackintosh explained that there had been a succession of "steps" in the growth of the wheat-staple economy. The first was the result of business-government cooperation in using railway technology to construct the Canadian Pacific Railway so as to link "Manitoba wheat" with the "Liverpool market" via the St Lawrence valley. The second was the elaboration of government legislation and administration over the grain trade. The third was the farmers' movement, based on the ethic of self-help, to make effective the cooperative marketing of grain. In each case, the basic conditions of the grain market and the characteristics of the wheat staple were essential. The evolved wheat economy created the wealth and the roles for business, government, and farmer alike. Again, a strong deterministic element in the history of the grain trade was clear to Mackintosh. But the equally significant consequence was the institutional framework that Canadians set up in response.[32] Farmers, businessmen, and governments had shaped a peculiar marketing system.

Agricultural cooperatives, Mackintosh suggested, had been conceived out of the "experience of Western Canada rather than by *a priori* cooperative principles." This judgment served further to distance Canadian cooperation from the European prototype – a confirmation of Michell's argument and his own about the peculiarities of the North American environment. It also led him to emphasize the ways in which the cooperative movement – like the railway-transportation system and government grain regulation – represented human beings' response to the environment. In that response, Mackintosh pointed out the margin of human control over the economic social order. Simultaneously, the cooperatives were bringing about greater efficiency in the capitalist-commercial system rather than its overthrow. Despite Michell's judgments, then, the major criteria by which the cooperative movement could be assessed were their financial and commercial successes. Mackintosh quickly and continually admitted that their educational and social effects were also significant, indeed perhaps more important in the long run. "One of the professed objects of cooperative marketing," he wrote, was "to enlighten that [commercial] ignorance and permit the effective participation of thousands of producers in the marketing process." With this in mind, Mackintosh examined the financial-commercial and the social-educational impact of the cooperatives in the body of his book. In both areas he advanced arguments to support the thesis that the cooperatives represented a fundamental force for economic and social transformation. That transformation, he tried to show, involved greater economic efficiency and greater social integration.[33]

After examining the varieties of the cooperative experience Mackintosh defined a "theory of cooperation" that concentrated on the economic and social benefits of cooperatives. He conducted this theoretical assessment chiefly through a discussion of the "educational" results of cooperation. For it was in that area that he found an indication of both his own emphasis on the significance of cooperation and the way in which human direction over and benefits from the material environment might occur. The "educational benefit in the [cooperative] marketing of grain," he explained, "is more important than any other. It is the end toward which financial success, competitive strength, etc., are merely means. This is so because of the wide gap between many producers in a frontier agricultural region and the ultimate market for wheat in Europe, with the consequent greater difficulty in relating producer to market ... For the present it is sufficient to note that the training of the farmer has meant the more complete commercialization of agriculture."[34]

Mackintosh was remarkably assertive in his statement about the educational impact of cooperation. As a result of cooperatives, the farmers themselves undertook to understand how, as informed and rational people, they might criticize and propose legislative as well as economic changes. In a 1925 discussion of the new "wheat pools" Mackintosh was to assert that the Prairie cooperative movement was "the most distinctive institution apart from our constitution that Canada has yet produced." If nothing else this was further proof to Mackintosh that the west was the new source of Canadian political and social vitality. In his book he emphasized that the cooperatives were created not merely to pay dividends to their members but also to sustain the place of the farmers both economically and politically. In both instances, the farmers not only demonstrated self-interest but also, through their self-help ethic and cooperative institutions, presented an example to the nation of reformist accommodation to the geographical-economic environment. Curiously enough, in his many allusions to the democratic and "educational" impact of the Prairies, Mackintosh never referred to the Progressives. He did acknowledge help from the "utopian" cooperator, E.A. Partridge, who rejected politics, but he emphasized the aid of "practical" cooperators W.R. Motherwell, C.A. Dunning, and T.A. Crerar, political leaders who at least partly accepted Progressivism. One cannot help but think that he, like Skelton, approved of their Progressive inclinations.[35]

The educational dimension of cooperation had even more important economic and social consequences. Mackintosh contended that the farmers' assessments of agricultural marketing led them to engage in precisely that revision of economic calculation and the reform of economic motivations which he had elsewhere divined from the contemporary economic order. His account of the "Psychologist and Economics," published in 1923, had prompted him to foresee that a more enlightened, more rational populace, including economically trained businessmen and well-motivated and rewarded workers, would move toward a new ethic and new motivation of non-pecuniary rewards and satisfactions. For farmers as for businessmen or industrial workers, the new economic motivations and calculations would change profoundly the economic order by making it more open to individual satisfactions.[36]

As proof of this benefit of cooperation, Mackintosh pointed to the fact that the cooperatives indeed had led to agriculture's "more complete commercialization." Ironically, the cooperative movement was divided over the question of whether profits were to be aimed at. But this was irrelevant, Mackintosh argued, because the integration of producers into a more efficient commercial system was the abiding result of the cooperatives. As the means by which western agriculture was fully commercialized, the cooperative movement was ushering in what Mackintosh saw as an agricultural revolution parallel to the commercialization of manufacturing in the industrial revolution. Like their effects on Canadian politics, the economic impact of the cooperatives was revolutionary in that they transformed the relationship between producer and consumer so that it was the most direct and therefore the most efficient possible. As he saw the process, commercialization was a phenomenal force indeed. "By thrusting forward through cooperation his business organization to the central market," he explained, "the farmer is enabled to organize his productive enterprise according to market results which he is in a position to distinguish and interpret." Mackintosh admitted that "the immediate cause of cooperative enterprise may be and usually is abuse of power by selling or purchasing firms," and he noted that "the results go far beyond the mere regulation of a trade, important as that is, and the benefits are not to be judged merely on the basis of quantitative efficiency, of getting the largest turnover with the smallest cost, but upon the effect of cooperation in relating the producer to his market." He grandiously concluded that "the agricultural producer can only enter the central market by cooperation."[37] The maximization of efficiency through cooperation benefitted both farmers and consumers, and not only economically. As Mackintosh put it, the efficiency induced did not involve simply "getting the largest turnover with the smallest cost." It was in fact a binding of consumer and producer into a commercial relationship which also allowed them to mutually learn about the other's situation. In other words, the education that men and women received was also one involving the producers' and consumers' appreciation of their economic and social interdependence. In his exposition Mackintosh spoke of an agricultural revolution that imposed the "complete commercialization" of and greatest market efficiency for agricultural production. This economic relationship, he reminded his readers, was precisely what Adam Smith had argued was the source of the capitalist system's many virtues. Both efficiency in material production and the effective social integration of all people resulted from the market relationship.[38]

Mackintosh also argued that it was imperative that much greater efficiency result from the agricultural production and marketing system. Otherwise, western farmers would continue to experience the frustrations and weaknesses that had brought about the whole reform movement. Here too, the purely economic significance of the cooperatives became clear. One way to maximize agricultural efficiency was to improve scales of production. In the Canadian west, however, economies of scale were considerable already, indeed stretched to their limits. The cooperatives represented the alternative means to sustain greater efficiency and commercialization. Mackintosh explained how the cooperatives effected this benefit through their impact on the price system. "Effective functioning of a market requires that the effective demand of the consumer exercise as direct and strong an influence as possible upon the productive enterprise of the producer and that the decisions of the consumer as to quantity and quality of commodities shall be clearly shown and effective in influencing production. Now the extent to which that result is attained depends upon the efficiency of various agents in communicating his decision to the producer. The more indirect the relation of the producer to his market, the greater the difficulty of making the relation economically effective."[39] Cooperation expedited the market relationship most effectively and thus contributed to the most efficient signalling of consumer demand to the producer. Under it, the utility of the price system was enabled to work best. This account is solidly based on neo-classical utility theory, a sign of Mackintosh's acceptance of the economic revolution that Adam Shortt had rejected and that Skelton was schooled in. To Mackintosh, like Skelton, the efficiency of market relations also resulted in significant social benefits, for the consumers' needs were the stimuli that sparked the producers' efforts, to their mutual understanding as well as benefit. Finally, the cooperatives were a human response to the challenge of enlarging economic efficiency and human interdependence. Economic efficiency, freedom, and social justice were intricately bound.

The cooperative movement, in Mackintosh's mind, resuscitated the market relationship. It brought about the most efficient possible binding of producer and consumer and hence the most efficient "flow" and distribution of goods and incomes. The agriculturalists themselves had become more complete economic calculators through the "training" that the cooperatives provided. In this regard the barriers that had sustained agrarian backwardness (that bane of Shortt's personal life and social thought) would dissolve. Simultaneously, the economic efficiency and social changes thus generated would lead to the new satisfaction and fulfilment of human needs. Mackintosh had followed Taussig and Veblen in predicting the transformation of men's and women's economic motives so as to provide for a more complete life for them. The revolution in agriculture was one means by which that transformation would come about. The integration of the settlement frontier with the other parts of Canada and the world also created a mutual change in social attitudes. As a result of this process, the democracy characteristic of the settlement frontier might well be diffused throughout the society, while the economic rationality long characteristic of industrial production would become typical of agricultural production.

The commercialization and efficiency as well as the democracy and reason that Mackintosh saw emerge from the "agricultural revolution" were similar in their ramifications to the "moralized market" which Skelton had foreseen in reformed capitalism. For Mackintosh as for Skelton, the efficient commercial economy was also a just one. Similarly, the rational economic evaluation was also the fulfilling one. In setting up the agricultural economy and society of the Prairies as the fount of renewed democracy, Mackintosh was showing his commitment to the goal of democratization. In seeking the integration of the agricultural economy into the commercial system shaped by the industrial revolution and capitalism, he was indicating his emphasis on material advancement. In both ways the political and social as well as the purely economic impact of the changing agricultural economy remained central in his analysis. For Mackintosh, greater individual satisfaction, increased commercial efficiency, and remarkable social harmony were the results of the economic revolution triggered by the western Canadian cooperative system.

THE CONCENTRATION OF QUEEN'S political economists on agriculture after 1918 was an indication of their concern for both the particular grievances of the farmers and the larger problems – social, political, and economic – that the nation faced because of its neglect of the consequences of agricultural settlement and commercial difficulties. This concentration also reflected the continued importance of the agricultural economy in spite of urban and industrial development. In 1921 agriculture employed one-third of the labour force and earned one-sixth of the gross national product.[40] Finally, the preoccupation with agriculture stemmed in part from the political economists' continued ambition – so well reflected in O.D. Skelton's postwar "blueprint" for research – to maintain their studies of the key Canadian problems. In pursuing this ambition, Queen's scholars again projected Kingston into the mainstream of Canadian life – a remarkable achievement for professors in a university located in a town so peripheral to the dynamic centres of political and economic development. It can be seen as a canny strategy, too, because it enhanced their own role.

Three main concerns were evident in the studies of Queen's political economists. Shortt and Swanson warned about the foolish economic directions and dangerous social results of the nation's disregard for the farmer's problems and position. Skelton concentrated (insofar as he could during a period in which his academic work was so prolific) on the farmers' equally vital place in the political reorganization of Canada. In his view, the latter was an important project indeed for the nation's health. Michell, Clark, and especially Mackintosh examined the phenomenon of agricultural cooperation as a crucial manifestation of the reforms that the farmers were demanding. From his studies (the most detailed and sustained ones, it need hardly be added), Mackintosh alone devised an account which not only put the agrarian movement into a national perspective but also provided a solution to several of the larger problems of Canada's political and economic development, problems that had long disturbed his predecessors at Queen's.

Mackintosh's work was the culmination of the Queen's school of political economists. His approach was rooted in the inquiries of Shortt and Skelton. It extended and modified them, yet followed the lines Shortt established in his environmentalist explorations into

Canadian economic history and political development as well as those made by Skelton in his discussions of the dimensions of political democracy and the capacities of the capitalist system. Also, Mackintosh unveiled in the 1920s the outlines of a summary theory about Canadian economic and political history – a theory very similar to that set out in the later writings of Harold Innis and Donald Creighton – through his elaboration of the staple thesis and his arguments about geographical determinants to Canadian development. In the process he suggested his resolutions to the problems of national autonomy, democracy, and agrarian discontent that his predecessors had concentrated on. Lastly, as shown in the previous chapter, Mackintosh led the diversion of his Queen's colleagues into the practical studies and the public service which provided the only serious outlet for their ambitions concerning national reconstruction and the role of the political economist.

Mackintosh's studies acknowledged the influence of Guy S. Callender's and Turner's economic history and Veblen's and Taussig's economic theory. Equally as important, his arguments owed much to the North American and environmentalist frame of reference established by Shortt and to the neo-classical economic reasoning and powerful liberal-democratic judgments of Skelton. But Mackintosh was not a mere follower of Shortt and Skelton. A child of the Laurier boom, Mackintosh, like Clifford Clark, actually worked for an extended period in the west, spending two summers as a schoolteacher and two years as a college professor as well as establishing close ties with agrarian leaders such as T.A. Crerar, Charles Dunning, and E.A. Partridge. In contrast, Shortt and Skelton made only brief visits to the west. Furthermore, while Mackintosh's debt to Shortt and Skelton was evident in his celebration of the material basis of renewed democracy and the social and political effects of the new economic order, there were also differences among them. Mackintosh's emphasis on the economic basis of changes extended beyond Shortt's or Michell's praise of the cooperatives for their social results or even beyond Skelton's support for the farmers as agents of a more democratic politics. Although he tried to contain each of these aspirations in his evaluation, Mackintosh concentrated on the fundamental impact of economic changes – changes that, he argued, were at the heart of a major transformation in Canadian life. This is why his analysis is so striking, whatever it may owe to his teachers.

Mackintosh has a central place among Canadian economic historians as a co-founder with Harold Innis of the staples interpretation. His account is often portrayed as a simple, optimistic, and favourable view of Canadian development, in contrast with Innis's complex, pessimistic, and critical interpretation. There is no doubt that recent theorists such as Glen Williams and Daniel Drache are right to emphasize the important distinctions between Innis's and Mackintosh's understanding of the tendencies of capitalist development in Canada. They have identified Innis's considerable unease about whether the Canadian economy would follow the example of successful national economies because of the debilitating effects of Canada's dependency on foreign capital and reliance on export staples. They have also noted Mackintosh's confidence that Canadian development would follow a set of stages from pioneer to mature economic development because it was using efficiently its great resource advantages and considerable attractiveness to foreign capital.[41]

To assess properly the merits of these arguments requires a much broader and more technical account of the tendencies of capitalist development than the present work can provide. Still, a couple of reservations need to be offered. While Innis strikes this author as too sinuous to categorize as a fundamental critic of capitalism, Mackintosh simply cannot be adequately understood without an appreciation of his deep perspective on the capitalist system. Like Adam Shortt, Mackintosh expected Canada to follow a pattern of development similar to that of the United States; like Oscar Douglas Skelton, he expected the economy to move to provide the equal opportunity and equitable rewards that alone justified its perpetuation. If Mackintosh was not quite as strident as Skelton in warning Canadian capitalists and politicians that the price of conserving the system was its basic reform, he nonetheless shared the sentiment. For him, as for Skelton, the future of Canadian capitalism was by no means assured.

9 An Agenda for Post-War Canada

> It is for the universities of this and other democratic countries, if they are not to be false to all the nobler traditions of learning and of liberty, if they are to deserve the trust the country has placed in them, if their idealism is to be more than a name, to take the lead in moulding the thought of the country along different lines.
>
> O.D. Skelton

By the end of the Great War, the economic and political difficulties of Canada had only changed their form. If the sheer horror of war was ended, momentous problems of reconstruction and readjustment remained. Apparitions of revolution and the reality of discontent were everywhere present and most obvious in the 1919 confrontation at Winnipeg and the 1921 emergence of the Progressives. There was also the clamour of reformers such as the social gospellers. Pressures for government-led reform came from organized manufacturers as well as organized farmers. Each sought a continuation of the regulatory state established during wartime. The hopes for a new era, however, did not lead to a new national consensus. Indeed, contradictory and competing pressures on government, especially the federal government, seemed to befuddle rather than inspire.[1]

Witnessing this cacophony of reformers and the confusion of governments and political parties were the political economists at Queen's. Their commentaries on the conditions of post-war Canada re-emphasized their arguments for national economic and political reorientaton. Still led by O.D. Skelton, the department had been invigorated by the appointments of Skelton's former students Clifford Clark and William Mackintosh, fresh from Harvard. These two young economists enthusiastically argued in favour of an elaborate role for government in supervising reconstruction. They also tried to link that role to the professional advice of social scientists, especially political economists. Skelton and his younger colleagues defined, as well, a systematic basis for Canadian reconstruction through the university. They began from the premise that the university should become the major agency of research into economic and social problems. They dared to hope that they could reform and influence public opinion by a program of research and teaching in business, economics, and social policy. Furthermore, they stressed that the state needed to move in the specific directions that they themselves had mapped out. By the mid-1920s, however, their various schemes for the university were in tatters. Frustrated, Clark and Skelton led a migration from Queen's to Ottawa. The legacy of their resignations from the university was a period of turbulence for Queen's and the beginnings of the transformation of the federal public service.

IN APRIL 1918, AT THE END of his first year of university teaching, Clifford Clark prepared an explanation of Canada's wartime problems in a long study of government regulation of prices. This was a momentous enough topic given the severe price inflation and popular unease at the shift toward greater government intervention. The particular problem of inflation led Clark to consider the more general characteristics of the price system in wartime and then to assess the capacity of economists, government officials, and business leaders to understand the economic system and economic policy.

Clark began by admitting that economics and many of its dogmas were severely challenged by the war. Partly this was because of the weaknesses of economic theory but to a far greater extent it was because of popular and governmental misconceptions about how the price system worked. Responding sympathetically to United States wartime price czar and engineer Herbert Hoover's dismissal of economic theory and economists, Clark tried to explain the price system in light of current economic theory. Prices, he said, were indicators rather than causes of shifts in the production and distribution of goods. He emphasized the extreme complexity of the way in which supply, demand, and valuation were signalled through the price system by referring to the work of the American economist Wesley C. Mitchell, a prominent theorist of the business cycle and pricing mechanisms who was himself a devotee of the work of Thorstein Veblen.

Prior to government intervention, proper understanding of the complexities of the economic order must be arrived at.[2] In light of the complexity and fragility of the allocation of goods and services, Clark emphasized the defects of any policies that regulated only economic indicators rather than the real factors which shaped economic operations. He maintained that the promise of price controls would be illusory – they would not ease the burdens on consumers or alleviate the problems of allocation which caused the inflation. A system of controls, he asserted, "fails to check waste and unnecessary consumption; it drives the commodity from the market and discourages production; it throws out of balance the sensitive mechanism of the price system; it involves endless frauds, with a general lowering of the moral standards of the community."[3] His moral and economic homily delivered – in the language of Adam Shortt – Clark admitted but one possible means to overcome his objections. If not only prices but also the production and consumption of goods were regulated, then and only then would price ceilings or controls work. Dryly, Clark commented that this course would be "impracticable" because of the logistics of such total planning. Still, the very basis of his objections show that he was engaged in something more than a defence of free enterprise or *laissez-faire*.

Moving from the specific remedy to the general problem of fiscal policy, Clark reached the nub of his argument. The new concept of social welfare – determining the ordinal preferences of society about the distribution of goods and services – was the framework on which economic policy and economic performance were now based. This was a major shift in economic theory from its previous basis on aggregate rather than ordinal output. Clark continued his discussion by stating that he did not wish "to deny the desirability of the state concerning itself in other ways with the problem which the war has created," but he warned that the concept of social welfare was paramount. "The conclusion reached above is not based on any doctrinaire belief in *laissez-faire* but on a study of the facts of experience. Other forms of state interference or state guidance can undoubtedly be justified by the same test, by the ability to contribute in actual practice to a greater measure of social welfare."[4]

In his own approach to state policy, Clark showed in 1918 that he shared the Skeltonian aims of economic efficiency and economic justice. He based his assessment on both the merits of economic efficiency via market forces and the calculation of what he termed the "moral standards of the community" or the" greater measure of social welfare." His dual agenda, like Skelton's, emerged from contemporary economic theory and sought to protect economic efficiency and take as its measure the well-being of all persons in the society. That well-being was to be determined by the hard evidence of the effective allocation of goods. Like Skelton, Clark then advocated a sharp expansion of income taxation designed to strengthen the capacity of the state to stabilize economic output. Clark also suggested a much more ambitious role for the state than Skelton did.

He aimed not just at stabilization, which was Skelton's goal, but also at the supervision of distribution and production. It was easy enough, therefore, for Clark to reel off the instruments for achieving his social-welfare goals: government watch-dogs should coordinate and direct industrial production; government should supervise and publicize consumption and production to encourage efficient and rational behaviour; and government should control excess profit-taking by effective, progressive taxation of personal and business incomes.[5] Each of these proposals had been proposed by Shortt and Skelton but in Clark's case they were presented in a coordinated fashion.

Clark's concern for the general welfare was developed in a second essay published in 1921. In a discussion of "business cycles" he was more explicit in his acknowledgment of Wesley Mitchell's work, mentioning too the writings of Veblen, J.A. Hobson, and the sociologist T.N. Carver. Clark was convinced about the general validity and regularity of economic cycles. Four factors accounted for the "wave-like motion" of expansion, crisis and depression: "the extreme specialization characteristic of modern industry, the large-scale production carried on months ahead of demand and in anticipation of demand, the intricate inter-locking of firms and places through the credit system, and the mob-mindedness of men." The problems of time and planning in the "intricate" system of firms and credit were set off by the subjective factor of human behaviour, with results that were predictable in their variability. The Clark of 1921 was somewhat more content to accept the inevitability of the business cycle than the younger scholar had been: the capacity of government to intervene, he now thought, was relatively limited. Yet he was ready to admit that both government policy and the influences of war, as well as general characteristics of business organization, had contributed to the present crisis. Consequently, he offered a rather conservative exhortation. To follow "the straight-and-narrow path of work, thrift and taxation" was to avoid the kind of over-expansion based on inflated currencies and over-production that had caused the present malaise.[6] While he was still grappling with the general causes of economic insecurity and disruption, he was not willing to apply the interventionist solutions he had previously favoured.

This change of mind should not be interpreted as a reversion to the traditional and fatalistic position that Clark's interpreters have often identified him with.[7] Clark strongly advocated the establishment of supervisory agencies to bring about the return to the "straight-and-narrow" path. In January 1921 he lauded the Board of Commerce, an administrative agency created by the Borden government in 1919. Depending on shaky constitutional and political support, the board was about to be dismantled when Clark defended it. Clark suggested that the board, rather than a politically motivated and probably inexpertly run body such as the once-proposed tariff commission, pointed the way to a new and important means for state economic coordination and stabilization. The need for such a regulatory body was established by the tendency of businesses, as a result of their defensible aim to seek stability and long-term profitability, to "co-operate" or merge. While that evolution of business organization would help to moderate the swings in the business cycle, its immediate effect on the public was somewhat disruptive. Business cooperation led to abuses of market-pricing mechanisms with attendant effects on the public interest. To ensure that the public interest was not severely harmed during the reorganization of business, he asserted, "we need a Board of Commerce."[8]

The newly perfected investigative skills of experts within the public service allowed government to create a supervisory body to regulate the changes in economic organization so that the effects of such changes were not severe. With the combination of business cooperation and state supervision, then, economic efficiency and protection of the public good could be provided for. Specifically, government supervision should tolerate business reorganization, provide codes for business practices, and supervise business by publicity or, occasionally, regulation. The power of publicity and the need for government-coordinated stability, beneficial for business and public alike, were compelling reasons to preserve the Board of Commerce. A rather typical Canadian, Clark thought that a combination of administrative supervision and business cartellization would "fortify" the "free enterprise" system.

To Clark, the old problems of commissions – their uneasy applicability to parliamentary government and the legislators' incapacity to follow disinterested advice – were now soluble. The application of "thorough research and scientific method" could be attuned to the dual aims of efficiency and social justice. Here Clark used the example of the advice tendered by the United States Tariff Board, a body directed by his dissertation supervisor F.W. Taussig. In Canada, political responsibility would be preserved through the subordination of such agencies to departmental organization. Clark looked to parliament as the forum where the public interest was to be defended but this parliament would rely on the advice of experts who could balance the goals of efficiency and justice.[9]

Accordingly, Clark emphasized the need to examine further the business cycle by the compilation of adequate statistical information. That task was taken up by many economists in the 1910s and 1920s.

Clark's one-time colleague, Humfrey Michell, wrote several papers on the business cycle for the fledgling *Canadian Forum*. Like Clark, Michell thought that the existence of such regular cycles was now unquestionable. What remained was to perfect the statistical measurement of this cycle so as to develop an "economic barometer" that would allow governments to prepare for fluctuations and possibly adjust the factors which brought changes about. That, Michell warned, was a task of years of statistical and theoretical inquiry. The massive ambition of it was obvious: "Solve the problem of the business cycle and the world will have advanced a great step towards mankind's control of the forces of nature." Later works such as the volumes *Statistical Contributions to Canadian Economic History*, edited by Michell, his McMaster colleague K.W. Taylor, and Queen's economist C.A. Curtis, indicated the fascination with measuring economic indicators as a means to begin to control their fluctuations.[10]

Skelton and Shortt had supported a Canadian "Bureau of Statistics" for precisely that purpose. Skelton's studies of Canadian federal finance were replete with serial statistical evidence which, he suggested, might be made the basis of predictions. That Clark shared this interest in statistics is seen by his membership in and contributions to the American Statistical Association.[11] All these scholars were convinced that, when data was collected, the basis for better prediction – and, of course, better policy – would be well established.

As their tone suggested, Queen's political economists thought that they were moving towards a better analysis of economic questions and that their information and proposals were very persuasive indeed. Their goal remained to gain more control over the economic process. A commitment to the potential mastery economic analysis might offer and to the social benefits of that mastery was exhibited by Clifford Clark's younger colleague, William Mackintosh. Like Clark, Mackintosh was emboldened by the disruptions and crises of war to offer a fundamental restatement about the direction of economic activities under the supervision of government. Mackintosh did so in light of the new proficiency he thought the economist could bring to that direction. He was quick to admit the theoretical and practical deficiencies of economics; the war, after all, had shown a number of flaws in the understanding and implementation of economic ideas. But the chief lesson of the war for economic thought and government policy making was that insufficient attention had been given to economic realities and to the comparison of practical developments with existing theory.[12]

Contemporary economic practice, claimed Mackintosh, clashed with classical Ricardian theory. Few economists, administrators, or politicians addressed this gap between theory and practice. For economists, in Mackintosh's view, the work of Thorstein Veblen was crucial in delineating the variations between contemporary practice and traditional theory, between facts and principles. Veblen's work suggested a way to devise the necessary "scientific" reinterpretation of economics on which more effective policy could be based. The particular weakness of analysis and policy was centred in their inability to deal with economic competition, which was itself central to the allocation of goods and services. Mackintosh elaborated on the present failings of economists and policy makers by reference to the alternative account of Veblen. For Veblen, "Industry is at present essentially dynamic; it is in motion. Without friction we could, in mechanics, have perpetual motion. Without friction we could have analogous results in industry and commerce. Some of our principles derived from frictionless or static economics are as useful to the administrator as that of perpetual motion to the mechanic. Veblen with more consistence than any other has laid emphasis on friction. Veblen's theory of business profits is that they represent the failure of competition to work; they represent frictional gains. They represent not competition but control."[13]

His analogy to mechanics and his declamation about the practice of "static" analysis suggested several points from which Mackintosh thought a new kind of economic analysis might begin. Mackintosh sought a practical direction to economic questions so that the "administrator" could repair the economic machine. Theory for its own sake was not his aim. He also indicated his skepticism about the "equilibrium" basis of neo-classical economics. Seeking the same kind of understanding that physical scientists such as engineers had achieved, he wanted to prod economists into considering the dimension of motion or time to their discipline. This can be seen as a plea for the kind of historical approach to economic problems that he himself was already pursuing and that his Queen's predecessors had followed. Even as he used the same mechanical analogy, he was dissenting from the assured view of neo-classical economists. To him, their understanding of the price system and its allocation of resources was predicated on an ill-founded assumption of natural efficiency and harmony.

Mackintosh's criticism of existing economic theory led him to call for much more analysis, particularly of economic competition. "The thesis presented here," he wrote,

is not that the competitive system is not justified by its results ... The argument rather is that at present numerous facts indicate that there are large and noteworthy gaps in our ordinary assumption of competition and that even where that system is effective as a means of control, it does not necessarily or even usually work according to the accustomed formulae. Further, we have not enough data at our disposal to know just how it does work. We know that competition exists and that friction exists. We know that there is an element of joint cost in most industries and that the effect of competition is decidedly "abnormal" in such cases. What we do not know is the extent to which these factors are involved. Once more we know the principles, but the facts are lacking. Moreover, the principles without the facts are like mathematics without measurements to apply them to, very pure but very useless.[14]

The search for data and revision of theory, for technical capacity to deal with the real industrial and commercial system, was again upheld by Mackintosh. His reference to overcoming economic "friction" (as well as theoretical fictions) shows that he was happy to aspire to work as the garage-mechanic of capitalism that historian Frank Underhill found so objectionable for economists. But this aspiration meant that an expanding role was needed for the economist, in line with his desire to achieve technical expertise along the lines Clark suggested, and especially a new general economic theory. It also meant a new role for the state, something socialist Underhill did not admit even though he himself called for a new Benthamite commitment to reform via administrators.[15] Mackintosh's criticism belittled the existing knowledge of economists and administrators, who could not achieve expertise and effectiveness until economic theory had been revitalized. It simply was not the case that a few administrative boards or the intrusion of professional economists could lead to the effective management of economy, despite the Underhills of the world.

For William Mackintosh, the problems of war and reconstruction demanded a reworking of economic theory and practice as well as supervision over the economy by the state. If nothing else were done, public discontent must be alleviated. The sources of that discontent were too broad and too serious to be ignored. Consumers knew that "through the failure of competition to work," prices as well as profits and productivity were askew. Moreover, "rising prices brought an unequal distribution of the burden of the war." Because economists and administrators had failed to respond, preachers and journalists were finding a receptive audience for their ignorant remedies. That chilling example of discontent, the Winnipeg General Strike, was not the result of conspiratorial or revolutionary zeal. On the contrary, the strike had been caused by deep-seated economic and social problems such as trade-union rivalries, inflation, "the slow racking of the poor," specific regional grievances, and the immediate effects of the post-war slump. The strike, in a nutshell, was made possible by the existence of what Mackintosh summarized as "potent fundamental evil; an evil so potent and so fundamental that the community becomes a co-partner in maintaining it." The strike also showed that at Winnipeg and elsewhere civil disobedience was "aimed directly at a public which had been ignorant of, or shirked its responsibilities." In his observations, Mackintosh offered an explanation which at least partially threatened that the consequences of economic injustice and inequality would be social upheaval. Simple prudence, as well as a sence of justice, dictated that economic reform and reorganization were vital.[16]

Skelton reached the same conclusion in his assessment of the Winnipeg strike. He also emphasized labour's goals of a fairer distribution of wealth and recognition of the inviolable right to collective bargaining. He too used the example of Winnipeg to call for more efficient taxation and business reform. Interestingly enough, Skelton's comments were published in the *Queen's Quarterly* while Mackintosh's more extended and critical analysis remained in manuscript; prudence applied to professors as well as to defenders of order, although Skelton criticized governmental reaction to the Winnipeg strike as "hysterical exaggeration."[17]

Mackintosh argued that the solution to social and economic problems rested on expert analysis, including statistics gathering and Veblenian rethinking of theory, and the expansion of state agencies to oversee economic activity. From 1919 to 1925 he urged the creation of economic commissions similar to the Commission on Conservation (that is, an investigative not a quasi-judicial body) as well as finance-department scrutiny of all banking operations, fundamental reform of the administrative arm of government by recruitment of economic and other administrative experts, and the redirection of economic policies to deal with the sectionalism, geographical barriers, and business practices that were at the root of Canada's difficulties.[18]

Like Adam Shortt and Clifford Clark, Mackintosh was eager to interpret national problems as administrative ones, although – and this was a continuing feature of their view of the public servant – he was also emphatic in maintaining a separation of the administrative from the political side of government. The sheer complexity of policy making defied the skills of economists or administrators alone, no matter how expert they became. On the other hand, the tendency of his proposals was towards the creation of a more powerful executive-administrative arm of government. In 1922 he observed that the

problems of the Canadian National Railways system were not amenable to "popular judgement." "The pressing railway problem is an
administrative problem," he claimed, and his conclusion was that
"only years of patient and ungloried economy, firm administration,
and not a little boldness in preparing for and stimulating the traffic
increases which the return of industrial prosperity will bring, can
solve the present difficulty. The result of that work, the public will
praise or blame, but popular judgement can contribute little or
nothing to railway policy."[19] Popular judgment, including by implication that of political advisors, was to be exchanged for the expertise
of autonomous administrators. The very folly and misdeeds of that
public which had "shirked its responsibilities" at Winnipeg were perhaps reason enough to choose experts over the populace. More generally, only by strengthening the civil service would the efficient and
economic administration of government policies be begun. Rede-
fining many national problems as administrative and economic ones
and solving them by technical expertise would enable the nation to
overcome the inequalities and inefficiencies reflected in sectional
protest and class discontent.

In addition, the expert's rational standards would improve the
efficiency of the market, and this would in turn lead to qualitative
and quantitative improvements in the condition of all people in
society. The cases of agrarian reform and economic ethics come to
mind. As agriculture became more efficient, an ethic of democracy
reflecting the farmers' own virtues was diffused throughout society.
Similarly, as business became professionalized, the "acquisitive" society
was displaced by a more humane and socially cohesive ethic. Like
Skelton and Clark, Mackintosh was identifying his arguments with
those of a strong reformist economist, in this case R.H. Tawney. In
fact, echoes of Tawney's argument reverberated in the language and
the arguments that Mackintosh often used. Like Tawney, he looked
forward to a social and economic transformation. With economic
well-being and efficiency as well as social justice and individual fulfilment as his goals, Mackintosh foresaw changes and the means to
achieve them which were similar to those of his predecessors at
Queen's. He aimed at the individual fulfilment within a reorganized
society that Shortt had posited as the broadest social goal. He anticipated the more equitable distribution of economic rewards and
opportunities that Skelton had also seen as within the capacities of
the capitalist system. To Mackintosh, the pace of the expert economist
in bringing about this transformation of social relations was as central
as that of the reforming agrarians in changing political ones.[20]

THE WORK OF SHORTT, SKELTON, Clark, and Mackintosh had established standards of economic responsibility for the state and new gauges of economic performance for the nation. Significantly, they claimed a similarly new set of goals and duties for the political economist. As well, they demanded numerous innovations in the federal government's approach to fiscal policy and the national economy. The reforms they suggested would provide for greater economic and social stability as well as a measure of economic and social effectiveness based on tenets of equality and calculations of efficiency.

Oscar Skelton led his colleagues in the elaboration of ideas and programs designed to engineer greater social justice. With the others, he explored ways to redistribute wealth and thus provide the basis for social security. These ways, of course, were applications of the tax reforms Skelton had developed during the war. Moreover, Clifford Clark and his Queen's classmate, Bryce Stewart, devised the system of labour exchanges that aimed at countering the bumpy effects of the business cycle and regional economic differences upon Canadian labour. In line with these ambitions, Queen's political economists also advocated the expansion of social-scientific research within the university so that they would more fully participate in the resolution of contemporary economic problems.

Discussing the 1919 Whitely report on industrial relations in the United Kingdom, O.D. Skelton suggested that wartime experiences and self-help traditions were allowing labour to bring exciting new approaches to the organization of industry. The addition of a new sense of collective bargaining rights meant that the next step in labour-capital relations would be an "equal partnership in industry," the"joint control by capital and labour" of the workplace. Both the impasse in labour-management relations and the model of hierarchical business organization were unlikely to remain, or so Skelton hoped. The alternatives to the present system and its current stalemate were the following: the state could step in to control labour-capital relations, thereby bringing about the likely expansion of state ownership; or workers could overthrow the authority of management and at least determine the direction if not capture the ownership of industry. In the interests of economic efficiency and social harmony, neither of these was acceptable. The "equal partnership" concept was the only choice that met the equitable claims of capital and labour and the prudential motives of society in seeking to maintain its liberal-democratic and capitalist orientations.[21] In many ways these views were similar to those of Skelton's collaborator Mackenzie King.

In fact, King's *Industry and Humanity* had been taken seriously enough by Skelton for him to review it – and very favourably.

Skelton himself claimed that he was really only sustaining arguments for a system of "representative government" in industry. Canadian whigs might have been inclined to conclude that before long "responsible" government in industrial relations might also come about. This was perhaps the sort of evolution Skelton foresaw in his hopes for the expansion of labour's right to share in the larger decisions about business operation. In any case, the provision of joint councils in industry suggested a major reorganization within industry. It also suggested the elaboration of further changes in the relations between industry and government. The expanding partnership between labour and management required that the state act as supervisor at least during the period of change.[22]

Such state participation was indeed necessary in directing the cooperation of the "partners" in industry. More generally, the reorganization of labour-capital relations was itself the necessary goal of full-scale post-war reconstruction, a point Skelton made forcefully to readers of the Canadian Bankers' Association *Journal* in January 1918. In this essay Skelton first warned his readers not to think of state-led initiatives as something to be leery of. He suggested that "there is room and need for a greatly increased measure of state activity before we approach the degree of national organization attained in other lands, or incur the rise of bureaucratic rule or undue centralization." He continued by arguing that "a nation-wide, if not national, system of labor exchanges is essential for the demobilization period, as well as for the future management of the problem of bringing man and job together." He went on to offer specific proposals as well as a blunt criticism of existing government policy: "A comprehensive system of technical education; an extension of the age of compulsory attendance, with the establishment of continuing schools; insurance on a contributory basis, against unemployment, sickness, invalidity, and possibly old age, are among the most obvious questions that call for full consideration – and a consideration much more serious, painstaking and informed than has been displayed by our Federal or most of our Provincial Governments in dealing with social questions in the past."[23]

Labour-market control, expanded educational facilities, and comprehensive social insurance were the crucial, minimal ways in which the state must act. In so doing it would reconstruct and reform the relations among people and the position of the individual in society. Once again, Skelton suggested that the dominion government was more remiss than at least some of the provinces in failing to adapt to the new demands on government. His emphasis on the necessity for federal initiative clearly did not emerge from a belief in its natural progressiveness. More likely, as has been noted in other instances, his commitment to federal action was based on his strong sense of the need for truly national social standards.

To each of these areas of state-induced reform, Queen's political economists of the post-war era devoted considerable attention. The provision for several kinds of social insurance had long been suggested by Skelton as a concomitant of the increased economic responsibilities of the state and of the enhanced economic capacity and interdependence of society. Prior to the war, Skelton had argued that these new reforms comprised a necessary "righting of wrongs" to which the alternative was "revolutionary agitation" by those who were not served by the unreformed order. Both then and after the war, Skelton thought that such provincial initiatives as workman's compensation showed the way for federal activity as well as the relevance of British model legislation. At this point it must be recalled that one of the reasons for Skelton's intention to strengthen the tax-gathering potential of the state was to provide it with the power to finance such reforms. Since he proposed an increase in taxation, Skelton suggested joint contributions by individuals and governments to social-insurance schemes, not total self-financing. He also proposed progressive income taxation in place of economically counter-stimulative and regressive "expenditure" taxes. The counter-cyclical fiscal policies he thereby envisioned amounted to a redistributive spending scheme of considerable scope. With his sights firmly fixed on a more secure treasury and the aims of economic stability and justice, Skelton ensured that the state indeed had the capacity to provide transfer payments to individuals. His schemes from 1911 to 1918 had depended on major taxation reforms so that such redistribution could result.[24]

A key field for state intervention and reform in Skelton's 1918 agenda was the labour market. Skelton's students Bryce Morrison Stewart and Clifford Clark worked in the Department of Labour at Ottawa during the reconstruction period to build a significant supervisory role for government. Both men had been undergraduates at Queen's prior to the war. Like Adam Shortt, Stewart had abandoned his original impulse to become a clergyman; instead, he took up political economy, eventually receiving an MA in 1911. After employment with the Methodist and Presbyterian churches' joint social surveys, he went to work for the federal government in 1914. Stewart actually spent two periods of his life working for the Department of Labour. From 1914 to 1922, he conducted policy studies, and much later, from 1940 to 1942, he served as deputy minister. Between his first resignation in 1922 and his 1926 entry into doctoral studies in industrial relations, he worked for the American Amalgamated Clothing Workers Union in the Chicago, the same union that recruited Clifford Clark. Stewart did his doctoral work at Columbia and, after completing his thesis, took on the post of industrial-relations director for the Rockefeller Corporation in New York, the billet Mackenzie King had once agonized over before returning to Canada. Stewart remained with "Industrial Relations Counsellors, Inc." except for his time in Ottawa during the Second World War.[25]

Prior to his 1914 move to Ottawa, Stewart had examined the problems of immigration and urbanization in an economy distinguished by severe seasonal variations in employment. To the new Canadian Political Science Association, he warned that "an army of industrial nomads" was being created. He concluded that both public and private efforts were necessary but that the major challenge was to strengthen Canadian social institutions in order to "Canadianize" the degraded but hardly dangerous foreigners. At the same time, he claimed that *laissez-faire* policies were no longer adequate in the present complex world.[26]

After the war, Stewart decided that the swings of the business cycle and the challenge they presented to the state's financial and administrative capacities must be addressed. Like Skelton, Clark, and Mackintosh, he held that the moderation of the business cycle by a systematic state response to economic difficulties would be the basis for resolving the problems of Canadian economy. That resolution would involve a "nice bit of social engineering that will take decades to accomplish." If his rhetorical turn suggested Stewart's enthusiasm for the task, his elaboration on the job of "social engineering" showed his grasp of its complexity. He suggested that the response must include the broad reform of higher education, especially technical education, the regulation of employment agencies and working conditions, and the "systematic distribution of public employment [and] unemployment insurance." By the end of the war he thought that the specific problem of converting the economy and the immense military force to peace-time endeavours necessitated the immediate attention of the government. Again, the national scope of the country's problems made it logical that the dominion government seize an initiative which until now had been left to the provinces.[27]

Like his Queen's associates, Stewart was convinced that systematic state-led reconstruction must begin in order to stabilize the economy and to create a more secure post-war society. The key to stability was the National Employment Service which he and Clark implemented at the Department of Labour during 1918 and 1919. The Employment Service was itself conceived as part of a larger program to grapple with the problems of the employment and economic cycles. Even if a larger scheme was not feasible, argued Stewart, the evident failure of private-employment agencies was so great that state action was necessary. Not only could a state-run employment service effectively get people and jobs together, it could also stabilize the employment cycle if it was coordinated with immigration and other policies. In any case, the state's "natural monopoly," as Stewart called it, over relations between labour and capital meant that an employment service was but an extension of existing supervisory powers. Stewart and Clark agreed on the long-term and highly technical nature of the problem of employment stabilization. Solving it, in their view, would require considerable statistical inquiry as well as the growth of expert administrators within the civil service. Still, Stewart also emphasized that employment problems must be seen from the "social viewpoint" as well as the economic. Focusing on the welfare of those who laboured with such insecurity under the private-enterprise labour market, he called for unemployment insurance to relieve short-term individual difficulties as well as contribute to long-term social stability.[28]

The National Employment Service experienced a rise and decline nearly as precipitous as the post-war problems that had encouraged the Borden government to support it in the first place. The employment service, its historian James Struthers has explained, floundered almost immediately even though it continued through the 1920s. The resistance of businessmen and politicians to innovation once the emergency of reconstruction was over, combined with the complexities of federal-provincial cooperation, led to its eclipse. Nonetheless, it represented an attempt to apply expert skills so as to resolve the worst effects of the economy on a large and vulnerable group. Ironically enough, Stewart's concerns about the place of the unskilled and semi-skilled and immigrant labour force were realized in the early 1930s when their efforts at self-help became the object of considerable official hostility during the "red scare" period. It had been the premise of Stewart – as well as of Skelton and Mackintosh – that reform through government intervention would draw the sting of radicals.[29] Finally, even if the specific attempt by Clark and Stewart was unsuccessful, it was a clear response by economists to the challenge to provide government with new policies. The failure of their efforts may have been a useful lesson to them that consulting policy-design work was ephemeral.

There was another factor that the Queen's political economists thought would contribute to the economic and social reconstruction of Canada – the expansion of the university as a centre for research and the teaching of economic questions. The importance they attached to this aim should not be underestimated. Skelton and his colleagues sought to devise an essential role for the university in shaping business as well as government and popular understanding of economic and social questions. Their ambitions for the university's further integration into the world of practical affairs, however, met with resistance. In that way, their experience was similar to the sociologists at McGill, who shared their hopes for university research and the university and who encountered the same kind of opposition. The difference between the two groups was that, unlike the McGill sociologists, Queen's political economists were able to transfer their skills to the government.[30]

At Queen's, Oscar Skelton emerged as the pivotal figure. In 1916 and 1918 Skelton and his departmental colleagues presented tightly argued proposals for major changes in the social sciences. As noted earlier, these were parallel to changes in the science faculty proposed by A.L. Clark. Both of the 1918 plans were launched by new deans who thought erroneously that Queen's was moving towards a new concept of service that included research but remained based on what Skelton had earlier suggested were the "nobler traditions of learning and liberty." In 1914 Skelton had believed that universities must remain aloof from war hysteria even if they should not limit the war effort. But by 1916 he thought that the universities must deal with the long-term consequences of the war. "The country," he wrote to Principal Gordon, "faces a period of rapid and far-reaching economic readjustment. The growth and transformation which the country experienced in the first dozen years of the century, the collapse of the boom before the war, the revolutionary effects of the war in Canada itself and in the world at large; have bequeathed us a host of questions which call for investigation and solution." He continued by arguing that he and his colleagues "believe that the Departments of Economics of our various universities, and not least Queen's should endeavour to take part more systematically and on a larger scale in the work of research alike in applied economics. English and American universities have undertaken some work in these fields ... but we think there is need for doing still more here." The universities should "take the lead in moulding the thought of the country along different lines," Skelton asserted. He had, of course, already decided that a vastly enlarged role for the universities was needed so that the intellectual "light we have" could actually be used. But during the war Skelton saw the university as the centre for the resolution of social and economic problems through research – research aimed at both commercial education and social and economic problems, at theoretical and practical questions. His plan was far more embracing and clear than Shortt's clarion call prior to the war.[31]

By 1918, Queen's political economy department was trying to set out the social and economic issues that demanded an innovative response from the social scientists within the university. Research into and teaching of a broad range of economic and social topics were, the political economists suggested, likely to yield highly important results.[32] This sense of optimism and self-confidence was derived from the political economists' assured explanations of how the social order actually worked, the result of their studies of Canada and the tenets of their discipline. But the university proved unsympathetic to their claims and proposals. The result was that the political economists were, to use the phrase Skelton once applied to Goldwin Smith, preaching to an empty house. Their own response to this rebuff was not to continue speaking into the void but rather to search for a receptive audience. For reasons that are somewhat outside the scope of this work – which reflect a convergence between Canadian political and administrative pressures and the social scientists' agenda – certain individuals in the federal government provided a ready audience indeed.[33]

Although they were willing to move to the public service, the Queensians held deep suspicions about the existing analytical and planning skills of governments. O.D. Skelton had been very critical of the democratic allies' reconstruction programs, reserving particular scorn for the Borden government. He noted with irony that "our sapient governments" seemed to have nothing to offer but such "futile" and "discredited" forms of intervention as commissions. The inadequacy of administrative tribunals, of course, did not mean that intervention was unnecessary or useless. With the undemocratic, uneconomic, and ineffectual government initiatives as a target, Skelton and his younger colleagues offered a post-war program of reconstruction based on effective government supervision of the economy. This program involved government reform, public re-education, and the expert social scientists' coordination of each.

Clifford Clark and William Mackintosh assessed critically the possibilities of government coordination and regulation of economic activity. Both men agreed with Skelton that the sort of regulation established by the Borden government was a futile – and perhaps harmful – attack on the indicators rather than the causes of economic activity. The government's policy, moreover, was to create agencies that handed down arbitrary judgments about particular instances of difficulty rather than measuring, publicizing, and cautiously regulating the complex system out of which the difficulties emerged. For Clark and Mackintosh, this distinction between intervention and regulation raised the point that there was a pressing need to reconsider how economic activity was conducted before regulation could be effective. Such a reconsideration was demanded of the economists, who did not, Mackintosh charged, fully understand the actual workings of the system. It was also demanded of the politicians and administrators who, Clark asserted, tried better than the economists to deal with the practical operations of the economy. Though a friendly debate about the scope of economic science and public administration ran through their writings, Clark and Mackintosh were agreed on the basic possibilities that rational economics and policies suggested. A high degree of economic efficiency through state regulation was now possible if scientific economic knowledge was applied to and by government, and such regulation would have important economic and social effects.

Yet no matter how great its possibilities were, regulation was only one aspect of the larger reorientation that was necessary – the economic goals and values of Canadians must also be changed. To bring about this reorientation, Clark repeated Skelton's arguments that justice could and should become an economic and social goal. One practical means to achieve this aim was a better system of taxation. Another was the labour-exchange network that Clark and Bryce Stewart established. But, for Mackintosh, the key change needed was social in nature and it could best be realized by the nourishment and harnessing of "instincts" other than the acquisitive one. Reviving Shortt's goal of reorienting humankind towards a more satisfactory conception of material and social fulfilment, Mackintosh drew on the contemporary economic theory developed by innovators such as Hobson and Veblen, Taussig and Tawney, to show how this change in human attitudes and behaviour would come about.

Mackintosh, in particular, defended the economists' perspective on the material order against the new behavioural scientists' claim to have founded a "scientific" means to manage people. These new managers thought that they could motivate and stimulate workers so as to produce the greatest possible efficiency and thus output. Yet it was not clear that their assessment of human motivation or the means of harnessing it were correct. The economists' concept of "man," he noted, had been developed from very long-term statistical observation and measurement of human behaviour as reflected in the market economy. In one way economists had been "behaviourists" long before psychologists. But the economists' assessment was more scientific and more valid since it was based on specific circumstantial factors rather than the psychologists' "deceptive common observations." Unlike behaviourists, economists did not "assume an 'economic man' let alone that individuals would conform to rigid theory." Mackintosh spoke like a direct student of Adam Shortt.[34]

Instead of the behaviourists' narrow conception of efficiency and of management, and the resulting aim to systematize work, Mackintosh urged the consideration of other human motives and ways of harnessing men's and women's energies. In particular, the "creative impulse" must be seen as a central counterpiece to the motivations usually appealed to by businessmen and honed to technical perfection by the scientific-management specialists. Mackintosh asserted that economists had begun to see that human nature contained potential untapped by existing social and economic relations. For instance, there were the findings of Taussig and Veblen. Taussig had argued that an "instinct of contrivance" was essential to economic activity while Veblen found an "instinct of workmanship" sustaining material life and progress. Each man showed that "there is a basic tendency for our natures to express themselves in some creative act." Mackintosh concluded: "The best work is done under this impulse but the bulk of the world's work is harnessed to the motive of self-interest ... Recent experience ... with widespread restrictions of output has made clear that the wage-incentive is not enough, that there must be some further incentive, some interest in or control over the work if the maximum efficiency is to be obtained."[35]

All researchers into economics and business must contend with this revelation, for it offered to change humanity's economic experiences considerably. One important task for academic and applied research would be to develop the "science of business" by professionalizing it. Businessmen, like the social scientists, should emulate the older, nobler professions. It would then be possible for business activity to shift from the limited and perhaps even economically stultifying profit motive to those of the creative impulses. With this shift, Mackintosh concluded, the "acquisitive society will pass from us." In an influential 1921 book that Mackintosh referred to, *The Acquisitive Society*, British economic historian and social democratic theorist R.H. Tawney had condemned pecuniary motives and saw great potential to cultivate the altruistic side of human beings. The acquisitive society of competing individuals would then evolve into a functional society of cooperating social groups. Mackintosh's adoption of Tawney's argument indicated his own attraction to an analysis both critical of the present order and hopeful in foreseeing its change, particularly by adopting the service-based advice of experts.[36]

MACKINTOSH'S, CLARK'S, and Stewart's hopes – like the various regulatory and welfare suggestions and plans they made – indicate how Queen's academics after 1918 were themselves reoriented. After the turn of the century, Shortt had devoted his time to public as well as university education as means to inform Canadians about the problems and choices they faced. He had sought greater influence – and social reform – through administrative work and administrative reforms. A bit later, Skelton had concentrated on the academic analysis and presentation of alternative proposals about Canada's difficulties. But with the end of the war, Skelton and the younger economists set out to bring about his previously defined aims of economic efficiency and social justice through the university.

There is considerable importance in the precise fashion in which they set out their agenda of research. Whereas in the 1900s Adam Shortt had made a grand appeal about the political economists' possible role, Clark could announce by the end of the Great War that social welfare was the new theoretical basis for economic policy. Skelton could then indicate specific problems for resolution and policies to solve them while Mackintosh could explain the role of the economist. The resolution of these problems required a central role for the political economist, rather than just for educated men and women. The political economists could propose and support a program of highly selective state regulation and social-insurance provisions. And, while they were not very informative about these provisions, they realized that the reforms were dependent upon the prior reorientation of popular expectations and public finance. Queen's political economists, after all, delivered homilies not on the virtues of private enterprise but rather on the weakness of current government supervision. The new programs demanded the expansion of a public administration which, to be effective, must be conducted by the expert social scientists who actually understood how the political and economic order worked. These scholars must be aided by the graduates of the new research- and policy-oriented social-science courses. Queen's political economists also looked to the transformation of business practices and popular thinking. Just as the agrarian economy could serve to stimulate the efficiency and rationality of the nation, so too the redirection of research and teaching in the university could contribute to this process by affecting those middle-class groups who were less experimental or innovative than the farmers.

The crucial director of this agenda and solutions was the social scientist. He could provide the intellectual analysis which might ensure proper state endeavours (regulatory and accountable, not judicial and arbitrary ones) and reassessment of economic activities and goals by the public, especially professional groups. Both were necessary. Reform could not be imposed by a regulatory state alone – for economic efficiency and human freedom as well as social justice were to be preserved. Neither could reform emerge merely from a reoriented public consciousness – the provision of justice required effective political intervention into the economic process. In this regard Queen's political economists were indicating somewhat less assurance about the power of the wheat economy than Mackintosh himself argued for. They were careful in setting out narrow conditions under which Canada might attain the social and economic goals of efficiency and justice. Those narrow conditions limited the role of the state and its new administrators, but not of the political economist. The latter was no longer simply a critic or analyst (as Shortt had once claimed) but rather the coordinator and educator of the professional classes, the government, and the populace.

Yet this very role was in one respect a continuation of the one that Shortt embraced. An increasingly complex world still demanded a sense of public responsibility from the more proficient social scientists. Following Shortt's lead, the new political economists did not advocate a retreat to very narrow problems or goals; they did not hide away in the bureaucracy implementing tariff schedules or freight rates. Like Shortt, they sought a general goal of economic and administrative reform. If the political economists betrayed something of the arrogance of the technical virtuoso or even technocrat in their exclusive claims to insights, they still held to Shortt's aims of seeking the preservation of economic efficiency as well as the movement towards economic justice and greater political and social opportunities for the individual. Their understanding of the complexity of the new order meant that strategic interventions and reforms could have an even more important impact than a well-meaning but ineffectual wholesale reconstruction.

In fact, only the expert could aspire to these goals. Clark's proposal for the administrative reform of the price system and Mackintosh's explanation of the political ramifications of greater agrarian efficiency and prosperity each demonstrated the need for both narrow economic expertise and its broad social effects. In the case of these men, the multiple impact of expert tinkering reflected the same appreciation of the interrelations between the complex factors of the social order that Shortt and Skelton previously had tried to set out as the basis for their strategic impact upon the nation. The optimism of Clark and Mackintosh most clearly reflects Skelton's assured understanding of the way in which the political and economic order worked. They were experts who still wished to solve general problems and still sought to preserve democracy and capitalism through a commitment to justice as well as efficiency.

10 Queen's Political Economists and the New Liberalism

The story of Queen's political economists, a group remarkable not only for their academic scholarship but also for their influence as bureaucrats and their commentary on public issues, reveals another band in the spectrum of early-twentieth-century political and economic debate. But their significance does not end there. The impact of the Queensians can also be seen in their consideration of the role of the scholar and scholarly research, and, more important, in their critical restatement of the actual workings and potential operations of political and economic institutions. The following examination of these subjects suggests some of their implications for our understanding of the debate about politics in the first half of the twentieth century in Canada. It is also intended to throw light on the intellectual conversation about political economy and the state that has informed Canadian social science.

Shortt, Skelton, Clark, and Mackintosh studied economics and politics in order to assess both the legitimacy and the possibilities of liberal-democratic political and economic institutions in Canada in the late nineteenth and early twentieth centuries. Responding to the serious changes reshaping these institutions, they posited arguments that challenged dominant interests, including their academic allies, who were content with the perpetuation of considerable inequalities and rather bleak prospects for most people. They also confronted that small minority of social and political critics who looked forward to the demise of liberal democracy in the changing social conditions. To Queen's political economists, the promise of democratic politics and capitalist economics had been thoroughly ignored, discredited, or rejected both by ostensible defenders and by the disenchanted. They were convinced that the truncated economic prosperity and limited political participation that marked early-twentieth-century Canada would have to be overcome if the legitimacy and promise of capitalist democracy were to be sustained.

Deeply committed to the idea of liberal democracy, Queen's social scientists were hopeful that a just and efficient market economy could be sustained and that an effective, representative parliamentary system of government could be nurtured. At the same time, however, they warned that a complex remaking of economic and political institutions and a reconsideration of the individual's role in society were necessary if the promise of liberal democracy was to be realized.

THE KEY QUESTION ABOUT the role of the intellectual focuses on the problem of whether intellectuals seeking influence in society constitute a "clerisy" or a "vanguard." Are intellectuals a clerisy, a separate group above society's normal activities? Or are they a vanguard, a class or part of a class that vitally participates in and influences society? If they are the former, how do they influence social change? If they are the latter, are they anything other than representatives of competing social groups and social forces?[1]

A widely accepted argument among Canadian political scientists and sociologists is that, by and large, social scientists have not been uncomfortable with their status as a clerisy offering mild commentary on society but not quarrelling with its basic structure or troubling to participate in non-academic matters. The few Canadian social scientists in the vanguard emerge as Harold Innis saw them, virtual collaborators with the élites and thus highly orthodox figures indeed.[2] One group that has often been charged with this Faustian sell-out is Queen's political economists. Accordingly, it is important to establish what Queen's social scientists actually did prior to striking that bargain with the devil which Canadian scholars since Innis have so often noted.

Clearly these people did not conceive of themselves as a clerisy seeking insulation from and only the most indirect influence over society. Yet, seeing themselves as a vanguard, they were very careful to define themselves as a separate group with a distinct role in society. They certainly did not want to subsume or even tie themselves to another group or class, not in the way they thought that so many of their contemporaries had done by their alliances with business or the churches.

To understand the particular position they defined, three points should be noted. First, the doctrine of academic autonomy that Shortt devised and Skelton and the others upheld was designed to prevent the subordination of the scholar's work to the goals of politicians. To insulate the scholar from both old-style political pressure and new-fangled expert consultation was to shift towards an autonomous role for the intellectual that has seldom been found in Canada. This form of autonomy, however, did not mean avoiding contact with government – Shortt, Skelton, and the others engaged in research with government agencies. They did this work partly because that was the only way to support their own inquiries into policy areas, and indeed their intellectual independence was never compromised. Shortt condemned the premises and direction of Mackenzie King's Industrial Disputes Act and Skelton's research during the reciprocity campaign of 1911 contradicted the results Mackenzie King wanted. In the 1930s, Mackintosh argued that the theoretical inquiries of the economists solved economic questions only. He warned that the broader social and political issues that disturbed society were not resolved by such technical inquiries. Mackintosh was not only stating the political economists' adherence to the distinction, commonly made by mainstream social scientists, between positive and normative work; he was also restating the longstanding Queen's insistence that the social scientist legitimately contributed to the normative choices society made but that they could not impose the positive results of economics as the basis for normative choices.[3]

Secondly, Shortt, Skelton, and Mackintosh were not the triumphant advocates of positions that governments adopted holus-bolus. In Ottawa, they found roles that allowed them to rethink the role of the public service, shape foreign policy, and create the structure of fiscal and social policy. But, if their roles as innovative policy architects became most visible during their years in government, they were hardly successful in imposing their own particular views. After all, Adam Shortt did not discredit the patronage approach to public-service appointments or the brokerage approach to policy making; Oscar Skelton did not lead Canada into Scandinavian-style autonomy in the area of foreign policy; William Mackintosh did not see the triumph of his Tawneyian vision of social transformation, not even in the adoption of a watered-down version of his goal of full employment. Even accepting that the influence of the senior mandarinate was itself considerable, it is not self-evident that there was more than an incomplete convergence of the political economists' analysis and the politicians' agenda in the middle decades of the century. The actual policies that were made resulted from social forces and decisions over which political-economy professors or other social scientists had little control. Civil servants have had influence, to be sure, but they have not controlled the strong interests – class, ethnic, religious, and usually territorial – that have dominated politics in twentieth-century Canada. While there is ample debate on the "autonomy" of the state as opposed to other centres of power in Canadian society, there is equally ample emphasis that the influence of bureaucrats emerges only within the structure of the plural sources of power in the country.[4]

Thirdly, the direction of Queensian social science was to try to distinguish between the parts of the political and economic orders that were amenable to voluntary human choice and the parts that were not. The discipline of political economy was so useful because it led to that important distinction. The basic operations of the market economy and the parliamentary system were the result of broad economic and political structural factors that were little open to human manipulation. Yet, unlike so many of their contemporaries, whose estimation of economic and political structures led to highly deterministic conclusions, Queen's political economists claim to have found a significant realm for state intervention. Their resistance to deterministic social science – Marxist and formalist alike – not only characterized their theorizing, sketchy though it was, but also shaped their view of the influence of the social scientist. The social scientists' place was to assess the sorts of intervention that were possible because the political-economy order was amenable to significant, if still limited, human intervention. Finally, Queen's political economists argued that analysis and intervention were neither so arcane nor so potent that the scholar acquired any special monopoly on or knowledge of social manipulation. Unlike the advocates of an intellectual clerisy – experts passionlessly commenting on a virtually deterministic social order – or the acolytes of an intellectual vanguard – revolutionaries enthusiastically nudging along the transformation of society – the Queensians held decidedly more restrained views about the direction of society and the role of the social scientist. They were, in short, neither a clerisy nor a vanguard.

Like other intellectuals of the so-called government generation, Queen's political economists participated in the remaking of the Canadian state in the first half of the twentieth century but did not control the results. Defining their own role extremely carefully, the Queen's scholars aimed to serve as brokers between the class and interest-group alignments in the nation and in that way they overcame their lack of power as academics and as bureaucrats at a time when knowledge was not power and government intervention did not yet drive the entire economy. Understanding the limited influence enjoyed by these scholars reminds modern-day historians that the nature of the public-policy debates of the early twentieth century and the goals of the participants may not be quite as well captured as they seem to think. There is a vocabulary to this debate which participants used but which historians, by proposing the triumph of a mandarinate, have overlooked or misunderstood.

In sum, Queen's political economists used their studies as the basis for vigorous participation in important public-policy debates and, of course, in later policy-making roles. Through their commited and persuasive writing, Shortt and Skelton worked to escape from the marginality that plagued the intellectual in Victorian and Edwardian Canada.[5] Themselves frustrated by their university's failure to accept their argument that research was central to the university and to society, Shortt, Skelton, Clark, and Mackintosh moved to the federal public service. To turn to the actual content of their analysis of Canadian society is to see how distinctive their analysis was in important ways, particularly in comparison with historians' portrayal of the welfare-state synthesis that did emerge during and after the Second World War.

THE MOST IMPORTANT ASPECT of their work lies in their diligent applications and at times exciting elaborations of the central arguments of the new liberalism developed in Great Britain and the United States in the early twentieth century. They conceived the study of political economy within the boundaries defined by John Stuart Mill and refined by the historical economists and the new liberals of the late Victorian era. This political economy maintained both normative and positive goals, seeking to understand social reality and to propose alternative directions.

Their own emphasis on reforming political and economic institutions was deceptively moderate, leading to a relatively small list of social reorientations, institutional changes, and government interventions. Nonetheless, Shortt advanced a social goal of the self-realization for all men and women, Skelton urged the goal of economic justice and political participation for all people, Clark supported the extension of state economic supervision, and Mackintosh dared to foresee the transformation of ethical values and economic behaviour in capitalist society.

To gain perspective on the importance of these underlying goals, it is helpful to consider the main tendencies of the broad liberal-democratic tradition in which Queen's political economy was developed. Especially useful in this regard is the significant distinction that political theorists, notably C.B. Macpherson, have made between, on the one hand, the egalitarian or developmental "democratic" stream of thought and, on the other, the possessive or individualist "liberal" stream.[6]

Recent work on the tenets of liberal-democratic theory has reflected Macpherson's studies in identifying the powerful, reformist stance that emerged with the new liberalism. This position is a shift towards an egalitarian and developmental interpretation of liberal democracy which has its roots in the critical restatements of liberalism by John Stuart Mill. Vastly modifying utilitarianism into eudemonism and transforming the estimation of both the economic capacity of capitalism and the rationality of human beings, Mill tried to accommodate the utilitarian and the idealist, the Benthamite and the Carlylean systems. Regardless of the technical success of his economic, political, or social theories, Mill's synthesis and restatement of liberal democracy have proven fundamental to subsequent political and economic theory and popular debate in the North Atlantic world.

Liberal-democratic theory was further developed and elaborated by influential writers in the late nineteenth and early twentieth century. Thomas Hill Green, John Hobson, and Leonard Hobhouse in Britain, and Robert McIver, John Dewey, and Thorstein Veblen in the United States, pushed liberal-democratic thought towards a self-described new liberalism that emphasized an extension of rights to mean equal participation in and fulfilment from the spectrum of social, political, and economic life. This enlargement of the concept of rights was supported by new economic theory which showed that the immense productive capacity of capitalism effectively provided for human wants. The new rights position did not advocate the abandonment of a market-based economy. But it argued in favour of a major role for the state as agent for the redistribution of economic and political rights because the state was the agent of the interests and needs of every human being in society. Above all, it argued for the extension of measures of human welfare from the utilitarian counting of aggregate income to the broad assessment of social well-being, opportunity, and satisfaction for all men and women. Liberal individualism was reinterpreted to include the equal "positive" rights of opportunity and security. These rights were distinguished from the old liberalism and its focus on the "negative" rights to individual property accumulation and to certain legal protections. Under the new liberalism, the individual's role is transformed and individual fulfilment thus resides in his or her full participation in society. Individual rights are economic as well as political; human welfare is social as well as economic.

It is in this stream that we can locate Queen's political economists. Shortt called for a society based on the self-realization of all and Skelton appealled for a nation based on social well-being, economic justice, and political rights for all. Shortt was attracted to Green's teachings about positive liberty and self-realization and Skelton endorsed McIver's "brilliant and stimulating" redefinition of the social purposes of the state by his adoption of Veblen's critique of Marxism. Clark cautiously hoped to control the business cycle and administer the financial system as well as implement the goal of social welfare as a basis of public finance. Mackintosh supported enthusiastically Tawney's call for the passing of the "acquisitive society" and hoped for the triumph of farmer cooperatives. All of these goals are reflections of their alignment with the developmental-democratic stream of the liberal tradition.

The new liberalism of the early twentieth century stands in contrast with earlier, pre-Millian constructs based almost entirely on a negative concept of liberty and a highly individualist notion of how freedom and fulfilment were attained. Liberal-democratic theory in the eighteenth and early nineteenth century posited a pessimistic account of how much wealth was available for distribution, an inegalitiarian assessment of how readily most individuals could discern their best interests, and a highly suspicious view of the state and democratic politics. It is here that the more cautious figures at Queen's, Michell, Swanson, and at times Shortt, can be placed.

The agenda of the new liberalism is at least partly reflected in the general approach subsumed under Keynesianism. This broad Keynesianism is chiefly identified by an optimistic account of the productivity of capitalism and an acceptance of intervention and limited redistribution as goals for government. In fact, the very conditioning terms that critics of Keynesian liberalism use in describing its tendencies indicate the extent to which developmental goals have permeated the individualist theory: the welfare of each is a key measure of the effectiveness of the economy and the intrusion of the state is a key means to ensure social and economic well-being. Even the now-abandoned goal of full employment – universally accepted in the 1950s and 1960s but repudiated as state policy in the 1970s and 1980s – was justified by tenets of social and political rights rather than purely economic efficiency.

Whatever the inadequacies of the Keynesian economic program, liberal-democratic theory has also been accompanied by a blossoming of developmental-democratic theory in the past three decades. Political theorists such as John Rawls and Ronald Dworkin (if not Macpherson himself in some of his writing) as well as economists such as John Kenneth Galbraith and Lester Thurow are the most notable adherents of a reformist liberalism supporting economic equality over efficiency, state intervention over corporate autonomy, and social claims to justice over individual claims to freedom.[7]

In recent years, libertarian and neo-conservative critics have found all too much public policy based on the theory and practices of reformist liberals. The resulting backlash has led to theoretical restatements in economics and political science based on strong scepticism about the productive capacity of regulated capitalism, fear for the effects on individual freedom of action from the interventionist state, and an individualist "libertarian" definition of social, political, and economic rights. The dominant restatements of the liberal position are identified with libertarian and conservative theorists such as F.A. Hayek, Robert Nozick, and James Buchanan. By measuring the welfare of the society as the total of individual welfare, by defining rights as "negative" individual ones, and by justifying continued élite dominance of political and economic life, this version of contemporary liberal-democratic theory adheres to tendencies much different from the goals of the no longer new liberalism. Contemporary conservative restatements of liberalism are descended from the possessive individualism defined by Lockean and one part of Benthamite philosophy.[8]

Indeed some critical liberal-democratic theorists such as Macpherson have suggested that even the Keynesian mainstream represents a shift away from developmental-democratic arguments towards acquisitive liberal arguments. In Macpherson's critical account, recent liberal theory is rooted in an economic analysis claiming that the wealth-generating capacity of capitalism depends on the incentives of unequal rights and the conditions of an essentially free or at least only partially regulated market. By this view, modern liberalism is also rooted in a political analysis that argues that individual rights, like economic productivity, are threatened by excessive state intervention and by manipulation of mass wants by political demagoguery. Critics of Keynesianism argue that it emphasizes individual economic accumulation and aggregate growth rather than equality of conditions or equal social well-being, that it accepts as proper the domination of political (and social) life and conditions by élites, and finally, that it sees the interventionist state as a threat to individual and corporate rights of accumulation and efficiency.

The interpretation holding that there are two streams of liberal-democratic thought not only makes some sense of the debate about the role of the state and the tendencies of liberal democracy in the past half century, it also stands in contrast to the conventional view of twentieth-century liberalism in Canada. Remarkably, Canadian historians and political scientists have virtually ignored the possibility that there was any Canadian participation in the democratic as opposed to the liberal version of liberal-democratic thought. If the ideas of Queen's political economists can be reintegrated into Canadian intellectual and political history, then the refusal to consider the other stream of liberal-democratic thought in Canada will no longer be viable. Moreover, Canadian political thought and political debate might well be reconsidered in terms of the tendencies of liberal-democratic thought rather than the categories so often used by Canadian historians – liberal, conservative, and social democrat. These categories obscure rather than clarify.[9]

WHY IT IS THAT HISTORIANS have so ignored the new liberalism and what have the consequences of their neglect been? The veil over the new liberalism in Canada can be explained by the very context in which Queen's political economists worked and by certain intellectual biases and generational presuppositions on the part of later scholars.

Leading contemporaries of Queen's political economists rejected the conclusions of the developmental stream in liberal-democratic theory. Highly relevant in this respect are the ideas of Mackenzie King, who become a key participant in the decision-making structure. King's understanding of political economy, it has been argued, was based on a view of the primary tendencies of liberal democracy that rejected the developmental for the individualist pole. King was at least dimly aware of the alternate version of liberal-democratic thought. But he was most comfortable in mediating between the goals of, on the one hand, wealth-generation and individual acquisition of property and, on the other, redistribution and individual equality or equity, indeed one of his biographers argues that he favoured property over equity in formulating his ideas about labour-capital relations. Like later critics of the welfare state, he seems to have been concerned that emphasis on equality would damage economic motivations and individual rights, not to mention the harm to the powerful vested interests that he knew dominated society and to his own influence and power first as a mediator and then as a politician. Thus the dominant figure in the policy-making structure of mid-twentieth-century Canada simply did not think that the direction of public policy and reform should be towards the egalitarian pole of liberalism.

From this conviction flowed his distrust of and occasional disdain for the Queen's professors.[10]

Two contemporaries of Mackenzie King, the prominent historians Frank Underhill and Arthur Lower, reflected carefully on the traits of liberal-democratic theory and practice. Yet they too ignored the alternate possibilities of liberal democracy. Underhill, a leading participant during the 1930s in the social-democratic League for Social Reconstruction, engaged in what proved to be a fruitless search for a reformist branch to Canadian liberalism. He turned to the completion of the liberal agenda in socialism precisely because he identified Canadian liberalism with the individualist stream of nineteenth-century Ontario Grits and its fiercely Protestant, capitalist, and individualist adherents George Brown and Edward Blake. Underhill totally disdained the populist protest tradition in Ontario; he also discounted the affinities between his socialism and contemporary liberalism, although he was well aware of such affinities in the Britain and United States from which he drew his intellectual sustenance. Lower, an active civil libertarian and cultural critic, defended in his work the "most famous stream" of liberal democracy against most forms of modern collectivism. He also identified this tradition with a negative view of liberty and a limited concept of the state, precisely the individualist liberalism that struck Underhill as so outmoded. Lower found Canada appallingly wanting even in its preservation of the individualist, negative liberties of civil rights while Underhill bitterly denounced the absence of positive rights and developmental goals in Canadian public life. Their reasons for doing so are unclear, although a clue may be found in the fact that the rather clerisy-oriented Lower and the decidedly vanguardist Underhill were not about to align themselves with political economists. Underhill derisively called them the "garage-mechanics of capitalism" and refused to view their version of interventionism as serious reform. Slightly more circumspectly, Lower described the political economists as power-players and empire-builders creating an interventionist state that would threaten the liberties he cherished. Liberal humanists simply did not consort with social scientists.[11]

If scholars sympathetic to egalitarian and liberal ends did not identify a reformist stream, many of the dominant historians of mid-twentieth-century Canada, especially W.L. Morton and Donald Creighton, were extremely critical of liberal politics and liberal historiography. They shared at least the posture of what later came to be defined by George P. Grant's conservatism and its profound contempt for liberalism and Liberal Party dominance. Creighton in particular scorned the historical interpretation of Shortt, Skelton, and Mackintosh as continentalist and reductionist. These liberal-nationalists, he charged, ignored the political and economic importance of the British connection and reduced Canadian history to a pre-determined evolution towards political autonomy and economic continentalism. Morton too railed against the centralist interpretation of the liberal nationalists for ignoring both the regional economic disparities that he condemned and the provincial and local centres of political and cultural power that he defended. It also appears that this generation was strongly influenced (perhaps intimidated is a better word) by the devotion to the concept of an intellectual clerisy held by Harold Innis. They certainly shared his strong disapproval of those scholars who left the academy and rejected the role of clerisy.[12]

In many ways, the criticisms levelled against Queen's political economists were not surprising; indeed, their carefully defined creed about the academic's place in society was opaque enough to support the views of critics then and since. Avoiding the roles of public crusaders, nationalist missionaries, or political-economic Cassandras, they chose a line of thought readily misunderstood by their contemporaries and perhaps therefore by subsequent writers. Also, their environmentalist and autonomist interpretation of Canadian nationhood placed them somewhat apart from the mainstream of contemporary and succeeding historians' advocacy of "British" Canadian nationalism. They did not think that Canadian society had a mission to sustain a conservative alternative to the United States or the British tradition in North America. Therefore they did not form a link between preceeding and succeeding defenders of the Canadian conservative inheritance. Lastly, their account of the potential of capitalism and parliamentary government was easily interpreted as comfortable and quietist doctrine as well as self-serving. They did not think that class relations and ethnic or regional conflict constituted continuing primary attributes of liberal democracy. Apart from their limited concern for the position of French Canadians in Confederation, they did not address the issue of minority rights and, though they never rejected gender equality, totally sidestepped the question of women's rights. Thus their views about the equalitarian capacities of liberal capitalism held little appeal to critics of capitalism such as Underhill or critics of regional inequality such as Morton.

From another source, historical accounts in Canada written since the 1960s have not reflected the re-evaluation of liberal-democratic thought simultaneously underway in Great Britain and the United States. Exemplifying this difference of perspective, the critique of

Canadian political ideas written in the mid-1960s by the political scientist Gad Horowitz did not recognize the alternate reading of liberal theory that other historically oriented theorists such as C.B. Macpherson were proposing. Ironically, both Horowitz and Macpherson wrote from within a strong socialist bent and in the same university department. More generally, whatever their dispositions towards liberal democracy, contemporary historians have grown up within the very Keynesian restatement of liberalism that emphasizes the continuities of liberal theory, from Locke to Keynes, as it were, but that ignores an alternative democratic theory, from the levellers and the populists to the new liberals and social democrats.

In Canadian scholarly terms, Gad Horowitz's brilliant critique of modern doctrines of liberalism, socialism, and conservatism has been immensely influential. This approach has been sustained by George P. Grant's powerful denunciation of liberal-democratic society and its political and economic expressions. To Horowitz and Grant, liberalism is identified by its essential continuing emphasis on individualism and inequality, competitiveness and human isolation, the characteristics that reflect social, political, and economic conditions in industrial societies. Rather neatly foreshadowing and complementing later work by historians on the Christian sources of Canadian reform, Horowitz and Grant argue that the dominant Canadian political position has been a conservative one, emphasizing community, order, and often religious faith as central to the shaping of political and economic activity. The sources of Canadian reform lie in this residue or "fragment," as Horowitz would have it in restating Louis Hartz's arguments, of conservative values. A Canadian conservative political tradition is thereby defined and distinguished from the dominant American tradition of Lockean liberalism. Canadian history yet again serves to demarcate our autonomy from the United States and our continuities with Great Britain. Creighton and Morton receive further endorsation.[13]

Writing prior to the recent rethinking of the history of the liberal tradition, Horowitz did not consider variations in the theoretical arguments, let alone the concrete manifestations, of liberal-democratic thought. This is chiefly because his conception of liberalism rested exclusively on the notion of negative liberty and the neutral state. To assess whether there was a "liberal" component to the political reforms of the mid-twentieth century, Horowitz draws on criticism of the individualist, inegalitarian, and economic bases of liberalism, including the post-1945 "welfare state," and notes the extent to which Mackenzie King and Louis St Laurent conceived their reforms as a strategic accommodation of the left. He therefore sustains the view that there was no theoretical liberal-democratic reformist position in modern Canada – or anywhere else in the English-speaking world. Similarly, Grant, writing in the shadow of Leo Strauss's anti-liberalism, partly follows a Horowitzian critique of the Keynesian welfare state and identifies virtually all aspects of the positive state in Canada as either residual conservative expressions of community or fiendish liberal appeasements of conservatism and socialism. Horowitz's influence, itself designed as a corrective to earlier views about an absence of political ideas in Canadian society, has perpetuated the argument that protest and reform were fed by everything but a reformist liberalism. Grant's views, in comparison, lead to the rejection of the entire liberal-democratic political and economic order, a position rather more un-compromising than that of most Canadian historians and political scientists.

Reflecting to a remarkable extent a Horowitzian judgment about the dimensions of Canadian political and economic thought, if not an explicitly Hartzean framework, recent studies of mid-twentieth century socialism perpetuate the division of the reformist laurels that excludes liberals as well as Liberals. These works argue that the sources of the goals of equality and redistribution and the effective positive state lie in the democratic-socialist movements of the 1930s and 1940s.[14] While it is certainly important to understand the emer-gence of a social-democratic political movement in Canada, it seems highly questionable whether social democrats in the League For Social Reconstruction such as Frank Underhill and developmental-liberal democrats such as Queen's political economists were really very different in their analysis of twentieth-century society. They disagreed over the productive capacity of capitalism and thus over the exact role of the state and they differed on the malleability of political institutions and therefore about the role of the intellectual. It is not at all clear that they really disagreed about the goals of equality and human rights, a factor that might explain the drift by the 1960s of social democrats such as Underhill, Eugene Forsey, and F.R. Scott towards political liberalism.

Equally questionable are views of reform set out in recent works on the rise of a "government generation" of public-service mandarins. Admitting the reform agenda's narrow base of popular support by the 1940s, but still emphasizing the role of the extremely small intellectual cohort which espoused that agenda, these studies have focused on the adoption of the novel Keynesian economic theory as crucial to the rise of the positive state in Canada. In this view, Keynesianism is understood to have been a narrow, technical approach to policy making while the political and economic change

advocated by the "government generation," including Queen's political economists, was the result of a Depression economy permanently
stuck at less than full output. To Doug Owram, reform meant "the
triumph of macro-economic management." It was achieved through
policies designed to redirect capital from savings to expenditure and
policy was implemented by an activist public service. Economic efficiency was thus the prime justification for this version of the welfare
state, which of course then rises and falls on the logic of economic
growth alone. Other studies of welfare-state programs, such as unemployment insurance, emphasize that it was precisely the fundamental
logic of capitalist efficiency rather than social justice that sold the
policies. The programs were designed to ensure the work ethic and
limit employer costs by stringent eligibility requirements and
financing measures.[15] Gone from this interpretation are arguments
favouring the extension of rights to include the full range of social
and economic as well as political rights and the measurement of these
rights equally rather than in aggregate. Gone, in other words, is any
version of developmental-liberal theory from the contributors to the
positive welfare state.

THE DEBATE ABOUT THE "welfare state" both before and since the
Second World War has not been shaped by a pragmatic searching
for the right "balance" between economic growth and social compas-
sion, or by the tactics of liberals in appeasing social democrats.
Rather, the debate has been between advocates of egalitarian/devel-
opmental and competitive/individualist visions of society, between the
primacy of economic and of non-economic models. The main point
at issue has not been just whether or how the technical arguments
favouring full employment and economic growth are implemented,
but whether and how the equal rights of all people to a satisfactory
way of life are to be achieved. Posed this way, was the post-war goal
of a "high level" of employment (much scaled down from W.A. Mackintosh's original 1945 proposal for "full employment") just an economic goal that would be traded off against economic efficiency? On
the contrary, it was a primary human right to which efficiency was
harnessed. The point of Clifford Clark's goal of social welfare was
identical. Those who emphasize the goal of economic efficiency in
the Keynesian agenda ignore the proposition that full employment
and the good of all society constituted a primary goal and not an
alternate strategy to be traded off against growth. At least W.A.
Mackintosh made this argument in the 1940s and he followed two
generations of Queen's political economists in presupposing the

primacy of developmental, positive rights over efficiency and negative rights.[16]

In the debate about Canadian public policy, the most striking element in the reflections of Skelton and Mackintosh on the political state of Canada after the Great War was precisely their commitment to democracy and politically rooted economic and social reform – a commitment that was in stark contrast to the views of mere progressive reformers, Christian and secular alike, in Canada and elsewhere. By the 1920s the Queen's interpretation of the new liberalism had led them to express a concept of reform that has seldom been credited to Canadian thinkers even though it was central to the arguments supporting the actual changes to the role of government and the relations between citizens and the state implemented during the 1930s, 1940s, and 1950s. Clearly they remained believers in both the productive capacity and the potential fairness of the market economy; they did not emerge as critics of a primarily market economy, any more than most of the new liberals did. Similarly, they did not intend their arguments to consider the rights of minorities or subordinate groups. What they did do was to make the perpetuation of the market subordinate to the well-being of the individual, and they conceived the rights of each as attendant upon the rights of all.

The new liberalism was something more than just a precursor to a technical explanation of how the economy worked and the extension of business-government planning and state-fiscal policy to expand aggregate income. The new liberalism was an argument for the provision of equal conditions for all men and women and the extension of the measure of well-being to include the totality of social, economic, and political life. That argument lies at the heart of the scholarly work of Shortt, Skelton, Clark, and Mackintosh. It also is their legacy to Canadian intellectual life.

Notes

1 Richard Allen, *The Social Passion: Religion and Social Reform in Canada 1914–1928* (Toronto 1973); Leslie Armour, *The Idea of Canada and the Crisis of Community* (Ottawa 1981); Ramsay Cook, *The Regenerators: Social Criticism in Late Victorian English Canada* (Toronto 1985); A.B. McKillop, *A Disciplined Intelligence: Critical Inquiry and Canadian Thought in the Victorian Era* (Montreal 1979); Marlene Shore, *The Science of Social Redemption: McGill, the Chicago School, and the Origins of Social Research in Canada* (Toronto 1987).

2 Norman Penner's *The Canadian Left* (Scarborough 1977) totally ignores the phenomenon, and Gad Horowitz's *Canadian Labour in Politics* (Toronto 1968) sharply criticizes its virility. Other key examples of accounts that emphasize radical as opposed to liberal sources of reform thought and activity are A. Ross McCormack, *Reformers, Rebels, and Revolutionaries: The Western Canadian Radical Movement 1899–1919* (Toronto 1977); Walter Young, *Anatomy of a Party: The national C.C.F., 1932–61* (Toronto 1969); Joan Sangster, *Dreams of Equality: Women on the Canadian Left, 1920–1950* (Toronto 1989). Somewhat correcting this approach are Paul Craven's study of Mackenzie King's connections with labour in *An Impartial Umpire: Industrial Relations and the Canadian State, 1900–11* (Toronto 1980) and Craig Heron's survey of the omission of the labourist position in labour historiography, "Labourism and the Canadian Working Class," *Labour*, 13 (1984), 45–76.

3 C.D.W. Goodwin, *Canadian Economic Thought: The Political Economy of a Developing Nation 1814–1914* (Durham, N.C., 1961); John H. Dales, "Canadian Scholarship in Economics," *Scholarship in Canada 1967*, R.H. Hubbard, ed. (Toronto 1968), 83–9; Daniel Drache, "Rediscovering Canadian Political Economy," *Journal of Canadian Studies* 11 (August 1976), 9ff; C.B. Macpherson, "The Social Sciences," *The Culture of Contemporary Canada*, Julian Park, ed. (Ithaca, N.Y., 1957), 190–7; Kenneth W. Taylor, "Economic Scholarship in Canada," *Canadian Journal of Economics and Political Science*, 26 (February 1960), 7–10.

4 The various interpretations of historical writing and their nationalist component are thoroughly reviewed in Carl Berger, *The Writing of Canadian History: Aspects of English-Canadian Historical Writing 1900 to 1970* (Toronto 1976) and in Ramsay Cook, *The Maple Leaf Forever: Essays on Nationalism and Politics in Canada* (Toronto 1977). See especially D.G. Creighton, "Macdonald and Canadian Historians" (1948) in his *Towards the Discovery of Canada* (Toronto 1972), 194–211; J.M.S. Careless, "Frontierism, Metropolitanism, and the Interpretation of Canadian History," *Canadian Historical Review* 35 (March 1954), 1–21. Accounts of the pedigree of economic thought are cited in note 3. But see also Wallace Clement and Daniel Drache, *A Practical Guide to Canadian Political Economy* (Toronto 1978).

5 F.H. Underhill, *In Search of Canadian Liberalism* (Toronto 1961); Hilda Neatby, *Queen's University 1, 1841–1917: And Not to Yield* (Montreal 1978); F.W. Gibson, *Queen's University 2, 1917–1961: To Serve and Yet Be Free* (Montreal 1983).

6 Doug Owram, *The Government Generation: Canadian Intellectuals and the State 1900–1945* (Toronto 1986); J.L. Granatstein, *The Ottawa Men: The Civil Service Mandarins 1935–1957* (Toronto 1982); James Struthers, *No Fault of Their Own: Unemployment and the Canadian Welfare State 1914–1941* (Toronto 1983); R.B. Bryce, *Maturing in Hard Times: Canada's Department of Finance Through the Great Depression* (Montreal 1985); H. Blair Neatby, *The Prism of Unity: Mackenzie King 1932–39* (Toronto 1976); Robert Bothwell and W. Kilbourn, *C.D. Howe: A Biography* (Toronto 1979).

7 C.B. Macpherson, *The Life and Times of Liberal Democracy* (Oxford 1977), chapters 3 and 4, and *Democratic Theory: Essays in Retrieval* (Oxford 1973), essay 2. See also Michael Freeden, *The New Liberalism: An Ideology of Social Reform* (Oxford 1978), chapter 1; John Allett, *New Liberalism: The Political Economy of J.A. Hobson* (Toronto 1981); Thomas Haskell, *The Emergence of Professional Social Science* (Urbana, Ill., 1977); Peter Clarke, *Liberals and Social Democrats* (Cambridge 1978); James Kloppenberg, *Uncertain Victory: Social Democracy and Progressivism in European and American Thought 1870–1920* (New York 1986).

CHAPTER ONE

1 Robert Craig Brown and Ramsay Cook, *Canada, 1896–1921, A Nation Transformed* (Toronto 1972), especially chapters 1–6.

2 James M. Gilmour, *Spatial Evolution of Manufacturing: Southern Ontario 1851–1891* (Toronto 1972); Gordon Bertram, "Economic Growth in Canadian Industry, 1870–1915," *Canadian Journal of Economics and Political Science*, 29, no. 2 (May 1963), 159–84.

3 John T. Saywell, introduction to *Lady Aberdeen's Canadian Journal* (Toronto 1960), passim; W.L. Morton, "Confederation, 1870–1896," *Contexts of Canada's Past*, A.B. McKillop, ed. (Toronto 1980), 208–28.

4 Brown and Cook, *Canada 1896–1921*, chapters 15 and 16.

5 H. Stuart Hughes, *Consciousness and Society: The Reorientation of European Social Thought, 1890–1930* (New York 1958), chapters 1 and 2; Reba N. Soffer, *Ethics and Society: The Revolution in the Social Sciences, 1870–1914* (Berkley and Los Angeles 1978); Thomas Haskell, *The Emergence of Professional Social Science* (Urbana, Ill., 1977).

6 Soffer, *Ethics and Society*, chapters 1 and 2 and 253–60; Mary O. Furner, *Advocacy and Objectivity: A Crisis in the Professionalization of American Social Science, 1865–1905* (Lexington, Ky., 1975), chapter 7 and 313–24.

7 O.D. Skelton, "Fifty Years of Political and Economic Science in Canada," Royal Society of Canada, *Fifty Years Retrospect, 1882–1932* (n.p. 1932), 85–90. From a great many works on the development of economics, see Robert L. Heilbroner, *The Worldly Philosophers*, 4th ed. (New York 1973); Eric Roll, *A History of Economic Thought*, 4th rev. ed. (London 1973); Joseph Schumpeter, *History of Economic Analysis*, Elizabeth Boody Schumpeter, ed. (New York 1954).

8 O.D. Skelton, "Fifty Years of Political and Economic Science in Canada," 89–90; Bernard Crick, *The American Science of Politics: Its Origins and Conditions* (Berkley 1962); Soffer, *Ethics and Society*, chapters 8 and 9.

9 See the works listed in notes 5, 6, and 7, especially Soffer, *Ethics and Society*, chapters 3–5.

10 Soffer, *Ethics and Society*, chapters 10 and 11; Hughes, *Consciousness and Society*, passim; Dennis F. Thompson, *The Democratic Citizen: Social Science and Democratic Theory in the Twentieth Century* (Cambridge 1970), 1–8 et seq.

11 Haskell, *The Emergence of Professional Social Science*, chapter 2; Furner, *Advocacy and Objectivity*, chapters 2–9, 322–4; Robert L. Church, "Economists as Experts," *The University in Society*, Lawrence Stone, ed. (Princeton 1974), chapter 2, 571–609.

12 A.B. McKillop, *A Disciplined Intelligence: Critical Inquiry and Canadian Thought in the Victorian Era* (Montreal 1979); S.E.D. Shortt, *The Search for*

an Ideal: Six Intellectuals in an Age of Transition (Toronto 1976); Leslie Armour and Elizabeth Trott, *The Faces of Reason: An Essay on Philosophy and Culture in English Canada 1850–1950* (Waterloo, Ont., 1981).

13 Ramsay Cook, *The Regenerators: Social Criticism in Late Victorian English Canada* (Toronto 1985), 7–15.

14 Shortt, *The Search for an Ideal*, 137–48.

15 McKillop, *A Disciplined Intelligence*, 229–32 and passim; Morton G. White, "The Revolt Against Formalism," *Journal of the History of Ideas*, 8 (April 1947), 131ff; David Nicholls, "Positive Liberty, 1880–1914," *American Political Science Review*, 51 (March 1962).

16 Hilda Neatby, *Queen's University, 1, 1841–1917: And Not to Yield* (Montreal 1978), passim; C.D.W. Goodwin, *Canadian Economic Thought: The Political Thought of a Developing Nation 1814–1914* (Durham, N.C., 1961), 109–51, 152–75. See also A.R.M. Lower, "The Development of Canadian Economic Ideas," *The Spirit of American Economic Ideas*, J.F. Normano, ed. (New York 1943); and Morley Wickett, "The Study of Political Economy at Canadian Universities," *Ontario Sessional Papers for 1897*, appendix 32.

17 Goodwin, *Canadian Economic Thought*, 176–84, 185–96; Kenneth W. Taylor, "Economic Scholarship in Canada," *Canadian Journal of Economics and Political Science*, 26 (February 1960), 6ff; Ian M. Drummond, *Political Economy at the University of Toronto: A History of the Department, 1888–1982* (Toronto 1983), 17–25, 26–31, 41–8, 61–5, 77–8, 96–7.

18 Biographical material has been compiled from a number of sources: *Canadian Journal of Economics and Political Science*, vols. 1–10; Taylor, "Economic Scholarship in Canada"; John H. Dales, "Canadian Scholarship in Economics," *Scholarship in Canada 1967*, R.H. Hubbard, ed. (Toronto 1968); Vincent W. Bladen, *Bladen on Bladen* (Toronto 1978), passim; Drummond, *Political Economy at the University of Toronto*, passim.

19 Hilda Neatby, *Queen's University, 1*; Charles Johnston, *McMaster University, 1, The Toronto Years* (Toronto 1976); Charles Johnston, *McMaster University, 2, The Early Years in Hamilton* (Toronto 1981).

20 Biographical material has been based on the following sources letters in Adam Shortt Papers, Queen's University Archives: Adam Shortt to his family, 13 October 1879; 8, 15, 22 November 1879; 6 April 1880; ? March 1883; George Bell, "re: Adam Shortt," 5 September 1885; G.M. Grant, "re: Adam Shortt," July 1885; A. Campbell Fraser, "re: Adam Shortt," 12 July 1885; John Watson to Adam Shortt, 24 April 1885, 25 December 1885; Adam Shortt to Elizabeth Smith (later Mrs Shortt), 29 July 1885, 20 December 1885, 18 May 1886. Also, from the same collection: Andrew Haydon, "Memo. Obtained from Dr. Shortt, August 1928."

21 W.A. Mackintosh, "Adam Shortt," in *Some Great Men of Queen's*, R.C. Wallace, ed., 38, no. 1 (April 1938), 6ff; Shortt, *The Search For an Ideal*, 95–102; Taylor, "Economic Scholarship in Canada," 6–8; Goodwin, *Canadian Economic Thought*; Queen's University *Calendars*, 1889–90.

22 Shortt, *The Search For an Ideal*, passim; Owram, *The Government Generation: Canadian Intellectuals and the State 1900–1945* (Toronto 1986), passim.

23 *Principal Grant's Inaugural Address* (Toronto 1885) 3–10; *Three Brief Addresses by Principal Grant on the Duty of the Legislature to the Colleges of the Province* (n.p., n.d.) 1–2, 2–5, 5–8; Hilda Neatby, *Queen's University, 1*, 153–66; Chad Gaffield *et al*. "Student Populations and Graduate Careers: Queen's University 1895–1900," *Youth, University and Canadian Society*, Paul Axelrod and John Reid, eds., (Montreal 1989), 3–25.

24 See Adam Shortt's correspondence cited in note 20.

25 Hilda Neatby, *Queen's University, 1*, passim; W.L. Grant and C.F. Hamilton, *Principal Grant* (Toronto 1903); Robin S. Harris, *History of Higher Education in Canada* (Toronto 1974), appendix 2.

26 Harris, *History of Higher Education in Canada*, chapters 8 and 9.

27 Adam Shortt to Andrew Haydon, 7 January 1894, Adam Shortt Papers. "Salutatory," *Queen's Quarterly*, 1 (July 1893), 1–3. A recent historical examination of this absence of free inquiry is found in McKillop, *A Disciplined Intelligence*, chapters 1 and 5. This work concentrates on the period from 1850 through the 1890s, the precise point at which the authors of the *Queen's Quarterly* introduction thought that a break from the intellectual constraints of Victorian Canada was possible.

28 All data from *McKim's Directory of Canadian Publications* 2nd and 18th editions (Montreal 1899 and 1925).

29 Grant, "Inaugural Address," 13; George M. Grant, "Important Changes in the Constitution of Queen's," *Queen's Quarterly*, 8 (October 1900), 104.

30 Adam Shortt, "Principal Grant," *Queen's Quarterly*, 10 (July 1902), 1–2.

31 Adam Shortt, "Aims of the Political Science Association," *Papers and Proceedings*, Canadian Political Science Association, 1 (1913), 9–17; W.A. Mackintosh, "An Economist Looks at Economics," *Canadian Journal of Economics and Political Science* 3 (August 1937), 316.

32 Hilda Neatby, *Queen's University, 1*, entitles two chapters "Queen's and a National Ideal" and "A National University" without examining the foundations for this national status; see Gaffield, "Student Populations and Graduate Careers."

33 George M. Grant, "The University Question," *Queen's Quarterly* 8 (January 1901), 220; Adam Shortt, "Reflections on the University Monopoly," *Queen's Quarterly*, 8 (January 1901), 221–2.

34 Shortt, "Reflections on the University Monopoly"; Grant, "Important Changes in the Constitution of Queen's," 101–4; Shortt, "The University Question," 219–20.

35 Daniel Miner Gordon, "Installation Address," *Queen's Quarterly*, 11 (January 1904), 319–25; Daniel Miner Gordon, "Queen's and Assembly's Commission," *Queen's Quarterly*, 11 (October 1903), 187–90; E.R. Peacock, C.F. Hamilton, Andrew Haydon, J. McD. Mowat, R.W. Brock, J. Strachan, J.R. Shannon, "To Our Fellow Graduates," pamphlet dated 20 December 1910, Daniel Miner Gordon Papers, Queen's University Archives. A memorandum prepared during the final stages of the secularization campaign leads to the conclusion that Queen's student population was not overwhelmingly Presbyterian. According to "Religious Denominations of Queen's Students, 1909–10 Session," the denominational composition of the student body was as follows:

Denomination	Number of Students	Percentage of Student Body
Presbyterian	712	46.9
Methodist	373	24.6
Anglican	162	10.7
Roman Catholic	175	11.5
Baptist	41	
Congregationalist	16	
Jewish	7	
Lutheran	5	
Disciple	3	
Plymouth Brethren	3	
Christian Scientist	3	
Others	9	
Unclassified	8	

Source: Queen's University Letters, volume 26, Queen's University Archives (by permission).

36 Adam Shortt, "Should We Revise the Constitution of Queen's?" *Queen's Quarterly*, 13 (October 1900), 112–14; Adam Shortt, "Current Events," *Queen's Quarterly*, 10 (July 1902), 122; James Cappon, "Current Events," *Queen's Quarterly*, 11 (October 1903), 219–20.

37 By this I mean the approach taken in Richard Allen, *The Social Passion: Religion and Social Reform in Canada, 1914–1928* (Toronto 1971), 3–17, 347–9; Stewart Crysdale, "The Sociology of the Social Gospel," *The Social Gospel in Canada*, Richard Allen, ed. (Ottawa 1975), 263–7, and Marlene Shore, *The Science of Social Redemption* (Toronto 1986), 72–8. The other approach is that of John C. Weaver, who finds class and business interests dominating proposals for reform; see his *Shaping the Canadian City* (Toronto 1978), 74–6, and his "Order and Efficiency: Samuel Morley Wickett and the Urban Progressive Movement in

Toronto, 1900–1915," *Ontario History*, 69 (December 1977), 218–19, 229–30.

38 Adam Shortt Papers: W. Bennett Munro to Adam Shortt, 16 September, 26 October 1898, 6 December 1905; Walter W. McLaren to Adam Shortt, 1 October, 17 November 1905, etc.; J.M. Platt to Adam Shortt, 7 April 1909; W.B. Wormwith to Adam Shortt, undated but probably 1908; Cecil Lavell to Adam Shortt, 2 December 1894, 3 April 1895; William Swanson to Adam Shortt, 10 November 1905, 13 January 1906, etc.; J.A. Donnell to Adam Shortt, 29 March 1903, 8 January 1908; A. Calhoun to Adam Shortt, 21 May, 9 September 1902, 30 October 1904; Oscar Skelton to Adam Shortt, 22 February 1902, etc., 29 June 1905, etc.

39 On Shortt's advocacy of Edward Peacock, see W.A. Mackintosh, "O.D. Skelton," *Canada's Past and Present: A Dialogue*, Robert McDougall, ed. (Toronto 1965), 62; Adam Shortt to Mackenzie King, 4 January 1905, 6 October 1905, W.L.M. King Papers, National Archives of Canada.

40 O.D. Skelton to Adam Shortt, 22 February, 1 March, 10 September 1902, 9 January, 14 and 26 March 1906, Adam Shortt Papers; Queen's University, *Calendars*, 1906–18.

41 W.A. Mackintosh, "O.D. Skelton," 115 ff.; *Macmillan Dictionary of Canadian Biography*, 4th ed., W.A. Mackay, ed. (Toronto 1978); Richard Storr, *Harper's University: The Beginnings* (Chicago 1966), passim; J.L. Granatstein, *The Ottawa Men: The Civil Service Mandarins 1935–1957* (Toronto 1982), 28–44.

42 Adam Shortt, Diary, 20 January 1908, Adam Shortt Papers.

43 O.D. Skelton to Adam Shortt, 29 April, 8 July, 11 July, 16 July 1907, 30 August 1908, Adam Shortt Papers.

44 O.D. Skelton to W.L. Grant, 12 February and 19 January 1904, W.L. Grant Papers, National Archives of Canada.

45 *The Canadian Who's Who*, C.G.D. Roberts, ed. (Toronto 1910); O.D. Skelton to Adam Shortt, 30 August 1908, W.W. Swanson to Adam Shortt, 31 August 1908, Adam Shortt Papers.

46 *The Canadian Who's Who*; W.W. Swanson to Adam Shortt, 10 November 1905, 13 January 1906, Adam Shortt Papers.

47 *The Canadian Who's Who*; O.D. Skelton to R.A. Falconer, 1 May 1915, J.C. Ross to R.A. Falconer, 1 May 1915, James Mavor Papers, University of Toronto Archives; Queen's University *Calendars*, 1906–18.

48 W.W. Swanson, "Independence in Canadian Politics" *Queen's Quarterly*, 19 (July 1911), 56.

49 O.D. Skelton to Adam Shortt, 24 November 1910, 27 July 1907, Adam Shortt Papers.

50 Adam Shortt, "Aims of the Association," *Proceedings and Papers*, Canadian Political Science Association, 1 (1913), 1–19, 10; Adam Shortt to Mackenzie King, 4 January 1905, W.L.M. King Papers.

51 Adam Shortt, "Aims of the Association."

52 G.W. Ross to Adam Shortt, 18 and 21 May 1904; W.B. Wilkinson to Adam Shortt, 22 and 24 June 1904; Edwin R. Seligman to Adam Shortt 30 June 1904, 24 September 1907; Adam Shortt to Mrs Shortt, 1, 3, 5, 9 July 1904, O.D. Skelton to Adam Shortt, 29 April, 8 June, 24 August 1907, 9 January 1908, Adam Shortt Papers.

53 Robert L. Church, "Economists as Experts," 571–4, 608–9; Furner, *Advocacy and Objectivity*, 322–4. In comparison to the neutralist position, see Skelton's remark in a review of Scott Nearing's eugenicist tract *Social Adjustment* that S.N. Patten was confirmed in his judgment that the economist must counter pseudo-science and that the "place of the economist is on the firing-line of civilization." *Journal of Political Economy*, 19 (April 1911), 350–1.

54 See Patricia Jasen, "The English Canadian Arts Curriculum: An Intellectual History" (PhD thesis, University of Manitoba 1987), chapters 2 and 3; A.B. McKillop, "The Research Ideal and the University of Toronto," in his *Contours of Canadian Thought* (Toronto 1987), 78–95; McKillop, *A Disciplined Intelligence*; Owram, *The Government Generation*; Shore, *The Science of Social Redemption*.

55 W.L.M. King to Adam Shortt, 2 September 1908, Adam Shortt Papers; Adam Shortt to W.L.M. King, 5 September 1908, W.L.M. King Papers; D.M. Gordon to Judge Maclennan, 10 September 1908, D. McIntyre to D.M. Gordon, 15 September 1908, O.D. Skelton to D.M. Gordon, 21 September 1908, D.M. Gordon Papers.

56 *The Canadian Who's Who*, C.G.D. Roberts, ed.

57 William Mackintosh, "William Clifford Clark and Canadian Economic Policy," *Canadian Journal of Economic and Political Science*, 19 (August 1953), 411–13; William Mackintosh, "William Clifford Clark," *Queen's Quarterly*, 9 (April 1953), 1ff.; Robert B. Bryce, "William Clifford Clark," *Canadian Journal of Economics and Political Science*, 19 (August 1953), 413–23; W.C. Good, *Farmer Citizen* (Toronto 1957), 137–8, 149; Granatstein, *The Ottawa Men*, 44–9.

58 M.C. Urquhart, "W.A. Mackintosh's Scholarly Work," Queen's University, Institute For Economic Research, *Discussion Paper*, no. 172 (1974), 1–10, especially 1–3; M.C. Urquhart, "John James Deutsch," *Canadian Journal of Economics*, 9 (November 1976), 685–8; Granatstein, *The Ottawa Men*, 153–8.

59 F.W. Gibson, *Queen's University, 2, 1917–1961, To Serve and Yet Be Free* (Montreal 1983), 11–58.

60 Department of political and economic science to Principal Taylor, "Memo on Economic Research and Social-Business Training," 15

October 1918, Queen's University Letters, volume 28 (by permission).

61 Ibid.

62 Information compiled from Queen's University *Calendars*, 1918–26, and *Historical Statistics of Canada*, 2nd ed., series D86–106.

63 J.M. Macdonnell, "The Decline of the Arts Faculty," *Queen's Quarterly*, 30 (January 1923), 310–18.

64 W.C. Clark, "University Training For Business: A Reply," *Queen's Quarterly*, 30 (January 1923), 319–23, 327–30, 333–4; both the Macdonnell and Clark essays were reprinted as Bulletin of the Departments of History and Political and Economic Science, no. 44 (1923).

65 O.D. Skelton, "University Preparation for Business," *Proceedings*, National Conference of Canadian Universities (Kingston 1923), 69–77, especially 77; Adam Shortt, "Current Events," *Queen's Quarterly*, 13 (October 1905), 187–90.

66 W.A. Mackintosh, "The Curriculum of a Course in Commerce," *Papers and Proceedings*, Canadian Political Science Association, 2 (1930), 95–8.

67 F.H. Underhill, "Commerce Courses and the Arts Faculty," *Proceedings*, National Conference of Canadian Universities (Toronto 1930), 74–80; Charles Norris Cochrane, "The Question of Commerce Courses in Universities," *Proceedings*, National Conference of Canadian Universities (Ottawa 1932), 61–9, especially 69; James Cappon, "Democracy and the Universities," *Queen's Quarterly*, 33 (February 1926), 362–3. Morley Wickett called for commerce courses in the universities as early as 1901, the year in which Toronto established a diploma program; see Morley Wickett, "Commercial Education at Universities," *Canadian Magazine*, vol. 17, no. 6 (October 1901), 561–3.

68 W.A. Mackintosh, "The Psychologist and Economics," *Queen's Quarterly*, 30 (January 1923), 299–310, 301–5. On Tawney see Peter Clarke, *Liberals and Social Democrats* (Oxford 1978), 218–22. Clarke points out that Graham Wallas thought that Tawney was too much a devotee of Tolstoy's views of human nature. Did Mackintosh, perhaps, think that such devotion was a recommendation?

69 Queen's University Letters, vol. 27: O.D. Skelton to Principal Gordon, 3 October 1916, O.D. Skelton to G.Y. Chown, 6 October 1916 (both by permission). The salaries of Queen's and Toronto professors can be followed intermittently for the inter-war period:

University of Toronto, Political Economy Salaries, 1919–20:

Rank	Salary
Professor	$5,000
Associate Professor	$3,500
Assistant Professor	$2,750

Rank	Salary
Lecturer	$1,500
Professor of Law	$4,000

Selected Political Economists' Salaries, Queen's University, 1920–37:

Year	Individual/Rank	Salary
1920	W.C. Clark (assoc. prof.)	$2,700
1920	W.A. Mackintosh (assist)	$2,300
1923	W.A. Mackintosh (assoc.)	$3,000
1931	Clifford Clark (professor)	$5,000
1931	Vincent Bladen (assoc.)	$4,200
1937	W.A. Mackintosh (professor)	$4,750
1937	Vincent Bladen (professor)	$5,400

Source: Queen's University Board of Trustees Minutes, Queen's University Archives (this was given to me by Prof. J. L. Granatstein); Vincent Bladen, *Bladen on Bladen*, appendix 2; Department of Political Economy, University of Toronto, series 1, Correspondence, Salaries 1919–20, University of Toronto Archives.

70 See sources cited in note 68 and Privy Council Office, orders-in-councils (RG2), C. #448, 30 March 1925; C. 2361, 24 October 1932.

71 O.D. Skelton to Mackenzie King, 27 January, 4 February, 26 May 1922; Mackenzie King to O.D. Skelton, 31 January, 8 February, 1 May, 30 May 1922; O.D. Skelton to Mackenzie King, 13 October 1922; Mackenzie King to O.D. Skelton, 16 October 1922; Mackenzie King to O.D. Skelton, 7 July 1923; O.D. Skelton to Mackenzie King, 9 July, 28 August 1923, W.L.M. King Papers. See also Gibson, *Queen's University 2.*

72 E.R. Peacock to Andrew Haydon, 6 July 1916, Adam Shortt Papers; Clifford Sifton to J.S. Willison, 13 May 1916, J.S. Willison Papers, National Archives of Canada; Clifford Sifton to J.S. Willison, 31 May 1916, J.S. Willison to Clifford Sifton, 16 May 1916, Clifford Sifton Papers, National Archives of Canada; O.D. Skelton to Adam Shortt, 20 October 1917, Adam Shortt Papers; O.D. Skelton to W.L. Grant, 19 March 1917, 13 August 1917, W.L. Grant Papers; D.M. Gordon to D. McColl, 28 April 1908, D.M. Gordon Papers.

73 O.D. Skelton to W.A. Mackintosh, 9 June 1925; W.A. Mackintosh to D.A. McArthur, 16 June 1925; W.A. Mackintosh to R. Bruce Taylor, 30 July 1925; W.A. Mackintosh to Rev. Neil Leckie, 15 March 1926, W.A. Mackintosh Papers, Queen's University Archives. Gibson, *Queen's University 2,* 56 ff.

74 W.L. Grant to J.M. Macdonnell, 17 April 1928; J.M. Macdonnell to W.L. Grant, 20 and 22 May 1929, W.L. Grant Papers. See also Gibson, *Queen's University 2,* 85–6.

75 See *Canadian Journal of Economics and Political Science*, vols. 1–20, and *The Canadian Who's Who*. On the "Frontiers of Settlement" series see R.C. Wallace Papers, file 3/2/6/3: W.A. Mackintosh to R.C. Wallace, 31 August, 16 September 1929; and W.L.G. Joerg to R.C. Wallace, 17 June 1929. See also Wallace's files on the "Frontiers" Series in the Wallace Papers, University of Alberta Archives, Granatstein, *The Ottawa Men*, 153ff, and Shore, *The Science of Social Redemption*, 166–76.

76 On Norman Rogers see the following letters in the R.C. Wallace Papers, file 3/2/6: D.A. McArthur to R.C. Wallace, 28 February 1931; W.H. Fyfe to R. C. Wallace, 5 October 1934; R.C. Wallace to W.H. Fyfe, 16 October 1934. Also: *The Canadian Who's Who*, C.G.D. Roberts, ed.; Harold Innis to Norman Rogers, 12 February 1935, and O.D. Skelton to Norman Rogers, 26 October 1935, Norman Rogers Papers, Queen's University Archives; J.A. Corry, *My Life and Work: A Happy Partnership* (Kingston, 1981), 48ff, 85–9, 104–12; F.W. Gibson, *Queen's University 2*, 168–71.

77 H.A. Innis, "Government Ownership and the Canadian Scene" (1933), in his *Essays in Canadian Economic History* (Toronto 1956), 78.

CHAPTER TWO

1 Robin S. Harris, *History of Higher Education in Canada* (Toronto 1974), appendix 2; *Historical Statistics of Canada*, 2nd ed., F.H. Leacey *et al.*, ed. (Toronto 1983), series A2–14; Richard Allen, *The Social Passion: Religion and Social Reform in Canada 1914–1928* (Toronto 1973), 10; A.B. McKillop, *A Disciplined Intelligence: Critical Inquiry and Canadian Thought in the Victorian Era* (Montreal 1979), 208–9; Hilda Neatby, *Queen's University 1, 1841–1917: And Not to Yield* (Montreal 1978), 231–5.

2 Alma Mater Society, *Sunday Afternoon Addresses*, 3rd series, 1893. Contributions to this volume included John Watson's "The Lesson of Ecclesiastes," Herbert Symonds's "Continuity and Progress," Rev. Dr Ross's "Christ and His Teachings Superceded?," Rev. Principal Caven's "Study and Spiritual Life," and Rev. Alf Gandier's "Motives to Missionary Work."

3 "The Influence of Daily Occupations on the Social Life of the People," *Sunday Afternoon Addresses*, 58–9.

4 Ibid., 58–61, 63–4.

5 H. Stuart Hughes, *Consciousness and Society: The Reorientation of European Social Thought, 1890–1930* (New York 1958), 33–66; Robert Heilbroner, *The Worldly Philosophers*, 4th ed. (New York, 1973), chapters 6–7.

6 "The Influence of Daily Occupations," 65–6.

7 A.R.M. Lower, *Great Britain's Woodyard* (Montreal 1973), 31–3, 130–2, 246–50; *Canada Investigates Industrialism: The Royal Commission on the Relations of Labour and Capital of 1889*, Greg Kealey, ed., 167–79 (Kingston), 179–92 (Cornwall), 192–210 (Ottawa).

8 Margaret Atwood, *Survival: A Thematic Guide to Canadian Literature* (Toronto 1972), 31–2, 49–64; George Altmeyer, "The Idea of Nature in Canada 1893–1914," *Journal of Canadian Studies*, 11 (1976), 21–34; Adam Shortt, "The Influence of Daily Occupations," 64–6.

9 Adam Shortt, "The Influence of Daily Occupations"; "The Great North-West," *Queen's Quarterly*, 2 (1895), 189–97; "Some Observations on the North-West," *Queen's Quarterly*, 3 (1895), 13–14.

10 Adam Shortt, "The Influence of Daily Occupations," 59, 65–6.

11 Adam Shortt, "The Nature and Sphere of Political Science" *Queen's Quarterly*, 1 (1893), 93–5.

12 Ibid. Remarkably similarly arguments about the debilitating effects of the division between political science and economics are made by contemporary revivalists of the "political economy" school. The most articulate exponent may be C.B. Macpherson, who has criticized the two disciplines for ignoring the interrelationship between economic theorems and political ones. Macpherson dates this divergence to the era of Adam Shortt, which witnessed the rise of marginal-utility economics, and later to the development of "positive" political science with its claims of "value-free" assessments, which both obscures and denies the "normative" and therefore "value-laden" content. Macpherson excepts Canadian social science to the extent that he recognizes Innis and to a lesser extent Mackintosh as theorists of a continuing "political economy" approach capable of both political and economic analysis, analytical and normative, descriptive and evaluative. Shortt was hostile to the marginalists and a clue regarding the origins of a Canadian "political economy" school is the fact that Shortt influenced both Innis and Mackintosh. Given this orthodox trio, it is interesting that Macpherson's foe, Harry Johnson, engaged in pure Marxist-baiting in rejecting Macpherson's claims about the importance of "political economy." See C.B. Macpherson, "The Economic Penetration of Political Theory: Some Hypotheses," *Journal of the History of Ideas*, 39 (1978), 101–3, and "After Strange Gods: Canadian Political Science," in *Perspectives on the Social Sciences in Canada*, T.N. Guinsburg and Grant Reuber, eds. (Toronto 1973), 60ff. See also Harry G. Johnson's commentary on Macpherson's paper in *Perspectives on the Social Sciences in Canada*, 79–84; and Daniel Drache, "Rediscovering Canadian Political Economy," *Journal of Canadian Studies* 9 (1976).

13 Adam Shortt, "The Nature and Sphere of Political Science," 96–7.

14 See notes 29 and 30, below.

15 "The Nature and Sphere of Political Science," 96, 100.

16 Ibid.; "Some New Books in Political Science," *Queen's Quarterly* 1 (1894), 228; "The Origins of Organized Society, or the State," mss., Adam Shortt Papers, Queen's University Archives.

17 "The Nature and Sphere of Political Science," 100.

18 John Watson, "Re Adam Shortt," 23 April 1883, Adam Shortt Papers, Box 1.

19 Adam Shortt, "Social Evolution According to Mr. Kidd," *Queen's Quarterly*, 2 (1895), 333–5. Kidd's imperialism is discussed in Carl Berger, *The Sense of Power: Studies in the Ideas of Canadian Imperialism* (Toronto 1970), 187.

20 "The Nature and Sphere of Political Science," 100; "Social Evolution According to Mr. Kidd," 329.

21 "Nature and Sphere of Political Science," 100; "Social Evolution According to Mr. Kidd," 329.

22 "The Basis of Economic Value," 71–3; "Some New Books in Political Science," 228–9.

23 "The Basis of Economic Value," 71–2.

24 Ibid., 72. Alfred Marshall was more sensitive to the problem of distinguishing between the ethical and the efficient and was surprisingly equivocal about the benefits of the allocation of goods under a laissez-faire position than Shortt gave him credit for. See Joan Robinson, *Economic Philosophy* (Harmondsworth, England), 51–7, and Eric Roll, *A History of Economic Thought*, 4th rev. ed. (London 1973), 402. Marshall's own thoughts are found in *Memorials of Alfred Marshall*, A.C. Pigou, ed. (London 1925), particularly "The Present Position of Economics" (1885), 153–6, and "The Old Generation of Economists and the New" (1897), 310–11.

25 "Adam Shortt, "The Nature and Sphere of Political Science," 96–9; "Some Characteristics of Canadian Economic History" mss., Adam Shortt Papers, 1; "The Anti-Dumping Feature of the Canadian Tariff," *Quarterly Journal of Economics*, 27 (1900), 250.

26 "The Basis of Economic Value," 71–2.

27 S.E.D. Shortt, *The Search for an Ideal*, 104–6; see also the views of historians Carl Berger and Ian Wilson cited in note 29.

28 James Kloppenberg, *Uncertain Victory: Social Democracy and Progressivism in European and American Thought, 1870–1920* (New York 1986), 6.

29 Adam Shortt, "Life in Kingston in the Year after Waterloo," *Queen's Quarterly*, 8 (1901), 181ff; "The Winning of Responsible Government in Canada," *Queen's Quarterly*, 10 (1902), 147; "Imperial Preferential Trade," 35–8, 60–1; "Life of the Settler in Western Canada Before the War of 1812," *Queen's Quarterly*, 22 (1914), 71. Cf. Carl Berger and Ian Wilson think that Shortt shared Arthur Doughty's patriotic approach to

history and thought it important chiefly as training for citizenship. Carl Berger, *The Writing of Canadian History: Aspects of English-Canadian Historical writing, 1900 to 1970* (Toronto 1976), 26–30; Ian Wilson, "Shortt and Doughty: the Cultural Role of the National Archives of Canada 1904–1935," *Canadian Archivist*, 2 (1973), 4–25.

30 Adam Shortt and A.G. Doughty, "Editors' Introduction," *Canada and its Provinces, 1* (Toronto 1914), 7–9; Adam Shortt to Robert Borden, 7 May 1915, "Memorandum on Publication of Historical Documents," Robert L. Borden Papers, Adam Shortt, "The Significance for Canadian History of the Work of the Board of Historical Publications," *Proceedings and Transactions, Royal Society of Canada*, series 3, 13 (1919), 104–5; Adam Shortt to Robert Borden, 3 May 1921, Adam Shortt Papers. Developments in historical thought are examined in various works such as Morton White, *Social Thought in America: The Revolt Against Formalism* (Boston 1957), passim, and James Kloppenberg, *Uncertain Victory*, passim.

31 "Books from the Library of the late Dr. Adam Shortt," Adam Shortt Papers.

32 Adam Shortt, "Some Aspects of the Social Life of Canada", 7; "Legislation and Morality," *Queen's Quarterly* 8 (1901), 354; "Social Evolution According to Mr. Kidd," 335; "The Influence of Daily Occupations," 68–9; "The Nature and Sphere of Political Science," 98.

33 Adam Shortt, "Personality as a Social Factor," *Clarkson Bulletin* 6 (1909), 3; "Legislation and Morality," 354ff; "Recent Phases of Socialism," *Queen's Quarterly*, 5 (1897), 11.

34 Adam Shortt to Andrew Haydon, 16 April, 31 July 1895, Adam Shortt Papers; Adam Shortt, "Life in Kingston in the Year After Waterloo," *Queen's Quarterly*, 8 (1901), 181.

35 "Some Aspects of the Social Life of Canada," *Canadian Magazine*, 11 (1898), 3–5, 7; "The Winning of Responsible Government," *Queen's Quarterly*, 10 (1902), 147; *Lord Sydenham* (Toronto 1908), 215–27, 315–16, 345–52. On LeSueur see *A Critical Spirit: The Thought of William Dawson LeSueur*, A.B. McKillop, ed. (Toronto 1977), 247–61.

36 "The Nature and Sphere of Political Science," 96. The notion of nineteenth-century individualism as reality and myth is accepted by Doug Owram, *The Government Generation: Canadian Intellectuals and the State 1900–1945* (Toronto 1986), 3–8, in contrast to the cultural context and legal realities analyzed by Alison Prentice, *The School Promoters: Education and Social Class in Mid-Nineteenth Century Upper Canada* (Toronto 1977), 170–84. Allan Smith, "The Myth of the Self-Made Man in English Canada, 1850–1914," *Canadian Historical Review*, 59 (1978), 189–219, examines the ambiguities of Canadian popular views

of the autonomy and potential of the individual in this period, although he tends to accept that the reality and concept of individualism were well entrenched, a view Adam Shortt would have criticized.

37 "Some Aspects of the Social Life of Canada," 7–10; "Legislation and Morality," 356–7; "Personality as a Social Factor," 5, 6.

38 "Some Aspects of the Social Life of Canada," 9–10 et seq.

39 "Historical Aspects of Town Planning," *Town Planning*, 1 (June 1921), 15–6; "One Method of Financing Town Planning," *Town Planning*, 1 (June 1922), 17–8.

40 For example: Berger, *The Sense of Power*, passim, and Ramsay Cook, *The Regenerators: Social Criticism in Late Victorian English Canada* (Toronto 1985), passim.

41 See S.E.D. Shortt, *The Search for an Ideal: Six Intellectuals and their Convictions in an Age of Transition, 1890–1930* (Toronto 1976), 102.

CHAPTER THREE

1 "Some Observations on the Great North-West, 1," *Queen's Quarterly*, 2 (January 1895), 184–95, especially 193–4; "Some Observations on the Great North-West, 2," *Queen's Quarterly*, 3 (July 1895), 12–22. Principal Grant was also critical of excessive promotion: see "Current Events," *Queen's Quarterly*, 1 (July 1893), 156.

2 "Some Observations on the Great North-West, 1," 194–5; "Some Observations on the Great North-West, 2," 12–15, 16–21; "Current Events," *Queen's Quarterly*, 9 (April 1902), 320–3; on immigration see "The Importation of Defective Classes," 1907 mss. Adam Shortt Papers.

3 James Mavor, "Agricultural Development in the North-West of Canada," *Report*, 29th Meeting of the British Academy for the Advancement of Science, Toronto 1904 (London 1910), passim; Stephen Leacock, "The Wizard of Finance," *Arcadian Adventures with the Idle Rich* (Toronto 1969; original edition 1914), and "The Speculations of Jefferson Thorpe," *Sunshine Sketches of a Little Town* (Toronto 1970; original edition 1912). Mavor's views on the Prairies are examined in S.E.D. Shortt, *The Search for an Ideal: Six Intellectuals and Their Convictions in an Age of Transition 1890–1930* (Toronto 1976), 123–4. Leacock's later decline is seen in *My Discovery of the West* (Toronto 1937), passim. The position Shortt was trying to rebut had a long history and undoubtedly one he observed closely, as shown by his library; see "Books from the Library of the late Dr. Adam Shortt," Adam Shortt Papers. The subject of expansionist promotion is surveyed in Doug Owram, *The Promise of Eden: The Canadian Expansionist Movement and the Idea of the West 1857–1900* (Toronto 1980), especially chapters 3, 5, 7.

4 "Some Observations on the Great North-West, 1," passim; "Mining Investment," *Queen's Quarterly*, 4 (April 1897), 269–74.

5 Sandford Fleming, "Build Up Canada," *Queen's Quarterly*, 11 (April 1904), 404–17.

6 In addition to Shortt's essays, the following exemplify the tone of the twenty-three papers published between 1901 and 1905: N.F. Carmichael, "Cobalt Nickel in New Ontario," 11 (July 1903); Richard Lees, "Forestry Problems of Ontario," 11 (July 1903), 109–13; Cecil Smith, "Ontario's Water Powers," 13 (October 1905), 127–33; J.J. Harpell, "University Men in Life Insurance," 10 (January 1903); A.H.U. Colquohoun, "Universities and the Press," 11 (July 1903), 85–100; A.T. Drummond, "The Need in Canada of Forest Engineering," 9 (April 1902), 307–13.

7 M.J. Patton, "Organized Conservation in Canada," *Queen's Quarterly*, 18 (July 1910), 26–33; Herbert T. Kalmus, "Conservation and Research," *Queen's Quarterly*, 20 (January 1913), 287–9; Rev. George Bryce, "The Crying Need for Industrial Research," *Transactions of the Canadian Institute*, 9 (1912), 223–35; W.L. Goodwin, "A School of Forestry for Ontario," *Queen's Quarterly*, 9 (July 1902), 77–80; A.T. Drummond, "The Need in Canada of Forest Engineering," *Queen's Quarterly*, 9 (April 1902), 307–13. See also Adam Shortt to editor of the *Globe*, February 1906, Adam Shortt Papers, Queen's University Archives.

8 Alma Mater Society, "The Influence of Daily Occupations," 3rd series, 1893, 66; "Some Observations on the Great North-West, 1," 20–2; *Imperial Preferential Trade* (Toronto 1904), 53.

9 Norman Penlington, *Canada and Imperialism, 1896–1899* (Toronto 1965), passim; Carl Berger, *The Sense of Power: Studies in the Ideas of Canadian Imperialism* (Toronto 1970), passim. See also O.D. Skelton, *Life and Letters of Sir Wilfrid Laurier* (Toronto 1921), 2 vols., 2:6–66.

10 O.D. Skelton to Adam Shortt, 1 March 1902, 9 January, 14 and 25 March 1906, Adam Shortt Papers.

11 G.M. Grant, "Review: Goldwin Smith's 'Canada and the Canadian Question,'" *The Week*, 8 (1 and 15 May 1891); G.M. Grant, "Current Events," *Queen's Quarterly*, 5 (July 1897), 85; "Current Events," *Queen's Quarterly*, 5 (October 1897), 166; "Current Events," *Queen's Quarterly*, 8 (July 1900), 75–8; "Current Events," *Queen's Quarterly*, 8 (October 1900), 153–7. Grant's views are examined in Carl Berger, *The Sense of Power*, 32–3 and passim, and in Allan Smith, "The Thought of George Monro Grant," *Canadian Literature*, no. 83 (Winter 1979), 90–109. Grant's son, William L. Grant, acknowledged the influence of Shortt on his father during the preparation of the only biography of Principal Grant and Shortt returned the compliment by noting the principal's impact on his own thinking. W.L. Grant to Adam Shortt, 28 June 1903,

15 February 1904, Adam Shortt Papers; Adam Shortt to W.L. Grant, 16 February 1904, W.L. Grant Papers, National Archives of Canada.

12 "Current Events," *Queen's Quarterly*, 6 (July 1898), 82–3; "Some Aspects of the Imperial Problem," *Canadian Magazine*, 18 (February 1902), 323–7.

13 "Current Events," *Queen's Quarterly*, 10 (July 1902), 111–12, 119–22.

14 *Imperial Preferential Trade*, 1–2, 57–8, 61–2.

15 Ibid., 4–9, 53–9,

16 Ibid., 13–21, 21–43, 35–6.

17 Ibid., 21–43. Arthur Lower, Shortt's collaborator on the Board of Historical Publications during the 1920s and his unofficial student for a History MA at the University of Toronto, developed a number of these themes in his own work. See *The North American Assault on the Forest* (Toronto, and New Haven, Conn., 1938) and *Great Britain's Woodyard* (Montreal 1973). Lower reviews his friendship with Shortt in *My First Seventy-Five Years* (Toronto 1967), 123–9.

18 Ibid., 26.

19 Ibid., 49; "Current Events," *Queen's Quarterly*, 10 (October 1902), 238–40; O.D. Skelton, "General Economic History 1867–1912," *Canada and Its Provinces*, 23 vols., Arthur G. Doughty and Adam Shortt, eds. (Toronto 1914–17), 9:148, 153–6, 205.

20 Ibid., 44–5.

21 Ibid., 44, 49.

22 Donald Creighton, *The Empire of the St. Lawrence: A Study in Commerce and Politics* (Toronto 1956; original edition 1937), passim.

23 "General Economic History 1867–1912," 4–5, 47–8, 61; "Preferential Trade Between Britain and Canada," *Proceedings of the American Economic Association 1904*, 12; "Some Characteristics of Canadian Economic History," 4–5, mss., Adam Shortt Papers. Shortt's thematic emphasis was reiterated in his surveys for *Canada and Its Provinces*: "General Economic History 1763–1840," 4:521–65, and "General Economic History 1841–1867," 5:185–7, 207–9.

24 *Imperial Preferential Trade*, 53; "Co-operation," *Queen's Quarterly*, 5 (October 1897), 129–33.

25 Shortt sarcastically considered Goldwin Smith's views as mere social observations in a review of Smith's "Political History of the United States," *Queen's Quarterly*, 1 (October 1893), 230–2. James Douglas, sometime board member and chancellor at Queen's and a New York mining mogul, took a similar view: *Canadian Independence, Annexation and British Imperial Federation* (New York 1894), 106–8. Goldwin Smith is examined in Elisabeth Wallace, *Goldwin Smith, Victorian Liberal* (Toronto 1957), 253–80. Erastus Wiman is studied in Ian Grant, "Erastus Wiman: A Continentalist Replies to Canadian Imperialism,"

Canadian Historical Review, 53 (March 1972), 1–20. Ramsay Cook analyzes the hereditarian and environmentalist perspectives in "Landscape Painting and National Sentiment in Canada," in *The Maple Leaf Forever*, 2nd ed. (Toronto 1977), 158–61.

26 *Imperial Preferential Trade*, 53–4.

27 "General Economic History 1841–1867," 185–6; "Preferential Trade Between Britain and Canada," 8–10, 12–13.

28 See: "Early History of Canadian Banking," *Journal of the Canadian Bankers' Association*, 4 and 5 (1896–97); "Canadian Currency and Exchange Under French Rule," *Journal of the Canadian Bankers' Association*, 5 and 6 (1898–99); "History of Canading Currency, Banking and Exchange," *Journal of the Canadian Bankers' Association*, 7–14, (1900–06). Shortt later wrote eleven essays for the *Journal of the Canadian Bankers' Association* collectively entitled "Founders of Canadian Banking," 29–33 (1921–25).

29 "Early History of Canadian Banking," *Journal of the Canadian Bankers' Association*, 4 (October 1896), 1–8.

30 "Early History of Canadian Banking," 10–17, 235–6. Shortt had noted that the Canadian tariff was a policy of economic development rooted in the North American struggle for markets and manufacturing capacity and was, from Galt to Macdonald, partly retaliatory against the United States. "Current Events," *Queen's Quarterly*, 10 (October 1902), 238–9; *Imperial Preferential Trade*, 49–50. Skelton, of course, reiterated this point: "General Economic History 1867–1912," 133–5.

31 "History of Canadian Currency, Banking and Exchange," *Journal of the Canadian Bankers' Association*, 8 (October 1900), 1–15; 8 (January 1901), 154–7; 9 (October 1901), 16ff.

32 "History of Canadian Currency, Banking and Exchange," *Journal of the Canadian Bankers' Association*, 8 (January 1901), 145–6, 149–50; 8 (April 1901), 227–43; 14 (October 1906), 26–7; 10 (July 1903), 29.

33 "General Economic History 1867–1912," 96–102.

34 Ibid., 97, 110–11.

35 *The Life and Times of Sir Alexander Tilloch Galt* (Toronto 1920), 217–22, 227–8, and passim; "General Economic History 1867–1912," 253–6, 133–5.

36 "General Economic History 1867–1912," 210–5, 274.

37 Ibid., 205–15, 238–42. Shortt had also noted the strong international economic influences at work during the periods when the Canadian economy had flourished and depended on the influx of foreign capital, especially British, as necessary for growth. See "Current Events," *Queen's Quarterly*, 6 (January 1899), 243–4; *Imperial Preferential Trade*, 49–50, 61; "General Economic History 1763–1840," 585–7.

38 "General Economic History 1867–1912," 192, 197–200, 133–5, 148.

39 *The Railway Builders* (Toronto 1916), 29–34, 34–5; *The Life and Letters of Sir Wilfrid Laurier*, 1:245–6. T.C. Keefer's views of 1850 are found in *The Philosophy of Railroads*, edited and introduced by H.V. Nelles (Toronto 1972), 16, 4–6, 14ff, especially 32.

40 *The Railway Builders*, 159. Galt's ideas are interpreted in *Life and Times of Alexander Tilloch Galt*, chapter 9.

41 *The Railway Builders*, 52–5.

42 "Early Banking in Upper and Lower Canada," in *History of the Canadian Bank of Commerce*, 3 vols., Victor Ross, ed. (Toronto 1920–34), 1 (1920): 1–25.

43 Adam Shortt, "Current Events," *Queen's Quarterly*, 15 (July 1907), 70; O.D. Skelton, "General Economic History 1867–1912," 191–2.

44 *Imperial Preferential Trade*, passim; "Current Events," *Queen's Quarterly*, 10 (October 1902), 242–5; "Some Aspects of the Imperial Problem," *Canadian Magazine*, 18 (February 1902), 323–7; "Current Events," *Queen's Quarterly* 9 (April 1902), 319–20.

45 On Laurier see: "Current Events," *Queen's Quarterly*, 10 (October 1902), 242–5; Adam Shortt to Wilfrid Laurier, 29 January 1902, 11 December 1905, Wilfrid Laurier Papers, National Archives of Canada. On Borden see: Adam Shortt to Robert Borden, 16 February 1921, Robert Borden Papers, National Archives of Canada.

46 "Current Events," *Queen's Quarterly*, 9 (October 1901), 148; ibid., 11 (January 1904), 328.

47 *Imperial Preferential Trade*, 148; Henri Bourassa to Adam Shortt, 28 March 1904, Adam Shortt Papers.

48 "Current Events," *Queen's Quarterly*, 6 (July 1898), 81–2. Also, Arthur J. Glazebrook to Adam Shortt, 21 November 1903, 10 October 1905; A. Steel-Maitland to Adam Shortt, 24 October 1908; Phillip Kerr to Adam Shortt, 20 April 1910; Lionel Curtis to Adam Shortt, 13 March 1911, Adam Shortt Papers.

49 Edward Peacock to Adam Shortt, 28 September 1903, 22 December 1908, 3 March 1911, Adam Shortt to Mrs Shortt, 14 November 1913, Adam Shortt Papers. Also: Adam Shortt to Sandford Fleming, 4 November 1905, 2 September 1907, Sandford Fleming Papers, National Archives of Canada.

50 On the Round Table movement see the following: James Eayrs, "The Round Table Movement in Canada, 1909–1920," in *Imperial Relations in the Age of Laurier*, Carl Berger, ed. (Toronto 1969), 66, 68–80; Ramsay Cook, *The Politics of John W. Dafoe and the Free Press* (Toronto 1963), 58–60, 85, 93–5; John Kendle, *The Round Table Movement and Imperial Union* (Toronto 1975), 64–8, 85, 93–5. Shortt's rejection of British military and constitutional aims and the need for formal ties is found in Adam Shortt, Diary, 6, 18, 21, February 1910, and Kenneth Bell to

Adam Shortt, 26 April 1912, Adam Shortt Papers; Adam Shortt to Sandford Fleming, 4 November 1905, Sandford Fleming Papers.

51 "Current Events," *Queen's Quarterly*, 6 (July 1898), 81–3; ibid., January 1899, 240–3, April 1899, 321–3. See also comments from Andrew Haydon and William Swanson reflecting on Shortt's apt characterization of social similarities in Canada and the United States: Adam Shortt to Andrew Haydon, 2 May 1897, William Swanson to Adam Shortt, 13 January 1906, Adam Shortt Papers.

52 Useful to discussion of the issue of nationalism and the state are the following: Elie Kedourie, Nationalism (London 1960), 9–30; David Cameron, *Nationalism, Self-Determination and the Quebec Question* (Toronto 1974), 25–66, 80–1; Ramsay Cook, *The Maple Leaf Forever*, 2nd ed., 1–11; S.E.D. Shortt, *The Search For An Ideal: Six Intellectuals and Their Convictions in an Age of Transition, 1890–1930* (Toronto 1976), 114–15. Shortt's use of the word "nationalism" suggests a sociological sense described by Cameron (16) rather than in a political sense with all the racialism that the term implied.

53 Shortt's views of French Canadians and French-English dualism are found in "Current Events," *Queen's Quarterly*, 1 (January 1894), 251–2; "Current Events," ibid., 11 (January 1904), 328; "Down the St. Lawrence on a Timber Raft," *Queen's Quarterly*, 11 (July 1903), 19–34; "General Economic History 1763–1840," 549; *Lord Sydenham* (Toronto 1908), 62–71, 93–4; Adam Shortt to W.M. Kennedy, 9 December 1918, Adam Shortt Papers.

54 "Some Characteristics of Canadian Economic History," mss., Adam Shortt Papers, 5–6.

55 "Current Events," *Queen's Quarterly*, 20 (July 1912), 108–11; "The Political Year in Canada," *Political Quarterly*, 1 (February 1914), 149–50.

56 *The Life and Letters of Sir Wilfrid Laurier*, 1:367; 2:60–6, 66.

57 Generally, see: *The Canadian Dominion* (New Haven, Conn., 1919), 212; *The Life and Letters of Sir Wilfrid Laurier*, 2:64, 291–2; "Canada, the Empire and the League," *Grain Growers' Guide*, 25 February 1920. On specific issues mentioned, see: "The Political Year in Canada," *Political Quarterly*, 1 (February 1914), 146–8, 154–5; "Current Events," *Queen's Quarterly*, 16 (April 1909), 377–80; ibid., 20 (April 1913), 469–74; ibid., 21 (July 1914), 100; "Canada and the Most-Favoured-Nation Treaties," *Queen's Quarterly*, 19 (January 1912), 231–52; "Extracts from an Address delivered by Professor O.D. Skelton at the Ottawa Canadian Club 21 January 1922," 1–3, Robert Borden Papers. Skelton was professionally acquainted with Borden. When Skelton became undersecretary at External Affairs, he often passed on essays and papers for Borden's comments; later, after Borden's return to private life Skelton was close enough to the former prime minister to ask him to look up

his son, Alex, a brilliant if erratic young man who was an Ontario Rhodes Scholar for 1927, on a planned visit to Oxford. See O.D. Skelton to Robert Borden, 24 January, 19 June, 23 July 1929, 24 October 1933, 19 December 1935; Skelton to Borden, misc. letters, July and August 1927, Robert Borden Papers.

58 O.D. Skelton to Adam Shortt, 1 March 1902, Adam Shortt Papers; "Current Events," *Queen's Quarterly*, 24 (April 1913), 469ff.; *The Life and Letters of Sir Wilfrid Laurier*, 2:292, 329–30.

59 "Canada and Foreign Policy," *Proceedings Canadian Club of Toronto*, 1921–22 (Toronto 1923), 144–6, 142–3, 147–8; "Canada, the Empire and the League," *Grain Growers' Guide*, 25 February and 3 March 1920; "Extracts ... Ottawa Canadian Club," Robert Borden Papers; *The Railway Builders*, 144.

60 D.M.L. Farr, introduction to *Life and Letters of Sir Wilfrid Laurier* (Carleton Library ed., Toronto 1965), 1:9–21; Carl Berger, *The Writing of Canadian History: Aspects of English-Canadian Historical Writing 1900 to 1970* (Toronto 1976), 47–52, notes this divergence but concentrates on the main "whig" historians of the 1920s. Canadian whiggery is examined in J.K. McConica, "Kingsford and Whiggery in Canadian History," *Canadian Historical Review*, 40 (1959), 108–20.

61 Adam Shortt, "Current Events," *Queen's Quarterly*, 6 (October 1898), 161–3; O.D. Skelton, "The Language Issue in Canada" and "Notes on the Language Issue Abroad," *Queen's Quarterly*, 24 (April 1917), 438–68, 469–77; O.D. Skelton to William Grant, 19 March 1917, 13 August 1917, W.L. Grant Papers, National Archives of Canada. The Bonne Entente is surveyed in J.L. Granatstein and J.M. Hitsman, *Broken Promises: A History of Conscription in Canada* (Toronto 1977), 41–2, and Brian Cameron, "The Bonne Entente Movement 1916–17," *Journal of Canadian Studies*, 13 (1978), 42–55.

62 O.D. Skelton to Adam Shortt, 4 March 1909, Adam Shortt to Mrs Shortt, 17 September 1908, Adam Shortt Papers. Shortt claimed that F.A. Acland, who became deputy minister of labour when Mackenzie King left the public service for politics in 1908, sought out Skelton, his former associate from their Philadelphia days. The overhaul of External Affairs under Skelton is surveyed in several places, most concisely and favourably in J.L. Granatstein, *The Ottawa Men: The Civil Service Mandarins, 1935–1957* (Toronto 1982), 28–44.

63 Norman Hillmer, "The Anglo-Canadian Neurosis: The Case of O.D. Skelton," in *Great Britain and Canada: Survey of a Changing Relationship*, Peter Lyon, ed. (London 1976), 62–4, 66–71; C.P. Stacey, *Canada and the Age of Conflict*, 2 vols. (Toronto 1981), 2:67.

64 On the Rainbow Circle see Peter Clarke, *Liberals and Social Democrats* (Cambridge 1978), 62–99; on the Anti-Imperialist League see Berkeley

Tompkins, *Anti-Imperialism in the United States, 1890–1920* (Philadelphia 1970), passim. For the conclusions of D.M.L. Farr and S.E.D. Shortt, see notes 52 and 60.

65 See J.A. Hobson, *Canada Today* (London 1905), 44–7; John Allett, *New Liberalism: The Political Economy of J.A. Hobson* (Toronto 1981), 131ff, especially 143.

CHAPTER FOUR

1 Adam Shortt, "Labour and Capital and the Cost of Living," *Industrial Canada*, 10, no. 7 (February 1910), 699–701.

2 W.W. Swanson, "The Increased Cost of Living and the Output of Gold," *Queen's Quarterly*, 17 (January 1910), 237–40, 242; O.D. Skelton, "General Economic History 1867–1912," *Canada and its Provinces*, 23 vols., Arthur G. Doughty and Adam Shortt, eds. (Toronto 1914–17), 9:270–2; O.D. Skelton, "Current Events," *Queen's Quarterly*, 22 (July 1914), 101–2; O.D. Skelton, Current Events, *Queen's Quarterly*, 20 (April 1913), 474.

3 See Craig Heron and Bryan Palmer, "Through the Prism of the Strike: Industrial Conflict in Southern Ontario, 1901–1914," *Canadian Historical Review*, 58 (December 1977), 423–58. This essay contains an interesting discussion of the dimensions and scale of labour's conflict with capital during the period from 1900 to the First World War.

4 Adam Shortt "Labour and Capital and the Cost of Living," passim; O.D. Skelton, "General Economic History 1867–1912," 272.

5 On these developments in Canada generally, see Robert Craig Brown and Ramsay Cook, *Canada, 1896–1921, A Nation Transformed* (Toronto 1972), especially chapters 5 and 6.

6 Adam Shortt, "In Defence of Millionaires," *Canadian Magazine*, 13 (1899), 496–8, 499.

7 Adam Shortt, "Current Events," *Queen's Quarterly*, 10 (October 1902), 235–7.

8 Ibid.; "Current Events," *Queen's Quarterly*, 13 (October 1905), 183; editorial, *Industrial Canada*, vol. 10, no. 7 (February 1910), 679. There was a remarkable similarity between Shortt's views on monopolies and trusts and those of his student Edward R. Peacock as found in the latter's 1898 essay. The very terminology, including the distinction between natural and artificial monopolies, is similar, doubtless reflecting the teacher-student relationship. See E.R. Peacock, "Trusts, Combines and Monopolies," *Queen's Quarterly*, 6 (July 1898), 1–34.

9 Shortt, "Labour and Capital and the Cost of Living," 699.

10 W.W. Swanson to Adam Shortt, 10 May 1910, Adam Shortt Papers, Queen's University Archives; J.C. Ross (editor, *Journal of Commerce*) to

R.A. Falconer, 1 May 1915, James Mavor Papers, University of Toronto Archives; W.W. Swanson, "Current Events," *Queen's Quarterly*, 17 (April 1910), 351–6; W.W. Swanson, "Current Events," *Queen's Quarterly*, 19 (July 1911), 79–80. On this question in general, see Michael Bliss, "Another Anti-Trust Tradition," *Enterprise and National Development*, Glenn Porter and R.D. Cuff, eds. (Toronto 1973), 39–50.

11 O.D. Skelton, "Current Events," *Queen's Quarterly*, 15 (January 1908), 252–3; O.D. Skelton, "General Economic History 1867–1912," 258–66, 273.

12 See A.J.P. Taylor, *Beaverbrook* (New York 1972), 35ff, 63–4.

13 G. M. Grant, "Current Events," *Queen's Quarterly*, 4 (April 1897), 315–16; W.L. Grant to Adam Shortt, 28 June 1903, 15 February 1904, Adam Shortt Papers; G.M. Grant to Wilfrid Laurier, 11 January 1899, 25 February 1899, 4 March 1899, Wilfrid Laurier Papers, National Archives of Canada; ibid., Wilfrid Laurier to G.M. Grant, 27 February 1899.

14 Adam Shortt Papers: Adam Shortt, Diaries, 7 March 1911, 22 September 1911; J. Laurence Laughlin to Adam Shortt, 1 December 1910, Albert J. Beveridge to Shortt, 12 May 1911; F.W. Taussig to Adam Shortt, 7 December 1910, 11 January 1911. Also: F.W. Taussig, "Reciprocity with Canada," *Journal of Political Economy*, 19 (July 1911), 542–9.

15 Adam Shortt, Diaries, 19 May 1911; O.D. Skelton to W.L.M. King, 9 August 1911, R.H. Coats to O.D. Skelton, 15 July 1911, W.L.M. King Papers, National Archives of Canada.

16 O.D. Skelton, "Current Events," *Queen's Quarterly*, 18 (July 1911), 329–35; O.D. Skelton, "The Canadian Reciprocity Agreement," *Economic Journal*, 21 (June 1911), 274–6; O.D. Skelton, "Reciprocity: The Canadian Attitude," *Journal of Political Economy*, 19 (February 1911), 89–96, 79–89, 97. A modern econometric analysis of the reciprocity proposals agrees with Skelton about its commercial impact: M.B. Percy, K.M. Norrie, R.G. Johnston, "Reciprocity and the Canadian General Election of 1911," *Explorations in Economic History*, 18 (1982), 432–4.

17 "Reciprocity: The Canadian Attitude," *Journal of Political Economy*, 77–8; "Current Events," *Queen's Quarterly*, 18 (July 1911), 331–2.

18 O.D. Skelton to W.L.M. King, 24 September 1911, W.L.M. King Papers; O.D. Skelton, "Canada's Rejection of Reciprocity," *Journal of Political Economy*, 19 (November 1911), 726–31.

19 W.L. Grant, "Current Events," *Queen's Quarterly*, 19 (October 1911), 172–5.

20 O.D. Skelton, "Current Events," *Queen's Quarterly*, 18 (April 1910), 332–3; O.D. Skelton, "Reciprocity: The Canadian Attitude," 97; O. D. Skelton to W.L.M. King, 27 June 1911, W.L.M. King Papers.

21 O.D. Skelton, "General Economic History, 1867–1912," 272–3.

22 John Hay, "A General View of Socialistic Schemes," *Queen's Quarterly*, 3 (April 1896), 292–3. Also symptomatic of the misperceptions that Shortt saw around him was an essay by the Nova Scotia attorney-general, J.W. Longley, who rejected the revolutionism of some socialist plans by accepting the need for a measure of socialistic social reform via government action, and another essay by John A. Cooper, sometime editor of the *Canadian Magazine*, who argued the same point: J.W. Longley, "Socialism: Its Truth and Error," *Canadian Magazine*, 6 (February 1896), especially 301, 324; John A. Cooper, "Canadian Democracy and Socialism," *Canadian Magazine*, 3 (August 1894), 332–6. Adam Shortt was acquainted and corresponded with both these men.

23 Shortt, "Recent Phases of Socialism," *Queen's Quarterly*, 5 (July 1897), 17–19.

24 Ibid., 11–13, 16–17; Shortt, "The Capitalist System" (mss., Univ. of Saskatchewan), 1–5. Adam Shortt, Diaries, 13 May 1908.

25 Adam Shortt, "Legislation and Morality," *Queen's Quarterly*, 8 (April 1901), 355, 358; "In Defence of Millionaires," 493–4, 495–7; Shortt's brother-in-law, Cecil Smith, was an engineer for that great early-twentieth-century-example of state activity, the Ontario Hydro-Electric Power Commission.

26 O.D. Skelton to Adam Shortt, 9 January, 25 March, 4 June 1906; W.W. Swanson to Adam Shortt, 3 July 1906, Adam Shortt Papers. Undoubtedly relying on personal testimony, William Mackintosh claimed that Skelton's mentor was Hoxie. It may well be that Hoxie's influence was significant, for he helped supervise Skelton's thesis. But contemporary evidence in Skelton's correspondence and his published writings modifies the "constant oral tradition" to which Mackintosh referred. Veblen was no friend of socialism, scientific or utopian, any more than Laughlin or Hoxie were. Unlike Laughlin, however, he was not a devotee of contemporary capitalism either. Veblen, like Laughlin, maintained a detachment from the neo-classical economic orthodoxy that Shortt had railed against. In his book on *Socialism*, Skelton used Veblen's work much more than any other writer's to buttress his position. Veblen received at least eleven citations; J.A. Hobson, two; Hoxie, along with Richard Ely, J.B. Clark, and Bohm-Bawerk, and so on, one. Skelton took a course on the history of socialism with Veblen, one on labour and capital with Laughlin, plus several with Professor Judson on politics. W.A. Mackintosh, "Oscar Douglas Skelton," *Canada's Past and Present: A Dialogue*, Robert L. McDougall, ed. (Toronto 1965), 61–2. Veblen's major essays are reprinted in *What Veblen Taught*, Wesley C. Mitchell, ed. (New York 1936).

27 O.D. Skelton, "Leaders of the Red Host," *Outlook*, 85, no. 12 (28 March 1907), 687, 690–1, 697–9; O.D. Skelton, "Current Events," *Queen's Quarterly*, 15 (October 1907), 157–9.

28 For example: *Socialism: A Critical Analysis* (Boston and New York 1911), 17, 5–6.

29 *Socialism*, 2ff, 15, 21–9, 29–40.

30 Ibid., 21–9.

31 Ibid., 29.

32 Ibid., 42–3, 43–6, 57–8, 46.

33 Ibid., 54–9.

34 Ibid., 46–54.

35 Ibid., 46.

36 Ibid., 95ff, 115ff, 137ff.

37 Ibid., 174.

38 Shortt's work and that of Hay are cited in notes 22 and 23. Stephen Leacock, *The Unsolved Riddle of Social Justice* (1920), *The Social Criticism of Stephen Leacock*, Alan Bowker, ed. (Toronto 1973), 115–32. Leacock admitted that Marxism was significant and yet he directed his arguments against revisionists and utopians: *Elements of Political Science* (Cambridge 1921), 366–80. This fact, and some reasons for Leacock's perspective (as well as his relationship with his mentor Thorstein Veblen) are discussed in Ramsay Cook, "Stephen Leacock and the Age of Plutocracy, 1903–1921," *Character and Circumstance*, John S. Moir, ed. (Toronto 1970), 168–78.

39 *Socialism*, 95, 115, 137, 171–4.

40 Ibid., 95ff, 112–13, 105–6, 111.

41 Ibid., 117–27, 130–6.

42 Ibid., 137ff, 141–51.

43 Ibid., 114, 176.

44 Ibid., 61, 183.

45 Ibid., 175ff, 187–90, 309–10.

46 Ibid., 49–50, quote 47–8. For a similar use of such terminology see O.D. Skelton's review of Goldwin Smith's "Labour and Capital" in *Queen's Quarterly*, 14 (April 1907), 330–2.

47 *Socialism*, 49–50, 52–4, 219: "Are We Drifting Into Socialism?" *Monetary Times Annual* (1913), 52; "General Economic History, 1867–1912," 95–6; "Current Events," *Queen's Quarterly*, 18 (April 1911), 337.

48 *Socialism*, 206–7; "General Economic History, 1867–1912," 273–4; "Are We Drifting Into Socialism?" 50–2.

49 Bonar's review is in *Queen's Quarterly*, 18 (April 1911), 328–9. Generally Bonar was very favourable about the work, apparently regretting that he, not Skelton, had written the essay on socialism for the *Encyclopaedia*

Britannica. See W.A. Mackintosh, "Oscar Douglas Skelton," 64ff. On the British penchant for blurring the socialist/liberal distinction, see Peter Clark, *Liberals and Social Democrats* (Cambridge 1978), 109–18.

50 John C. Weaver, "Order and Efficiency: Samuel Morley Wickett and the Urban Progressive Movement in Toronto 1900–1915," *Ontario History*, 69 (December 1977), 218–30; W.L. Mackenzie King, *Industry and Humanity* (Toronto 1973; originally published 1918), passim, 103–4, 106–8, 108–12, 335–6. Both Wickett as interpreted by Weaver and King as interpreted by David Jay Bercuson, who edited *Industry and Humanity* for republication, suggest that their subject saw the possibility or else inevitability of social harmony. Either through commission government manned by efficiency experts, in the case of Wickett, or through human beings' apprehension of universal laws, in the case of King, political, economic, and social problems were to be obliterated. Like others of the Queen's department, Skelton differed from Wickett in his acceptance of the "political" and, it seems, from King in his acceptance of social conflict.

51 In addition to works cited in note 50, see John English, *The Decline of Politics: The Conservatives and the Party System, 1901–20* (Toronto 1977), W.L. Morton, *The Progressive Party* (Toronto 1950), and Richard Allen, *The Social Passion: Religion and Social Reform in Canada 1914–1928* (Toronto 1973), for characterizations of the three positions I have in mind.

52 O.D. Skelton, "Are We Drifting Into Socialism?," 52.

53 *Socialism*, 208–9.

CHAPTER FIVE

1 Examples of the political corruption of the day are well summarized by such amusing contemporary accounts as Hector Charlesworth's *More Candid Chronicles* (Toronto 1928), 123–43, and Stephen Leacock's *Arcadian Adventures* (1914) and *Sunshine Sketches* (1912). See also James Bryce, *Modern Democracies* (London 1921), 555–65, especially 563–5; André Siegfried, *The Race Question in Canada* (Toronto 1966, originally published 1907), 112–42, especially 125–9. Most political histories are interspersed with examples and explanations of what F.H. Underhill termed "brokerage politics." Recent works that examine the nature and significance of political corruption with a detailed explanation of its relevance to later reformism are John English, *The Decline of Politics: The Conservatives and the Party System, 1901–1920* (Toronto 1977), 8–30, 222–9; Gordon Stewart, *The Origins of Canadian Politics* (Vancouver 1986), 60–90. Another equally intriguing study raises similar questions about the Ontario in which Shortt and Skelton lived: Peter Oliver,

"Scandal in Ontario Politics: The Jarvis-Smith Affair, An Ontario Dreyfus Case," in his *Public and Private Persons* (Toronto 1975), 182–4, 253–63.

2 An excellent summary of Shortt's views on political reform is "The Party System," *Social Services Congress Report, Ottawa, 1914* (Toronto, 1914), 297–9.

3 Ibid. See also G.M. Grant, "Current Events," *Queen's Quarterly*, 3 (January 1896), 239. James Cappon, "Current Events," *Queen's Quarterly*, 11 (April 1904), 434–5.

4 Adam Shortt, "The Party System," 298; Adam Shortt, "The Relation Between the Legislative and Executive Branches of the Canadian Government," *American Political Science Review* 7 (May 1913), 192.

5 O.D. Skelton, "Current Events," *Queen's Quarterly*, 25 (October 1917), 219, 219–22.

6 On the Industrial Disputes Act see Paul Craven's *An Impartial Umpire: Industrial Relations and the Canadian State, 1900–11* (Toronto 1980), 299. Craven's book sustains the view that King and Shortt did not share the former's benign analysis of how social order would come about.

7 W.A. Mackintosh, "Adam Shortt," *Some Great Men of Queen's*, R.C. Wallace, ed. (Toronto 1941), 124–6, and S.E.D Shortt, *The Search for an Ideal*, 99.

8 "The Canadian Industrial Disputes Act," mss. Adam Shortt Papers; this was later published in the American Economics Association *Publications*, series 3, 10 (1909). See Andrew Haydon, "Memo. Taken from Dr. Shortt," 1928 mss., Adam Shortt Papers, 10.

9 "The Canadian Industrial Disputes Act," 1–2, 4–5, 6. Also from the Adam Shortt Papers: Adam Shortt Diaries, 5 July 1910; D. Campbell to Adam Shortt, 19 February 1908; C. Birmingham to Adam Shortt, 5 March 1908; F.A. Acland to Adam Shortt, 23 May 1908.

10 "The Canadian Industrial Disputes Act," 2–6; J.G. O'Donoghue to Adam Shortt, 21 August 1908.

11 Adam Shortt to Mrs Shortt, 11, 14, 16, 20, 21, 25 July 1908, Adam Shortt Papers.

12 "The Canadian Industrial Disputes Act," 8–10; "Current Events," *Queen's Quarterly*, 10 (January 1903), 398–9.

13 Ibid.

14 "The Canadian Industrial Disputes Act," 11–14.

15 *Lord Sydenham* (The Makers of Canada Series, Toronto 1908).

16 Victor S. Clark, "The Canadian Industrial Disputes Investigation Act of 1907," *Bulletin of the Bureau of Labor*, no. 76 (May 1908), 657–80. See also Paul Craven's contrary interpretation in *An Impartial Umpire*, 312–14; O.D. Skelton, "A Canadian Experiment in Industrial Peace," *The Outlook*, 88 (4 January 1908), 32–7; O.D. Skelton, "Current Events,"

Queen's Quarterly, 15 (July 1907), 68–70; O.D. Skelton, "The New Partnership in Industry," *Canadian Author and Bookman*, 1 (April 1919), 62.

17 J.E. Hodgetts, *et al.*, *The Biography of an Institution: The Civil Service Commission of Canada, 1908–1967* (Montreal 1972), 28–41, especially 35–9, and Doug Owram, *Building for Canadians: A History of the Department of Public Works 1840–1960* (Ministry of Supply and Services, Canada, 1979), 207–13. Adam Shortt to Robert Borden, 12, 14 October, 8, 13, November, 12, 14 December 1911, Robert Laird Borden Papers, National Archives of Canada. See also C. 1774, 7 August 1911, RG 2, 768, file 366E.

18 Robert Borden to Adam Shortt, 19 February 1912, Adam Shortt Papers, Queen's University Archives; Adam Shortt to G.M. Wrong, 1 April 1915, G.M. Wrong Papers, University of Toronto Archives; Adam Shortt to W.L. Grant, 18 March 1915, W.L. Grant Papers, National Archives of Canada; Adam Shortt, "Reply to Personal Attack," Memorandum, Adam Shortt Papers, Box 27. Also in the Shortt Papers: George R. Parkin to Adam Shortt, 5 January 1909; Gilbert McIntyre to Adam Shortt, 5 May 1911; Miscellaneous letters of Col. Samuel Hughes to Shortt, for example, 28, 29 January 1914.

19 "Memorandum on Improvements Required in the Canadian Civil Service," Robert Borden Papers, mfm. reel C-4408, 1–2. See also Walter Lippmann, *Drift and Mastery* (Englewood Cliffs, Calif., 1961; original ed. 1914), 158–77.

20 "Memorandum on Improvements,", 4–7. On the topic of British reform, see *Studies in the Growth of Nineteenth Century Government*, Gillian Sutherland, ed. (Totawa, N.J., 1972).

21 Ibid., 7–8.

22 Ibid., 5.

23 Sir George Murray, "Report on the Organization of the Public Service of Canada," Canada, *Sessional Papers*, 1912, no. 57a, 9–27.

24 Adam Shortt, "Confidential Memorandum for the Prime Minister on the Report of Sir George Murray." Robert Borden Papers, mfm, reel C-4408, 1–4, 4ff, 13–4, 26–7.

25 Shortt, "Confidential Memorandum." See also these letters in the Adam Shortt Papers: Adam Shortt to William Foran, 28 March 1918, Adam Shortt to George Warburton, 4 January 1918, Adam Shortt to E.R. Peacock, 19 January 1918, Adam Shortt to G.M. Wrong, 16 February 1918, G.M. Wrong to Adam Shortt, 25 February 1918. As civil service commissioner, Shortt established links with academics such as Wrong and Archibald McMechan who acted as examiners as well as more informal recruiters.

26 J.A. Corry's work is briefly discussed in Doug Owram, *The Government Generation: Canadian Intellectuals and the State 1900–1945* (Toronto 1986), 166.

27 Adam Shortt, "The Aims of the Canadian Political Science Association," *Papers and Proceedings*, Canadian Political Science Association, 1 (1913), 1–19, 10.

28 Hodgetts *et al.*, *The Biography of An Institution*, chapters 5–7; W.A. Mackintosh, "Adam Shortt," *Some Great Men of Queen's*, 121–2. S.E.D. Shortt's *The Search For An Ideal: Six Intellectuals and Their Convictions in an Age of Transition, 1890–1930* (Toronto 1976), 100–1, summarizes the scholarly consensus in overstating both Shortt's initial influence and the impact of the conflict with Rogers.

29 Adam Shortt to Mrs Shortt, 13, 26 March 1917, 29 January 1918; Adam Shortt to George F. Chipman, 14 March 1918, Adam Shortt Papers. Also: Adam Shortt to Robert Borden, 22 January 1918, Robert Borden Papers; Adam Shortt to W.L. Grant, 16 March 1923, W.L. Grant Papers. See, as well, correspondence cited in note 17.

30 W.A. Mackintosh, "Current Events," *Queen's Quarterly*, 31 (February 1924), 330; W.A. Mackintosh, "Adam Shortt," 132–3. On the problems of the Canadian civil service in the 1920s see Hodgetts *et al.*, *The Biography of an Institution*, chapter 5, and Robert Bryce, *Maturing in Hard Times: Canada's Department of Finance through the Great Depression* (Montreal 1986), chapter 2.

31 O.D. Skelton, "Current Events," *Queen's Quarterly*, 10 (January 1903), 398–9.

32 Adam Shortt, "The Influence of Daily Occupations and Surroundings on the Life of the People," *Sunday Afternoon Addresses, Third Series* (1893), 398–9; Adam Shortt, "Current Events," *Queen's Quarterly*, 6 (April 1899), 31–2. On the shift in American social science see Thomas Haskell, *The Emergence of Professional Social Science* (Urbana, Ill., 1977), chapter 1. This book builds on a theme clearly explained by Morton White, *Social Thought in America: The Revolt Against Formalism* (Boston 1957), chapter 2.

CHAPTER SIX

1 O.D. Skelton, "Current Events," *Queen's Quarterly* 16 (January 1909), 292–5; O.D. Skelton, "Current Events," *Queen's Quarterly*, 17 (January 1910), 263; O.D. Skelton, "Current Events," *Queen's Quarterly*, 21 (April 1914), 507–15.

2 Skelton, "The Referendum," *University Magazine*, 12 (April 1913), 212–13.

3 Adam Shortt to Andrew Haydon, 31 December 1895, Adam Shortt Papers, Queen's University Archives; Adam Shortt, "Current Events," *Queen's Quarterly*, 13 (July 1905), 75–77; "There is every reason to hope that war will come to an end says Prof. Skelton," Peterborough *Daily*, 24 January 1914, Daniel M. Gordon Papers, Queen's University Archives;

O.D. Skelton, "Current Events," *Queen's Quarterly*, 23 (July 1915), 109; O.D. Skelton, "Current Events," *Queen's Quarterly*, 24 (July 1916), 146–7. See also Maurice Hutton, "Militarism and Anti-Militarism," *University Magazine* 12 (April 1913), especially 196. The typicality of Hutton's views among the imperial-minded nationalists of pre-war Canada is shown in Carl Berger, *The Sense of Power: Studies in the Ideas of Canadian Imperialism* (Toronto 1970), chapter 10.

4 Adam Shortt, "War and Economics," *Address*, Canadian Club of Montreal, 1914–15, 309–11; Adam Shortt to W. L. Grant, 29 May 1915, W.L. Grant Papers, National Archives of Canada; Adam Shortt, "Some Aspects of Canadian War Finance," *Proceedings National Tax Association*, 10th Conference, 1916 (New Haven, Conn., 1917), 164.

5 O.D. Skelton, "The European War and the Peace Movement," *Queen's Quarterly*, 21 (October 1914), 205–14; O.D. Skelton, "Current Events," *Queen's Quarterly*, 23 (July 1915), 105–10; W.L. Grant, "Current Events," *Queen's Quarterly*, 22 (October 1914), 219–23, 223–31.

6 O.D. Skelton, "Canada in Wartime," *Political Quarterly*, no. 6 (May 1915), 58–69; O.D. Skelton, "Current Events," *Queen's Quarterly*, 23 (July 1915), 11–15; O.D. Skelton, "Current Events," *Queen's Quarterly*, 26 (July 1918), 122; O.D. Skelton, "Canadian Federal Finance," *Queen's Quarterly*, 26 (October 1918), 202.

7 O.D. Skelton, "Current Events," *Queen's Quarterly*, 24 (July 1916), 143; O.D. Skelton, "Current Events," *Queen's Quarterly*, 17 (January 1910), 262–7; O.D. Skelton, "The Referendum," *University Magazine*, 196–214.

8 O.D. Skelton, "Current Events," *Queen's Quarterly*, 15 (January 1908), 248–51; O.D. Skelton, "Current Events," *Queen's Quarterly*, 18 (April 1911), 336; O.D. Skelton, "Current Events," *Queen's Quarterly*, 16 (January 1909), 290, 291.

9 W.W. Swanson, "Current Events," *Queen's Quarterly*, 19 (July 1911), 80; O.D. Skelton, "A Canadian Experiment in Industrial Peace," *The Outlook*, vol. 88, no. 1 (4 January 1908), 33, and his *Socialism*, 193–8; Adam Shortt, "Current Events," *Queen's Quarterly*, 13 (October 1905), 181–3. On this issue see Michael Bliss, "Another Anti-Trust Tradition: Canadian Anti-Combines Policy, 1880–1910," *Enterprise and National Development*, G. Porter and R. Cuff, eds. (Toronto 1973), 47–50.

10 W. Bennett Munro, "Should Canadian Cities Adopt Commission Government," *Queen's Quarterly*, 20 (January 1913), 262–71 (Bulletin of the Departments of History and Political and Economic Science, no. 6, 1913); W. Bennett Munro, "Boards of Control and Commission Government in Canadian Cities," *Papers and Proceedings*, Canadian Political Science Association, 1 (1913); S. Morley Wickett, "City of Government in Canada," *Municipal Government in Canada*, University of Toronto Studies, History and Economics, 2 (Toronto 1908), 3–23; F.H. Underhill, "Commission Government in Cities," *The Arbor*, 8 (April 1911), 284–94.

11 O.D. Skelton, "A Canadian Experiment in Industrial Peace," 33; O.D. Skelton, "Current Events," *Queen's Quarterly*, 24 (July 1917), 143; O.D. Skelton, "Current Events," *Queen's Quarterly*, 18 (April 1911), 337; O.D. Skelton, "Current Events," *Queen's Quarterly*, 15 (July 1907), 75–8; O.D. Skelton, "Of the Canadian Taxpayers' Bill," *Monetary Times Annual* (1914), 179.

12 O.D. Skelton, "The Referendum," *University Magazine*, 12 (April 1913), 198–200; 214; O.D. Skelton, "Of the Canadian Taxpayers' Bill," *Monetary Times Annual*, 1914.

13 O.D. Skelton, "Current Events," *Queen's Quarterly*, 24 (July 1916), 141–2; O.D. Skelton, "Current Events," *Queen's Quarterly*, 21 (April 1914), 515–6; O.D. Skelton, "Current Events," *Queen's Quarterly*, 23 (July 1915), 103–4; O.D. Skelton to W.L.M. King, 5 March 1921, W.L.M. King Papers, National Archives of Canada.

14 O.D. Skelton to W.L. Grant, 19 March 1917, 13 August 1917, W. L. Grant Papers, National Archives of Canada; O.D. Skelton to Wilfrid Laurier, 15 November 1918, Wilfrid Laurier Papers, National Archives of Canada; O.D. Skelton, "Current Events," *Queen's Quarterly*, 26 (July 1918), 125–6, 129.

15 O.D. Skelton to Wilfrid Laurier, 15 March, 23 March, 15 November 1918, Wilfrid Laurier Papers; O.D. Skelton, "Current Events," *Queen's Quarterly*, 26 (July 1918), 129.

16 O.D. Skelton, "Current Events," *Queen's Quarterly* 21 (October 1921), 202–5; O.D. Skelton, *Life and Letters of Sir Wilfrid Laurier*, 2 vols. (Toronto 1922), passim.

17 Adam Shortt, "The Relations Between the Legislative and Executive Branches of the Canadian Government," *American Political Science Review*, 7 (1913), 192–3, 196.

18 O.D. Skelton, "Current Events," *Queen's Quarterly*, 24 (July 1916), 132–40; O.D. Skelton, "Current Events," *Queen's Quarterly*, 25 (October 1917), 224–6; J.L. Granatstein and J.M. Hitsman, *Broken Promises* (Toronto 1977), chapters 2 and 3.

19 Robert Craig Brown, *Robert Laird Borden, A Biography, 1914–37*, 2 vols. (Toronto 1975–1980), 2:70–82, 28–35, etc. On the gap between the public and government see John English, *The Decline of Politics: The Conservatives and the Party System 1901–20* (Toronto 1977), chapter 6.

20 O.D. Skelton, "Current Events," *Queen's Quarterly*, 24 (July 1916), 140–1, 135–9; O.D. Skelton to W.L. Grant, 19 March 1917, W.L. Grant Papers; O.D. Skelton to Wilfrid Laurier, 29 October, 1917, Wilfrid Laurier Papers.

21 O.D. Skelton, "Canada in Wartime," *Political Quarterly*, 6 (1915), 58–69; O.D. Skelton, "Current Events," *Queen's Quarterly*, 24 (July 1916), 132–4; O.D. Skelton to Wilfrid Laurier, 30 May 1917, Wilfrid Laurier Papers; O.D. Skelton to W. L. Grant, 13 August 1917, W.L. Grant Papers; on

Bonne Entente see R.M. Bray, "A Conflict of Nationalisms," *Journal of Canadian Studies*, 15 (1981), 18–30.

22 O.D. Skelton to Wilfrid Laurier, 1 January 1918, Wilfrid Laurier Papers; O.D. Skelton, "Current Events," *Queen's Quarterly*, 25 (October 1917), 227; O.D. Skelton, "Current Events," *Queen's Quarterly*, 25 (July 1911), 136–9.

23 O.D. Skelton, "Current Events," *Queen's Quarterly*, 24 (July 1916), 137–8.

24 O.D. Skelton, "Current Events," *Queen's Quarterly*, 24 (July 1916), 136–7; O.D. Skelton, "Current Events," *Queen's Quarterly*, 25 (October 1917), 226–7.

25 O.D. Skelton, "The Language Issue in Canada," *Queen's Quarterly*, 24 (April 1917), 446–52, 460–3, 468 (Bulletin of the Departments of History and Political Economic Science, no. 23, 1917).

26 Ibid.

27 O.D. Skelton, "Canadian Federal Finance," *Queen's Quarterly*, 26 (October 1918), 228 (Bulletin of the Departments of History and Political and Economic Science, no. 29, 1918).

28 O.D. Skelton to W.L. Grant, 13 August 1917, W.L. Grant Papers; Skelton, "Current Events," *Queen's Quarterly*, 25 (October 1917), 223–4; O.D. Skelton, "Current Events," *Queen's Quarterly*, 24 (July 1916), 139; Skelton, "Canadian Federal Finance," *Queen's Quarterly*, 26 (October 1918), 228.

29 Adam Shortt, "The Origins of Organized Society, or the State," mss. Adam Shortt Papers, 16–18; John Watson, "German Philosophy and the War," *Queen's Quarterly*, 23 (April 1916).

30 O.D. Skelton, "Current Events," *Queen's Quarterly*, 25 (October 1917), 223; O.D. Skelton, "Current Events," *Queen's Quarterly*, 24 (July 1916), 139.

31 O.D. Skelton, "Current Events," *Queen's Quarterly*, 26 (July 1918), 125–6; O.D. Skelton, *The Canadian Dominion* (New Haven, Conn., 1919), 276.

32 Bernard Crick, *The American Science of Politics* (Berkeley and Los Angeles, 1964), chapters 8–12. C.B. Macpherson, *The Life and Times of Liberal Democracy* (Oxford 1977), chapters 3 and 4.

CHAPTER SEVEN

1. Adam Shortt, *Early Economic Effects of the War upon Canada* (New York 1918), 1–2; Adam Shortt, "The Economic Effects of War upon Canada," *Proceedings and Transactions of the Royal Society of Canada*, series 3, no. 10 (1916), 65.

2   Adam Shortt, "Early History of Canadian Banking," *Journal of the Canadian Bankers' Association*, 4 (July 1897), 344–5; Adam Shortt, "History of Canadian Currency, Banking and Exchange," *Journal of the*

Canadian Bankers' Association, 8 (October 1900), 1–15, 8 (January 1901), 146ff.

3 Adam Shortt, "Current Events," *Queen's Quarterly*, 10 (January 1903), 396–8; Adam Shortt, "Current Events," *Queen's Quarterly*, 11 (January 1904), 328–30; Adam Shortt, "The Banking System of Canada," *Canada and Its Provinces*, 23 vols., Arthur G. Doughty and Adam Shortt, eds. (Toronto 1914–17), 10:660.

4 Adam Shortt, "Railway Construction and National Prosperity: An Historic Parallel," *Proceedings and Transactions of the Royal Society of Canada*, series 3, no. 8 (1914), 295–308.

5 *Ibid.*

6 Adam Shortt, "The Economic Effects of the War upon Canada," 65–74.

7 Adam Shortt, "The Effects of the War on Canadian Trade," *Proceedings, Canadian Club of Toronto*, 1914–15, 18–24; Adam Shortt, "War and Economics," *Addresses, Canadian Club of Montreal*, 1914–15, 312–30; Adam Shortt, "Early Economic Effects of the War upon Canada," 9–11.

8 *The Early Economic Effects of the War upon Canada*, 9–10, 13–16, 19–25.

9 Adam Shortt to Gordon Philip (Secretary, London Chamber of Commerce), 12 May 1923, Adam Shortt Papers, Queen's University Archives; Adam Shortt, "Recent Conditions Relating to Investment," *Monetary Times Annual 1921*, 83–5.

10 Adam Shortt, "Some Aspects of Canadian War Finance," *Proceedings, National Tax Association* (New Haven, Conn., 1916), 165–75; Adam Shortt, "Financing After-the-War Industry," *Monetary Times Annual*, 1919, 75–7.

11 Adam Shortt Papers: Adam Shortt to Thomas White, 13 November 1918; Adam Shortt to W.G. Gates, 1 February 1919; Adam Shortt to K.N. Robins, 10 April 1919; Adam Shortt to L.D. Woodworth, 29 October 1919; Adam Shortt to David Kinley, 17 February 1918.

12 O.D. Skelton, "Canada at War," *Political Quarterly*, 6 (May 1915), 58–69.

13 Ibid.

14 O.D. Skelton, "Current Events," *Queen's Quarterly*, 15 (October 1907), 159–62; O.D. Skelton, "The Taxation of Mineral Resources in Canada," *Proceedings, National Tax Association* (Toronto 1908), 385–94; Adam Shortt, "The Taxation of Public Service Corporations," *Proceedings, National Tax Association* (New York 1907), 622–34. For a good source on how taxation policy towards resource industries developed in this period, see H.V. Nelles, *The Politics of Development* (Toronto 1974), chapters 4 and 5. A useful summary of the history of taxation is J.H. Perry, *Taxes, Tariffs and Subsidies: A History of Canadian Fiscal Development* (Toronto 1955), chapters 7–10, 13–14.

15 See sources cited in note 14.

16 O.D. Skelton, "Current Events," *Queen's Quarterly*, 20 (July 1912), 112–3.

17 O.D. Skelton, "Current Events," *Queen's Quarterly*, 17 (January 1910), 267.

18 O.D. Skelton, "Current Events," *Queen's Quarterly*, 20 (April 1913), 475–6; O.D. Skelton, "Of the Canadian Taxpayers' Bill," *Monetary Times Annual, 1914*, 178–9; O.D. Skelton, "Current Events," *Queen's Quarterly*, 21 (April 1914), 516.

19 O.D. Skelton, "Federal Finance," *Queen's Quarterly*, 23 (July 1915), 60–77 (Bulletin of the Departments of History and Political and Economic Science, no. 16, 1915).

20 Ibid., 77. On the People's Budget and taxation policy see James E. Cronin and Terry G. Radtke, "The Old and New Politics of Taxation," *Socialist Register, 1987*, Ralph Miliband, Leo Panitch, and John Savile, eds. (London 1987), especially 263–8, and H.V. Emy, "The Impact of Financial Policy on English Politics Before 1914," *Historical Journal*, 15 (1982), 103–27.

21 O.D. Skelton, "Federal Finance," 77–9, 79–82, 82–6.

22 Ibid., 86–93.

23 Ibid. On the Wisconsin Plan see Robert Maxwell, *La Follette and the Rise of the Progressives in Wisconsin* (Wisconsin 1956), chapter 7.

24 O.D. Skelton, "Federal Finance," 86.

25 Ibid., 87.

26 See Canada House of Commons, *Debates*, 1917, xxxff, and W. Thomas White, *The Story of Canada's War Finance* (Montreal 1921), 33–4, 54–5. The most available summary of wartime finance is Robert Bothwell *et al.*, *Canada 1900–1945* (Toronto 1987), 179–83.

27 O.D. Skelton, "Current Events," *Queen's Quarterly*, 25 (October 1917), 214–19.

28 O.D. Skelton, "Canadian Federal Finance," *Queen's Quarterly*, 26 (October 1918), 195–207 (Bulletin of the Departments of History and Political and Economic Science, no. 29, 1919). This article appeared in truncated form in the *Monetary Times*, 20 December 1918 and 3 January 1919. O.D. Skelton, "Current Events," *Queen's Quarterly*, 25 (October 1917), 219.

29 O.D. Skelton, "Canadian Federal Finance," 210–12. See also Bothwell *et al.*, *Canada 1900–1945*, and Robert Craig Brown, *Robert Laird Borden 2, 1914–1937* (Toronto, 1980), 43–4, 95, 137.

30 O.D. Skelton, "Canadian War Finance," *American Economic Review*, 7 (December 1917), 818–31; O.D. Skelton, "Canadian Capital Requirements," *Annals of the American Academy of Political and Social Science*, 68 (November 1916), 216–25; O.D. Skelton, "Current Events," *Queen's Quarterly*, 25 (October 1917), 218–19.

31 See sources listed in note 30.

32 W.W. Swanson, "The Financial Power of the Empire," *Queen's Quarterly*, 22 (April 1915), 400–9, 411, 427–8 (Bulletin of the Departments of History and Political and Economic Science, no. 14, 1915); W.W. Swanson, "Prices During and After the War," *Monetary Times Annual*, 1918, 23–4; W.W. Swanson, "Growth of a National Economy," *Monetary Times Annual 1920*, 23–5; W.W. Swanson, *Depression and the Way Out* (Toronto 1931), passim.

33 Stephen Leacock, "The Canadian Balance of Trade," *Journal of the Canadian Bankers' Association*, 22 (April 1915), 165–72; Stephen Leacock, "The Economic Aspect of War," *Journal of the Canadian Bankers' Association*, 24 (1917), 302–15; Stephen Leacock, "The Unsolved Riddle of Social Justice," *The Social Criticism of Stephen Leacock*, Alan Bowker, ed. (Toronto 1973), chapter 7.

34 O.D. Skelton, "Current Events," *Queen's Quarterly*, 16 (April 1909), 376.

35 Joseph Schumpeter, *History of Economic Analysis* (New York 1954), 945–6; Robert Ekelund and Robert Tollison, "The New Political Economy of John Stuart Mill: The Means to Social Justice," *Canadian Journal of Political Science*, 9 (May 1976), 213–31; *Classics in the Theory of Public Finance*, R. Musgrave and A. Peacock, eds. (New York 1967), passim.

36 O.D. Skelton, "Current Events," *Queen's Quarterly* 23 (July 1915), 72–3.

37 See chapters 4 and 9.

38 O.D. Skelton, "Current Events," *Queen's Quarterly* 27 (July 1919), 128; O.D. Skelton, "Memorandum on Economic Research," 15 October 1918, Queen's University Letters, volume 28 (by permission). On Keynes see Donald Moggridge, *John Maynard Keynes* (Harmondsworth 1976), chapters 4 and 5.

39 John English, *The Decline of Politics: The Conservatives and the Party System 1901–20* (Toronto 1977); Tom Traves, *The State and Enterprise* (Toronto 1980); John Herd Thompson, *Decades of Discord, Canada 1922–39* (Toronto 1985), chapters 2–5.

40 *Historical Statistics of Canada*, 2nd ed., F.H. Leacey *et al.*, ed. (Toronto 1983), Series H1–18, Federal Budgetary Revenue; series H19–34, Federal Budgetary Expenditure; series F1–13, Gross National Product.

CHAPTER EIGHT

1 G.M. Grant, "Current Events," *Queen's Quarterly*, 4 (April 1897), 318.

2 Adam Shortt, "Current Events," *Queen's Quarterly*, 11 (July 1903), 216–18.

3 See chapter 5.

4 The best general overview of agrarian organization and politicization is W.L. Morton, *The Progressive Party in Canada* (Toronto 1950), chapters 1

and 2. On the economic conditions and the excitement behind the agrarian ferment, see Paul F. Sharp, *The Agrarian Revolt in Western Canada* (Minneapolis 1948).

5   Adam Shortt, "The Influence of Daily Occupations and Surroundings on the Life of the People," *Sunday Afternoon Addresses, 3rd Series*, 1893, passim; Adam Shortt, "Some Observations on the Great North-West, 2," *Queen's Quarterly*, 3 (July 1895), 12–22.

6   Adam Shortt, "The Social and Economic Significance of the Movement from the Country to the City," *Addresses*, Canadian Club of Montreal, 1912–13 (Montreal 1913), 62–71; Adam Shortt, "Historical Aspects of Town Planning," *Town Planning*, 1, nos. 4 and 5 (June 1921), 15–18. A fellow political economist who later became a statistician with the Department of Labour, S.A. Cudmore of the University of Toronto, surveyed the movement of rural population. He supported its "economic benefits" and downplayed agrarian dismay. See S.A. Cudmore, "Rural Depopulation in Southern Ontario," *Transactions*, Royal Canadian Institute, 9 (1912), 261–6, 267. The views of Ontario farm leaders were, of course, far less composed. They are examined in an excellent essay by W.R. Young, "Conscription, Rural Depopulation and the Farmers of Ontario, 1917–19," *Canadian Historical Review*, 53 (September 1972), 289–319.

7   Adam Shortt, "Equalizing Production and Consumption," *Monetary Times*, 62 (23 May 1919); William Swanson, "Canadian Industry and Western Agriculture," *Monetary Times*, 61 (13 December 1918); William Swanson, "Growth of a National Economy," *Monetary Times Annual*, 64 (9 January 1920).

8   O.D. Skelton, "Reciprocity: The Canadian Attitude," *Journal of Political Economy*, 19 (February 1911), 91; O.D. Skelton, "Canada's Rejection of Reciprocity," *Journal of Political Economy*, 19 (November 1911), 727–31; O.D. Skelton, "The Political Year in Canada," *Political Quarterly*, 1 (1914), 165; O.D. Skelton, "General Economic History, 1867–1912," *Canada and Its Provinces*, 23 vols., Arthur G. Doughty and Adam Shortt, eds. (Toronto 1914–17), 9:243–6; O.D. Skelton, *Socialism: A Critical Analysis* (Boston and New York 1911), 159–63, 305–6.

9   W.L.M. King Papers, National Archives of Canada: O.D. Skelton to W.L.M. King, 17 February 1914; W.L.M. King to O.D. Skelton, 23 February 1914; O.D. Skelton to W.L. Grant, 19 March, 13 August 1917, W.L. Grant Papers, National Archives of Canada; O.D. Skelton to Wilfrid Laurier, 18 October 1917, 15 November 1918, 27 November 1918, Wilfrid Laurier Papers, National Archives of Canada.

10 O.D. Skelton to Wilfrid Laurier, 15 November 1918; Wilfrid Laurier to O.D. Skelton, 25 November 1918; Skelton's letter to Laurier contained the enclosure "Suggestions for Farmers' Platform," a typescript dated 1

October 1918 (microfilm reel C918, 201867–76), Wilfrid Laurier Papers.

11 "Suggestions for Farmers' Platform," 1–10.

12 O.D. Skelton to Wilfrid Laurier, 18 October 1917, Wilfrid Laurier Papers; O.D. Skelton to W.L.M. King, 5 March, 28 March 1921, 24 November, 25 November 1921, 8 December 1921, W.L.M. King Papers. Also: O.D. Skelton to W.C. Good, 10 January 1919, W.C. Good Papers, National Archives of Canada; O.D. Skelton to C.B. Sissons, 16 October 1920, C. B. Sissons Papers, National Archives of Canada; O.D. Skelton, "Book Review" (Good's *Production and Taxation in Canada*), *Queen's Quarterly*, 27 (October 1919), 220–3.

13 Skelton's strategy was similar to King's practical response to the Progressives. See R.M. Dawson, *William Lyon Mackenzie King, 1874–1923* (Toronto 1958), 317–8.

14 Adam Shortt, "Co-operation," *Queen's Quarterly*, 5 (October 1897), 124–8, 129–34.

15 William Swanson, "Current Events," *Queen's Quarterly*, 21 (July 1913), 122–7; William Swanson and P.C. Armstrong, *Wheat* (Toronto 1930), 132–6, 149–50, 272–82. Swanson conceded the social benefits of cooperation in his *Depression and the Way Out* (Toronto 1931).

16 Humfrey Michell, "The Problem of Agricultural Credit in Canada," *Queen's Quarterly* 21 (January 1914), 328–32, 349–50 (Bulletin of the Departments of History and Political and Economic Science, no. 10, 1914).

17 Ibid., 333–45, 347–9; H. Michell, "The Grange in Canada," *Queen's Quarterly*, 22 (October 1914), 164–83 (Bulletin of the Departments of History and Political and Economic Science, no. 13, 1915).

18 Humfrey Michell, "Profit-Sharing and Producers' Co-operation in Canada," *Queen's Quarterly* 25 (January 1918), 299ff, 323 (Bulletin of the Departments of History and Political and Economic Science, no. 26, 1918); Humfrey Michell, "The Co-operative Store in Canada," *Queen's Quarterly* 23 (January 1916), 318–19 (Bulletin of the Departments of History and Political and Economic Science, no. 18, 1916); Humfrey Michell, "The Grange in Canada," *Queen's Quarterly* 22 (October 1914), 175–83 (Bulletin of the Departments of History and Political and Economic Science, no. 13, 1915).

19 Humfrey Michell, in "The Rise of Co-operation in Canada," *Canadian Forum*, 1 (December 1920), 90, explained his view that the two kinds of cooperatives were the only successful Canadian adaptations of the movement.

20 C.B. Sissons, "The Rise of Co-operation in Canada," *Canadian Forum*, 1 (October 1920), 8, 16. See also Sissons's and Michell's letters in the *Canadian Forum*, 1 (December 1920), 90. Michell authored "Social

Services News and Notes" for the *Canadian Churchman* in the late 1910s
and 1920s. See Richard Allen, *The Social Passion: Religion and Social
Reform in Canada 1914–1928* (Toronto 1973), 37, 106, 109. On the
ideas and aims of the cooperative movement in the period under discussion, see Ian MacPherson's *Each for All: A History of the Co-operative
Movement in English Canada, 1900–1945* (Toronto 1979), 46–8 and
especially 106–9. MacPherson distinguishes between "practical," "utopian," and "occupational" reformers. He explains that the "utopians"
were the most influential and important in maintaining unity among
producers' and consumers' groups. The agrarian exclusivism and
almost millenialist hopes of the "utopians" were the very points that
Michell, Shortt, and, as we shall see, Clark and Mackintosh found
objectionable. Their analyses emphasized the integration of rural and
urban Canadians and their mutual participation in the market
economy which the "utopians" were rather hostile to.

21 W.C. Clark, "The Country Elevator in the Canadian West," *Queen's
Quarterly*, 24 (July 1916), 46–68, especially 53–6, 68 (Bulletin of the
Departments of History and Political and Economic Science, no. 20,
1916). O.D. Skelton praised the cooperatives as a confutation of the
Marxist contention that the only alternative to private property was
"state control"; "Trotzky," *Queen's Quarterly*, 25 (April 1918), 422–3.
W.C. Good, *Farmer Citizen* (Toronto 1957), 137–8.

22 I am thinking here of the interpretative essays written by J.M.S. Careless, John H. Dales, Daniel Drache, and Carl Berger which are cited in
chapter 1.

23 Here the identification of the continuity of the Queen's school is noted
by A.R.M. Lower, John H. Dales, and Daniel Drache. See also Doug
Owram, *The Government Generation: Canadian Intellectuals and the State
1900–1945* (Toronto 1986), 316–17.

24 W.A. Mackintosh, "Economic Factors in Canadian History," *Canadian
Historical Review*, 4 (March 1923), 12–13.

25 Ibid., 23–5.

26 Ibid., 15–16, 178, 19–21. See also W.A. Mackintosh, "The Laurentian
Plateau in Canadian Economic Development", *Economic Geography*, 2
(October 1926), 537–40. In a manuscript apparently dating to the
1920s and entitled "Economic Development of Canada" – the fact that
it is marked "Chapter 1" suggests that he intended to write an economic history of Canada – Mackintosh revised his account of the geographical "determinants." Here he noted that the St Lawrence and
Hudson–Mohawk as well as the Mississippi River systems provided the
primary access to the rich interior of North America. He also noted
that these three routes were complemented by the Hudson Bay–
Saskatchewan system and potentially significant Mackenzie–Peace River

system as access routes. See W.A. Mackintosh Papers, Box 9, File 217, mss., Economic Development of Canada, 1–18, National Archives of Canada. It is no wonder that Mackintosh was writing about Canada's "northern frontier" as a "perpetual frontier" in the 1950s. See W.A. Mackintosh, "The Canadian Economy and its Competitors," *Foreign Affairs*, 34 (October 1955), 127. This observation was later taken up by another conservative historian, W.L. Morton, in his speculations about the Canadian "identity." See Morton's "The Relevance of Canadian History" (1960), reprinted in *Context of Canada's Past*, A.B. McKillop, ed. (Toronto 1980), 163–7. Just as Mackintosh had derived the lesson from his 1955 essay that Canadian history and development was distinct from that of the United States in part because of their different "frontiers," so did Morton five years later.

27 "Economic Factors in Canadian History," 2.

28 Ibid., 21–3.

29 Ibid., 25; H.A. Innis, *The Fur Trade in Canada: An Introduction to Canadian Economic History* (New Haven, Conn., 1930). On the triumph of the "environmentalist" mode of thought in the 1920s, see Ramsay Cook, "Landscape Painting and National Sentiment in Canada," in his *The Maple Leaf Forever*, 2nd ed. (Toronto 1977), 158ff.

30 Kingston and Toronto, 1924. The book was published jointly by the Ryerson Press and Queen's University.

31 *Agricultural Cooperation in Western Canada*, 6, 8.

32 Ibid., 3–4, 7–9, 9–15, 16–33.

33 Ibid., 58, 72ff, 81ff, 87–9, especially 87.

34 Ibid., 88–9.

35 Ibid., 89, and 140ff.; W.A. Mackintosh, "The Canadian Wheat Pools," *Queen's Quarterly* 32 (November 1925), 142 (Bulletin of the Departments of History and Political and Economic Science, no. 51, 1926); E.A. Partridge to W.A. Mackintosh, 24 November 1924, William Mackintosh Papers; Mackintosh, *Agricultural Cooperation in Western Canada*, 7. On Partridge's Christian millenialism, see Carl Berger, "A Canadian Utopia: The Cooperative Commonwealth of Edward Partridge," *Visions: Twenty/Twenty*, Stephen Clarkson, ed. (Toronto 1970), 257–62.

36 W.A. Mackintosh, "The Psychologist and Economics," *Queen's Quarterly*, 30 (January 1923), 299–305.

37 *Agricultural Cooperation in Western Canada*, 148.

38 Ibid., 145–9.

39 Ibid., 147.

40 M.C. Urquhart and K.A.H. Buckley, *Historical Statistics of Canada*, series C1–7 and series E1–12.

41 Glenn Williams, *Not for Export: Toward a Political Economy of Canada's Arrested Industrialization* (Toronto 1983), 130–7, 148–50; Daniel Drache,

"Rediscovering Canadian Political Economy," reprinted in *A Practical Guide to Canadian Political Economy*, Wallace Clement and Daniel Drache, eds. (Toronto 1978), 1ff.

CHAPTER NINE

1 On these pressures and their result on government policy, see Tom Traves, *The State and Enterprise* (Toronto 1980), chapter 2, and Robert Craig Brown, *Robert Laird Borden, A Biography, 1914–37*, 2 vols (Toronto 1975–80), 2, chapters 13 and 14. Each of these studies elaborate on the interpretation of the pressures on government and society first noted in Robert Craig Brown and Ramsay Cook, *Canada, 1896–1921: A Nation Transformed* (Toronto 1972), chapters 15 and 16.

2 W.C. Clark, "Should Maximum Prices be Fixed?" *Queen's Quarterly*, 25 (April 1918), 435–58.

3 Ibid., 456–7.

4 Ibid., 458.

5 Ibid., 458–61.

6 W.C. Clark, "Business Cycles and the Depression of 1920–21," *Queen's Quarterly*, 29 (July 1921), 62–83 (Bulletin of the Departments of History and Political and Economic Science, no. 40, 1921).

7 See Doug Owram, *The Government Generation: Canadian Intellectuals and the State 1900–1945* (Toronto 1986), 202, and John Bacher, "W.C. Clark and the Politics of Canadian Housing Policies, 1935–50," *Urban History Review* 17 (June 1988), 5–15.

8 W.C. Clark, "Current Events," *Queen's Quarterly*, 27 (January 1921), 302–8, especially 306–8. On the board see T.D. Traves, "The Board of Commerce and the Canadian Sugar Refining Industry: A Speculation on the Role of the State in Canada," *Canadian Historical Review*, 54 (1974), 159–75. What would Traves make of Clark's position in light of the "reality" of state regulation which he so excellently portrays in his essay and his subsequent volume *The State and Enterprise*? Clark's speculations do not enter into his discussion.

9 W.C. Clark, "Current Events," *Queen's Quarterly*, 27 (January 1921), 302–8, especially 306–8.

10 Humfrey Michell, "The Business Cycle," *Canadian Forum*, 3 (June 1923), 286; (July 1923), 318; (August 1923), 350; (September 1923), 380; *Canadian Forum*, 4 (October 1923), 30; Humfrey Michell, "Comparative Prices in Canada and the United States," *Annals of the American Academy of Political and Social Science*, 107 (May 1923), 149–54; *Statistical Contributions to Canadian Economic History*, 2 vols., H. Michell, K.W. Taylor, and C.A. Curtis, eds. (Toronto 1931).

11 File on "Commission on Statistics," June – September 1912, Adam Shortt Papers, Box 27, Queen's University Archives; O.D. Skelton,

"Current Events," *Queen's Quarterly*, 20 (July 1912), 106; O.D. Skelton to W.L.M. King, 27 January 1922 (supporting R.H. Coats's attempt to reorganize the Bureau of Statistics) W.L.M. King Papers, National Archives of Canada.

12 W.A. Mackintosh, "Economics, Prices and the War," *Queen's Quarterly*, 26 (April 1919), 452–8 (Bulletin of the Departments of History and Political and Economic Science, no. 31, 1919).

13 Ibid., 454.

14 Ibid., 458–62.

15 See F.H. Underhill, "The Conception of a National Interest," *Canadian Journal of Economics and Political Science*, 1 (August 1935), 404, and "Bentham and Benthamism," *Queen's Quarterly*, 39 (November 1932), 666.

16 W.A. Mackintosh, "Revolution at Winnipeg," mss., 1–8, W.A. Mackintosh Papers, Queen's University Archives.

17 O.D. Skelton, "Current Events," *Queen's Quarterly*, 28 (July 1919), 122–28.

18 W.A. Mackintosh, "Economics, Price and the War," 464–5; W.A. Mackintosh, "Current Events," *Queen's Quarterly*, 21 (October 1923), 220; W.A. Mackintosh, "Current Events," *Queen's Quarterly*, 29 (February 1922), 313–16.

19 W.A. Mackintosh, "Current Events," Queen's Quarterly, 29 (February 1922), 309–10. Mackintosh's reflections on government policy making came later: "An Economist Looks at Economics," *Canadian Journal of Economics and Political Science* 3 (August 1937), 311–21, and in "Government Economic Policy: Scope and Principles," *Canadian Journal of Economics and Political Science* 16 (August 1950), 324–6.

20 W.A. Mackintosh, "The Psychologist and Economics," *Queen's Quarterly*, 30 (January 1923), 299ff; W.A. Mackintosh, "Economic Factors in Canadian History," *Canadian Historical Review*, 4 (March 1923), 12f.

21 O.D. Skelton, "Industrial Unrest and the Way Out," *Journal of the Canadian Bankers' Association*, 25 (January 1918), 119–23. See also "Current Events," *Queen's Quarterly*, 22 (October 1913), 214.

22 O.D. Skelton's review of King's *Industry and Humanity* in *Canadian Author and Bookman*, 1 (April 1919), 62.

23 O.D. Skelton, "Industrial Unrest and the Way Out," 124.

24 See chapter 8. A summary of Skelton's views can be found in Joseph Levitt, "In Praise of Reform Capitalism: The Economics Ideas of O.D. Skelton," *Labour*, 11 (Spring 1983), 143–54.

25 B.M. Stewart to Principal Gordon, 28 September 1908, D.M. Gordon Papers, Queen's University Archives; Richard Allen, *The Social Passion: Religion and Social Reform in Canada* (Toronto 1973), 14, 25; *Macmillan Dictionary of Canadian Biography*, W.A. Mackay, ed. (Toronto 1978); *The Canadian Who's Who*, 8th ed.

26 Bryce M. Stewart, "The Housing of Our Immigrant Workers," *Papers and Proceedings*, Canadian Political Science Association, 1 (1913), 99–111. The history of the social and economic conditions of this period sustains Stewart's diagnosis. See Donald Avery, *Dangerous Foreigners: European Immigrant Workers and Labour Radicalism in Canada, 1896–1932* (Toronto 1978), chapter 1.

27 Bryce M. Stewart, "Public Employment Bureaus and Unemployment," *Canadian Municipal Journal*, 12 (October 1916), 522–3; Bryce M. Stewart, "The Employment Service of Canada," *Queen's Quarterly*, 27 (July 1919), 37–45 (Bulletin of the Departments of History and Political and Economic Science, no. 32, 1919); B.M. Stewart, "Report of a Social Survey of Port Arthur," Methodist Church of Canada and Presbyterian Church in Canada, *Reports of Investigations of social conditions and social surveys* (Toronto 1913–14).

28 Bryce M. Stewart, "Public Employment Bureaus and Unemployment"; Bryce M. Stewart, "The Employment Service of Canada," 45–53. Also note Stewart's "Problems of the Employment Service," *Monetary Times Annual, 1920*, 18–20, as well as his "Unemployment and the Organization of the Labour Market," *Annals of the American Academy of Political and Social Science*, 107 (May 1923), 286–93.

29 James Struthers, "Prelude to Depression: The Federal Government and Unemployment 1918–29," *Canadian Historical Review*, 58 (September 1977), 277–88. On the vicissitudes of immigrant labourers generally and their actions and government reaction in the early 1930s in particular, see Donald Avery's *Dangerous Foreigners*, especially chapters 1, 2, and 5. Stewart's later views can be found in "Some Aspects of Unemployment Insurance," *Papers and Proceedings*, Canadian Political Science Association, 3 (1931), 32–44, and "The Employment and Social Insurance Bill," *Canadian Journal of Economics and Political Science*, 1 (August 1935), 456–64.

30 On McGill see Marlene Shore, *The Science of Social Redemption: McGill, The Chicago School, and the Origins of Social Research in Canada* (Toronto 1987), 262–70.

31 O.D. Skelton to Principal Gordon, "Memo. on Economic Research," Queen's University Letters, 27, 1916 (by permission); O.D. Skelton, "The European War and the Peace Movement," *Queen's Quarterly*, 22 (October 1914) 214; O.D. Skelton, "Current Events," *Queen's Quarterly*, 27 (July 1919), 128.

32 Department of Political and Economic Science to Principal Taylor, "Memo on Economic Research and Social Business Training," 15 October 1918, Queen's University Letters, 28 (by permission).

33 On the political pressure to grapple with the general welfare, see Doug Owram, *The Government Generation*, passim and 5. Seymour Wilson,

"Mandarins and Kibitzers," *Canadian Public Administration*, 26 (Fall 1983), 456–61.

34 W.A. Mackintosh, "The Psychologist and Economics," *Queen's Quarterly*, 30 (January 1923), 301.

35 Ibid., 303–4.

36 Ibid., 305.

CHAPTER TEN

1 Stephen Brooks and Alain Gagnon, *Social Scientists and Politics in Canada: Between Clerisy and Vanguard* (Montreal 1988), 3–4, 9.

2 Innis's views are discussed in Donald Creighton, *Harold Adams Innis* (Toronto 1978), 80–3, 91–5, and Doug Owram, *The Government Generation: Canadian Intellectuals and the State 1900–1945* (Toronto 1986), 166–7. Innis's reasoning is exemplified in "Government Ownership and the Canadian Scene," *Canadian Problems* (Toronto 1933), 69–90, and "Economics for Demos," *University of Toronto Quarterly*, 3 (1934), 389–95.

3 W.A. Mackintosh, "An Economist Looks at Economics," *Canadian Journal of Economics and Political Science*, 3 (August 1937), 319–21.

4 John Porter, *The Vertical Mosaic: An Analysis of Social Class and Power in Canada* (Toronto 1965); Wallace Clement, *The Canadian Corporate Elite: An Analysis of Economic Power* (Toronto 1975). Public administration expert Seymour Wilson criticized historian J.L. Granatstein for presuming that the bureaucrats had achieved this degree of influence by the 1940s. See Seymour Wilson, "Mandarins and Kibitzers," *Canadian Public Administration*, 26 (1983), 456–61; see also J.L. Granatstein, *The Ottawa Men: The Civil Service Mandarins 1935–1957* (Toronto 1982) and his *A Man of Influence: Norman A. Robertson and Canadian Statecraft 1929–1968* (Ottawa 1981). The broad framework of the issue of the autonomy of the state and its apparatus is surveyed in Leslie A. Pal, "Relative Autonomy Revisited: The Origins of Canadian Unemployment Insurance," *Canadian Journal of Political Science*, 19 (1986), 71–92. Pal's book on unemployment insurance, *State, Class and Bureaucracy: Canadian Unemployment Insurance and Public Policy* (Montreal 1988), and Tom Traves's book on industrial policy, *The State And Enterprise* (Toronto 1980), lean towards the autonomy position for the mid-twentieth century, unlike a work such as Jim Struthers's *No Fault of Their Own: Unemployment and the Canadian Welfare State 1914–1941* (Toronto 1983).

5 S.E.D. Shortt, *The Search for an Ideal: Six Intellectuals and Their Convictions in an Age of Transition, 1890–1930* (Toronto 1976), 9–10, 145–7; J.M. Bumsted, "Canadian Intellectual History and the 'Buzzing Factuality,'" *Acadiensis*, 7 (1977), 120–1.

6 My account of the two traditions of liberal-democratic theory argued in
this and subsequent paragraphs has been shaped by the following:
C.B. Macpherson's three books, *Democratic Theory: Essays in Retrieval*
(Oxford 1973), *The Life and Times of Liberal Democracy* (Oxford 1977),
and *The Rise and Fall of Economic Justice* (Oxford 1985); Virginia Mac-
Donald, "A Model of Normative Discourse for Liberal-Democratic Man:
Another look at the Is/Ought Relation," *Canadian Journal of Political
Science*, 8 (1975), 381–402; Gerald F. Gauss, *The Liberal Theory of Man*
(London 1983); R.J. Halliday, *John Stuart Mill* (London 1976); John Pla-
menatz, "Liberalism," *Dictionary of the History of Ideas*, 3:36–61; Dennis
F. Thompson, *The Democratic Citizen: Social Science and Democratic Theory
in the Twentieth Century* (Cambridge 1970). The classic formulation
about negative and positive liberty is Isaiah Berlin, "Two Concepts of
Liberty," in his *Four Essays on Liberty* (Oxford 1969), 118–72. Among
historical accounts, see works cited in earlier chapters: Michael
Freeden, *The New Liberalism: An Ideology of Reform* (New York 1978);
Stefan Collini, *Liberalism and Sociology: L.T. Hobhouse and Political Argu-
ment in England*, (Cambridge 1979); Peter Clarke, *Liberals and Social
Democrats*, (Cambridge, 1978); John Allett, *New Liberalism: The Political
Economy of J.A. Hobson* (Toronto 1982).
7 For a recent brief review of liberal-democratic theory since the 1960s
see Michael Walzer *et al.*, "The State of Political Theory," *Dissent*,
Summer 1989, 337–70, especially Amy Gutman, "The Central Role of
Rawls's Theory," 338–42.
8 See H. Scott Gordon, "The New Contractarians," *Journal of Political
Economy*, 84 (1976), 573–90; H.L.A. Hart, "Between Utility and
Rights," *The Idea of Freedom: Essays in Honour of Isaiah Berlin*, Alan
Ryan, ed. (Oxford 1979), 77–98; Charles Taylor, "What's Wrong With
Negative Liberty," *The Idea of Freedom*, 111–29.
9 For example, W. Christian and C. Campbell, *Political Parties and Ideologies in Canada* (Toronto 1990).
10 Paul Craven, *An Impartial Umpire: Industrial Relations and the Canadian
State* (Toronto 1980), 11–30, 353–8.
11 F.H. Underhill, *In Search of Canadian Liberalism* (Toronto 1960), 3–21,
107–9, 172–81; Arthur Lower, *This Most Famous Stream* (Toronto 1954),
passim, and his *My First Seventy-Five Years* (Toronto 1967), 317–20.
12 W.L. Morton, "Clio in Canada" (103–12) and "A Northern Nation"
(163–85), *Contexts of Canada's Past*, A.B. McKillop, ed., (Toronto 1980);
Donald Creighton, "Towards the Discovery of Canada" (46–64) "Macdonald and Canadian Historians" (194–210), in his *Towards the Discovery
of Canada* (Toronto 1972). See Creighton's singular interpretation of
Innis, *Harold Adams Innis*, for the most complete statement of the
clerisy view of scholarly work.

13 This and the subsequent paragraph are based on Gad Horowitz, "Conservatism, Liberalism and Socialism in Canada: An Interpretation," in his *Canadian Labour in Politics* (Toronto 1968); George Grant, *Lament for a Nation: The Defeat of Canadian Nationalism* (Toronto 1965), and *Technology and Empire: Perspectives on North America* (Toronto 1969), especially "Canadian Fate and Imperialism." A recent and critical account of the Hartz-Horowitz thesis applied to Canada is H.D. Forbes, "Hartz-Horowitz at Twenty: Nationalism, Toryism and Socialism in Canada and the United States," *Canadian Journal of Political Science,* 20 (1986), 287–315.

14 Michiel Horn, *The League For Social Reconstruction: The Intellectual Origins of the Democratic Left in Canada 1930–42* (Toronto 1980); R. Douglas Francis, *Frank H. Underhill: Intellectual Provocateur* (Toronto 1986).

15 Doug Owram, *The Government Generation*, especially chapters 10–12; J.L. Granatstein, *The Ottawa Men*, especially chapter 6; James Struthers, *No Fault of Their Own*; Robert Bothwell and William Kilbourn, *C.D. Howe: A Biography*; Robert Bothwell *et al.*, *Canada Since 1945* (Toronto 1981), chapters 10, 17.

16 W.A. Mackintosh, "Trade and Fiscal Policy," *Canada Looks Ahead,* National Liberal Federation (Ottawa 1948), 6–14, especially 12; *Twenty Years After: The White Paper of 1945,* Canadian Trade Committee (Ottawa 1965), passim; R.B. Bryce, "The White Paper in Retrospect," in Queen's University Institute For Economic Research, *Discussion Paper,* no. 172, 1974.

A Note on Sources

The chief sources for this work are the published writings of Queen's political economists. Virtually complete bibliographies of the writings of Shortt, Skelton, and Swanson were published with their obituaries, as were somewhat less complete lists for Clark and Michell. Regrettably, there is no bibliography of Mackintosh's writings. The printed bibliographies are listed below; the publications used in this work can be found in the notes to the chapters.

In addition to published work, manuscript sources, particularly correspondence, were used. Adam Shortt's papers are extensive, William Mackintosh's rather less so, and Oscar Skelton's correspondence was destroyed by a fire in the late 1940s. The manuscript sources consulted are also listed below.

Other published sources, contemporary and secondary, used in this study are found in the notes.

PRIMARY SOURCES

Manuscript Collections

NATIONAL ARCHIVES OF CANADA

R.B. Bennett	Robert Borden
Arthur Doughty	Sandford Fleming
W.C. Good	G.M. Grant
W.L. Grant	W.L. Mackenzie King

Wilfrid Laurier	Arthur Meighen
Clifford Sifton	C.B. Sissons
O.D. Skelton	F.H. Underhill
J.S. Willison	

QUEEN'S UNIVERSITY ARCHIVES

W.C. Clark	T.A. Crerar
C.A. Curtis	D.M. Gordon
W.D. Gregory	F.A. Knox
Norman Lambert	W.A. Mackintosh
Norman M. Rogers	Adam Shortt
R.B. Taylor	John Watson

The following official Queen's University material was made available by permission of Queen's Board of Governors through the university archivist, Mrs Anne MacDermaid:

Board of Trustees Minutes	Faculty of Arts Minutes
Principal's Files	Queen's University Letters

UNITED CHURCH ARCHIVES, VICTORIA UNIVERSITY, TORONTO
Salem Bland

UNIVERSITY OF ALBERTA
R.C. Wallace

UNIVERSITY OF TORONTO, UNIVERSITY ARCHIVES

H.A. Innis	Innis Family
Department of Political Economy	

UNIVERSITY OF TORONTO, THOMAS FISHER RARE BOOK COLLECTION

John Charlton	James Mavor
George M. Wrong	

Published Sources, Bibliographies

W.A. Mackintosh, "William Clifford Clark and Canadian Economic Policy," *Canadian Journal of Economics and Political Science*, 19 (August 1953).

"Humfrey Michell," *Proceedings and Transactions*, Royal Society of Canada, 4th series, vol. 8 (1970).

R.F. Neill, "Adam Shortt: A bibliographic comment," *Journal of Canadian Studies*, 2 (February 1967).

W.A. Mackintosh, "Oscar Douglas Skelton," *Canadian Journal of Economics and Political Science*, 7 (May 1941).

G.W. Simpson, "William Walker Swanson," *Canadian Journal of Economics and Political Science*, 17 (August 1951).

Index

DATE DUE